ORTHODOX CHRISTIANITY IN IMPERIAL RUSSIA

ORTHODOX CHRISTIANITY IN IMPERIAL RUSSIA

A SOURCE BOOK ON LIVED RELIGION

EDITED BY HEATHER J. COLEMAN

INDIANA UNIVERSITY PRESS   *Bloomington & Indianapolis*

This book is a publication of

INDIANA UNIVERSITY PRESS
Office of Scholarly Publishing
Herman B Wells Library 350
1320 East 10th Street
Bloomington, Indiana 47405 USA

iupress.indiana.edu

Telephone orders 800-842-6796
Fax orders 812-855-7931

© 2014 by Indiana University Press

All rights reserved

No part of this book may be reproduced or utilized in any form or by any means, electronic or mechanical, including photocopying and recording, or by any information storage and retrieval system, without permission in writing from the publisher. The Association of American University Presses' Resolution on Permissions constitutes the only exception to this prohibition.

♾ The paper used in this publication meets the minimum requirements of the American National Standard for Information Sciences–Permanence of Paper for Printed Library Materials, ANSI Z39.48–1992.

Manufactured in the
United States of America

Library of Congress
Cataloging-in-Publication Data

Orthodox Christianity in imperial Russia : a source book on lived religion / edited by Heather J. Coleman.
    pages cm
   Some materials translated from the Russian.
   Includes bibliographical references and index.
   ISBN 978-0-253-01313-2 (cloth : alk. paper) – ISBN 978-0-253-01317-0 (pbk. : alk. paper) – ISBN 978-0-253-01318-7 (ebook) 1. Christianity – Russia. 2. Christianity – Russia – History – Sources. 3. Christian life – Russia. 4. Spiritual life – Russkaia pravoslavnaia tserkov'. 5. Russkaia pravoslavnaia tserkov' – Russia. 6. Sermons, Russian. 7. Miracles – Russia. I. Coleman, Heather J., [date] editor of compilation.
   BR935.5.O78 2014
   281.9'47 – dc23

2014001386

1 2 3 4 5   19 18 17 16 15 14

Contents

- *Acknowledgments* · vii
- *A Note on Spellings and Dates* · ix
- *Maps* · x

- Introduction: Faith and Story in Imperial Russia
  Heather J. Coleman · 1
1 The Miraculous Healing of the Mute Sergei Ivanov, 22 February 1833 · *Christine D. Worobec* · 22
2 The Miraculous Revival and Death of Princess Anna Fedorovna Golitsyna, 22 May 1834
  Christine D. Worobec · 31
3 Monastic Incarceration in Imperial Russia
  A. J. Demoskoff · 43
4 Letters to and from Russian Orthodox Spiritual Elders (*Startsy*) · *Irina Paert* · 58
5 Sermons of the Crimean War · *Mara Kozelsky* · 72
6 The Diary of a Priest · *Laurie Manchester* · 85
7 "Another Voice from the Lord": An Orthodox Sermon on Christianity, Science, and Natural Disaster
  Nicholas Breyfogle · 95
8 A Ukrainian Priest's Son Remembers His Father's Life and Ministry · *Heather J. Coleman* · 107

9 Akathist to the Most Holy Birth-Giver of God in Honor of Her Miracle-Working Icon Named "Kazan" · *Vera Shevzov* · 131

10 A Nineteenth-Century Life of St. Stefan of Perm (c. 1340–96) *Robert H. Greene* · 139

11 Written Confessions to Father John of Kronstadt, 1898–1908 *Nadieszda Kizenko* · 152

12 An Obituary of Priest Ioann Mikhailovich Orlovskii *Laurie Manchester* · 172

13 Not Something Ordinary, but a Great Mystery: Old Believer Ritual in the Late Imperial Period · *Roy R. Robson* · 184

14 Orthodox Petitions for the Transfer of the Holy Relics of St. Stefan of Perm, 1909 · *Robert H. Greene* · 192

15 Dechristianization in Holy Rus? Religious Observance in Vladimir Diocese, 1900–1913 · *Gregory L. Freeze* · 208

16 Petitions to the Holy Synod Regarding Miracle-Working Icons · *Vera Shevzov* · 229

17 Missionary Priests' Reports from Siberia *Aileen Friesen* · 249

18 Petitions to "Brother Ioann" Churikov, 1914 *Page Herrlinger* · 262

19 Archimandrite Toviia (Tsymbal), Prior of the Trinity-Sergius Lavra: Memoirs and Diaries (Selections) *Scott M. Kenworthy* · 269

20 "From Ignorance to Truth": A Baptist Conversion Narrative *Heather J. Coleman* · 288

- *Glossary and Abbreviations* · *313*
- *Further Reading* · *315*
- *List of Contributors* · *319*
- *Index* · *321*

Acknowledgments

THIS BOOK HAS BEEN A TRANSNATIONAL AND COLLECTIVE effort from its inception, and it is a pleasure to thank the many people who have made it possible.

My first debt is to the contributors who responded so enthusiastically to my initial proposal and have shaped my thinking about lived Orthodoxy in imperial Russia. I thank them all for their interesting contributions, but also for help in conceptualizing the project, for reading drafts of the introduction, for answering innumerable questions about Orthodox theology and practice, and for helping to solve various translation puzzles.

I am grateful to colleagues in Russia who assisted with the acquisition of copies of archival and published documents and images, including Alexander Polunov and Ksenia Sak in Moscow, Pavel Rogoznyi, Irina Poltavskaia, and Boris Kolonitskii in St. Petersburg, Oksana Mykhed in Kyiv, and the very helpful staff of the State Archive of Vladimir Oblast.

Contributors first presented their work to one another at a workshop, "Faith and Story in Imperial Russia," held at the University of Alberta, Edmonton, Canada, on October 1–2, 2010. I am grateful to the Canada Research Chairs Program, as well as the Department of History and Classics at the University of Alberta, for sponsoring that event. Mariya Melentyeva provided logistical support and linguistic advice during and after the gathering. Even her family in Kharkiv got involved in sorting out the mysteries of nineteenth-century Ukrainian agricultural implements and other translation challenges! Many thanks to Melanie Marvin of the Department of History and Classics for all her help with travel and local arrangements for the colloquium. I would also like to thank cartographer Michael J. Fisher for his careful professionalism.

Janet Rabinowitch at Indiana University Press was enthusiastic about the project from the start. I am grateful for her sound advice and for shepherding the manuscript through the contract stage. Many thanks also to the "anonymous" readers, Paul Vallière and Patrick Lally Michelson, for their attentive reading of the manuscript and their valuable and encouraging comments. After Janet's retirement, Dee Mortensen took over the project with grace. I thank her, production editor Michelle Sybert, and copyeditor Candace McNulty for their careful work to prepare the manuscript for publication.

And finally, because they are the ones I really get up for in the morning, I would like to thank my husband, François Bégin, and our children, Nicolas and Anne, for their support and love.

A Note on Spellings and Dates

WE HAVE PRESERVED THE GEOGRAPHIC TERMS IN THE FORM they are given in the sources. Thus, Ukrainian cities such as Kyiv or Kharkiv are rendered as Kiev or Kharkov in the text. Where a standard English-language form is accepted, such as for the Dnieper River, we have followed it. For simplicity, soft-signs in place names have been dropped.

All dates are given in the Julian Style used in prerevolutionary Russia. In the nineteenth century, these dates were twelve days behind the Gregorian calendar used in western Europe and North America.

Biblical quotations are rendered in English using the Revised Standard Version. The psalms were numbered differently in the Russian Bible. We have indicated this where relevant.

Maps

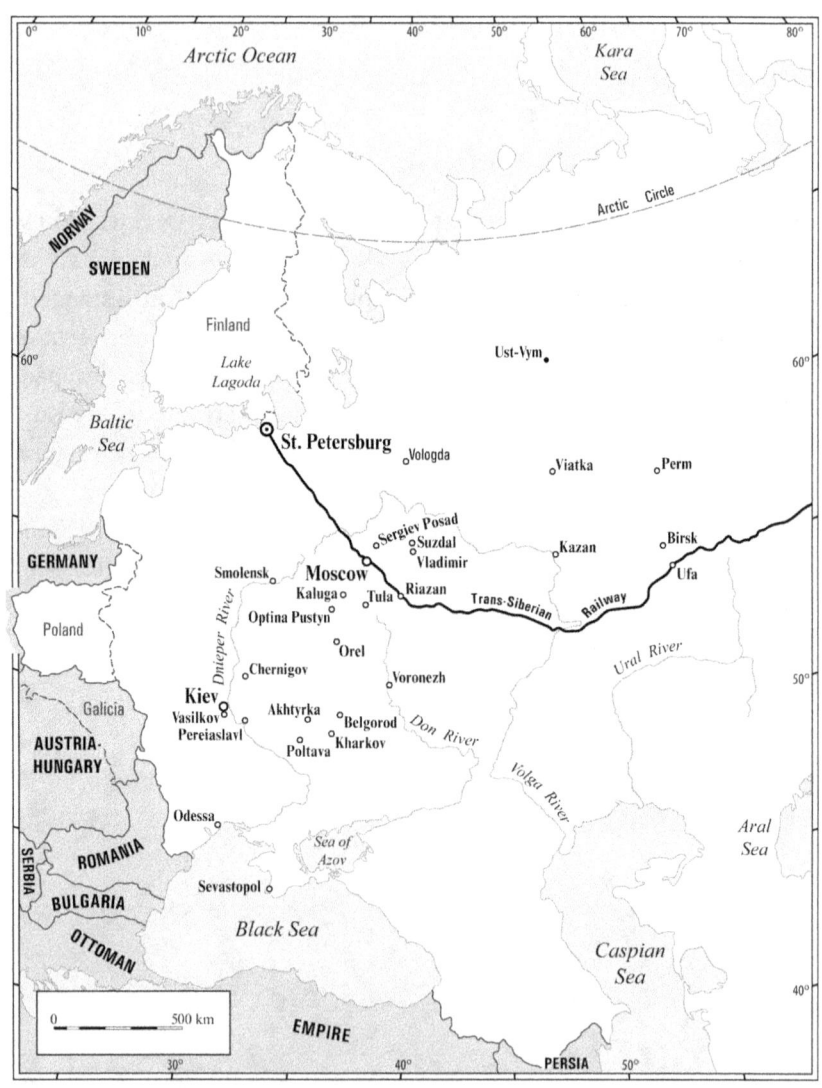

Map 1. European Russia in 1900. Michael J. Fisher, Cartographer.

Maps   xi

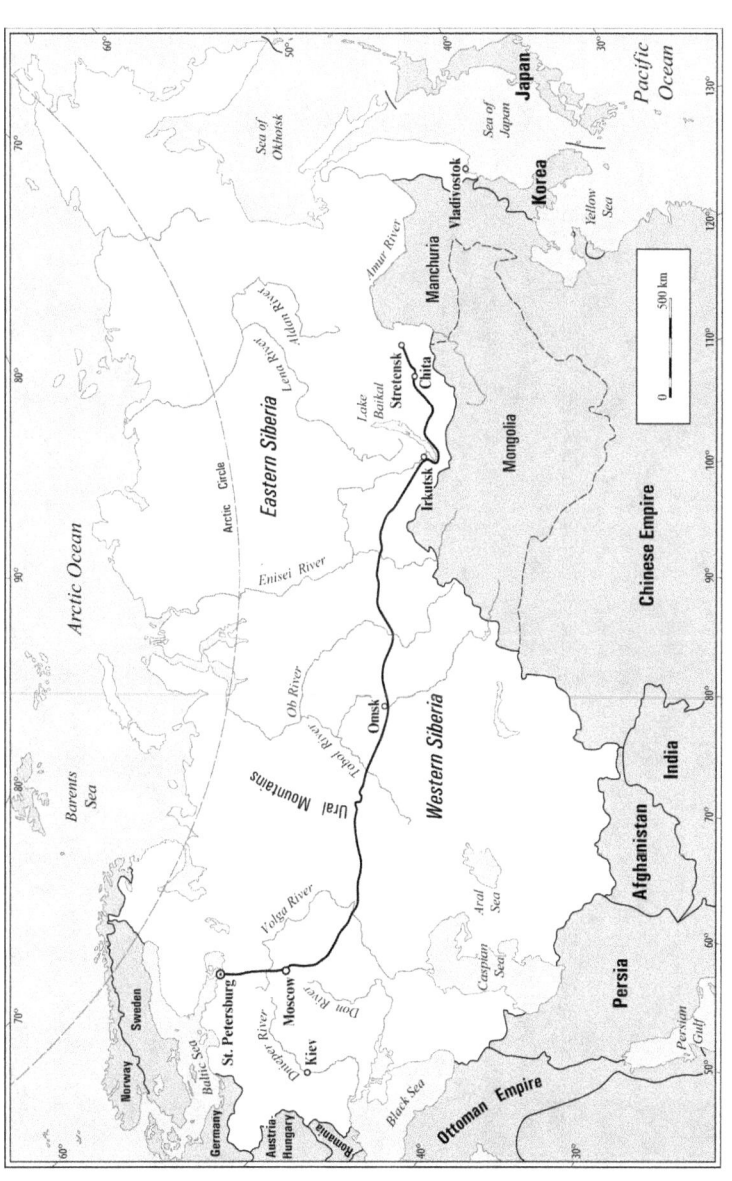

Map 2. The Russian Empire in 1900. Michael J. Fisher, Cartographer.

ORTHODOX CHRISTIANITY
IN IMPERIAL RUSSIA

INTRODUCTION

Faith and Story in Imperial Russia

Heather J. Coleman

STORIES LIE AT THE HEART OF EVERY FAITH, OF EVERY FAITH community, and of every individual's religious identity. Each religious tradition shares a central story that explains, orders, and thereby gives meaning to, the universe. A set of narratives of the collective experience of that story becomes the basis for religious communities, whether denominational, national, or local. And individuals develop their religious identities as they use these public stories to make sense of their own autobiographies.[1]

This collection invites readers to explore how nineteenth- and early twentieth-century-Russians lived out Eastern Orthodoxy – a major Christian tradition that is relatively little known in Western scholarship and culture. Through both public narratives such as sermons, lives of saints, hymns, and clerical reports, and personal stories of faith told in diaries, memoirs, miracle tales, and confessions, the documents offered here provide new insights into the lived religious and social experience of imperial Russia.

Everyday life in imperial Russia comes alive in these texts. They are religious narratives but in most cases they also document social and political and cultural history, affording a new window into a dynamic society undergoing an accelerating and wrenching modernization. In the century before the revolution of 1917, the imperial Russian government grappled with the challenges presented by the economic, social, and political modernization of its European competitors. Despite continual – and frequently secret – efforts at reform, the two brothers who ruled Russia in the first half of the nineteenth century, Alexander I

(r. 1801–25) and Nicholas I (r. 1825–55), never fully came to grips with the real need for structural transformation of their empire's increasingly archaic serf-based social and economic system and autocratic political order. Such fundamental change would come only after the humiliating debacle of the Crimean War (1853–65), which provided the impetus for the Great Reforms of the 1860s and 1870s, undertaken by Nicholas's son, Alexander II (r. 1855–81). This comprehensive program of state-directed modernization emancipated the serfs in 1861 and launched a series of further reforms to deal with the consequences of this great transformation in such spheres as education, local administration, the judicial system, the military, and the church. Virtually all the fundamental institutions of the land were overhauled, except the autocracy itself. Alexander II's son, Alexander III (r.1881–94), in vain sought to stem the change, tamp down the growing unrest, and even undo some of the reforms. But modernization – which unleashed enormous tensions as well as growth – opened the door to severe political and social friction that precipitated a revolution in 1905, when Nicholas II (r. 1894–1917) at last agreed to the introduction of a semi-constitutional system. Historians debate the long-range prospects of this Duma monarchy: was it too little too late or would it have provided the basis for the peaceful evolution of Russia toward a constitutional order more like that of its western European neighbors and competitors? What is certain is that the monarchy did not survive World War I. In February 1917, after two and a half years of war, the population again took to the streets, and this time none of the key institutions of imperial Russia rose to defend the tsar's regime. Deprived of the support of the police, the army, and the church, Nicholas II abdicated on 2 March 1917. The revolutionary ferment only intensified, however, ultimately leading to the Bolshevik seizure of power in October 1917 and an attempt to build the world's first communist state.

It was not only a matter of social and economic change: the empire experienced a veritable "printing and reading revolution." A profusion of works – secular and spiritual, political and literary – were published, distributed, and read across the land. This was due both to the expansion of the press and the sharp rise in literacy rates. At the beginning of the nineteenth century, very few Russians were literate. Indeed, rural literacy rates in the 1860s are estimated at approximately 6 percent. But after the Great Reforms, with the dramatic expansion of primary education, the number of readers grew apace. By 1917, over 22 percent of rural and 61 percent of urban women could read.[2] Figures had especially improved for young men: literacy rates rose from 21 percent of new army recruits in 1874, to 68 percent by the 1913 draft.[3] These youths often read aloud to their unlettered elders and sisters, meaning that far more people came into contact with the written word than literacy figures might suggest at first glance. And publishing in the Russian Empire increased exponentially in these years. In the second half of the nineteenth century, mass-circulation newspapers, magazines, popular prints, and simple books flooded the market. A similar expansion in religious literature took place. Whether through the scholarly journals published by the theological academies, the diocesan newspapers (*eparkhial'nye vedomosti*) that began publication in the 1860s, other journals aimed at priests such as *Guidance for Village Pastors* (*Rukovodstvo dlia sel'skikh pastyrei*), or the wide range of lives of saints, prayer and hymn books, and, after a long delay, the Gospels in the Russian vernacular that became widely available from the 1860s and 1870s and were avidly read by the laity, the Russian Orthodox Church participated in this expanded universe. Reading huts and libraries, as well as book peddlers traveling through the villages and villagers working in the factories, brought the countryside, where the vast majority of Russian subjects still resided, increasingly into contact with this new culture of the written word.[4] As communications theorists and scholars of nationalism have shown us, the expansion of literacy and the emergence of a mass-circulation press facilitated the diffusion of common discourses or stories throughout modernizing societies.[5] Even the relatively censored Russian press provided space for reworking or countering these discourses and generating new narratives.

Numerous Christian groups populated the multinational Russian Empire in the nineteenth century. These included adherents of Orthodoxy, Roman Catholicism, Greek Catholicism, Protestantism, the Armenian Gregorian Church, Old Belief (which had broken with the official Russian Orthodox Church in the seventeenth century), and a range of small Christian groups such as the Dukhobors and the Molokans. Although this volume makes reference to this multiconfessionality, its focus is on Orthodoxy, in particular that of the eastern Slavs (Russian, Ukrainian, and Belarusian speakers). There are good reasons for such an emphasis. After all, Orthodoxy was both the majority faith in the Russian Empire – approximately 70 percent subscribed to this faith in the 1897 census – and the state religion;[6] until 1905, it was illegal for someone baptized into Orthodoxy to convert to another creed. Despite this predominance, however, the Orthodox experience remained a neglected area of study until the 1990s, when research in Russian religious history – and Orthodoxy in particular – blossomed. However, few documents are available in English that provide insight into the sources undergirding this work and the rich spiritual tradition that such scholarship explores. This book aims to fill this gap by presenting a varied compilation of the personal and collective narratives that Orthodox believers, clergy and laity, told themselves and others about their faith and their church in the century before the Russian Revolution.

THE RUSSIAN ORTHODOX CHURCH

By the nineteenth century, Orthodoxy had been associated with the eastern Slavs and the Russian state for some 900 years – ever since Grand Prince Vladimir of Kiev formally converted his people to Christianity in 988. The faith came to the eastern Slavs from the Greeks, centered in the eastern capital of the Roman Empire, Constantinople (present-day Istanbul, Turkey). Over the centuries after the late third century, when the Roman Empire had been divided into eastern and western parts, each with its own emperor, two different church cultures had emerged in Europe, the Greek Byzantine and the Latin Roman ones. In 1054, a couple of generations after the conversion of Kievan Rus to Christianity, eastern and western Christendom formally split and the fate of Kievan Rus would be culturally tied henceforth to the Greek Orthodox world.

One of the key issues leading to the schism in 1054 was the refusal of the Eastern Church to accept the bishop of Rome's claim to supremacy in Christendom as pope. Indeed, the Orthodox Church continued to develop into a network of autochthonous (self-governing local and often, but not necessarily, national) churches, located primarily in Eastern Europe, Russia, and the eastern Mediterranean. The patriarch of Constantinople held a position of special honor within this family but had no right to intervene in the affairs of local churches.[7]

Already by the time the Mongols sacked Kiev in 1240, the eastern Slavic principalities had fallen into disunity. The future Ukrainian and Belarusian lands to the south and west would find themselves under Polish-Lithuanian rule in the late medieval and early modern periods, while, in the northeast, the new Russian state of Muscovy arose and grew to encompass Siberia by the seventeenth century. This complex political history brought religious change. Just as Muscovy was rising to prominence in the fifteenth and sixteenth centuries, Byzantium's thousand-year history was coming to an end. After the Ottoman Turks conquered Constantinople in 1453, Muscovy remained the only major independent Orthodox state in Europe and began to develop an ideology of itself as the Third Rome, the last true Christian nation. By 1589, the Muscovites would found a self-governing (autocephalous) Moscow patriarchate, separating themselves religiously from the jurisdiction of the Greek patriarch; the Kiev Metropolitan, whose authority extended over the Orthodox eastern Slavs in neighboring Poland-Lithuania, remained subordinate to the patriarch of Constantinople. After Kiev and the Ukrainian lands east of the Dnieper River came under Muscovite rule in the second half of the seventeenth century, the Metropolitan of Kiev would swear allegiance to the Muscovite patriarch in 1686. This was no easy "reunification," however. The eastern Slavs, the Russians to the northeast, and the Ruthenians (Ukrainians and Belarusians) to the south and west had evolved different regional Orthodoxies in the centuries of separate political life; in particular, the Ruthenians were both more exposed to and open to Western influences, living under their Polish and Lithuanian Roman Catholic rulers, than were the Muscovites. Moreover, this act severed the enormous territory of the Kiev Metropolitanate, leaving the Orthodox in Right-Bank Ukraine (lands west of the Dnieper that remained under Polish rule until the partitions of Poland in the late eighteenth century) isolated from Kiev and also from Constantinople.[8] Muscovy/Russia would make the protection of the Ruthenian Orthodox a salient feature of its foreign policy rhetoric in the century that followed. And Ruthenian Orthodox clerics would play an influential role as reformers in the Muscovite church. Indeed, one of the causes of the great schism that took place in the Russian church in 1666–67, leading to the emergence of Old Belief, was precisely the reform of church ritual inspired by the encounter with scholarly Kievan monks and the way that Orthodoxy was practiced in Ukraine and Greece.

Whereas the Orthodox Church had played a major (at times, dominant) role in the history of Russia before 1700, the reign of Peter the Great (r. 1682–1725) brought a major realignment in church-state relations. When the patriarch died in 1700, Peter did not summon a church council to elect a successor and left the position empty for almost a generation. As part of his reform of the state administration into colleges, in 1721, he abolished the post of patriarch and established a board of bishops, the Holy Synod, as the supreme administrative organ directing spiritual affairs in Russia. Its overseer was a layman, the chief procurator, whose purpose was to be the "sovereign's eye" in the Synod.[9] Although the Church retained much operational autonomy in the eighteenth century (the state lacking either the means or interest to intercede), in 1764 Catherine the Great achieved what several predecessors had failed to do and secularized church lands and peasants, thereby further reducing the church's independent institutional strength.

These developments gave rise to one of the most long-lived traditions in the historiography of Russia, the view, widely held by prerevolutionary, Soviet, and foreign students of Russian history, that the 1721 Ecclesiastical Regulation turned the Russian church into a moribund branch of the state bureaucracy. Certainly, the Russian state, starting with Peter the Great, modeled itself on other "enlightened" European states that sought, on the one hand, to compartmentalize religion, placing the church in charge of the "spiritual domain," and, on the other, to use the clergy as "a spiritual arm of the state, requiring them to report schismatics, compile vital statistics, read state laws aloud in Church, even violate the confidence of confession if a parishioner revealed 'evil intentions.'"[10] The fuzziness of the line between church and state spheres was exemplified by the practice of housing prisoners convicted for both church and state crimes in some Orthodox monasteries. But by the nineteenth century, there was an increasingly widespread view, not just outside the church but within, that Orthodox religious life needed reforming. A largely state-initiated effort in the 1860s to reform the institutions of the church from administration to education to the parish itself ironically led only to disillusionment on the part of both bishops and parish clergy. Indeed, Gregory Freeze called for a rethinking of the position and potential of the Russian Orthodox Church in imperial Russian society as an institution and a moral force in a famous 1985 article questioning the old view of the church as the "handmaiden of the state." Without denying the structural obstacles the church faced, Freeze challenged scholars to view the church as increasingly spiritualized, internally differentiated, and interested in renegotiating its relationship with the state.[11]

The documents offered here provide insight into the inner workings of the church and the aspirations of its members. They include a number of narratives by and about clergymen, as well as by lay believers. The Orthodox clergy was divided into two separate groups, the "black" monastic clergy and the "white" parish clergy. The hierarchy of the church – metropolitans, archbishops, bishops, and suffragan (vicar) bishops – was made up exclusively of male monks. By the middle of the nineteenth century, they all had higher theological education, and had mostly gained their initial administrative experience as rectors of the seminaries that were established in each diocese to train the sons of priests to serve the church. In the post-reform era, the episcopate came increasingly to consist of widowed priests – who were forbidden to remarry, sometimes took monastic vows, and rose in the hierarchy. A much larger group of monastic clergy participated in the great contemplative renewal that began in the second quarter of the century. Monasteries in this period experienced a profound spiritual renaissance, in particular through the emergence of the phenomenon of the *startsy*, charismatic spiritual elders who counseled and disciplined monks as well as attracting pilgrims in search of spiritual guidance. Their numbers also grew dramatically, as did the population of monks, nuns, and novices, which rose from 11,080 to 94,629 between 1825 and 1914. Women, who had once been a minority in the monasteries, made up over three-quarters of this total by the early twentieth century.[12]

The "white," married, clergy served in the parish churches. They were divided into two categories: the ordained priests and deacons and the non-ordained sacristans. The priests conducted the liturgy and dispensed the sacraments; they were also responsible for administering the parish and overseeing the rest of the clergy. About half of the parishes also had a deacon, whose main role was to lead the singing during services. The sacristans assisted at services and other rites, read and sang parts of the liturgy, rang the bells and helped maintain the church building.[13]

A combination of social, legal, and educational barriers transformed the parish clergy into a closed social estate. For one thing, it was in priests' interest to develop family networks in individual parishes that would provide jobs and retirement security; thus, priests' sons married priests' daughters and took over their father's or father-in-law's parishes. Furthermore, because members of the clerical estate were exempt from the poll tax, the state had an interest in preventing peasants and townspeople from entering the clergy. Finally, isolation was a by-product of the increasing professionalization of the clergy: priests' sons (and, increasingly, daughters in girls' schools) were educated in a separate system of church-run elementary schools and seminaries, popularly known as the *bursa*, leading to higher education in the theological academies. By 1880, virtually all priests had a seminary diploma. Since bishops insisted on a theological education for appointment and the seminaries were reserved for priests' sons (young noblemen were educated through the parallel state gymnasia after the Great Reforms), the educational system reproduced the clergy's social – and cultural – isolation from both the uneducated classes and the nobility.[14]

The colloquial names used for the clergy reflected the mixture of affection and contempt with which the population viewed their ministers. On the one hand, the priest was regularly addressed as *batiushka*, an honorific meaning "little father." Believers wanted a priest in their parish and valued his presence as a spiritual leader, a performer of the liturgy, a teacher, and a community mediator.[15] On the other hand, by the nineteenth century the term *pop*, which had previously been used in official documents to describe priests, had taken on such a derogatory sense that the authorities ceased to employ it; the same applied to the two sacristan ranks of *d'iachok* and *ponomar'*, which were replaced in the 1860s reforms by *psalomshchik*. Likewise, the words *popovich* (priest's son), *seminarist*, and *bursak* (student of the *bursa*) came to serve as pejoratives, evoking images of a poverty-stricken, uncultured, drunken, and benighted clerical milieu.[16] These resentments were not entirely unfounded. Although villages were required to set aside a plot of land for their priest to farm, these were virtually never large or fertile enough to support a family; the only other source of support available to the pastor came from gratuities for the performance of rites (*treby*) such as baptism or marriage, payments that were deeply resented by impoverished villagers as a form of extortion. Moreover, clergymen and their sons were themselves notoriously negative about their bursa experience, describing violence, poverty, and rote learning of impractical subjects.[17] Because the privileged classes, especially the gentry, were so socially and educationally isolated from the clergy, they tended to perpetuate this view.[18] Yet clerical culture was also changing in the nineteenth century. In particular, from the 1840s onward, the Russian church saw the development of an active pastoral care movement among priests who sought to reinvigorate their service to their flocks by complementing their liturgical role with social and educational activism.[19] These priests aimed to develop an informed piety among parishioners through a new emphasis on the sermon, but also through Christian education discussions and organizing village schools. They also launched sobriety circles and got involved in local charitable work.

The documents included below offer a range of perspectives on the clergy in imperial Russia. The selections introduced by Gregory Freeze provide a taste of what have traditionally been some of historians' most frequently used sources: the diocesan reports that bishops submitted annually to the Holy Synod in St. Petersburg, as well as other materials generated by the consistories (the boards of parish priests that administered the dioceses under the authority of the bishop) such as local deans' reports. A little "closer to the ground" are the articles from the diocesan press by priests working with Siberian settlers introduced by Aileen Friesen, on the one hand, and the report on the status of prisoners incarcerated at the Spaso-Evfimiev Monastery in Suzdal presented by A. Joy Demoskoff. These and other selections, such as the correspondence with the Holy Synod in the cases translated by Christine Worobec, Vera Shevzov, and Robert Greene, allow the reader to explore the stories that the church told itself about the challenges it faced and the nature of lay piety. They also illuminate the workings of the church bureaucracy, the relationship between church and state, and ordinary believers' attempts to negotiate the official system to promote their spiritual objectives.

Other texts here shed light on the culture of the clergy, both parish priests and monks. Scott Kenworthy presents the memoirs and diaries of Archimandrite Toviia, the prior of Russia's leading monastery, the Trinity-Sergius Lavra, in the early twentieth century. Laurie Manchester introduces us to two personal narratives, one a priest's diary where we see the struggle of a young pastor to minister to his flock, the other a hagiographic obituary written by a priest's son about his father, which were clearly intended to serve as models for the new-style activist pastor. By contrast, in a selection that I introduce, another priest's son describes with affection his father's career as an old-school parish priest in Kiev diocese from the 1830s to the 1850s. The sermons of the famous Archbishop Innokentii (Borisov) and of an unnamed urban parish priest, presented here by Mara Kozelsky and Nicholas Breyfogle, provide insight into the development of preaching in this period. Whether it is in the laity's petitions to the Synod or in priests' discussions of their ministry among the settlers who flocked to Siberia following the building of the trans-Siberian railway from the 1890s, these documents illuminate clerical and lay ideals of the priest and the monk, clerical spirituality, and the concrete relationships between priest and parishioner. Sometimes there were tensions between clerics and the laity, but more often than not they interacted in a larger ecclesial community.

Indeed, these documents remind us that the diverse community of lay believers made up "the church" just as much as did the clergy. As Vera Shevzov has argued, by the late nineteenth and early twentieth century, discussions of the nature of *tserkovnost'*, a term meaning "churchness" or "ecclesiality," and the "churchly" qualities of various practices and organizational principles, were widespread in the writings of lay commentators on religious matters. And, as she points out, issues of authority and of the nature of the Orthodox community also underlay tussles between communities at the grassroots and their bishops or the religious authorities in St. Petersburg over the legitimacy of various local practices.[20] In the pages below, she presents two cases of conflict between local communities and the church leadership about locally venerated icons that illuminate these dynamics.

Orthodox Spirituality

All of the sources here illuminate the lived religious experience of Orthodoxy in prerevolutionary Russia. The Incarnation – the doctrine that God became fully human in the form of Jesus Christ, yet remained fully God – is at the center of Orthodox theology and spiritual practice. The aim of the Christian life is to preserve and intensify the union between God and humans that God exemplified by becoming man.

This assimilation is a complex process bringing together the mind, body, and soul. Scripture lies at the heart of Orthodoxy: the Bible is read during services and it imbues the words of the liturgy, while icons represent the stories of the Old and New Testaments and often depict the saints studying the Word. Furthermore, the Russian Orthodox Church, especially after the 1862 publication of a new vernacular translation of the New Testament, actively encouraged the distribution of scripture to the laity. At the same time, Orthodoxy is a profoundly "embodied" expression of the Christian faith: the liturgy is not just about words, but about gestures, images, sounds, tastes, and scents that, together with the words, express the truths of the faith. This embodiment extends beyond ritual to the material world. Religious images adorn Orthodox churches, chapels, and private homes, and each individual receives an icon at his or her baptism. Their purpose is not decoration but to serve as revelations of the spiritual world and channels to venerate God, the uncreated spiritual prototype of the painted icon.[21] In nineteenth-century Russia, writes Vera Shevzov, sermons about icons regularly discussed "the relationships between icons and the Incarnation, the image and the prototype, the written word (scripture) and drawn image (icon), and sight and sound in the human quest for the knowledge of and communion with God." Icons were and are integrated into the liturgical activity of congregations during services, and certain icons enjoy liturgies and hymns in their honor.[22] These hymns, according to Shevzov, "associated the making and veneration of the icon directly with the Incarnation and consequently with human salvation; only because the divine nature was 'pleased to take flesh and be circumscribed' could and did believers depict the form of the Son of God incarnate."[23] For our volume, Shevzov introduces one of the most important of these hymns, the akathist to the icon of the Kazan Mother of God. Numerous other sources presented here also reveal the central place of icons in Orthodox spirituality and community life.

In similar fashion, the relics of saints remind believers that when God took a material body, God proved that matter can be redeemed. In the early 1870s, the relics of some 455 saints were officially venerated across the Russian Empire, as were the bodies of many more dead men and women recognized as saints by believers but not formally canonized. Whether they had been miraculously preserved from decay or not, relics constituted a channel of divine power in the Orthodox understanding. Church publicists and priests in their sermons treated the presence of many uncorrupted holy bodies in Russia as a sign of God's special favor; as a writer in the popular religious magazine *Kormchii* (The Helmsman) noted, the example of incorruptible bodies was God's way of "convinc[ing] us of the resurrection of our own bodies" and showing "the truth of the Orthodox faith we profess." Clergy and laity shared an intimate relationship with their saints and a faith in their miraculous involvement in human life.[24] Readers will taste this reverence as they read the account of the miraculous cure of a deaf-mute at the shrine of St. Sergei of Radonezh presented by Christine Worobec, or the correspondence, introduced by Robert H. Greene, between the inhabitants of Perm and the Holy Synod when they appealed to have the relics of the medieval evangelizer of their region, St. Stefan of Perm, moved from Moscow to their own city.

With its incarnational and experiential spirituality, Orthodoxy by its nature lends itself to the material culture and "lived religion" approaches that have emerged in the study of western Christianity since the 1980s. These approaches challenged earlier tendencies in religious history that privileged the "scriptural" or "doctrinal" mode of religiosity over a material or "imagistic" type. Scholars emphasized the interpenetration of these categories and the centrality of words, images, objects, and spaces to ways in which Christians of various denominations have lived out their faith. They shifted their gaze to what Colleen McDannell calls believers' "hearing, reading, seeing, [and] touching," in search of a "more nuanced understanding of the relationship between body and mind, word and image."[25] Such a perspective implies also a move away from interpretive frameworks that set up a sharp dichotomy between "elite" and "popular" religion.[26] Particularly influential for much of the new work on Russian Orthodoxy has been the "lived religion" approach. Practitioners aim to explore what the historian of American religion Robert Orsi calls "the mutually transforming exchanges between religious authorities and the communities of practitioners."[27] They also take seriously believers' own assertions that what they were doing was Christian, even if their practices may appear to differ substantially from official teaching.[28]

Despite the potential fruitfulness of such inquiry for studies of Orthodoxy, it was only in the 1990s and especially in the twenty-first century that historians of Russian religion, many of them contributors to this volume, embraced the shift toward the study of materiality and practice in religious studies in order to rethink our understanding of Orthodoxy and its role in private and public life in imperial Russia. Russian history until after the fall of the Soviet Union in 1991 remained focused around explaining (and, especially in the Soviet Union, justifying) the Bolshevik revolution of 1917. Whether they regarded the church as having been too weak to stand up to the state and provide a viable alternative to revolutionary ideology, or as simply increasingly irrelevant in a modernizing and secularizing age, the political, social, and labor historians who dominated the profession in the West generally paid little attention to religious factors. In Russia, both before and after the revolution, the discounting of the ritualistic and visual components of religious practice also underlay the longstanding scholarly tradition of describing the religion of the peasantry as *dvoeverie* or "dual faith." According to this view, Orthodoxy remained merely a thin veneer over the fundamentally pagan beliefs of Russian villagers.[29] In Russia as elsewhere, such views of so-called popular religion were often also derived from or reinforced by the writings of clerics themselves who were involved in the great "rechristianization" campaigns that sought to reform popular practice and create a more "conscious" faith among the laity in the early modern and modern eras. The notion of dual faith served Soviet Marxist researchers of popular culture well, allowing them to portray the alleged preservation of paganism as a form of social protest against the dominant ideology. Thus, a perception that Orthodoxy was a religion that emphasized form over content played no small role in the longevity of the view of the Russian Orthodox Church as a state-bound and moribund institution in imperial Russia.[30] It also underlay the longstanding neglect of the history of Russian religious thought, of modern Russian Orthodox theology, and of religion as it was practiced.[31]

In many of the documents below, we encounter the intertwined worlds of scripture and physical practice. Roy Robson presents an Old Believer poster that brings together images and an ancient sermon by St. John of Chrysostom about the correct manner of making the sign of the cross to assert the theological importance of proper physical worship. Whether in a priest's struggle in his diary to make services meaningful or in the confessions infused with scriptural quotations from the liturgy that Nadieszda Kizenko introduces, these narratives of personal religious experience reveal how religious practices enacted the stories of faith.

These sources offer an opportunity to wade into the discussion of the nature of Orthodoxy as it was lived, as readers listen to various voices, many of a type rarely heard, telling their stories of religious experience or seeking to evaluate that of others. "Peasant" religiosity looks quite different, for example, in the memoirs of Archimandrite Toviia of his youth in the village than in the reports of priests. Women and workers reveal their understandings of faith as they write to their spiritual advisors, whether they are the legitimate startsy Paert presents or the popularly acclaimed but unsanctioned "Brother Ioann" Churikov introduced by Page Herrlinger. Readers can experience the challenge of hearing the mediated voices of believers whose words were recorded by others in the abbot's report of his interviews with prisoners at the Spaso-Evfimiev Monastery translated by Demoskoff or the official depositions recorded by the commission investigating the peasant Sergei Ivanov's miraculous cure that Worobec presents. They can also assess how Orthodoxy was at once shared across class, ethnic, and gender lines and inflected by these differences, for example in the selection of written confessions translated by Kizenko.

Stories of Faith as Narratives of the Self, the Nation, and Modernity

Religious narratives provide a particularly valuable arena for exploring the relationship between individual experience, prescribed texts, and discourses abroad in a society. Religious organizations, writes Nancy T. Ammerman, "are suppliers of 'public narratives,' accounts that express the history and purposes of a cultural or institutional entity. These organizations create widespread social arenas in which religious action can occur, and they supply structured religious biographical narratives – the saved sinner, the pilgrim – within which the actor's own autobiographical narrative can be experienced." Sacred stories are at once tales of uniqueness and tales of belonging: believers draw on the church's public narratives, but they also remember, adapt, create, and re-tell those stories in ways that make sense of their own personal experiences and that interact with the other "stories" within which they live.[32] Among the documents included in this collection are examples of prescriptive texts that were widely known through both reading and re-telling, such as the *Life of St. Stefan of Perm*, translated by Greene, or the akathist in honor of the icon of the Kazan Mother of God; other sources here reveal how believers used such texts and acted upon them. First and foremost, believers who told stories of faith sought to recount personal religious experience. But elaborations of the self, of modernity, and of the nation can all be found intimately interwoven through these sacred stories.

The recent surge of interest in religious history has coincided and intersected with a lively scholarly discussion of personal narratives, autobiographical practices, and constructions of the self in imperial Russia. Russian personal narrative developed in an atmosphere quite different from the individualistic culture to which much scholarship on western European or North American autobiographical texts attributes the flourishing of the genre in the modern era. The emerging western model of the self-defining, rational, individual self contributed to a dialogue about the individual personality in nineteenth-century Russia, but both an authoritarian political culture and important cultural elements quite skeptical of individualism militated against any unquestioning adoption of western patterns.[33] Russian theologians and church publicists engaged actively in this discussion of personhood, drawing on Orthodox teachings about both the possibility of and the need for Christian men and women to pursue moral self-perfection in quest of salvation.[34] Nineteenth-century seminarians were urged to keep diaries precisely to chart their own spiritual development, but also that of their parishioners.[35] The priest's diary introduced by Manchester and the excerpts from Archimandrite Toviia's diary show us this genre that was both individual and collective. The letters to and from Orthodox elders introduced by Irina Paert or the confessions written to the charismatic priest Father John of Kronstadt offer glimpses into how religious texts and practices, personal experience, and dialogue with a spiritual advisor combine in this process of self-perfection. These and other very private sources, together with the more public accounts of spiritual experience translated below, reveal how religious faith and ideas about religion contributed to and were shaped by evolving notions of gender and class identity, of the individual and the collective in imperial Russian society.

These documents also chart the continuing relevance of the sacred in modernizing societies and of religion as a framework for understanding the modern. Modernity's rationalizing impulse shaped official Orthodox attitudes toward miracles (as it did the Roman Catholic Church's in western Europe). Thus, in selections introduced by Worobec, Shevzov, and Greene, we see church authorities carefully investigating alleged miracles before giving them the official stamp of approval and increasingly seeking the support of modern scientific medicine for confirmation of healings.[36] Continuing anxiety about balancing belief in God's active power in the world with the findings of modern science emerges in sermons following the devastating earthquakes that rang in the New Year of 1862 in the Lake Baikal region, such as Breyfogle presents, or the description (most likely by a priest) of a near-death experience, translated by Worobec. The intellectual challenge of modern science's increasing understanding of the physical world was but one aspect of the secularizing forces that the Russian church, like its western neighbors, confronted in the nineteenth and early twentieth century. By 1905, changing social configurations and new political ideas seemed to threaten traditional views of community, authority, and the individual. The documents Freeze presents from Vladimir diocese reveal the church administration struggling to understand the relationship between modernization and the piety of the population; those of Friesen show how modern physical mobility could interfere with equally modern impulses to standardization and nationalization, as the church sought to create new parishes among migrants to Siberia. Religious faith was also implicated in the elaboration of modern identities. Stories of young, disoriented peasant workers in the city discovering new revolutionary identities are a staple of studies of the emergence of the working class in late imperial Russia. In the conversion narrative that I have translated below, Vasilii Skaldin tries on a revolutionary identity as a newcomer to the city, but simultaneously seeks meaning in Orthodox practices before settling on the Baptist teaching that finally helps him to make sense of his new self in the urban environment. In so doing, he followed a perceived pattern that church authorities increasingly worried about, especially after the revolution of 1905: the susceptibility of the peasant-worker to religious sectarianism or political radicalism. Indeed, Brother Ioann Churikov, who would ultimately be excommunicated in 1914, sought, as a lay preacher and healer, to help the inhabitants of the capital's working-class neighborhoods to live lives of faith in the city. In the prayer requests that they wrote to him, translated by Herrlinger, we see their daily struggles and their spiritual hopes. They express no sense that they are operating outside of the faith of their forebears in their quests.

Both religious narrative and physical religious experience contributed to the development of ideas about the Russian nation in imperial Russia. One modernizing component of Nicholas I's rule in the 1830s was the development of a state ideology, Official Nationality. Its slogan, "Orthodoxy, Autocracy, and Nationality," would be repeated down to the revolution of 1917. This triad would link the Orthodox Church with the state and with evolving notions of Russian nationality. In the eyes of the enemies of autocracy, Official Nationality would further tarnish the church's reputation, but it also provided a powerful creative framework for religious patriots who seized on the rather vague slogan and elaborated its significance.[37] In the Crimean War sermons of Archbishop Innokentii, for instance, we see such creativity at work. While Innokentii drew on these themes in a very public attempt to construct rhetorically the idea of Crimea's ancient Christian heritage and a Russia-wide Orthodox patriotism, other texts presented here show a physical landscape being shaped by the faith of pious laypeople. As pilgrims traveled to monasteries and shrines near and far or when they sought the "repatriation" of "their" local saints' relics; when they thrilled at the sight of the roadside cross outside of their home villages or fought to keep a miraculous icon in their midst, believers traced out a religious basis for local, regional, and national identity.

In these varied ways, the sources presented here reveal the complex relationships between memory and faith and identity, both individual and collective. By making these voices audible to the English-speaking reader, we hope to provide insight into modern Orthodoxy as it was lived in imperial Russia, into the many genres of spiritual narrative in that society, and into the role of the Orthodox Church and Orthodox religiosity in the social, political, and cultural history of the Russian Empire.

NOTES

1. Nancy T. Ammerman, "Religious Identities and Religious Institutions," *Handbook of the Sociology of Religion*, ed. Michele Dillon (Cambridge: Cambridge University Press, 2003), 215; Lewis R. Rambo, *Understanding Religious Conversion* (New Haven, CT: Yale University Press, 1993), 137–38, 158.

2. Boris N. Mironov, "The Development of Literacy in Russia and the USSR from the Tenth to the Twentieth Centuries," *History of Education Quarterly* 31, no. 2 (Summer 1991): 241.

3. Jeffrey Brooks, *When Russia Learned to Read: Literacy and Popular Literature, 1861–1917* (Princeton, NJ: Princeton University Press, 1985), 4.

4. Stephen K. Batalden, "Colportage and the Distribution of Holy Scripture in Late Imperial Russia," *Christianity and the Eastern Slavs*, vol. 2: *Russian Culture in Modern Times*, ed. Robert P. Hughes and Irina Paperno (Berkeley: University of California Press, 1994), 83–92.

5. See, for example: Ernest Gellner, *Nations and Nationalism* (Ithaca, NY: Cornell University Press, 1983); Benedict Anderson, *Imagined Communities*, rev. ed. (London: Verso, 1991)

6. For debates at the time about the number of dissidents among these eastern Slavs, see: Irina Paert, "Two or Twenty Million? The Languages of Official Statistics and Religious Dissent in Imperial Russia," *Ab Imperio* no. 3 (July 2006): 75–98.

7. Timothy Ware, *The Orthodox Church*, new ed. (London: Penguin, 1997), 5–7, 43–44.

8. Barbara Skinner, *The Western Front of the Eastern Church: Uniate and Orthodox Conflict in Eighteenth-Century Poland, Ukraine, Belarus, and Russia* (DeKalb: Northern Illinois University Press, 2009), 6, 34–35.

9. For the text of this decree, which established the basic framework of church-state relations for the rest

of the imperial period, see: Alexander V. Muller, trans. and ed., *The Spiritual Regulation of Peter the Great* (Seattle: University of Washington Press, 1972); see also: James Cracraft, *The Church Reform of Peter the Great* (Stanford, CA: Stanford University Press, 1971).

10. Gregory L. Freeze, *The Parish Clergy in Nineteenth-Century Russia: Crisis, Reform, Counter-Reform* (Princeton, NJ: Princeton University Press, 1993), 7.

11. Gregory L. Freeze, "Handmaiden of the State? The Orthodox Church in Imperial Russia Reconsidered," *Journal of Ecclesiastical History* 36 (1985): 82–102.

12. Gregory L. Freeze, "Russian Orthodoxy: Church, People and Politics in Imperial Russia," *The Cambridge History of Russia*, vol. 2, *Imperial Russia, 1689–1917*, ed. Dominic Lieven (Cambridge: Cambridge University Press, 2006), 291. On the *startsy*, see: Irina Paert, *Spiritual Elders: Charisma and Tradition in Russian Orthodoxy* (DeKalb: Northern Illinois University Press, 2010). On nuns, see: Brenda Meehan-Waters, *Popular Piety, Local Initiative, and the Founding of Women's Religious Communities in Russia, 1764–1907* (Washington, DC: Wilson Center, Kennan Institute for Advanced Russian Studies, 1987); William Wagner, "The Transformation of Female Orthodox Monasticism in Nizhnii Novgorod Diocese, 1764–1929, in Comparative Perspective," *Journal of Modern History* 78 (December 2006): 793–845.

13. Gregory L. Freeze, *The Parish Clergy in Nineteenth-Century Russia*, 53. Following Sophia Senyk's usage in "Schools for Priests: Orthodox Education in Eighteenth-Century Ukraine," *Orientalia Christiana Periodica* 70, no. 2 (2004): 289–312, in most cases we have chosen to translate the various terms by which they were known, including *tserkovnik, prichetnik, d'iachok, ponomar', d'iak*, and, after the 1860s, *psalomshchik*, as "cantor," which describes their primary role.

14. Freeze, "Russian Orthodoxy," 292–93.

15. Vera Shevzov, *Russian Orthodoxy on the Eve of Revolution* (New York: Oxford University Press, 2004), 80.

16. Freeze, *Parish Clergy*, 102–103; Laurie Manchester, *Holy Fathers, Secular Sons: Clergy, Intelligentsia, and the Modern Self in Revolutionary Russia* (DeKalb: Northern Illinois University Press, 2008), 14–15.

17. See for example: I. S. Belliustin, *Description of the Clergy in Rural Russia: The Memoir of a Nineteenth-Century Parish Priest*, transl. and intro. by Gregory L. Freeze (Ithaca, NY: Cornell University Press, 1985); Dmitrii Ivanovich Rostislavov, *Provincial Russia in the Age of Enlightenment: The Memoir of a Priest's Son*, transl. and ed. Alexander M. Martin (DeKalb: Northern Illinois University Press, 2002).

18. Gregory L. Freeze, "A Case of Stunted Anticlericalism," *European History Quarterly* 13, no. 2 (April 1983): 179; Manchester, *Holy Fathers, Secular Sons*, 123–27.

19. Manchester, *Holy Fathers, Secular Sons*, 19–21, 70; Jennifer Hedda, *His Kingdom Come: Orthodox Pastorship and Social Activism in Revolutionary Russia* (DeKalb: Northern Illinois University Press, 2008), esp. ch. 3.

20. Vera Shevzov, "Letting the People into Church: Reflections on Orthodoxy and Community in Late Imperial Russia," in *Orthodox Russia: Belief and Practice under the Tsars*, ed. Valerie A. Kivelson and Robert H. Greene (University

Park: Pennsylvania State University Press, 2003), 66, 70–73.

21. Chris Hann and Hermann Goltz, eds., *Eastern Christians in Anthropological Perspective* (Berkeley: University of California Press, 2010), 12.

22. Vera Shevzov, "Poeticizing Piety: The Icon of Mary in Russian Akathistoi Hymns," *St. Vladimir's Theological Quarterly* 44, no. 2–4 (2000): 344.

23. Vera Shevzov, "Between Purity and Pluralism: Icon and Anathema in Modern Russia, 1860–1917," in *Alter Icons: The Russian Icon and Modernity*, ed. Jefferson J. A. Gatrall and Douglas Greenfield (University Park: Pennsylvania State University Press, 2010), 56–57.

24. Ware, *The Orthodox Church*, 33; Robert H. Greene, *Bodies like Bright Stars: Saints and Relics in Orthodox Russia* (DeKalb: Northern Illinois University Press, 2010), 4, 8–9, 34.

25. Colleen McDannell, *Material Christianity: Religion and Popular Culture in America* (New Haven, CT: Yale University Press, 1995), ch. 1, esp. 13–15; Meredith McGuire, "Embodied Practices: Negotiation and Resistance," in *Everyday Religion: Observing Modern Religious Lives*, ed. Nancy T. Ammerman (New York: Oxford University Press, 2007), 187–89. See also: Harvey Whitehouse, *Modes of Religiosity: A Cognitive Theory of Religious Transmission* (Walnut Creek, Calif.: AltaMira Press, 2004); Jonathan Z. Smith, *Imagining Religion: From Babylon to Jonestown* (Chicago: University of Chicago Press, 1982).

26. Thomas Kselman, *Belief in History: Innovative Approaches to European and American Religion* (Notre Dame, IN: Notre Dame University Press, 1991), 1–7; Ellen Badone, ed., *Religious Orthodoxy and Popular Faith in European Society* (Princeton, NJ: Princeton University Press, 1990), 3–9.

27. Robert Orsi, "Everyday Miracles: The Study of Lived Religion," in David D. Hall, ed., *Lived Religion in America: Toward a History of Practice* (Princeton, NJ: Princeton University Press, 1997), 62.

28. John-Paul Himka and Andriy Zayarnyuk, "Introduction," in *Letters from Heaven: Popular Religion in Russia and Ukraine*, ed. John-Paul Himka and Andriy Zayarnyuk (Toronto: University of Toronto Press, 2006), 5.

29. Eve Levin, "*Dvoeverie* and Popular Religion" in *Seeking God: The Recovery of Religious Identity in Orthodox Russia, Ukraine, and Georgia*, ed. Stephen K. Batalden (DeKalb: Northern Illinois University Press, 1993), 29–52; Stella Rock, *Popular Religion in Russia: "Double Belief" and the Making of an Academic Myth* (Abingdon, UK: Routledge, 2007), esp. ch. 3.

30. Influential accounts that make this assumption include: Richard Pipes, *Russia Under the Old Regime* (New York: Penguin Books, 1974), ch. 9; John Shelton Curtiss, *Church and State in Russia: The Last Years of the Empire, 1900–1917* (New York: Octagon Books, 1965).

31. Recent work that addresses Orthodox thought, including the long-neglected subject of thought within the theological academies, includes: Judith Deutsch Kornblatt and Richard F. Gustafson, *Russian Religious Thought* (Madison: University of Wisconsin Press, 1995; Paul Valliere, *Modern Russian Theology: Bukharev, Soloviev, Bulgakov: Orthodox Theology in a New Key* (Grand Rapids, MI: Eerdmans, 2000); Hyacinthe Destivelle, *Les Sciences théologiques en Russie: Réforme et renouveau des Académies*

ecclésiastiques au début du XXe siècle (Paris: Les éditions du Cerf, 2010); Patrick Lally Michelson, "'The First and Most Sacred Right': Religious Freedom and the Liberation of the Russian State, 1825–1905," (PhD diss., University of Wisconsin–Madison, 2007); Judith Deutsch Kornblatt and Patrick Lally Michelson, eds., *Thinking Orthodox in Modern Russia: Culture, History, Context* (Madison: University of Wisconsin Press, 2014).

32. Ammerman, "Religious Identities," 217, 219; McGuire, "Embodied Practices," 187.

33. Jochen Hellbeck, "Introduction," *Autobiographical Practices in Russia – Autobiographische Praktiken in Russland*, ed. Jochen Hellbeck and Klaus Heller (Göttingen: V&R Unipress, 2004), 11–14; Laura Engelstein and Stephanie Sandler, "Introduction," *Self and Story in Russian History*, ed. Laura Engelstein and Stephanie Sandler (Ithaca, NY: Cornell University Press, 2000), 2–6.

34. Manchester, *Holy Fathers, Secular Sons*, 47–48; William G. Wagner, "'Orthodox Domesticity': Creating a Social Role for Women," in *Sacred Stories: Religion and Spirituality in Modern Russia*, ed. Mark D. Steinberg and Heather J. Coleman (Bloomington: Indiana University Press, 2007), 125–26; Gary M. Hamburg and Randall A. Poole, eds., *A History of Russian Philosophy 1830–1930: Faith, Reason, and the Defense of Human Dignity* (Cambridge: Cambridge University Press, 2010).

35. Manchester, *Holy Fathers, Secular Sons*, 72.

36. Christine D. Worobec, *Possessed: Women, Witches, and Demons in Imperial Russia* (DeKalb: Northern Illinois University Press, 2001), 54–58.

37. See, for example: John D. Strickland, "Remembering Rus' In Modern Russia: The Orthodox Church and Its Cultural Mission Before the Revolution," *Modern Greek Studies Yearbook* 14 (1998): 149–67.

ONE

The Miraculous Healing of the Mute Sergei Ivanov, 22 February 1833

Christine D. Worobec

POSTHUMOUS MIRACLES BEFORE SAINTS' RELIQUARIES AND AT gravesites that local believers thought contained the remains of holy individuals were ubiquitous across early modern and modern Orthodox Russia. They attested to the need and desire of communities to have their own protectors and intercessors before God in an uncertain world of illnesses, epidemics, and chronic conditions. Although miracles during or after the life of the holy person provided evidence of God's grace and rationale for sanctification, the process for sainthood in the medieval and early modern periods was not regularized. The political objectives of the monastic institutions' princely patrons, as well as local community and monastic interests, spawned petitions for canonization, to which the pre-modern church generally acquiesced.

Beginning with the mid-seventeenth-century church reforms and culminating in Peter the Great's 1721 Spiritual Regulation and replacement of the patriarchate (established in 1589) by the Holy Synod to oversee ecclesiastical affairs, changes in the official recognition of saints occurred. Skepticism about certain devotional practices and beliefs among the laity and fears about false miracles and saints, as well as unregulated saints' cults, made ecclesiastical hierarchs hesitant to acknowledge new saints and accept new miracles without verification. Such concerns were fueled by the growing strength of the Old Believer movement, which opposed the seventeenth-century church reforms, and the development of sectarian movements, along with the influences of the Protestant Reformation, Catholic Counter-Reformation, and Enlightenment. Accordingly, the eighteenth and nineteenth centuries witnessed few canonizations.

In the battle against superstitions, including what the Holy Synod viewed as excessive veneration of saints and miracle-working icons, the Russian Orthodox Church was unable to stem the disaffection of believers to Old Belief, sectarianism, Protestantism, and ultimately scientific rationalism. Consequently, in the 1830s the Synod somewhat softened its stance toward the laity's steadfast belief in miracles in their contemporary world. It now understood that the recognition of some miracles, while still subjected to the greatest of scrutiny, could improve its chances of success in the battle for control of the faithful. That relaxation resulted in the printing of unusual miracle stories in the church's newly established religious journals or in pamphlet form. With the explosion of print literature, by the late nineteenth century miracle tales appeared regularly in all religious publications, especially those geared toward the growing pilgrimage trade.

Generally, printed miracle stories were dramatically redacted versions of the miraculous cures. Following the medieval formula, a miracle tale recorded the name, estate, and residence of the recipient of the miracle as well as the nature of the individual's illness prior to the miracle; the ways in which the person prepared for the miraculous event; the nature of the saint's intervention; and finally, the type of thanksgiving the recipient bestowed upon the holy intercessor. The archival documents are much more elaborate in detailing the stories of the recipients of the miraculous cures and those of the eye-witnesses. While the components of the medieval genre remain, the testimonies include more personal information about the recipients and more detail about the miraculous cures. Some also provide insight into the verification process.

The archival file regarding the healing of the nineteen-year-old freeholder peasant Sergei Ivanov, who had been mute for nine years, at the reliquary of St. Sergius on 23 February 1833, located in the Trinity–St. Sergius Lavra (the term "*lavra*" denoting a monastery of exceptional importance and size) in Sergiev Posad (just over 78 kilometers northeast of Moscow) is fairly lengthy. Only a sampling of the documents is included below. In addition to Ivanov's sworn testimony to the miracle he had witnessed and the eyewitness account from the monk who was in charge of overseeing St. Sergius's reliquary, the monastery's investigative council took statements from eight others, mainly staff from the monastery's kitchen who could affirm that Ivanov had in fact been a mute. Some could attest to the miracle itself. The council also contacted Ivanov's village elder to ensure that he had the proper passport to travel to the monastery. In the end, Metropolitan Filaret and the Holy Synod accepted the council's recommendation that further inquiries were unnecessary, given the irrefutable signs that Ivanov had been the beneficiary of God's grace. An imperial decree signed by Nicholas I was issued on 30 March 1833 announcing the miraculous cure, and just two months after the miracle's occurrence an imperial censor allowed the publication of Ivanov's oral testimony as a pamphlet.

Sergei Ivanov was typical of Russian Orthodox pilgrims in traveling on foot to a number of holy sites before receiving his miraculous healing. Walking hundreds of kilometers was part of the arduous process of fulfilling a pledge to God and various saints to visit the holy men's and sometimes women's shrines. Prior to his 1833 pilgrimage to the Trinity–St. Sergius Lavra, Ivanov had made a pilgrimage tour the previous spring of the holy sites in Moscow, Sergiev Posad, and finally the distant city of Kiev, which housed the first Orthodox monastic institutions in the Rus lands, including the Caves (Pecherskaia) Lavra. Such an ambitious route exemplified Ivanov's resolve to demonstrate his sincerity in leading a committed Christian life. Other popular nineteenth-century pilgrimage tours included the locations that he visited as well as one or more of the following: the monastic complex at Solovki on the White Sea, the Valaam monastery in Karelia, the Sarov monastery in Nizhnii Novgorod province, and the Optina hermitage in Tula province.

Ivanov's testimony describes visions of a man he probably thought was St. Sergius. Visions and dreams of saints and particular miracle-working icons of the Mother of God were not uncommon in other miracle tales, although the timing of the miraculous cures varied. Some occurred immediately after the vision; others had to wait until a visitation to the particular saint's relics was possible. In the event of an immediate cure, the recipient of a miraculous cure was obliged to give proper thanks to the saint or Mother of God by visiting the saint's reliquary or miracle-working icon and ordering the appropriate prayer service.

Setting up the Investigative Commission

To the Governing Council of the Trinity-Sergius Lavra[1]
Most Humble Report of the Lavra's Dean Hieromonk Innokentii
   On this 23 February during the conduct of the hours [of the Divine Office] a miraculous healing before the relics of God's St. Sergius of the peasant Sergei of the village Shchiuch'evo [elsewhere in the documents Shchuch'evo], Venetskii district, Tula province, who had been mute for nine years, occurred; accordingly, it would be good if the Governing Council would carry out the necessary investigation of this occurrence of grace and report it to the authorities.
   23 February 1833
   Signed Dean Hieromonk Innokentii

Oath administered to witnesses

I, the undersigned, swear and bow before the Almighty God that I will under questioning by you inform you according to God's Christian commandment of the absolute truth, neither for the sake of friendship nor property, nor for gifts or donations, nor out of fear, nor out of envy or friendship; but I only want to and should say completely unadulterated only what I heard and saw, and I will add nothing upon pain of what awaits me on Christ's Judgment Day when he judges the dead, and with that absolute truth I kiss the words and cross of my Savior, Amen.
   Signed by the witness, the retired cavalryman [Christian name illegible] Mindin, from the Aleksandrov factory on behalf of the peasant Sergei Ivanov of the village Such'ia [sic] of Tula province because of Ivanov's illiteracy and the Lavra Council's steward Hieromonk Tikhon
   28 February 1833

Eyewitness testimony of the Holy Trinity Sergius Lavra's dean of the grave Hieromonk Innokentii before the Governing Council

Having noticed a mute man always zealously praying for about four weeks, I found out that he had the father prior's permission to live in the brothers' kitchen; I ordered him to come and see me sometimes since he often came to see Hieromonk Ilarii, the custodian of the brothers' refectory, who lived with me in the same building. Extending sympathy to him, especially when I saw a pious attitude in him, I advised him to pray fervently to the Saint [i.e., Sergius] about his inability to speak. Once, seeing him visit the monk Ilarii and figuring out from his gestures that he was preparing to go home, we talked him into staying and praying to the saint. During the second week of Lent, having my turn to say prayers before the saint's relics and seeing him, I ordered him to stand at the head of the saint's [grave] for prayer; and at eight fifteen, during the saying of the hours [and] seeing him in such devoted prayer on his knees, I summoned him, gave him some oil from the votive lamp in front of the holy relics to drink and ordered him to kiss the relics. [As a result of] being distracted from him by other pilgrims [and having to] conduct memorial services, I did not notice what state he was in. After I served memorial services for everyone and had supper, I entered Hieromonk Ilarii's cell, where I saw that mute noticeably enraptured by the fact that he was growing stronger in his ability to speak. Hieromonk Ilarii and I began to demand that he say his ABCs, and he talked with effort. Later, in the same manner he was able to say [the word] God, and having said this, he began to speak freely and explained that he had received this ability through the saint's relics. He did not believe that he could in reality speak, and out of joy and with tears, could only say: "O Lord My God! Holy Father Sergius, forgive me, a sinner!"

Soon after this they called us to Vespers; I went into the Church, and the healed [man] went there also, crying and praying before his Holiness, repeating those same words. All the laypersons in the Church and the brothers, learning about the beneficial healing, joyously praised the wondrous Lord and his saints. Upon the conclusion of Vespers, I brought him to the cell of the prior, who upon seeing his excited state, did not

think it appropriate to question him in detail, but [instead] ordered that prayers of thanks to the saints be said [and] ordered the healed [man] to prepare his confession so that he could partake of the holy mysteries, which was carried out with God's help.
Dean of the Grave Innokentii so testified.
Prior Archimandrite Antonii was present for this testimony.

Sworn Testimony of the freeholder Sergei Ivanov of the village Shchuch'evo, Vinevskii district, Tula province, to the Governing Council

On 24 February 1833 the freeholder Sergei Ivanov of the village Shchuch'evo, Vinevskii district, Tula Province, after kissing the cross, testified to the following in the presence of the Governing Council:

I am 19 years old; because of my being mute I gave a silent confession[2] each year and partook of the holy mysteries. When I was 9, I was given over to the parish priest, Father Aleksandr, to learn to read; and during the first year of my learning I experienced a seizure in my sleep, as a consequence of which, when I awoke, I began to lose control over my tongue and as a result of that lost the ability to speak, without losing my hearing. Then I began to have more convulsions every month; during a new moon they occurred three times in thirty-six hours, in the morning, at night, and then in the morning of the next day, during which I hurt my left arm, which I could no longer lift up without feeling cramps.

I lived in that state the whole time, trying to work as far as it was possible in various places, more often than not, at soldering factories and in my village. Wishing to receive God's grace through healing, I went after Easter of last year to Moscow and to St. Sergius; and then walked to Kiev. Having returned from Kiev and having been home one week, I saw one night in a dream that someone was talking to me: "You were at St. Sergius's; come again to him [and] maybe you will also be able to talk." When I awoke, I rejoiced [as one who] had taken a vow; I began to get ready to visit the Holy man. My uncle by birth and my little brother began to ask me where I was headed; with signs I showed them that I was going off to pray to God; I pointed to my earring, by which [sign] I explained that I was going to Trinity-Sergius. My uncle asked the township elder, Lavrentii Ivanov, for a pass to [allow me to] go to Trinity[-Sergius]. I arrived at the saint's body with it [the pass].

With permission of the head [of the monastery] I lived in the kitchen where I helped the cooks in the preparation of the brothers' repasts; I together with the other laypersons ate leftovers from the brothers' meals; then I went also to the church to pray to St. Sergius. During my stay I often went to the father dean who always ordered me to pray and to believe in the grace of the holy man, which strengthened my hopes in the saint, steadfastly wanting a loosening of my tongue. Having lived in the hermitage almost two weeks and not seeing any improvement in myself, and after that, during the full moon during Cheesefare Week,[3] having had once again a habitually strong seizure before everyone in the kitchen as before, three times, in the morning, in the evening, and in the morning of the second day, I thought, after gaining consciousness, about heading home. Both the dean and Father Ilarii counseled me to eat bread and not work. [They] tried to convince me to stay and pray some more but I was determined to leave. One night I saw someone in a dream quietly and joyfully telling me: "Why are you rushing home? Stay awhile, maybe God will give you back your tongue; you will stay and speak." After that I stayed and began to pray zealously to the saint at night, [and] to go to his services to ask for his grace. On the Thursday of the second week, while standing at the head of the saint's relics, by the father dean of the grave, near the end of the hours during my prayers, someone said in my ear: "Wait for an hour [and] God will give you back your tongue; you will be able to speak." Because of that voice, I rejoiced and became afraid, I trembled all over; having collected myself, I looked around me and could not see who could have told me this information; I fell to my knees and tearfully prayed to the holy man. At that time the father dean gave me some oil from the holy lamps before the saint's relics to drink and ordered me to kiss the holy relics. I could feel my tongue becoming unstuck, and it was as if something had come undone or broken apart inside of me, and I could raise my arm; I fell before the saint with tears, not knowing what had happened to me. Having prayed until everyone had left the church, I went to the holy man's cell with great joy and kissed the three relics there. After I left there, I glanced over to the Cathedral of the Assumption and heard myself say, "O Lord my God! St. Sergius! Pray for us sinners." As I said the words I didn't think it was my tongue doing the talking; overjoyed and not believing myself, I went to Father Ilarii's cell, to which the father dean also came. They began to order me to say my ABCs, then [the word] God. At first it was difficult for me to talk; it was as if all my vocal cords were cut. When I said the word "God" after them, then I was able to talk freely.

Because of the above-mentioned freeholder Sergii Ivanov's illiteracy, his spiritual father, the Lavra's Hieromonk Sergii, appended his signature to the evidentiary document.

Present for the taking of the deposition:
Prior Archimandrite Antonii
The Council's steward Hieromonk Tikhon

NOTES

1. RGADA, f. 1204, op. 1, d. 4736, ll. 1, 4, 5–7.

2. According to the priests' manual, a deaf mute could communicate with signs and gestures. In the event that a mute was literate, the priest might have the penitent read the questions asked in confession and answer each in turn with either an affirmative or negative gesture.

Rukovodstvo dlia sel'skikh pastyrei 1 (1888): 411.

3. Cheesefare Week, sometimes called Butter Week, refers to the week before Great Lent when meat cannot be consumed, but dairy products can be eaten even on the customary fast days of Wednesday and Friday.

SUGGESTED READINGS

Freeze, Gregory L. "Institutionalizing Piety: The Church and Popular Religion, 1750–1850." In *Imperial Russia: New Histories for the Empire,* ed. Jane Burbank and David L. Ransel, 210–49. Bloomington: Indiana University Press, 1998.

Greene, Robert H. *Bodies like Bright Stars: Saints and Relics in Orthodox Russia.* DeKalb: Northern Illinois University, 2010. Chapter 2.

Kenworthy, Scott M. *The Heart of Russia: The Trinity-Sergius Monastery under Tsars and Soviets.* Oxford:

Oxford University Press, 2010. Chapter 5.

Thyrêt, Isolde. "Muscovite Miracle Stories as Sources for Gender-Specific Religious Experience." In *Religion and Culture in Early Modern Russia and Ukraine,* ed. Samuel H. Baron and Nancy Shields Kollmann, 115–31. DeKalb: Northern Illinois University Press, 1997.

Worobec, Christine D. "Miraculous Healings." In *Sacred Stories: Religion and Spirituality in Modern Russia,* ed. Mark D. Steinberg and Heather J. Coleman, 22–43. Bloomington: Indiana University Press, 2007.

TWO

The Miraculous Revival and Death of Princess Anna Fedorovna Golitsyna, 22 May 1834

Christine D. Worobec

TWO UNDATED COPIES OF THIS EYEWITNESS ACCOUNT OF Princess Anna Fedorovna Golitsyna's miraculous revival after being pronounced dead by medical experts and of her subsequent death have survived in two different Russian archives in separate files devoted, in one case, to miracles attributed to both icons and saints and, in the other, to the full or partial biographies of spiritually uplifting individuals, most of whom had been monks. The shorter of the copies found in the latter category lists the author as Golitsyna's spiritual adviser, the parish priest Mikhail Lavrent'evich.[1] The editor of the redaction presented below is identified only by the initials G. K. The comments that G. K. made in the narrative itself, which he bracketed with the markings // and which I have kept in the translation and added where necessary, suggest that he was preparing either a sermon (if he, too, was a priest) or publication of the noblewoman's experiences for the edification of both Orthodox believers and non-believers. The record does not contain any evidence that the supposed miracle underwent investigation or the process of verification, although the original author is careful to note that he is relaying eyewitness testimonies. Such verification had become standard by the late eighteenth century. In polemical language the editor G. K. reveals his concerns about the dangers of the triumph of scientific rationalism over religious faith as well as the popularity of Pietism and other Protestant influences among members of the Russian nobility and his belief in the strength of the Orthodox God, whose omnipotence and grace, as demonstrated in this miracle story, ultimately triumph over both science and Protestantism.

Ironically, the recipient of this miracle belonged by marriage to the aristocratic Golitsyn family. Alexander N. Golitsyn had been head of the Russian Bible Society, which translated the entire Bible into Slavonic, and had been appointed by Alexander I in 1816 to head the Ministry of Education and a year later the amalgamated Ministry of Spiritual Affairs and Education. In a backlash against the mysticism of Alexander I, the Pietism and religious toleration of Golitsyn, and Quaker and Evangelical influences in state affairs, the Russian Orthodox Church was reasserting its authenticity and its primacy over religious affairs under the more conservative government of Nicholas I (1825–55).

That political agenda should not, however, diminish the piety and beliefs of Princess Anna Golitsyna. Her deathbed story illuminates an Orthodox noblewoman's understanding of her relationship to God, which ultimately transcended her love of husband and children. In all likelihood Golitsyna had been inspired by the popular Byzantine *Life of St. Basil the Younger* (d. 944), which, among other things, contains Blessed Theodora's depiction of paradise as well as her explanation that the truly repented could bypass the torments that the soul faced in the minor judgment.[2]

In the miracle story we see the application of the Orthodox Rite for the Anointing of the Sick, referred to here as the Unction of Consecrated Oil. One of the seven sacraments, it celebrates life in Christ and the Holy Spirit. It is usually administered to a sick conscious person, either on the deathbed or in a less serious condition. Unlike the Roman Catholic Church, which uses the rite in terminal cases, the Eastern Church has never used the phrase "Extreme Unction" to describe the rite, preferring instead to focus on repentance, the forgiveness of sins, and the healing of both mind and body. Indeed, the Anointing of the Sick may be administered to an individual more than once. According to the Orthodox theologian John Meyendorff, "The sacrament of oil bestows a new dimension of existence in the 'new Adam,' where there is no more disease or death."[3] The officiating priest first hears a penitent's confession and administers the Eucharist. Then he anoints the forehead, chin, cheeks, hands, nostrils, and breast with oil, while intoning a modified prayer from the Euchologian of Serapion: "O Holy Father, physician of souls and bodies, who sent your only begotten Son, Our Lord

Jesus Christ, who heals every infirmity and delivers from death: heal also your servant (name) from the infirmities of body and soul which afflict her, and enliven her with the grace of your Christ; through the prayers of our most-Holy Lady, the Theotokos and ever-virgin Mary... and of all saints."[4] Other prayers are part of the rite as well. In the nineteenth century clerics gave the consecrated oil to healthy individuals once a year on the Thursday of Holy Week in Moscow's Cathedral of the Assumption and in the main church of the Holy Trinity Sergius Lavra in Sergiev Posad, among other significant places of worship, where the preparation of the consecrated oil involved the participation of seven clerics.

In Princess Golitsyna's case, she was given the Eucharist and then the Unction of Consecrated Oil by virtue of the severity of her illness and her likelihood of dying. Having recently given birth to twins, she would not have undergone the purification ritual of churching, which occurs forty days after parturition. The sacrament of the Anointing of the Sick had the added benefit of cleansing her of impurities. After receiving the rite, Golitsyna was pronounced dead by the attending physicians, only to awake and articulate her belief that she had entered the heavenly Kingdom and experienced an angelic life. Even today, individuals who revive after having been pronounced clinically dead often talk about out-of-body experiences.

The Miraculous Revival and Death of Princess Anna Fedorovna Golitsyna, 22 May 1834

/Just as the incomprehensible, mysterious aspects of man's spiritual and physical nature boggle the mind when laid bare, so too, when confronted with the holy mystery of the divine, must even the most supreme intellect place the finger of silence upon his lips and with reverent humility prostate himself before the unassailable glory of nature's creator.[5]

The true and evident occurrence described here is one of those that solves many of our scientific perplexities about the soul and reveals several mysteries. It is an out-of-body experience./

Princess Anna Fedorovna Golitsyna, née Boborykina[6] [in 1807], was simple and ordinary, by all appearances a Christian; in terms of goodness a wife and mother; she was married for just over eleven years; by nature she had a weak, nervous constitution; a quiet, calm, almost always even temper. Simple-hearted and unwavering in her Orthodox faith, she was not at all brought up reading those books that easily entice and sometimes cause a woman to have a pretentious spiritual feeling and give them a disposition toward either Pietism or simple daydreaming. Preferring always to occupy herself more with her family responsibilities, which alone defined all of her earthly pleasures, she loved only her domestic circle, to which she was tied by her affection for her husband and children; under her cold reasoning, fashionable society and noisy gatherings, worldly essentials for others, held no attraction for her. Her favorite places for outings were to a large extent either their secluded summer houses with gardens, or the cemetery, or sacred cloisters where with great happiness she looked at tombstones. In ordinary domestic conversations with her husband she did not discuss with much thought anything about such matters as her future life, preparation for death, and about the situation of the dead beyond the grave. She frequently was visited by grace-filled dreams which she did not relay beyond her domestic circle, and did not recount them with any particular excitement [but rather] with a childlike simplicity of thoughts. She did not show herself to be particularly spiritual or pious, aside from the fact that, not counting the annual attendance at confession and communion, every time she was pregnant, when she was close to giving birth, she partook of the holy mysteries without fail. But Almighty God knows hearts and minds, and what he hid in matters of faith from the wise and intelligent, he revealed to babies.[7]

On 7 May 1834, after a very difficult and sickly pregnancy, she gave birth to twin boys. Even before the births she had a vision of Christ appearing as he is depicted on painted icons in full height with a red background and light blue riza [icon cover], with a beard split at its end, with fine brows and eyes the color of the heavens, with his hand making the sign of a blessing (just as she herself related with rapture), and in response to her persistent request that he appear before her as he did before his disciples he answered: "Why do you want that, for you will see me this way on my second coming and in all my glory." She responded to this: "Because I, like other people, would then be very afraid, but I would like it now because I very much love you," to which he replied: "Wait until Holy Week," and in response to her question about what day it would be, he did not specify but promised only that he would appear. At dawn on 22 May she suddenly felt such a change (although she had evidently recovered after giving birth) that she feared for her life. At that time she asked for a confessor. Although she was extremely weak and her tongue was already inert, she managed in full consciousness to partake of the holy mysteries. Everyone noticed that soon after taking communion her lackluster eyes brightened up again and some sort of unfamiliar animation was reflected on her bright and calm face. Without a doubt this was an act of blessed grace. Then she took leave of her grief-stricken husband with a rather strong spirit. Blessing her children and asking forgiveness from all of the servants, she said: "Pray to God for me, and I will also pray for you, if I am deemed worthy." Then, through her husband, she asked her spiritual father solicitously to grant her a few minutes of his presence at her deathbed, so that she could take from him the remaining instructions for an eternal life and the Unction of Consecrated Oil which she herself desired. "For I," she said, "will not live long with you." When the rite of the consecrated oil began, she said to her husband, whom she had summoned to her with the wave of a hand: "Do you hear that singing?" /she had apparently already lost her sense of hearing/ "How do you like it?" And in response to his answer that it was very comforting for a Christian, she added, "Yes, that singing is useful and important for people on earth; it can only be comforting for them, accustomed to it as am I and the children and the servants; but I will soon hear another, better Angelic singing there, only you, do not cry for me." After the rite with consecrated oil, which she experienced in full consciousness, she closed her eyes quickly out of fatigue and fell into deep unconsciousness: /which lasted more than an hour/ it was as if she were sleeping, but one could see, from her faint breathing, the gradual quiet parting of the soul from the body, so that the rite for the departure of the soul was performed by the priest!

    With this occurrence one after another doctors R[il'ter] [and Pavel Nikolaevich] K[il'biushevskii] appeared quickly. Upon taking her pulse, they announced without a moment's hesitation that all life had departed the body, for on her face a massive cold deathly sweat had already appeared. – But there was a startling moment: only when one of the doctors, who had continued to observe her situation carefully [and] in whose hand her pulse had stopped, pronounced to those standing [by the bedside], "She has passed away," did she, beyond all expectation, open her bright and fresh eyes, and with a rather strong and expressive voice, as if having fallen from the world into darkness, begin to say, "Where am I?" The expressions of the amazed doctors were a sight to see, as they experienced in all its force how God rejects the rational minds of intellects. One had to see the condition of the joyful husband, or more precisely the husband who was beside himself with joy, and the speechless ecstasy of amazement of all those present in order to understand this event. If this wasn't a miracle of Resurrection, couldn't one at least call this a miracle of an unexpected revival, when even the doctors, as far as they did not try to subsume this incident under the general laws of reason and nature, solemnly declared: "God is great!"? What good is all our knowledge in those places where God's finger clearly acts, where His strength acts upon sickness? /original words G. K./ Let others judge this as they wish. Let them call it a frequent, common occurrence such as being rooted to the spot or fainting. [But] what does it mean that the revived woman was somehow completely alien from all flesh? She no longer knew anyone around her, she no longer understood anything that was earthly and human. It was as if she were newly born, and completely divine, spiritual, and holy. She spoke with rapture as an inhabitant of heaven, with precision of a Higher knowledge of self, with harmony of the soul. Having already tasted the power of things to come,[8] she could explain in positive and optimistic terms the condition of her life in which she found herself after awakening more than nine hours later! Whether in the body or out of the body, I do not know, God knows.[9]

Let's propose for discussion for those who are curious the following details, noticed and upheld by the witnesses on hand [and] written down intentionally from the revived woman's actual words.

"Where am I?" she began to say after she awoke; "Tell me, someone. Is it possible that I am again in that dark, nasty, stuffy, and tedious world? Oh, why have I parted from that world where I saw the Savior? All have such beautiful faces there, but here they are all unsightly, coarse, repulsive!"

"Is it possible that you don't recognize us, Princess? This is your husband, Prince N[ikolai] N[ikolaevich], and these are your children / naming them all by name/," said one noble person.

"Husband, children! No, I don't know anyone, and I don't even understand your very words. True, I saw beautiful children there, but these ones are so grotesque." /After some silence [she said]/ "I didn't want to leave there; everything there is so nice, bright, happy; how easy it was for me there! I was completely healthy there, but here it is so difficult, painful, tedious! But the Savior told me: go and live some more where you were, and when you are no longer needed there, I will take you back. What can one do? Having taken a deep breath, I came back [to experience] an ordeal, suffering, but one can never disobey the Savior. He is our God, He saved us, but He will soon, soon send for me again!" /silence/ "How I want to see my Savior again! Give me His icon!" /They gave her an icon of the Dormition of the Mother of God and the icon with the relics of Saint Vasilii of Paria./[10] "No, this isn't the right icon. Here there are many representations of saints. They should also be revered and the Mother of God [should be] esteemed. She gave birth to God the Savior for us. Put those icons in their place and give me an icon of the Savior! I love only Him and seek only Him! I seek [only Him]."

Then, giving her an open prayerbook, her husband said, "Here is an image of the Savior."

"No," she answered. "I don't want to kiss a picture; give me the true icon of the Savior!" As soon as they gave her the icon of the Savior Not Made by Hands,[11] a rather handsome painting, she said, overjoyed: "That's Him! My Savior, whom I saw!" Firmly taking the icon in her hands, she covered it in ardent kisses, saying, "I love you, my Savior, I love only you; take me again to you!" Then turning to those around her, she said: "And you, do you love the Savior? If you love Him, then all of you, all of you, kiss Him. He is our God; He is our Redeemer; it is impossible not to love Him!" And when all those present had kissed the icon, she ordered that it be placed in front of her and gazed at it with joy.

The delighted husband, having come close to the bed, unintentionally sat with his back to the icon [and] leaned toward his wife, who quickly scrutinized him [and] said: "They tell me that this is my husband; what kind of husband is he who is so disrespectful of the Savior? Turn around and bow before Him: He is our God, our Redeemer." Her order was immediately obeyed.

After that, seeing the betrothal ring on her husband's hand, she asked, "What is that you have on your hand?"

"That is a betrothal ring, my friend."

"I don't understand the meaning of the word 'ring.'"

"Why, that is the same ring with which the priest betrothed us when we married."

"Why then don't I have such a ring on my hand?"

"Because of your illness, my friend, it was taken off your hand to [make things] easier [for you]."

"Why was that done? No, give me my ring; it is said that what therefore God has joined together, let not man put asunder!"[12]

When they gave her her ring and put it on her, she said, "Now I know that when the priest betrothed us, you became my husband."

The doctor came up to her and said: "Do not talk a lot, Princess: you are weak, take some medicine or Holy water, fall asleep, close your eyes, ..."

"And who do you think you are! What are these words 'weak,' 'medicine,' 'sleep'?! How abstruse and incomprehensible your language is! We don't have anything like that there. No one talks like that! What right do you have to give me orders? If my husband orders me to close my eyes, I will listen because God Himself ordered a wife to obey her husband."

"What ails you, Princess?" said the doctor.

"And what concern is it of yours? And I am closing my eyes not because I want to sleep, but because it is offensive for me to look on all of you freaks! ... ."

"Recently, my friend, you took better medicine – the body and blood of Christ," her husband said.

"Yes, I remember it well. How afterward it became easy and pleasant for me! I'm not ill, but healthy; I saw the Savior there, but He sent me again to you freaks."

"Didn't He, by way of you, give us some commands?" asked her husband.

"Yes, He ordered that you pray more zealously and live better."

"Tell me, my friend, am I worthy of being where you were recently?" her husband asked further.

"Yes! You'll be [there], only pray to God."

"By the way, my dear," asked her aunt. "Did you see dear Volodia[13] there? /That was her [the princess's] newborn baby who died after he was christened/. Did you see the other children?"

"You need not know whether I saw them or not; and if I did see [them], I wouldn't tell you; and I cannot for it is unworthy, don't you understand me? How wicked you all are; you are all merely curious but do not want to believe." /Having become quiet for awhile, [she then asked]/ "You, who questioned me, who are you?"

"I am your aunt M[aria] D[mitrivna Boborykina], the godmother who took your children out of the [baptismal] font."

"Well, you have a different name there... And what do you call me here?"

"Your name is Anna, my dear."

"Is there some other way to identify one another here? What [else] do you call me here?"

"Your Highness, Princess Anna Fedorovna."

"What nonsense! There is nothing like that there. Oh, how tedious it is to be with you!"

In the meantime, her confessor, the parish priest, had entered the room [and] sat down by the ill woman; no one had announced his arrival, but she immediately recognized him and with a smile expressed her pleasure, saying, "How pleased I am, because of you, Father! Thank you for administering the sacrament and unction to me. I saw the Savior, and it is so nice to see you. After all, you are carrying His image on you; go away, everyone else!

When those standing nearby had moved to the side, she quietly and already in a lifeless manner said to him, "In the name of the Almighty bless me, Father, on my journey."

The priest blessed her, placed a hand on her, and said the following prayer in everyone's hearing:

"May the Lord Merciful God provide for you; may the Lord Jesus Christ grant you every positive petition; may the Almighty God save you from all misfortunes; may the Lord teach you; may the Lord enlighten you; may the Lord help you; may the Lord save you; may the Lord defend you; may the Lord keep you safe; may the Lord cleanse you; may the Lord fill you with the joy of the Holy Spirit; may the Lord be your Protector; may the Lord as merciful and lover of men forgive your sins; may the Lord God Jesus Christ, on the Day of Judgment, forgive you and bless you for all of your living days, Amen!" /From the service book/[14]

After that, she kissed his hand and said, "How easy and pleasant it is for me now! Thank you, Father."

Upon the priest's departure, she frequently recalled him to those remaining as if she wanted to see him again; then she asked for the icon of the Savior and the cross with the holy relics; for the last time she kissed them and ordered that they be put back in their place, and with a weakened voice ordered those around her to pray with her, "Repeat after me," she intoned. "In the Name of the Father and Son." This last word – "Son" – [which] she repeated a few times, froze on her lips and she quietly passed away /at age 27/.[15]

It is likely that this type of revival was the result or fulfillment of some former pledge to her husband /just as he had asked her/ so that she could console him with news of her activity beyond the grave; and what the Savior himself said is even truer: "He who believes in me, though he die, yet shall he live."[16]

/Miraculous – worthy of rejoicing!/

NOTES

1. RGB, f. 304, part II, no. 250, ll. 429–39 as reproduced on www.stsl.ru/manuscripts/book.php?col=2&manuscript=250 (accessed 15 January 2013).

2. Gregory's *Life of St. Basil the Younger* may have been translated into Slavonic as early as the eleventh century. By the beginning of the sixteenth century, there were at least two Russian versions in circulation. See John-Paul Himka, *Last Judgment Iconography in the Carpathians* (Toronto: University of Toronto Press, 2009), 18; and David M. Goldfrank, "Who Put the Snake on the Icon and the Tollbooths on the Snake? A Problem of Last Judgment

Iconography," *Harvard Ukrainian Studies* 19 (1995): 180.

3. See Paul Meyendorff, *Marriage: An Orthodox Perspective* (Crestwood, NY: St. Vladimir's Seminary Press, 1975), 73.

4. Translated in Paul Meyendorff, *The Anointing of the Sick* (Crestwood, NY: St. Vladimir's Seminary Press, 2009), 164.

5. RGADA, f. 1191, op. 1, d. 1064, ll. 37–440b. I have used the version contained in RGB, f. 304, part II, no. 250, ll. 429–39 to fill in the names of individuals presented in the redaction only by their initials.

6. In nineteenth-century texts, the family name Boborykin sometimes appears as Babarykin or Bobarykin.

7. Matt. 11:25.

8. The phrase appears to come from Heb. 6:5 ("And have tasted the good word of God and the powers of the world to come...").

9. 2 Cor. 12.

10. St. Vasilii had been Bishop of Paria, who in the early ninth century fought against iconoclasts in the Byzantine Empire. His saint's day is celebrated on 12 April; *Pravoslavnaia entsiklopediia* http://www.pravenc.ru/text/150497.html (accessed 25 April 2011).

11. According to legend, Christ miraculously created the first icon in his own image, the so-called "Not Made by Hands," on a mandylion or towel, which he sent to the ailing King Abgar of Edessa. The image healed the ruler.

12. Mark 10:9, which is quoted in the Russian Orthodox marriage service.

13. Volodia is the diminutive of Vladimir. He was born on 7 May 1834 and died two days later. The surviving twin was named Aleksei Nikolaevich (d. 1 September 1868). Nikolai Mikhailovich (Romanov), *Moskovskii nekropol'*, 3 vols. (St. Petersburg: Tip. M. M. Stasiulevicha, 1907–1908), 1:295, 293.

14. This is one of the prayers said over a person receiving communion. For E. V. Shann's translation of the complete prayer, see his *Book of Needs of the Holy Orthodox Church* (London: David Nutt, 1894), 125, at http://www.ccel.org/ccel/shann/needs/Page_125.html (accessed 25 April 2011).

15. Golitsyna was buried in Moscow's Vagankovo cemetery. (Romanov), *Moskovskii nekropol'*, 1:295.

16. John 11:25.

SUGGESTED READINGS

Himka, John-Paul. *Last Judgment Iconography in the Carpathians.* Toronto: University of Toronto Press, 2009. Appendix 3.

Marker, Gary. "God of Our Mothers: Reflections on Lay Female Spirituality in Late Eighteenth- and Early Nineteenth-Century Russia." In *Orthodox Russia: Belief and Practice under the Tsars,* ed. Valerie A. Kivelson and Robert H. Greene, 193–209. University Park: Pennsylvania State University, 2003.

Meyendorff, Paul. *The Anointing of the Sick* (Crestwood, NY: St. Vladimir's Seminary Press, 2009).

Nastol'naia kniga sviashchennika: Reshenie nedoumennykh voprosov iz pastyrskoi praktiki (Kiev: V tip. Kievskogo Imperatorskogo universiteta imeni Sv. Vladimira, 1903), 104–12.

Wigzell, Faith. "Reading the Map of Heaven and Hell in Russian Popular Orthodoxy: Examining the Usefulness of the Concepts of Dvoeverie and Binary Oppositions." *Forum for Anthropology and Culture* no. 2 (2006): 364–67.

Zacek, Judith Cohen. "The Russian Bible Society and the Russian Orthodox Church." *Church History* 35 (1966): 411–37.

THREE

Monastic Incarceration in Imperial Russia

A. J. Demoskoff

DURING THE IMPERIAL PERIOD, RUSSIAN ORTHODOX MONAS-
teries often served a life-giving function, in both a spiritual and a physical sense, as centers of pilgrimage and charity.[1] It would be remiss, however, to deny a more controversial side to their history. The practice of incarcerating individuals in Russian Orthodox monasteries would doubtless fall into this latter category. Peter the Great is a well-known example, since he consigned his half-sister, Sophia, to a convent in order to seize the throne in 1689. But political intrigue represents a very small percentage of the people who were confined in monasteries. More frequently, members of the clergy, landowners, and even peasants were sentenced to perform public penance by the ecclesiastical courts or by one of the many secular regional authorities.

Most people who served time in monasteries did so within the context of traditional practices of public penance. The "crime" was most likely to be a sin under biblical or church law, with sexual sins such as fornication and adultery being at the top of the list. Missing confession and communion as well as heresy and apostasy were also common reasons to be sentenced to public penance. Indeed, avoiding confession and communion was at times a way of concealing sectarian belief. A sentence of public penance usually involved living under monastic rule, attending church services within the monastery and answering to a confessor. The goal was reformative rather than punitive, so good behavior and outward signs of repentance could result in the reduction of a sentence.

It is significant to note, however, that punishment by incarceration in a monastery was not merely for religious disobedience or "sin" as it was understood by the church authorities. The secular courts also sent individuals to monasteries for a variety of reasons, including social disturbance, mental illness, and sometimes for violent and/or political crimes. The blurred boundaries between sin and crime and the frequent negotiations between the secular and religious powers demonstrate the complicated relationship between the church and state establishments. The authority structure was not always clear. At times the ecclesiastical authorities seemed to dictate the conditions, and at other times they submitted to the secular rulers.

For the most part, incarceration in a monastery was seen as a light sentence and the physical burden was not onerous. There were even times when the church authorities gave permission for the sentence to be fulfilled in the local parish for reasons of circumstance. There were two monasteries, however, where the crimes were of greater political import, the punishment more rigorous, and the facilities more prison-like with the inmates being kept under military guard – Solovetskii Monastery in Arkhangelsk diocese and Suzdal Spaso-Evfimiev Monastery in Vladimir diocese.

The first document in this section is a decree sent from the Kaluga Spiritual Consistory to the rector of the Borovskii Pafnut'evskii Monastery regarding a sentence of church penance given to a peasant for failure to attend confession and take the Eucharist. This is a typical example of the communications that were sent from the ecclesiastical or secular authorities to the person who would oversee the fulfillment of the penance, outlining the conditions of the sentence. The second document is a report from Lavrentii, the father superior and archimandrite of Suzdal Spaso-Evfimiev monastery in Vladimir diocese, sent to the governor of Vladimir in 1840. From the last quarter of the eighteenth century monasteries were required to submit similar reports to the Holy Synod (the highest administrative organ of the Russian Orthodox Church) every six months. These semi-annual reports took the form of a chart as established by the Synod. The chart was to include the following information: name of monastery, name and age of each prisoner, date sentenced and by whose authority, for what crime and length of sentence, state of mind (sanity) and behavior during captivity. The second document is in most respects representative of these reports. It differs slightly in format but contains the same fundamental information, providing basic biographical and situational details regarding the prisoners and their sentences. Unlike the hundreds of other such reports, however, Lavrentii went into greater detail on the behavior of the prisoners, often with his own unique and rather inarticulate turns of phrases. He described not only their mental health and spiritual well-being, but also measures taken to bring individuals to repentance, and even snippets of actual conversations between himself and the prisoners, providing us with a glimpse into the religious narratives embraced by these individuals. While it is important to keep in mind that these conversations have been filtered through Lavrentii's own worldview and therefore represent his own sacred categories (including what it meant to be Orthodox or heretical), they nevertheless preserve for us glimpses into the mindset of the prisoners themselves and how they articulated their own beliefs and situations. When this same document was forwarded to the Holy Synod, the behavioral reports were reduced by the local consistory to a simple "good" or "bad."

These documents invite further study in several areas. Was the rehabilitation of prisoners an issue of concern among the authorities? Are there differences between the reports on prisoners who were sent by the ecclesiastical authorities as opposed to the ones who were sent by a secular authority? In what ways are religious and political narratives intertwined in these documents, and what does this tell us about life in Imperial Russia? And to what extent do these documents deal with narratives that are specifically Orthodox?

A File on Public Penance in Kaluga Diocese (1825)

A file on the fulfillment of church penance by various persons assigned by the Spiritual Consistory for criminal offences, failure to perform church rites and other [reasons].[2]
19 May 1825 (received 22 May)

A decree of His Imperial Majesty the All-Russian Autocrat from the Kaluga Spiritual Consistory, to its member of the Kaluga Seminary, the rector of the Borovskii Pafnut'evskii Monastery, Father Archimandrite Venedikt. This consistory has heard the file initiated according to the report of the Kaluga Provincial government which lays out the decision of the Kaluga Criminal Court, about conferring church penance [on] Mikhail Nikitin, a peasant from the village of Liudskov on the estate of titular counselor Peter Smirnov of Vereiskii uezd, for failure to attend confession and to take the Eucharist for six years. With the same notice from the above-mentioned provincial government about its sending the peasant Nikitin to this consistory . . . from that date (May 4) a receipt of an excerpt from the law [was] attached to the report sent to the provincial government. They ordered, and His Eminence Damaskii, the bishop of Tul'skii and Belevskii, confirmed that: . . . on the basis of the decrees of November 4, 1765, October 19, 1797, and January 26, 1801, as someone who does not attend to the benefit of his soul, and who does not fulfill the duties imposed by the Holy Church, to assess a month of church penance, to be fulfilled by him, Nikitin, at the Borovskii Pafnut'evskii monastery. During all of that time, he is to consume only dry food, go to church every day to all the services, and at these services he is to make twenty-five prostrations [while repeating] the prayer of the Publican.[3] For the proper fulfillment [of these things] a decree is sent to you, father Archimandrite Venedikt, with instructions that, upon the fulfillment of penance assigned to him, the peasant Nikitin, and after he has been convinced not to avoid his soul-saving Christian duty, and having tested his conscience in confession through a confessor, [he is] to receive the Holy Mysteries of Christ if he is worthy. Then send him, Nikitin, along to the Borovskii District Court for settlement to his place of residence, and report back to the consistory.

May 19, 1825.
Annunciation Archpriest Grigorii.

Кто такой, и каких лет, каждый из ниже показанных лиц, с какого времени находится в Арестантском отдел. Спасо-Евв. Монастыря; от кого, и по какому случаю, прислан в оное.	Какой образ мыслей или дух вообще, имеет кто либо из содержащихся в Арестантской, и каков по жизни.
1., Г-н Статский совет-ник, Пилецкий Он 59-ти лет; находится в Арестант-ском отделении Спасо-Евфимиева монастыря с 1837 г., 19го Мая; прислан ли в это отделе-ние, по Высочайшему повелению, от Его Высо-копревосходительства, Владимирскаго Губерна-тора, при отношении, за составление тайнаго союза, и установлении своего образа молений, вопреки духу нашей Истинно-Христианской церкви, и Высочайшим узаконениям.	Имеет ныне понятие о Религии Христианской, возвышенное, и несколько по видимому непритво-ное внутренному ея составу; таковой образ мыс-лей своих христианских внушает, по возмож-ности, и в самой своей жизни; именно он ве-дет себя постоянно, особенно хорошо, или, как Христианин. При Богослужении бывает он во вся-кое время, без меры строг в отношении к себе самому, а к другим, и преимущественно к обу-мнимыми из человечества, исполнен он любви живейшей, истинной. Вообще, в мышлении чистейшим, и деятельности Духовной, он зна-чительно усовершен и утвержден.

Софроний |

3.1. First page of the Report on the Condition of Inmates in the Monastic Prison at Spaso-Evfimiev Monastery in Suzdal (1840). GAVO, f. 578, op. 1, d. 165, 1840, l. 14. Reproduced with permission.

Report on the Condition of Inmates in the Monastic Prison at Spaso-Evfimiev Monastery in Suzdal (1840)

Column A: Identity and age of each of the individuals listed below. How long has he been in the prisoners' section of Spaso-Evfimiev Monastery, who sent him there, and under what circumstances?	Column B: What manner of thinking or what general spirit does the person who is being held among the prisoners have, and what kind of life?
1. General State Adviser Piletskii. He is 59 years old and has been in the prisoners' section of Spaso-Evfimiev monastery since 19 May 1837. He was sent to this section by imperial command, by His Excellency the Governor of Vladimir, for the creation of a secret union, and the establishment of its manner of praying, contrary to the spirit of our True Christian Church and imperial laws.	At present he has an understanding of the Christian religion that is elevated, and by appearance, not in the least contrary to its inner structure; the same manner of his Christian thinking is conveyed also in his own life as far as possible. Namely, he always manages himself particularly well, or as a Christian. Any time he is at liturgy, he is immeasurably strict with respect to his own self, but toward others, and especially to the impoverished of humanity, he is full of living, true love. In general, he is significantly committed and confirmed to pure thought and spiritual activity.
2. Former Priest Aleksandr Chernyshev, who by his own desire left the cloth, but not without the consent of higher authorities. He is 39 years old and has been kept in the prisoners' section since 16 October 1836. He was sent there by command of the Sovereign Emperor, from the Governor of Vladimir, because of the breakdown of his mental capacity.	At the present time, he judges and reasons correctly and not incoherently in almost every instance. He has good health and not the kinds of infirmities that are sometimes present. He does not forget the Liturgy of the church. In his manner of life, he is well disposed with regard to himself and also toward others. A disposition of hostility has not become apparent in him. In short, he is in rather good condition. Through his learned household activities, little by little he gets stronger and better, both in the strength of his soul and body, and, it seems, he will soon come to a regular condition.
3. Gavriil Lektorskii, Former Muromskii Archpriest He is 61 years old and has been kept in the prisoners' section since 16 April 1832. He was sent there by	At present he thinks and judges according to the spirit of the Holy Scriptures – in a Christian manner, soundly. A special disposition to attend liturgy can be seen in him; he is as observant of himself as possible, and not at

imperial command, by His Excellency the Governor of Vladimir, for performing reprehensible deeds, harmful for both himself and others, after suffering brain damage.

some specific time, but at any time without distinction, he is prudent and unreserved in his treatment of others, but in a considerable [number of] cases he is open and in disclosing some matter, it is possible to say, he can be generous. His sincere stories are accompanied for the most part with some sort of anger. In a word – Christian simplicity and candor form the essential traits of his character.

4. Hieromonk Filaret, Novgorod diocese, Kirillo-Belozerskii Monastery.

He is 73 years old; he has been in the prisoners' section of Spaso-Evfimiev Monastery since 22 April 1836. He was sent there by order of the Supreme Spiritual Authority, by letter from the town governor of Suzdal, being found to have a deranged mind, and in prevention of the harmful actions of which a person in his condition is capable.

At present he too is found in a downcast state. His intellectual abilities are not functioning properly. Namely, he does not sufficiently know himself, nor can he exactly recognize others. He is often vexed and complains about himself and about everything around him. Even in casual dealings with people, especially those who have an influence on him, he is extremely angry. Such a disorder in his spirit is probably caused by a physical disorder, and to be precise, from an illness that is revealing itself in his legs. But he is zealous toward the liturgy and strict with himself.

5. Dosifei, Irkutsk diocese, Selenginskii Monastery Hieromonk, stripped of the priesthood and monkhood.

He is 45 years old and has been kept in the prisoners' section since 8 November 1834. He was sent there by imperial command, by decree of the Vladimir Spiritual Consistory, for the dissemination of doctrine contrary to Christian teachings among the residents of Trinity Savskaia fortress. He was also sent there for his collaboration in the alteration of the rites of the Divine Liturgy, which clearly involved the abasement of the sacrament of the Eucharist.

At present he has an elevated, pure spiritual, Christian tendency, is deep within himself, or is closed within himself, and he believes in the invariable and special habitation of the Spirit of God in himself. He also sees Christ in his spirit all the time, and he allegedly must instruct or teach him directly, in every case, and especially when studying Holy Scripture and he, in this instance, according to his understanding, should be some sort of extraordinary internal Interpreter, and internal, unmediated teacher. When he says the name of Jesus, and especially during rather lengthy discussion about this Eternally benevolent person, he experiences a strong change followed by strange bodily movement. That is to say in this condition he jumps and claps his hands while repeating the words, "Jesus my light, light, light, light, light," and so on. He attends liturgy and he

6. Simon Shvetsov, head of the Molokan Sect, Merchant of the town of Shatska in Tambov province.

He is 75 years old and has been in the prisoners' section of Spaso-Evfimiev monastery since 13 December 1835. He was sent there by imperial command, referred by the Shatska district police officer Maskatilev, for his own personal Molokan delusions and his effort to attract others to the same sect.

is very zealous and often demonstrates the condition described above. Toward others he is good; to himself he observes moderation.

At present he is still not leaving his delusion, nor does he intend to do so. He does not recognize even one of the regulations of our church as true and necessary for salvation. In his understanding it [our church] appears too refined and free, without limits. To be precise, he considers our church to be nothing, since in his unfounded opinion, he considers it a human invention devised for imperfect people, but not for the perfect and, so to speak, for those who manage without such things in their search for God. For the latter, all that is perceptible and imagery is of no use. They are not elevated by this, but they grow dull in their feelings or these become very limited. He is so elevated in his nature, and that is why exercise in the perceptible and objective is not necessary for him – so he constantly asserts about himself. He has a perfect spirit and he is united with God and that is why the means for merging with the Higher Being are entirely superfluous for him. "For example," he says, "I can see God without images and bow to Him in my own soul." And in his understanding, all other church-approved methods for our spiritual elevation, for example fasts, are of little value to him. Such institutions can have more of a place for the simple, but not for those who are able to triumph over their own selves, or can conquer all their passions spiritually within themselves. "These same rites," he maintains, "or the observance of one or another of such regulations, will achieve nothing for us with respect to our salvation." In general he has an aversion to outward appearances and he is interested only in that which is distant from our sight, the spiritual, that is, not determined in our thoughts or ideas. And it is not his way of life that deserves attention – indeed it is extremely ordinary – but rather his aversion.

7. Kodrat Feodorov, peasant of Countess Litty.

He is 70 years old and has been kept in the prisoners' section since 3 December 1825. He was sent to that section by imperial command, by decree of the Vladimir Spiritual Consistory, for his deviation to the Jewish delusions.

Until now he has had very simple ideas about religion in general, and more so about Christianity. For example, in his mistaken opinion, Jesus Christ was not equal to God the Father, but far lower in his essence, and this is also why he does not rank as the true God in the proper sense of this word. The Savior, in his quite superficial judgment, is nothing more than a human, albeit an extraordinary human, imbued with God-given gifts and clothed with extraordinary power such that during His sojourn in this world, He did many things that exceeded normal, human powers. He also dreams up ideas about the rest of our Christian doctrine. For example, in his very limited understanding, allegedly the dead who pleased God should receive life once again, but those who did not submit themselves to the will of the Lord, who have finished their earthly existence, will not ever return to life. And he maintains a moral doctrine that is in many ways incorrect. Thus he does not accept representations of the Holy. He says that icons are not necessary. It is possible to see the image of God or of any holy person in every living person since each of us can fully represent, in himself, God Himself. And further – he considers Saturday an important holiday, and to be precise, he also honors this day as we honor our Sunday. And in general, he is unrestrainedly devoted to everything to do with the Old Testament. Thus he holds the Old Testament feasts in great esteem since, he says, God himself established them. In like manner also, he has great respect for the Holy people of the Old Testament. He also studies only the Old Testament, mainly through reading the Psalter; but as for Christianity, which he does not understand, he simply has no respect for it whatsoever. His way of life is very normal and, it can be said that it is rather low. In general – he does not differ from followers of the Jewish faith.

8. Mikhail Timofeev, a schismatic of the re-baptizing sect, peasant of Moscow province, Ruzskii district, from the village of Iakshina.

He is 41 years old and has been held in the prisoners' section in a special room since 28 November 1838. He was sent to this section as a result of imperial command, by decree of the Vladimir Spiritual Consistory mostly for the misinterpretation of the Revelation of Saint John, and for the resulting resolute assertion that the Antichrist was born in Moscow, and that the time of his birth was 1666 – namely, the time when Nikon was installed as Patriarch, and therefore, so he thinks, it is possible to consider Peter I as the first "Emperor Antichrist," and the presently reigning sovereign, Nikolai Pavlovich, as the last.

To this day he is immeasurably bound to his schismatic prejudices and has no intention to deviate from them. According to his unreasoned view, everything in their society is lawful, pious, and worthy of God. But in our true, Christian society, everything is criminal and that is also why God is not pleased with our most perfect service of Him. He resolutely says that at the present time, God does not reveal His divine, gracious presence in the Christian church, since everything in its sacred services happens according to the new way; namely you have changed every form of the liturgy in contrast to the former way. He says constantly and to all who preserve the Christian faith in purity and without prejudice that you have your prayers too, and they are pronounced in their own way, and the actions at the time of the sacred service are not the right ones, are not correct, but are your own, invented ones, they are nothing other than the work of the Antichrist, and your clergy are not worthy of the service that they must perform. And they do perform it since their lives are not in good order; thus, they give themselves up to many unpermitted things – they trim their moustaches and the arrangement of their fingers when praying is not as it ought to be, and they are not alien to self-interest. In short, their behavior is very normal, but that is why they cannot be, for that important quality, that at their ordination they did not receive God's divine grace for performing the sacraments, since they were ordained according to the new books. And thus in the so-called Christian church one does not receive salvation, nor is there the possibility to receive any sort of salvation in Her [the Church]. And that is why all those who take measures to turn us to the Christian faith are justly called tyrants. Keeping to an allegedly true Christian faith they try to turn us from the True Faith to their untrue one; if they cannot make us voluntarily stray from our religion, then they subject us, or are prepared to subject us, to the same punishments that Nero and Domitian, in their hard and steadfast opposition to Christianity, subjected true believers to in former times. It is exactly the same with us, or I should say, directly, the supreme authorities do precisely the same thing with me by keeping me here in such confinement for a long time. In truth, times of cruelty for us true Christians have begun or have returned – the times of Nero and Domitian, tormentors of humanity, the times of the Antichrist. This is the way of thinking of this schismatic about our Faith and about the supreme authorities, and about the currently reigning Sovereign Emperor Nicholas the First! And the life of this prisoner is quite low but that is why it is also detestable; it is most empty because he is not able to achieve anything for his salvation, nor is he able to achieve anything through it.

9. Ivan Poliakov, Kiev townsman, Schismatic.

He is 56 years old and has been kept in a separate room in the prisoners' section since 14 June 1837. He was sent to that section by imperial command by the Suzdal town governor because at the request of the military command he did not take our oath.

He is fully occupied with his schismatic biases, such that by fully keeping faith, he hopes to save himself. He considers everything truly Christian insufficient for this task, since according to his rather undefined understanding, genuine Christianity is imperfect; in the form of its religious teachings it is connected with considerable delusions. Everything in it is erroneous; most importantly, its liturgy is untrue, it is from the Antichrist. In such service to God a person does not sanctify himself but makes himself more impure. And that churches in which it takes place are not churches but outhouses. And those who perform the liturgy are not true servants, but people who just use the name of such ones. Their sacraments are such in name only but not in reality. And likewise both prayers and actions during the sacred services are allegedly against their Old Faith. In general, according to his delusion he is against our Church and completely belongs to one of the

| | Old Believers' sects – the so-called Priestly Old Believer sect. Also he conducts himself rudely and, sometimes, forgetting his current situation, without distinction, is not humble with anyone who talks to him. |

10. Evfimii, Kaluga diocese, former Hieromonk of Borovskii Pafnutiev monastery, deprived of the priesthood and monkhood for false denunciations.

He is 62 years old and has been kept in the prisoners' section since 25 December 1833. He was sent there from Solovetskii Monastery by imperial command, by decree of the Vladimir Spiritual Consistory, for the same reason that he was kept in Solovetskii – namely, for the false interpretation of dogmatic teaching.

At present, he apparently understands dogmatic teaching in agreement with the Scriptures, in a Christian spirit. In discussion with him about some dogmas, there is revealed in him some sort of special readiness of spirit and a respect toward the holy subject under discussion. And in such a case, he is not content with simply upholding some truth, but also demonstrates his readiness to defend it as best he can and he defends it actively. For example, when talking about the future judgment, he said that the Lord is called omniscient and that is why he is a just judge, and incidentally he said that that is why by serving him in spirit, he receives a worthy prize for his spiritual, Christian service. In like manner he also keeps moral doctrine correctly and almost without any deviation from our usual understanding of it. There is only one thing in him that causes doubt, and that is that while he was talking about the statutes of the church, he said that he tries to observe and does follow all the regulations of the church and the fasts in the purity of his conscience, except when infirmity happens to him or could occur. About his way of life, he himself testifies, calling himself a slave of the Lord Jesus. Indeed he conducts a strict, selfless, spiritual-Christian life. He is fully committed to the authorities. On this subject, he expressed himself as follows: "The authorities have full power over me, and they can treat me, an unfortunate prisoner, however they want." In short, he has almost reformed his way of thinking and in life he is much, much improved, so that one sees little of the laboriousness and dissatisfaction in him that used

11. Tikhon Sal'nikov, Perm province, Osinski district, Dubrovskaia Volost, peasant, schismatic.

He is 64 years old and has been kept in the prisoners' section of Spaso-Evfimiev Monastery since 27 March 1838. He was sent there by imperial command referred by the Perm Provincial Governor, mostly because he bothered the heir-tsarevitch for permission to serve the liturgy in his own Old Believer way, with a petition from 10,000 people who did not have this in mind.

to occur at times, even in insignificant cases. It is especially wonderful that he has in him a special disposition to attending liturgy, and a readiness to express it during the service in frequent outward worship of God.

He is in no way improving nor does he think about his correction. Namely, he holds his Old Believer faith and is convinced that it is true, and therefore he finds it fully sufficient for receiving salvation. He considers anything else in this respect to be excessive. For example, he regards our manner of divine service as nothing, and therefore when he was supposed to attend, he did not. And there is little prospect for hope, given his complete disregard toward such a Holy matter, that he will at some point conceive a resolve to participate in our Holy services. However to all who enter into conversation with him, he insists that when he is liberated he will go to hear the Divine Service at some church that is located in his home region and he will take the sacraments there from the local clergyman. He behaves very normally, or, he leads a most simple life. That is, he does not occupy himself with anything that concerns his spiritual perfection, but only keeps himself busy by eating and sleeping.

12. Egor Ivanovich, Vishniakov, Deacon of the village of Novoe Prokudino, Iurevskii district.

He is 51 years old and has been in the prisoners' section since 14 November 1815. He was sent to this section from Florishchevaia Pustyn, referred by the abbot, by order of the authorities, because of mental derangement.

Even now he remains in an extremely sick condition, to the point that he has perfectly shattered strength, both spiritually and physically. To be precise, his reason is not functioning and he is decisively unable to judge about anything in any way. Like a child he merely looks at everything in his field of vision, without ascending to its foundation or to the sort of knowledge by which something is usually defined from one angle or another. And so I have had occasion to ask him, more than once, has he long been housed in this place of confinement. He gave me a short answer, "I don't know, I don't know how long I've been here." I asked him whether it had been ten years and he answered, "It seems so." When I asked him what day of the week it was or what this day was called (we were speaking together on a Sunday), he said to me likewise, "I don't know." "Is it Thursday?" I said to him. And he confirmed my suggestion, "Probably Thursday." But then I addressed him again and said, "Today is Saturday." And he responded, "Yes, so it is. Today is Saturday." In a similar manner, he is not able to give a good response about the state of his health. He hardly moves and is unable to do any activities, but spends all his time in sleep. Nevertheless, he does not forget the liturgy, and in general, as a very sick person, his life is very calm.

13. Mikhail Ofer'ev, Novice of Solbinskaia Pustyn.

He is 42 years old and has been in the prisoners' section of Spaso-Evfimiev Monastery since 23 April 1825. He was sent there by order of the authorities, by a decree of the Vladimir Spiritual Consistory, because of the derangement of his mind.

He is also disturbed beyond measure, both in spirit and in body. In the first place, his mental powers remain without any activity. He is also unable to distinguish between days. He is not even able to distinguish white from black. In general his mind is in an unsound condition. Furthermore, his physical powers are very weak and he is quite unable to function. And more, in such a pitiful condition, he gives himself up to sleep. However, he goes to the Divine Service and conducts himself meekly but not swiftly.

14. Lev Vasil'evich Strelkov, Constable of the Orel Police.

At 69 years of age, last 17th of November 1840, in the evening at five o'clock, his life ended naturally. That is to say that from time to time he experienced exhaustion and in the end, on that day and hour, he completely lost his strength and died.

Abbot Archimandrite Lavrentii
Source: GAVO, f. 578, op. 1, d. 165, 1840, ll. 14–20.

NOTES

1. My thanks to Heather Coleman and Scott Kenworthy for their insightful comments and detailed assistance with these translations. Also, thanks to Christine Worobec for providing the first document.

2. RGADA: Borovskii Pafnut'evskii Monastery Fond 1198, op. 2, d. 4498 (1825), l. 2.

3. From Luke 18:13: "God, have mercy on me, a sinner."

SUGGESTED READINGS

Freeze, Gregory L. "Handmaiden of the State? The Church in Imperial Russia Reconsidered." *Journal of Ecclesiastical History* 36 (1985): 82–102.

———. "The Wages of Sin: The Decline of Public Penance in Imperial Russia." In *Seeking God: The Recovery of Religious Identity in Orthodox Russia, Ukraine and Georgia,* ed. Stephen K. Batalden. De Kalb: Northern Illinois University Press, 1993.

Kenworthy, Scott M. *The Heart of Russia: Trinity-Sergius, Monasticism, and Society after 1825.* New York: Oxford University Press, 2010.

Robson, Roy R. *Solovki: The Story of Russia Told through Its Most Remarkable Islands.* New Haven, CT: Yale University Press, 2004.

Schrader, Abby M. *Languages of the Lash: Corporal Punishment and Identity in Imperial Russia.* DeKalb: Northern Illinois University Press, 2002.

FOUR

Letters to and from Russian Orthodox Spiritual Elders (*Startsy*)

Irina Paert

SPIRITUAL ELDERS (*STARTSY*) WERE PERSONS OF EXCEPTIONAL spiritual insight who provided religious directorship to neophytes. Even though many of the elders were priests or monks, or both, being an elder was not a church office, but rather an informal ministry. The reputation of an elder was established "from below" by ordinary believers and an elder's disciples. While the practice of spiritual guidance (*starchestvo*) has long been cultivated within monasticism, in nineteenth-century Russia it spread beyond monasteries and penetrated the lives of lay people. Many spiritual elders were heralds of the neo-Hesychast revival, which was characterized by an interest in mystical theology and the centrality of mental prayer in spiritual life. This interest was stimulated by the publication in 1794 of an anthology of early Christian writings on ascetic life, prayer, and the importance of spiritual guidance, under the title of *Dobrotoliubie* (*Philokalia*, literally "the love of beauty," in Greek, or "the love of good," in Russian), translated from Greek by St. Paisii Velichkovskii.

The phenomenon of the Russian elders cannot be separated from the revival of women's monasticism in the nineteenth century, a phenomenon that had socioeconomic as well as religious reasons. The involvement of male elders with women's celibate communities had an impact not only on religious women but also on the "careers" of elders who, like St. Seraphim of Sarov, often had far fewer supporters among the brethren of their own monasteries than among women. There were different forms the relationship between elders and religious women could take. Spiritual elder St. Zosima (Zakhariia Verkhovskii 1766–1833),[1] for example, as seen in the first document, composed in 1819 a "spiritual pledge" that he and his spiritual daughters signed in declaration of their "eternal spiritual friendship." He went on to found a women's community in the Siberian town of Turinsk in 1822, for which he wrote the communal Rule and acted as a benefactor (*popechitel'*). It started as an informal spiritual friendship between St. Zosima, who had neither priestly nor official monastic status, and three unmarried women. The solemnity of the pledge is perhaps a result of the precariousness of St. Zosima's position as a leader of this informal community as well as his belief in the sacredness of the spiritual bond between the spiritual father and his disciples, on the one hand, and among the disciples themselves, on the other. It is interesting that, according to the pledge, this spiritual bond continued in the afterlife, with each member of the spiritual union responsible for the salvation of the rest, emphasizing a collectivist aspect of the Russian Orthodox concept of salvation. In practice, however, it was difficult to keep the pledge. The women's community guided by St. Zosima went through a series of internal conflicts in the 1820s. In particular, some sisters were inclined to replace St. Zosima with an elected mother-superior. The Synod in 1822 ruled that St. Zosima had to leave the convent; together with fifteen sisters, he established another community, the Troitse-Odigitrievskaia Pustyn (hermitage) in the Vereisk district of Moscow province.

The spiritual style of St. Zosima, who felt that he had to be personally involved in the management of the women's community as well as guiding nuns individually, can be contrasted here with that of the elders of Optina Pustyn in Kaluga province, who encouraged women to become spiritual mothers, as in ancient times. The second document, Elder Makarii's letter to a nun, suggests that a frequent (almost daily) revelation of one's deep thoughts, anxieties, and feelings to a person experienced in ascetic struggle was crucial for spiritual progress, especially for monks and nuns. He patiently explained to his addressee that within convents novices should seek such guidance from experienced spiritual mothers. Consulting with male spiritual mentors, including priests, should not substitute for the everyday relationship between spiritual mothers and novice nuns. The Optina elders' encouragement of spiritual eldership within female monasticism was sometimes misunderstood. Elder Leonid of Optina in 1841 was banned from receiving visitors by

Bishop Nikolai of Kaluga. The formal reason was the Belev convent affair (1839–41) in Tula diocese: one of the nuns who acted as a spiritual mother to a group of nuns had the approval of Leonid, but not of the mother superior. The latter, who was unfamiliar with the practices and teaching of the Dobrotoliubie, suspected heresy and reported the guilty nuns to the bishop of Tula. In this context the letter from St. Makarii to a nun (written after the Belev convent affair) may be treated as a defense of or an apology for the ancient practice of spiritual guidance by women, who in imperial Russia had to run the risk of being accused of "heresy."

Even though lay men and women did not have such an intensive relationship with elders as monks and nuns, they nevertheless established strong personal bonds. Lay men and, overwhelmingly, women met spiritual elders in the context of visits to monasteries during which they stayed in monastic hostels and took part in the sacraments. Some members of educated society corresponded with the elders, especially when they could not pay a personal visit. An example of such a relationship is the third document. Princess Shakhovskaia's letters are addressed to elders Leonid[2] and Makarii[3] of Optina Pustyn, both reputable spiritual advisors for monks and laity. We do not know much about the author of the letters. Anna Antonovna Shakhovskaia (née Petrovskaia) was a landowner in Orel province. She assisted monasteries and convents in organizing purchase and delivery of food provisions, and served as a mediator between Optina monks and their lay friends. Her correspondents, Elder Leonid and Elder Makarii, were instrumental in the promotion of the Hesychast literature and spirituality in Russia. St. Makarii, for example, published translations of the Hesychast authors with the help of the Slavophile philosopher Ivan Kireevskii and his wife Natal'ia.

Lay people approached elders for various reasons: to receive advice or a blessing in the critical moments of one's life, such as during illness, before marriage, or before entering a convent or monastery. It appears that more women (both nuns and lay women) than men sought the advice of reputable male elders, such as the Optina elders. This was not a specifically Russian phenomenon: spiritual friendship between pious women and renowned spiritual mentors was also characteristic of medieval religion in the West and the Catholic Reform. Not all elders had a reputation as clairvoyants, but most of them were believed to be wiser and holier than ordinary Christians. It was not unusual for elders to have to deal with mundane, practical matters as well as spiritual concerns, and none of these was dismissed as irrelevant. As the final two documents illustrate, lay people could share with elders their worries about land transactions and family matters (notably, in the second letter, Shakhovskaia asks the monks to recommend a governess). Shakhovskaia was also involved in the economic transactions of the Optina monastery, mediating between suppliers and the monastery, providing the Optina monks with the fabric to make monastic clothes.[4] Shakhovskaia was not untypical in her role as a manager of the family economy, nor was she unusual in her longing to withdraw from the "world" and her appreciation of monastic life. Her letters are an example of piety among the Orthodox Russian nobility: she lives according to the Orthodox liturgical calendar; all mundane events are assessed against the sacred meaning of specific seasons of the Orthodox year. Even though Shakhovskaia could not be immune to the dominant ideology of domesticity, according to which the woman's role as mother and wife was divinely ordained, she had a genuine interest in the Hesychast theology and practice that could be seen as an alternative to "Orthodox domesticity" and a coping strategy to deal with the pressure of social expectations and everyday concerns.[5] The style of the letters could be identified as lament (*plach* or *prichitanie*), a literary and folk genre overwhelmingly practiced by women.[6] This is a recitation of afflictions and troubles that affect a woman's life, presenting the author as an innocent victim of circumstance and the external world.[7] Shakhovskaia's letters betray a strong emotional attachment to her spiritual advisors. She ponders her real or imaginary "offence" to Elder Leonid and bemoans her separation from the elder due to the bishop's ban. This emotional content was typical of the largely informal relationship between elders and their spiritual children.

Elders and Women's Monasticism

Pledge Letters (zavetnnye pis'ma)[8]

2 February 1819
In the name of the Father, the Son and the Holy Spirit, Amen.

I, sinful elder Zosima, named Zakhariia, in witness of myself before God, have written in reassurance of you, my spiritual sisters Onisia, Nataliia, and Evdokiia.

First, if I do not take care of you with all my heart and soul to such an extent that I do not want to enter Kingdom of God without you, let me forever be deprived of God's Kingdom.

Second, if my love of you is sinful, that is, impure and insincere, let me suffer God's abomination.

Third, if I do not care for your salvation as much as for mine own, let my soul be damned.

Fourth, if I decide to desert you without an honorable reason or neglect your needs, let me be forsaken by God.

Equally we, your undersigned spiritual daughters, in confirmation of our eternally bound spiritual friendship with you and among ourselves, pledge before God Himself. If any of us lacks sincere loving feelings toward you, our spiritual father, or toward other sisters, so that she would not even want to inherit the Kingdom of God without the others; or if she will not be honest before you in everything, or not desire to live in obedience to you and act according to your direction and advice; or will desire to leave you or to separate herself from her sisters without your consent, then such a person as untrustworthy and having fallen away and having violated this, our covenant before God, should be removed from it and divested of our association with her. And from henceforth she should not be counted among us in our harmonious, eternally unbreakable union in Christ, which we hereby affirm.
Onisiia Koniukhova, Nataliia Vasil'eva, Evdokiia Ramanava.

We pray to God regarding our pledge: Lord and God of all, who has power over all living creatures. You know that with our trust and hope in you and with the intention to serve you we made this consensual and eternally bound friendship.

This is why we pray as one to You, our Lord, do not put us to shame, who made this union in Your name, but grant us to be undivided, even after our death, in accordance with our covenant on earth. As we have bound ourselves by pledge and promise with trust in Your merciful kindness.

Unless all four of us will be saved through Your grace and mercy, one without the others does not desire to inherit the eternal Heavenly bliss or enter your kingdom as You have prepared it for those who love and serve You.

In confirmation of this spiritual pledge in God, and of our determination to be together in the afterlife, we give our signatures:

I, sinful elder and your spiritual friend, yet unworthy servant named Zakhariia and known as Zosima, pledge myself and my soul before God, his eternal Son and Holy and life-giving Spirit. If you preserve your friendship with me and among yourselves and be obedient, meek, and pure-hearted in honesty toward me, and keep it all your life, should I be saved among those who pleased God. I promise to keep this pledge. That is: I will pray to God to grant his eternal blessedness to you first, and then to me.

Likewise I, your spiritual daughter Onisiia, pledge before God, if you, father, and sisters remain with me and among yourselves in such spiritual friendship as here described, then, if I have God's mercy and will be joined to his saints, then I will do as our father promised to do.

Equally I, your spiritual daughter Natalia, promise before God to do as the sister has promised above. Equally and I, your spiritual daughter Evdokiia, promise before God to do the same.

A Letter from Hieromonk Makarii (Ivanov) of Optina Pustyn to a Nun[9]

24 May 1845
Beloved in Christ N. N.

In response to your perplexity (*nedoumenie*) I offer my reasoning, not even mine but that of the Holy Fathers. St. John of Ladder wrote that those who relied on themselves and not on the spiritual doctor fell into delusion. It is important to disclose one's thoughts as brethren did in the old times; some of them even recorded all the thoughts they had during the day and then disclosed those [to their spiritual father]. St. Abba Dorotheus teaches that "in an abundance of counselors there is safety" (Prov. 11:14) but to consult not with many, but with the one you ought to (your spiritual father) and about everything: not keeping anything from him but revealing everything on your mind. He also says that the enemy hates even the voice of acknowledgment and leads away from this.[10]

St. Symeon the New Theologian recommends revealing one's thoughts daily to one's mentor and not doing anything without the latter's advice.[11] St. Kallistos and St. Ignatius wrote two substantial chapters 14 and 15 about this.[12] St. Cassian writes that we have to confess not only what we do but also what we think and not to trust our own thought but follow in everything the words of the elders; and we take [them] as gold even if they test us.[13] In addition, St. John of the Ladder writes that "humility is born out of obedience"; obedience is connected with disclosure of thoughts and rejection of one's will and reason. In such a way spiritual life begins, proceeds, and achieves completion; and only following this, with God's help, can one avoid delusion through which one can be exalted or be thrown down.

You may ask whether in your situation it is possible to have such a constant relationship with your spiritual father. Yet all the above is relevant for spiritual mothers who have experience of spiritual life and can guide, guard from harm, and support [neophytes] in spiritual warfare (*bran'*). God Himself teaches spiritual mothers to say a word and give good advice to the benefit of those who came with faith. When the seekers reveal their thoughts and with obedience reject their own reasoning and self-will, they will learn spiritual life and humility.

This was exactly the way of life of women ascetics in the past as we see in their lives: where could they find [male] spiritual mentors in convents where the male sex was banned? They had but a priest who came occasionally to give them Holy Communion, but they had no priests in residence as we have now. In particular, some used [the advice of male spiritual mentors] as some do now but not on a regular basis but only occasionally. This form of spiritual life is not the same as a formal confession to a priest, which has to be done in certain periods of the year (during which one does not hide anything and receives the absolution of sins), but this is a [form of] guidance in spiritual life. Is it really possible to discuss every aspect [of the spiritual life] with a priest when one has no more than five to ten minutes every two or three months? In the meantime, one lives with a burdened conscience and a darkened mind, yet after disclosing one's thoughts, even without an absolution, one receives peace of mind, decrease in inner warfare and advice on how to resist temptations. "Sinful thoughts which have been revealed to fathers (or mothers) lose their power and have no influence [on the soul of the ascetic]" (St. Cassian). By revealing your thoughts to your spiritual mother, you do not mean to hide the sin from the spiritual father and, if your spiritual mother finds it important, you can confess this sin to the priest and receive absolution without waiting for the time of formal confession.

The above will help you to find profit from disclosure of thoughts to spiritual mothers in your convent.

Blame yourself, not others, for their distrust of you and say to yourself: "This means I deserve this and it is God's will that they do not trust me." This reasoning will help you obtain humility, while justifying yourself shows that you feed on proud thoughts; but it is not up to me to see other people's weaknesses while I have plenty of my own, I just feel I have to say the truth.

Remaining the well-wisher of your salvation, sinful I[eromonakh]. M[akarii].

Laity and Elders

Letters from A. A. Shakhovskaia to Elders Leonid (Nagolkin) and Makarii (Ivanov) of Optina Pustyn

11 April 1841

Most-reverend batiushki, Father Leonid and Father Makarii![14]

We had the honor of receiving your precious letter. We thank you, reverend batiushki, for the books, and doubly for your kind Christian benevolence to us sinners; believe me that your love in Christ to us so far has not made me proud but brought me to my senses because I know from the Holy Scripture that our Lord came to save not the righteous but sinners, among whom I am the most wretched and prone to anger. Oh, batiushka, how much I suffer for the grief I have caused you: troubles and temptations (*iskusheniia*) don't leave me since my return from you

[Optina]. First, for a long time I felt pangs of conscience thinking of my foolishness before you! Secondly, the prohibition [from the bishop] for you to receive us, sinners, worries me and many others. Why have we been deprived of such strong support, [our] guide (*putevoditel'*) to God?

Then I had another temptation: [it happened] on Friday of Cheesefare Week when my soul soared to God – because all these days I had the Last Judgment in my head and I wanted nothing worldly,[15] our neighbor, a landlord, proposed that we buy his estate adjacent to ours. The first thought I had was of Batiushka Leonid's words "Why do you need to buy another estate when you already have enough worries?" Then I thought about my abhorrence of the world so I thought: "Why do I have to tie myself even more to the world, how could I take under my supervision another fifty souls while I am so wary of power over those which I have already?" I, a sinner, resorted to God with tears, praying that He, All-knowing (*vseznaiushchii*), might reveal whether [this estate] was needed for our children, or not. But how could I be sure that my sinful prayer was heard? The Prince [Shakhovskoi], however, rejected the offer with indifference and we've offered this estate to the Prince's brother and have even lent him money [to help with the purchase].

When they had completed the purchase and came to thank us for our help, however, the Prince started to feel regret and blame me for depriving our children of such comfort because the neighbor's land was interspersed among ours (*cherezpolosnaia*).[16] I became depressed because I felt it was my fault. My grief was compounded when someone returned us a debt, several thousand rubles, and no one was there at the time to whom we could lend it, so it lay without profit. Finally we found a borrower, but everybody now said he was unreliable. This [chain of troubles] started from the first Monday of Great Lent and continued until the next terrible blow.

During the fifth week of Lent I went with Mariia Egorovna [Shakhovskaia's cousin or sister-in-law] to the Sevsk convent to rest from worldly worries, where we found consolation and partook in the Holy Mysteries. But as soon as we came back Mariia Egorovna sent for me on the sixth week. Unsuspectingly, I took the risk of traveling by flooded river only to find her quarrelling with her husband because of his infidelity. I tried in vain to reconcile them and, eventually, despite my reservations, she came to stay with us. The mistress of her own household, the poor thing spent Holy Week, Easter, and Bright Week[17] with us. The Prince visited his brother-in-law twice, and [as a result], she reunited with her husband on Bright Friday.

We had just managed to reconcile them, yet yesterday they both again came to us determined to divorce. Since I kept reminding her that Batiushka did not give his blessing to divorce, she asked me to write to you about this and ask for advice and prayer. But they don't love each other, and their reconciliation is unsteady because it is insincere and based on [material] interest. My sister lost much weight and has fainting fits. It is heartbreaking enough for me to console her, and yet her husband and his family spread rumors that I have looted their property and break up their marriage for my own sake.

Batiushka, hasten to console her with your letter and help her to make a decision. Please pray for them and for us, sinners.

We send you with thanks 87 rubles and 50 kopeks. We would like to purchase St. John of the Ladder and Dobrotoliubie, Spiritual Healer (*Dushevnoe vrachevanie*), Lenten Triodion, General Menaion, the Epistles which are used in churches. Could you order these books for us? If no opportunity arises, keep the books until our arrival. If God is willing and Batiushka will have permission to see us, the Prince wants to accompany me and the children to Optina after the feast of Korennaia.[18] Let us know how things are with you, give us some joy. Bless our household and me, wretched Aleksandra Shakhovskaia.

We are sending our sincere respect and love in Christ to reverend Father Hegumen, Father Ioann S., to Batiushka's Makarii, and to all the blessed brethren.

Batiushka, let us know if Father Petr needs the book, we could promptly send it.

[30 June 1841]
Reverend Fathers Leonid and Makarii!

From my heart I thank you holy elders for your love for us! An ailing neighbor of ours came back recently from Optina and passed on your love for me. How precious is this memory to me. If you could only see my joy and tears when I listened to her!

So you remember us sinners. I have confirmation of this every week when we receive the Sunday sermon from Optina with gratitude and renewed love in Christ. I could not exchange all the treasures of the world for your love!

You have shown to me the greatest treasure, the way to the Lord. Sustain me now with your prayers, instructions, and most importantly strict reprimand for misdeeds.

I could just fly to you to ask your advice about things, but my sister Mariia Egorovna (who still lives with us while there is building work in her village two versts from us) cannot come now and asked me to wait for her.

Batiushka, misfortunes trouble me. Starting on the sixth week of Lent Maria E. and her husband several times came together and then separated again and everybody blames me for [breaking up the family] because of my interest. But I pray to God that nothing of hers might tempt me and be given to me, it would be better that through my [disinterestedness] the Lord not reject me, my children and husband. She does not want to live with [her husband], yet while separated from him, misses him badly, fainting and getting hysterical. I do not know what to do with her: she is naive and undiscerning, probably, because of her affliction. She is in love with him but does not want to believe in this.

Besides, I have troubles of my own. I was given a six-year-old orphan girl to foster, the daughter of my late sister Varin'ka Karazina, so now altogether I have five children. Give me your blessing, Batiushka and pray for us to God and the Heavenly Queen for this undertaking. And guess what? The next day [after she was made my ward] my governess decided to leave us. What did it cost me! How could I [on such a short notice] find another governess and know that she would not be capricious. I beseeched the Lord with tears to torment me for my sins but not to leave the children. I thank God for these bitter moments, but the governess was persuaded to stay even though she already had a carriage waiting.

I wanted to come to you for advice about how to find a new governess: you have connections in the capitals so [could you assist me] in the case of necessity? Woes don't leave me: it seems that some other trouble will loom yet, by the Lord's grace, dark clouds pass me by. I see the Lord's providence in everything. My Lord, do not leave me in heaven for my suffering. There is so little that attracts me and makes me happy in this world, with the exception of Optina and Sevsk, as my motherland in heaven, where I go to forget my worries and hide from the world.

Repeating my deep gratitude to you for the Sunday readings I ask not to forget me in your holy prayers not only here on earth, but also in Heaven.

Yours, sinful Aleksandra Shakhovskaia

PS: The Prince, the children and my sister ask for your blessing and prayers. Please, pass on five rubles from us to Sergei Egorovich Lakhtionov and a letter from his father.

NOTES

1. Elder Zosima, a nobleman from Smolensk province, left military service at the age of twenty-one and became a monk, joining an unofficial community of hermits in the forests of Orel province, among whom was a peasant elder, Vasilisk, the author of the mystical text "On the effects of the prayer of the heart." In his search for an ideal ascetic retreat, Zosima accompanied his teacher Vasilisk to the Siberian taiga where he found followers among the local merchants and nobility. In 2004 Zosima and Vasilisk were canonized as saints of the Russian Orthodox church.

2. Leonid Nagolkin (1768–1841) came from a merchant family in Karachev (Orel province); in 1797 he became a novice and in 1801 he took monastic vows at Beloberezhskaia Pustyn. St. Lev (Leonid) learned Hesychast prayer and the tradition of spiritual guidance through his spiritual mentor Feodor (Pol'zikov), a member of Paisii Velichkovskii's community, and in 1829 introduced it into Optina Pustyn. St. Lev was known to his correspondents and brethren by the name Leonid, as the Holy Synod did not recognize his Great Schema (a second tonsure recognizing the highest level of spiritual attainment as a monk, which was accompanied by a change of name and the pledge to a stricter rule of fasting and solitude) because it had been executed without the formal Synodal procedures. Here we use Leonid, as it corresponds better to the sources.

3. St. Makarii (Ivanov, 1788–1860) came from a noble family in Kaluga province. Like Leonid, St. Makarii had a connection with St. Paisii Velichkovskii's disciples and shared the same ideals (he was a secretary to Leonid, drafting and co-signing many of his letters to lay and religious correspondents). Lev (Leonid) and Makarii were canonized together with twelve other monks of Optina Pustyn as saints of the Russian Orthodox Church in 2000.

4. OR RGB, f. 213, kart. 83, d. 19, ll. 1–4.

5. On "Orthodox domesticity" see William G. Wagner, "Orthodox Domesticity: Creating a Social Role for Women," in *Sacred Stories; Religion and Spirituality in Modern Russia*, ed. Mark D. Steinberg and Heather J. Coleman (Bloomington: Indiana University Press, 2007), 119–45.

6. Russian ethnographer Tatiana Bernshtam, for example, speaks about "lament culture" (*plachevaia kultura*). T. Bernshtam, "Svadebnyi plach v obriadovoi kul'ture vostochnykh slavian," in *Russkii Sever: Problemy etnokul'turnoi istorii, etnografii, fol'kloristiki* (Leningrad, 1986), 82–100.

7. It is also possible to compare Shakhovskaia's style to what Nancy Ries called litanies, "those passages in conversation in which a speaker would enunciate a series of complaints, grievances, or worries about problems, troubles, afflictions, tribulations, or losses and then often comment on these enumerations with a poignant rhetorical question ('Why is everything so bad with us?')." Nancy Ries, *Russian Talk Culture and Conversation during Perestroika* (Ithaca: Cornell University Press, 1997), 84.

8. A. L. Beglov, "'Vechnost'iu nerazrushimoe sodruzhestvo.' Stranitsy russkogo starchestva XIX veka: prepodobnyi Zosima (Verkhovskii) i ego dukhovnaia sem'ia v 1818–1825 gg.," *Alfa i Omega* 29 no. 3 (2006), 205–40. Translated with permission.

9. *Sobranie pisem blazhennyia pamiati optinskogo startsa ieroskhimonakha Makariia k monashestvuiushchim* (Moscow, 1862), 39–42.

10. St. Makarii refers here to Abba Dorotheus of Gaza (sixth century), the author of popular homilies and instructions on the ascetic and spiritual life.

11. Probably, St. Makarii refers to the compilation of St. Symeon the New Theologian's writings in the Dobrotoliubie. *Dobrotoliubie v russkom perevode, dopolnennoe*, 2nd ed., vol. 5 (Moscow, 1900).

12. Makarii refers to chapters by St. Kallistos and St. Ignatius Xanthopulos in *Dobrotoliubie*, vol. 5.

13. St. John Cassian (ca. 360–435) in *Dobrotoliubie*, 2nd ed., vol. 2 (Moscow, 1895).

14. OR RGB, f. 213 (Optina Pustyn'), karton 75, d. 48.

15. Cheesefare (*miasopustnaia*) Week was the last non-fasting week before Great Lent. During it the Orthodox Church reminds its members of the Last Judgment and calls to repentance and forgiveness.

16. This should not be confused with a practice of redistribution of strips of land of different quality between peasant households, a common risk-averse strategy. Perhaps, in Shakhovskaia's case, the lack of consolidated land property was a result of the Russian property laws that allowed divisions of estates among male and female heirs. See Michelle Lamarche Marrese, *A Woman's Kingdom. Noblewomen and the Control of Property in Russia, 1700–1861* (Ithaca, NY: Cornell University Press, 2002).

17. In the Orthodox calendar the week following Easter is called Bright (*Svetlaia*) Week.

18. She probably means the feast of the Kurskaia-Korennaia Icon of the Mother of God "Znamenie" icon on the ninth Friday after Easter.

SUGGESTED READINGS

Hausherr, Irénée. *Spiritual Direction in the Early Christian East.* Translated by Anthony P. Gythiel. Kalamazoo, MI: Cisterian Publications, 1990.

Nichols, Robert. "The Orthodox Elders of Imperial Russia." *Modern Greek Studies Yearbook* 1 (1985): 1–30.

Paert, Irina. *Spiritual Elders, Charisma and Tradition in Russian Orthodoxy.* DeKalb: Northern Illinois University Press, 2010.

Sederholm, Fr. Clement. *Elder Leonid of Optina.* Platina, CA: Saint Herman Press, 1990.

Stanton, Leonard. *The Optina Pustyn' Monastery in the Russian Literary Imagination: Iconic Vision in Works by Dostoevsky, Gogol, Tolstoy and Others.* New York: Peter Lang, 1995.

FIVE

Sermons of the Crimean War

Mara Kozelsky

THE CRIMEAN WAR (1853–56) STARTED AS A LOCALIZED DISPUTE between the Russian and Ottoman Empires over the protection of Orthodox subjects of the Sultan living in the Danubian principalities of Wallachia and Moldavia (part of modern-day Romania). Fearing Russian expansion after its early success at the Battle of Sinope (30 November 1853), England and France joined sides with the Ottoman Empire by March of 1854. Their entrance shifted the primary theater of war to the Crimean peninsula and entailed protracted violence for more than a year. One of ten wars between Russia and the Ottoman Empire from the reign of Peter I through World War I, the Crimean War was the most pivotal conflict of the Eastern Question, a complex international debate stemming from Europe's presumption to manage the affairs of the Ottoman Empire.

From Russia's official declaration of war, religion figured prominently. Priests actively participated through deed and rhetoric. They worked on the front lines to comfort parishioners and to protect churches from plunder. Continuing an old tradition, monks served alongside sailors and soldiers, ministering to those in need. In a new development, monks supervised the activities of the Russian Sisters of Mercy, the Russian counterpart to Florence Nightingale and her nurses. At the end of the war approximately 200,000 Muslim Tatars emigrated from Crimea to the Ottoman Empire. Bulgarians and other Orthodox refugees from Ottoman territory settled in their vacated villages.

Beyond the battlefield, sermons communicated the war to the wider Russian public and emphasized that the Allies attacked one of the holiest places in Slavic Christianity. A chief publicist of the war effort, the Russian Orthodox Church depicted the conflict as a holy war. Sermons depicted the war as a struggle between Orthodoxy and Islam. Sermons also portrayed Orthodox Christianity as the true Christian faith in comparison with Protestantism and Catholicism. Religious rhetoric played a particularly prominent role once the war reached Crimea, for the peninsula held special symbolic value among Russian nationalists as the cradle of Russian Christianity. According to the medieval Chronicle of Nestor, Prince Vladimir of Kiev traveled to Crimea – specifically to the ancient coastal trading town of Chersonesos – where he accepted Orthodox Christianity from Byzantine priests in the tenth century.

Delivered in church squares and reprinted in journals, pamphlets, and newspapers, sermons reached both the literate elite and the illiterate masses.[1] These texts constituted an important stream in public discourse as they interpreted worldly events through an Orthodox lens. Sermons, such as those delivered during the Crimean War, could influence policy and shape local and imperial views of the world. Few texts, religious or otherwise, had greater authority, or greater ability, to connect with as wide an audience.

With one exception, Archbishop Innokentii (1800–1857) authored the documents collected here. His see included Odessa and Crimea. The texts span the early phase of fighting in Crimea, when most Russians anticipated a quick victory, to the height of the siege of Sevastopol, when more than a thousand Russian soldiers died daily. Archbishop Innokentii aimed these particular sermons at those associated with the military, an audience composed of men and women, Russians and non-Russians. Local residents in attendance constituted a secondary audience. Russians throughout the empire who later read the sermons reprinted in their local newspapers became the tertiary and the largest audience. Indeed, one contemporary commented that Innokentii's sermons were "read and reread by all people from all estates, from high and low, and Innokentii's name resounded in all of the immeasurable borders of Russia."[2]

Military and civil officials similarly recognized the contribution from the Orthodox Church. After the bombardment of Odessa in April

1854, for example, General Osten-Saken praised Archbishop Innokentii "for inspiring devotion to the throne, love for the Fatherland and instilling calm with his edifying words after each service."[3] The governor of the province concurred, writing that "without any doubt" the archbishop's steadfast performance of church services and delivery of sermons "supported the city during a very difficult time, and helped to keep peace and order."[4]

Archbishop Innokentii delivered his most famous sermon on 26 June 1855 in Sevastopol, where he met the Russian military at their crumbling defenses. With bombs exploding in every direction, he blessed the soldiers and sailors with icons sent from all over Russia. The moment became woven into the myth of the defense of Sevastopol, described in memoirs and recreated in an imperial broadside. The sermon itself went through several publications and is translated here. For this sermon, Archbishop Innokentii received the ribbon of the Order of St. George, the medal created especially for the heroes of Sevastopol.[5]

Today, Orthodox theologians remember Archbishop Innokentii for pioneering practical theology and homiletics – the study and practice of sermons. His contemporaries called him the *Russkii Zlatoust*, or Golden-tongued Russian, a descriptor evoking the great preacher and father of the early church, St. John Chrysostom, and one that some Orthodox theologians have revived today.[6] His sermons addressed any number of themes, including teaching believers how to apply the Gospels to everyday life and educating parishioners about their local history. The Crimean War sermons, therefore, represent a worldly subset within the genre and highlight the rhetorical and political applications of speeches delivered in the church.

Because churches served as a gathering place for all strata of Russian society, priests and bishops typically disseminated news of the empire and read official pronouncements to their congregations. Naturally, some chose to express their own views after their reading. Thus the first two documents, the official declaration of war signed by Nicholas I and Innokentii's subsequent sermon, operate as a pair, providing a rare window into the church–state dialogue. The other four sermons each offer something unique, whether in their choice of spiritual metaphors, or political exposition. Together, the documents in this selection raise questions about Orthodox notions of war, patriotism, Russian identity, and faith during an era of international conflict.

Nicholas I, Declaration of War[7]

In our Manifesto dated 14 June earlier this year, We announced to our beloved subjects the reasons leading us to demand that the Ottoman Porte firmly protect the holy rights of the Orthodox Church.

We then protested that all of Our friendly measures to persuade the Porte to conscientiously observe the treaties remained useless; this is why We concluded it was necessary to move our troops to the Danubian Principalities. But, having taken this measure, we still retained hope that the Porte, recognizing its error, would decide to fulfill our just demands.

Our expectations were not realized.

In vain even the main European powers tried with exhortations to sway the stubborn obstinacy of the Turkish government. But the Porte answered the peace-loving powers of Europe with a declaration of war. Our patience and suffering met with denunciation of Russia. Finally, having accepted the rebels of every nation into the ranks of its troops, the Porte opened hostilities in the Danube.[8]

Russia has been called to battle. With hope in God she must resort to the strength of guns in order to compel the Porte to observe the treaties, to find satisfaction for the insults with which the Porte responded to our most moderate demands and for Our legitimate concern to defend the Orthodox faith in the East, the faith which is the Russian people's as well.

We are firmly convinced that Our faithful subjects join Us in warm prayers to the Almighty: His Right hand blesses our arms, raised by us for a holy and just cause, the zealous champion of our devout ancestors. O Lord, in Thee have we put our trust. Let us never be confounded.[9]

Read at Tsarskoe Selo, on 20 October, in the year of Jesus Christ 1853, the 28th year of our reign.

Archbishop Innokentii

> Excerpt from the sermon accompanying a reading of the War Manifesto given in the Odessa Cathedral on 21 October 1853.[10]

"What Did We Do to Turkey?"

We asked only what was just and necessary. We asked that the Orthodox churches and their servitors be given their inviolable freedom, which we have given to Muslims and their mosques in our borders from time immemorial; we asked that the holy places of Jerusalem, where thousands of devout Russian people flow every year, not be transferred from hand to hand, like some place bought and sold [...] we asked that the Orthodox faith not be reproached for its faith in Muslim eyes; we asked that when necessary, we could intervene to defend our suffering brothers of faith, with the right to point out their wounds and shackles. This we demanded for the benefit and peace of the Ottoman power, in those places where there are three or four Muslims for dozens of Orthodox.

> Delivered at the prayer service on the Odessa Cathedral Square for the 11th Division of the 4th Infantry before their departure for Crimea, 9 October 1854.[11]

Christ-loving and Victorious Soldiers!

Christ-loving and therefore victorious [soldiers]! You have not had long to rest from your labors and feats in the Danube! According to the call of the Monarch, you must rise again and go to the Tauride peninsula to deliver a resounding defeat to our arrogant enemies, who, blinded by pride and evil, dared to sail across the sea to invade our ancient region, where the great Apostle-like Prince Vladimir was baptized and from where, together with him, the Christian faith spread to the whole Russian land.[12] We welcome you on this new campaign, which will be combined with a devout pilgrimage to the cradle of our Christianity and Orthodoxy!

Worship, worship [this cradle] with reverence, in the name of the whole Russian land, and stand with your characteristic bravery against the fanatical worshippers of Islam and their impudent minions for the glory of the faith and the Cross of Christ, for the tears and blood of our brothers in faith.

If you remember for whom and for what you suffer, if you wage war as befits lovers of Christ, distinguishing yourselves not only by courage and bravery, but also by faith and trust in God, by enduring need and difficulty in good humor, by gentleness to the peaceful inhabitants, and by magnanimity toward the vanquished – then God himself will stand among you. Angels of heaven will fight invisibly for you within your ranks. The enemy arriving *as one* will beat *ten lines* of retreat, fleeing, but with no possibility of escaping your sword. Meanwhile, let it be known that, wounded on all sides, [the enemy] doubtlessly would wish that the wind would be in their sails sending them back; but the fire of our brave military will not allow them to leave. It will remain only to deliver the last blow and throw them from our shores, like an ugly corpse, into the deep. It is an honor that has been presented to you and your courage: hurry to take advantage of such a rare opportunity. For the joy of all of Russia and the glory of our beloved Monarch, so that we too may soon have the comfort of seeing you victorious and together with you exclaim in joyful gratitude, "Glory be to God on high! Peace on earth! Goodwill toward men!"

> Delivered at the prayer service to the Greek Battalion at the Odessa Cathedral before dispatching them from Odessa to Sevastopol.[13]

Odessa, 14 January 1855.
Brave and Christ-loving Hellenes!

Each time we send detachments of our Orthodox soldiers to the Tauride peninsula from this church with our prayer and blessings, we are sincerely touched by the readiness and zeal with which they take their very lives there for the faith, tsar and fatherland. But seeing you off now to the same place and for the same goal, we experience, in addition to these earlier sentiments, a special kind of feeling, which originates deep from within our souls.

You are not our countrymen, and not even of our race; however, like our own military, you hurry now to the battle and thus to death itself for us! Should one not bow with particular respect before such devotion and selflessness, when the word of God says "There is no greater love than that of a friend who lays down his soul for another."[14]

This is the meaning of the unity of faith that ties us to you! And this is why – and for no other reason – the Great Autocrat of All Russia, despite all manner of dangers and difficulties, stood bravely, against virtually the entire West, for Orthodoxy and our fellow believers in the East. This unity now drives you too, having left your peaceful homes, to go to a distant war far removed from you in our borders, and seek out the battleground, ready to fight side by side with Russians.

You surely know that the present struggle originated not for worldly advantages and not for earthly goals, but for the faith and Orthodoxy; you are fully convinced that the fruit of war must not be any kind of increase in the might or borders of Russia, which are already almost boundless, but exclusively freedom of conscience and the protection of the rights of man for Eastern Christians. You know and are convinced of this, I say, and therefore you hurry to prove to yourselves and your comrades that you are not inferior, that you are worthy of all the great efforts and sacrifices that your Russian co-religionists now make for you.

May God bless your path! Go forth, beloved, in this affair, which evidently is not ours alone, but also yours, and, indeed, more yours than ours. Its beginning came from us but its end will be entirely for you and your brothers in the East. Go forth and show our common enemy and all the world that for the Hellene there is nothing higher and dearer than the faith and the fatherland and that he, with the cross upon his heart and sword in hand, is prepared to search out the latter to the very ends of the earth.

In support of your feat, consider the very memory of the holy meaning of this place where the flames of war now rage and where you will fight with enemies. After all – have you considered this? – it is not just any place, but it is a holy place named Tauric Chersonesos, where nine centuries ago, Russia accepted the faith and holy Baptism from Orthodox Greece . . . And here, as well, in this memorable and holy place, in your person, this ancient and holy union between two great peoples, the Russians (*Rossov*) and Greeks must now be renewed and strengthened.

In the first case, this union was constituted through baptism by water and the Spirit, which Orthodox Greece, like a mother, gave and which Russia, like an obedient daughter, accepted for her spiritual enlightenment. Now, to reinforce this ancient union, a baptism is again being administered, not by water only and by the Spirit, but by fire and blood (Matt. 3:2) in which, therefore, mother and daughter must participate equally, forever united and reborn, for a new common life in the East. At this, though, who among you does not take heart and forget the difficulties of the feat ahead?

In memory of our current prayers and fond wishes, take from us this icon of Saint Nicholas, the Saint of Christ. May it recall for you the memory of the heavenly defender and protector of the Orthodox military – the Bishop of Myra, and the earthly Supreme Commander[15] of Russia and all Orthodox Christians, our devout Sovereign Nicholas I. Amen.

Sermon for the Russian Sisters of Mercy[16]

Delivered in the Odessa Cathedral 12 June 1855, while raising the Cross for the Sisters of Mercy, who cared for the wounded soldiers.

Two feelings rage in our souls as we look upon you, newly selected sisters of mercy! The expansion of your society and your circle of activity naturally leads to the conclusion that the number of our Orthodox military demanding tender care is not decreasing, but grows quickly, a bitter and staggering thought.[17] But we take heart, seeing the product of your tremendous service to the sufferings of the defenders of the fatherland from the first news of this need. The true-Christian work of yours in this feat demonstrates a comforting truth: if human evil tirelessly brings pain and wounds, the love of Christ is equally tireless in healing and doctoring them.

Thanks to God, more than once already we have had the comfort, even the joy, to hear about the success of your predecessors who zealously pursued their blessed calling, that with the help of God, they endured equally the great temptations in their care for the ill. We call to mind the holy comments of the Apostle: "Suffering produces endurance, and endurance produces character, and character produces hope, and hope does not disappoint us."[18]

Similarly we expect from you, sisters, beloved of God, that your tribulation will produce success! And why would we not expect this? Is there less love in your heart for God and humanity? Are you less animated by the blessings and life-giving spirit of Christ? Are your vows here on the Gospel less impressed by the majestic, great name of God? Do you not kiss the same Cross of Christ and like your predecessors carry it on your shoulders?

Oh, to fall from these holy heights would mean also to fall from heaven . . . Lord save us all from such a fall! You leave all that is easy and comfortable, to give up tranquility and quiet, joy and gaiety, for grief and tears, to live in the midst of groans and suffering. Concerning bodily pain, the Apostle has said that suffering of the flesh will be the end of sin.[19] Now it is you who will be served with the suffering of the flesh – and what terrible suffering! It must be said that you, in your destination and type of occupation, will [be] further than others from the seduction of worldly temptations. Oh, sickness and death are not only weak words of ours: but are the most eloquent instructors of faith and good deeds.

Soon a new enemy might threaten you with depression and low spirits, as you must enter and work in the midst of gloom and the shade of death. But, remember how many defenses you have, beloved, against all depression and forms of low spirits. Do you not have all the prayers and blessings of the holy Church? Do you not have all the cares and maternal kindness of the August Foundress[20] of the Christ-loving society of yours? Is it not with you, working in the affairs of human love, that skilled doctors will work serving bodily health while spiritual fathers and experienced pastors serve the health of the spirit? Was not the Cross of Christ, that invincible weapon of the Christian, raised for all of you? And will you be in despair? Or succumb to poor spirits? No, beloved, fortified in faith, buoyed by love, inspired by hopes of eternal life, you will possess as much spirit and fortitude, in order to save from low spirits and enliven with faithful care all those you help who are under the weight of physical suffering.

Go forth on your path in peace. Allow us soon to hear about your blessed work, in order that we can thank God for you, who together with planting in our hearts the seeds of good and pure intentions will allow them the strength to grow and come into maturity. Amen.

Blessing the defenders of Sevastopol with Holy Icons, sent to them from various places in Russia.[21]

Given in Sevastopol, after the service in the Nikolaev square, 26 June 1855.

Praise and gratitude to you, Christ-loving defenders of Sevastopol, in the name of the whole Russian land. Thanks to God you stand here strong and steadfast for the fatherland, for the pious Tsar, and for our universal mother, the Orthodox Church. May you also know that Holy Russia, too, strongly remembers and fiercely loves all of you. Let it be known that the Orthodox Tsar, too, delights in you and is diligently preparing rewards for you for your unprecedented exploits. Know also that the holy Church, as your true mother, blesses your courage with both hands. Day and night she prays for you to God. She prays both for the living – may God grant you strength and victory above – and all the more so for the deceased, that they may be honored with a heavenly halo.

Look at these holy icons! This is a holy gift to you from all the Russian land! This is a maternal blessing to you – from the Orthodox Church!

Here is the image of the Dormition of the Mother of God from the Kievan Monastery of the Caves, which was once received by the Lavra's holy architects as a blessing for this monastery from the hands of the Queen of Heaven herself! This is the icon of the Mother of God of the Sign, before whom, once upon a time, the large army of the Prince of Suzdal suddenly faltered and returned unsuccessfully beyond the walls of Novgorod.[22] These are the first bishops of Moscow – tireless champions and eternal defenders of our fatherland. And here is the image of the newly-brought-to-light saint of God and miracle worker, Mitrofan of Voronezh; may it be a sign among you of my pastoral devotion and love for you in Christ![23]

Soldiers of Christ! Take these gifts with the very faith and love with which each was sent to you from various places of Russia and are now entrusted to you by me as a guarantee of success in battle and a sign of God's grace upon you.

Dark creatures from the West in the service of evil continue to swell our enemies' numbers; but as I have seen in my travels, not only do your many brothers in arms rush to your ranks, but as you yourself see, so do even the saints of God, even the Queen of the heavenly army. Who is against us, if God and his Holy Saints are for us? Complete this holy affair with the courage and glory with which you began it! Stand fearlessly against the enemy, who being Christian had the misfortune to dishonorably stand against the cross of Christ and for the fraud of Mohammed. Let them, in blinded mind and bitter heart, lay their hopes in human strength, wisdom and skill. Our strength and fortress always was and will be God our Father! Our immutable trust is in God the Son! Our indissoluble protection and shelter is in God the Holy Spirit!

Holy and almighty Trinity, bless and fortify the Orthodox host. Protect and save the Russian land! Amen.

NOTES

1. The original nineteenth-century Russian titles given to the documents translated here use the words *rech'* (meaning speech, discourse, or address) and *slovo* (speech or homily) and not *propoved'* (homily or sermon). I use the word sermon here, however, to encapsulate the wide range of Innokentii's oration, which was often political and religious, delivered at a variety of prayer services and not necessarily as a component of liturgies. Further, the term "sermon" conveys the spirit of preaching for which Innokentii was known among contemporaries and by biographers.

2. Bishop Makarii of Tambov, "Biograficheskie zapiski o Vysokopreosviashchennago Innokentiia," 19–39, *Venok na mogilu Vysokopreosviashchennago Innokentiia, arkhiepiskopa tavricheskago* (Moscow: V. Tip. M. P. Zakharova, 1864), 27.

3. General Osten-Saken to Count Protasov, RGIA, f. 797, op. 24, d. 16, 6.

4. From the office of the General Governor of New Russia and Bessarabaia to Count Protasov, 17 April 1854, RGIA, f. 797, op. 24, d. 16, 5.

5. About permitting Archbishop Innokentii and a few clerics in Kherson diocese to wear medals for their defense of Sevastopol, RGIA, f. 796, op. 137, d. 408, 29 January 1856, 2–3.

6. A recent survey of Orthodox homiletics includes Innokentii along

with three others: Dmitrii of Rostov, Metropolitan Platon, Metropolitan Filaret. V. P. Zubov, *Russkie propovedniki: ocherki po istorii russkoi propovedi* (Moscow: URSS, 2001). His reputation as the Russkii Zlatoust has been cultivated in the post-Soviet period. The prerevolutionary biography by T. Buktevich, *Innokentii Borisov, byvshii Arkhiepiskop Khersonskii* (St. Petersburg: I. L. Tuzov, 1887), for example, has been recently reissued under the new title *Russkii Zlatoust: zhizneopisanie, slova i propovedi sviatitelia Innokentiia, Arkhiepiskopa khersonskago* (Edinets, Moldova: Edinetsko-Brichanskaia eparkhiia, 2005).

7. PSZ series 2, t. 28, (1853) ch. 1, no. 27628

8. Nicholas I is refering principally to the Hungarians and Poles who entered the Ottoman Army, Poles who were freedom fighters, and Hungarians who were displaced by the Russian invasion of 1849.

9. Ps. 25.

10. Innokentii, Archbishop of Kherson and Tauride, "Rech' po prochtenii Vysochaishago Manifesta o voine s Turtsiei," *Sochineniia Innokentiia, Arkhiepiskopa khersonskago i tavricheskago*, vol. 8 (St. Petersburg: M. O. Vol'f, 1874), 9.

11. Translated from *Sochineniia Innokentiia, Arkhiepiskopa khersonskago i tavricheskago*, vol. 12 (St. Petersburg: M. O. Vol'f), 282–83.

12. According to the medieval *Chronicle of Nestor*, the tenth-century Prince Vladimir received baptism from the Byzantine emperor in Chersonesos, an ancient city located near Sevastopol, whose ruins are visible today.

13. Translated from *Sochineniia Innokentiia, Arkhiepiskopa khersonskago i tavricheskago*, vol. 12 (St. Petersburg: M. O. Vol'f, 1901), 287–290.

14. John 15:13.

15. Innokentii uses the term *arxistrategos* here, thus underscoring the relationship between Archangel Michael and Tsar Nicholas.

16. Translated from *Sochineniia Innokentiia, Arkhiepiskopa khersonskago i tavricheskago*, vol. 12 (St. Petersburg: M. O. Vol'f, 1901), 318–20.

17. Nearly 900,000 Russian soldiers died during the Crimean War, the majority from cholera, typhus, and malaria, rather than battle wounds.

18. Rom. 5:3–5.

19. 1 Pet. 4:1, "Since therefore Christ suffered in the flesh, [for you] arm yourselves also with the same intention (for whoever has suffered in the flesh has finished with sin)."

20. Grand Duchess Elena Pavlovna founded the Russian Sisters of Mercy, and established the *Krestnovozdvizhenskaia obshchina* (Elevation of the Cross Society) in October 1854, where they worked under the mentorship of Crimean War surgeon Nikolai Pirogov and the spiritual authority of Crimean monks.

21. Translated from *Sochineniia Innokentiia, Arkhiepiskopa khersonskago i tavricheskago*, vol. 12 (St. Petersburg, M. O. Vol'f), 303–305.

22. According to most versions of the legend, just as the Prince of Suzdal's army was about to break through Novgorod's defenses, the Mother of God of the Sign Icon flickered on city walls and repulsed the army. For the various myths associated with the Novgorod Mother of God of the Sign icon and the appropriation of her story in imperial narratives see, Gail Lenhoff, "Novgorod's Znamenie Legend

in Moscow's Steppennaia Kniga," in *Moskovskaia Rus': Spetsificheskie cherty razvitiia* (Budapest: Lorand Eotvos University Press, 2003), 178–86.

23. St. Mitrofan (1623–1703) established the main cathedral in Voronezh, where Innokentii attended seminary. Innokentii might also have seen a parallel between Mitrofan's efforts at battling the Old Belief in the reign of Peter I and his own efforts at the same during the reign of Nicholas I. The church canonized Mitrofan in 1832. See http://days.pravoslavie.ru/Life/life6741.htm (accessed 9 September 2013).

SUGGESTED READINGS

Curtiss, John Shelton. "Russian Sisters of Mercy in the Crimea, 1854–1855." *Slavic Review* 25, no. 1 (March) 1966: 84–100.

Figes, Orlando. *The Crimean War: A History*. New York: Metropolitan Books, 2011.

Goldrank, David M. *The Origins of the Crimean War*. London: Longman Group, 1994.

Kozelsky, Mara. *Christianizing Crimea: Shaping Sacred Space in the Russian Empire and Beyond*. DeKalb: Northern Illinois University Press, 2010.

Wagner, William G. "Orthodox Domesticity: Creating a Social Role for Women in Late Imperial Russia." In *Sacred Stories: Religion and Spirituality in Modern Russia*, ed. Mark D. Steinberg and Heather J. Coleman, 119–45. Bloomington: Indiana University Press, 2007.

SIX

The Diary of a Priest

Laurie Manchester

BEGINNING DURING THE GREAT REFORM ERA OF THE 1860S, Russian Orthodox priests were encouraged by the bourgeoning clerical press to keep confessional diaries. In these personal diaries they were to chart not only their own spiritual progress, but, in contrast to the Puritan practice of individual diary keeping, to some extent that of their parishioners as well. In part, this was a practical necessity born of the high illiteracy rates of Russian Orthodox parishioners. But it also underscores the greater authoritative power Orthodox priests, endowed with sacramental authority, had over their parishioners. As the Russian revolutionary movement spread and the autocratic government unsuccessfully sought to control the process of modernization, reform-minded publicists within the Russian Orthodox Church interpreted the crisis engulfing Russia primarily as a moral crisis. Asking priests to keep diaries was part of a movement to save Russia by elevating the morality and erudition of its priesthood. Diaries were to serve as mirrors to priests' souls, as a means to identify and correct existing imperfections. Given the social isolation many rural priests suffered, diaries were also to serve as a much needed friend. In turn, because few rural priests could afford to buy many books, diaries could afford a means of working on self-improvement at no cost. In keeping with the church's disregard for any dichotomy between public and private, diaries were to chronicle a priest's parish work as well as his domestic life. Priests were instructed to note anything good or bad they had done each day, everything that had made an impression on them, and their feelings about the main events of the day.

A few priests' diaries – including the one excerpted below – were published in the 1870s in the same national theological journals that were prescribing diary keeping for priests. They were thus undoubtedly chosen by the editors to serve as prescriptive models and are probably not representative of the genre at the time. Because of the acute persecution of the clergy during the early Soviet period, most unpublished diaries of priests were lost forever, making it impossible to gauge how many priests actually kept diaries. The few unpublished rural priests' diaries from the late nineteenth century that have survived differ from those published in the 1870s; entries are far less lengthy, and authors are less self-reflexive. They also write more about their family life (which is actually more in keeping with the prescriptive manuals) and complain more about their financial hardships. A few book-length diaries were published or serialized in the early twentieth century; they resemble the prescriptive genre more, indicating that over time priests began to interiorize prescriptive models of clerical diary writing.

The excerpts below, from the last two sections of Archpriest I. G.'s diary, were serialized in four parts in 1871. He wrote them during his first year as a priest, in the 1850s, before the clerical press began its campaign encouraging the genre. The first part includes a preface on his childhood memories. He was orphaned at age eight, and although he does not mention his social estate background, his apparently free-of-charge clerical education indicates he was from the clerical estate. In entries in the first two parts he wrestles with whether or not he is worthy to enter a profession he considers to be the highest calling, and describes his actual ordination. He remains intimidated by his vocation in the passages below, having clearly interiorized the church's campaign to elevate the priesthood, and even quotes John of Chrysostom – whose writings were translated and widely read by the nineteenth-century clergy – on how priests possess a higher authority than angels. His knowledge of theology and his reference to the many sermons he is writing and delivering reflects the improvements in clerical education; by the second half of the nineteenth century the majority of priests had completed a rigorous seminary education. Some of the themes these entries raise – such as clerical exhaustion, complaints about excessive drinking by the masses, the perceived feminization of piety, and the tension between priests having to deal with worldly material concerns while serving God – are commonplace in priests' autobiographical narratives. The deep personal piety the author expresses – for example, in reconciling his fears about the possibility of drowning an infant during baptism – is not. Whereas we see the author striving for self-improvement in the entries below, he is not charting the spiritual progress of his parishioners. However, he does describe his individual encounters with them in detail, both below and in the untranslated entries, and attempts to learn from each of these interactions. Finally, the albeit limited social commentary we witness in the final entry, when he confesses an impoverished, dying tailor, foreshadows subsequent generations of progressive Russian Orthodox priests who increasingly endeavored to heal parishioners' minds and bodies as well as their souls.

"The Diary of a Priest," by Archpriest I. G.[1]

Translated by Heather Coleman

185 ... My week is over. I can breathe easier. To tell the truth, it's sort of hard to serve the Divine Liturgy day after day. Maybe my fellow priests don't feel such a burden as I experience during the week. I am ashamed to ask others about this and it is sinful to feel oppressed by God's service. And in fact it is very possible that my colleagues don't find the week hard to endure; they are already accustomed to the work of God and have steeled themselves with thoughts of the greatness of this service and of the Christian exploit. But I'm still a novice at this. Be pleased, O God, to deliver me! O Lord, make haste to help me![2] But the Lord helps those who help themselves, as the proverb goes. And so I need to find both outside and within myself some motivations to guide my untiring service of the Lord God in my ordained state. But where will I find them? Surely not in profits – in other words not in the revenue received during the offertory from those who ask for their living and dead relatives to be remembered in prayer, or from the administration of rites, which is paid for through voluntary donations? What a worthless and pathetic motiva-

tion for the worthy carrying-out of the service of God! ... Are there no higher motivations for this? There must be! Here is what the Holy Church Fathers write about the great importance of pastoral service: "He (i.e. the Pastor) should stand with the angels, glorify with the archangels, offer sacrifices at the mountain altar, perform religious rites along with Christ, reconstitute Creation, restore the image of God, work for peace from on high."[3] "If anyone reflects on how great a thing it is," writes Saint John Chrysostom, "for someone, being still a man, and clothed in flesh and blood, to assist near that blessed and pure nature, he will then clearly see what great honor the grace of the Spirit has bestowed on priests. Through them the sacrifice is celebrated, and others, too, accomplish great service with regard to our dignity and our salvation. They still live and circulate on earth but they are entrusted with the administration of things which are in Heaven, and have received an authority which God has not given to angels or archangels." Here is a great incentive for the worthy carrying out of the priestly service. One needs to reflect more often on the importance and holiness of the sacraments of the holy Orthodox Church in order to be always ready to serve the liturgy with joy and enthusiasm. But on the path to thoughts of God stands the bustle of life, or, better put, one is confronted with urgent demands. How does one avoid this? And because of this, how does one find time – or, can one always find time for reflection on such important and holy subjects? Time must be found! At the very least, while getting ready to perform the holy rites, while performing those rites, can one not detach oneself from those worldly concerns and ascend in mind and heart to God? And the very prayers that are laid out in what is called the *Prayer Rule Before Holy Communion* and that serve as preparation for celebrating rites, as well as the prayers that are in the *Book of Needs* – can they really not arouse the spirit and direct it toward the worthy celebration of these rites? "Well, of course," one of my colleagues once said to me when we were discussing how we must and can perform our pastoral responsibilities irreproachably; "I agree with you, but is it really always possible? For example, you're kneeling in prayer, saying the *Prayer Rule*; suddenly your wife comes in and asks your advice on something, asks about various domestic matters. Or a workman comes in while you're praying and preparing to celebrate the rites and wants to know what he should do, what to keep busy with . . .

How's that for thoughts of God? ..." It's not hard to resolve such a quandary. When we prepare to celebrate the Divine liturgy, no one should come to us for any advice or orders. Before getting started, one should make sure one has given all necessary directions to one's household. "But when you pray," says the Lord, "go into your room and shut the door and pray to your Father who is in secret; and your Father who sees in secret will reward you." (Matt. 6:6). In this way we avoid vainglorious prayer, for which the Lord criticized the Pharisees, and can give ourselves over freely, if only for a few minutes, to thoughts of God....

185... Monday. The Holy Church on this day holds a service in honor of the incorporeal heavenly hosts who, among the saints, are in the first place after the Mother of God, the most honored Cherubim.[4] Thus, in accordance with longstanding tradition, on this day before the liturgy in our parish church the akathist to the Archangel Michael with all the heavenly Powers is chanted. I chanted this hymn for the first time. There weren't many people in the church; mostly women were in attendance. At the end of the liturgy, at the usual time, I gave a short homily. In this homily, I mostly tried to explain the significance of this day, of Mondays, with regards to church services. In particular, I said that the Holy Church on this day glorifies the heavenly host. I laid out the dogma of the division of the nine orders of angels into three spheres and explained the name of each sphere in particular, which reveals their relationship to God, to one another, and to us, sinners. Then I addressed the superstition that exists among the common folk that Monday is allegedly a difficult day and as a result they don't undertake anything important on this day. I tried to show that God doesn't have any difficult days for us. On the contrary, Monday should be considered the easiest of days, if we can put it that way, because it is the first day after Sunday, on which the Lord was raised from the dead and, having destroyed hell and conquered death, He gave us eternal life. Moreover, on that day, the Holy Church prays especially to the holy angels who are our invisible teachers, leaders, helpers, protectors. And I concluded my sermon, that in accordance with the teaching of the Church and its regulations, we too always need to turn to the petitioning and intercession of the angels, our protectors, in our prayers at home and at church, and should therefore not believe the superstition that Monday is a difficult day. Upon leaving the church,

I asked the cantor: "Are there always so few people on this day, that is, on Mondays?" "Always," he answered. "Most of those who come on this day are all old women, the so-called *Monday ladies*" (*ponedel'koviia*). And the artisans, especially the apprentices, are hung over on this day," added my sacristan with a smile. What a pitiful people! All week they work diligently and don't eat or sleep enough; but when they're paid their hard-earned penny on Sunday, they've squandered it by Monday. I was preoccupied by another thought, by the way, as well, which the cantor had casually mentioned, the idea of *Monday ladies*. I wondered whether there was any kind of basis for the so-called *Monday ladies*. It would seem that there is no sort of canonical basis for fasting on this day, even for a very few people. Fasting on Mondays is nothing other than a vow made to God by a few people or something along the lines of a voluntary penance. There are two categories among the *Monday ladies:* some eat absolutely nothing until sundown, whereas others eat only fast-day fare at the usual times. Of course, such a vow is not unpleasant to God if it is given in a thoughtful way and lived out precisely and with zeal, as a sacrifice of love and gratefulness to God for His mercy. . . .

Thursday. 18$. – Today we commemorated Holy Philip the Apostle, one of the Seven Deacons.[5] In my homily I laid out the life of Saint Philip in some detail, based on material from *Sunday Reading.*[6] In front of me, before the lectern, stood an elderly, honored soldier, a broad-shouldered, portly old man whom the burden of years had already begun to bow toward the earth. At the end of the liturgy, when I left the church, this old man stopped me, having apparently intentionally awaited my exit.

– "We humbly thank you for the sermon, Father," he said, accepting a blessing.

– "And what did you take away from the sermon that was edifying for you, old man?"

– "What was edifying, indeed! Here I have lived out my whole lifetime, I'm about seventy years old, and up to now I did not know the life of my patron. It is a well-known thing – we are illiterate people and I've never had the chance to ask a literate person to read me the life of my saint: because you don't know where to find such a life of this saint, in what book it is written, where to acquire that book. And now, although I'm in my old age, I finally got to hear and know the life of my saint. But surely it is not enough to just know the life of the saint whose name we bear, we also need to imitate his life.

– Now I also don't understand this, spiritual father: how can I imitate in my own life the life of St. Philip? You were saying that he was first a deacon and then even a bishop and that he preached the Word of God as other apostles did.

– Listen; here's how you can imitate him: St. Philip was a family man, he had four daughters who were even honored with the gift of prophecy. Why did the Lord God honor them with this holy gift? Because they lived in purity and chastity. They were raised under the supervision, of course, of their father, in the true faith and in all manner of Christian piety. Most likely you too have a family, have children. You, too, should raise them in the same spirit of faith and Christian piety. This is the great and holy responsibility of every father of a family.

– But the point is this, my spiritual father, that the Lord did not give us children. We have lived in marriage with the old woman almost four decades but God does not send children. For that reason, indeed, my wife and I thought, for comfort in our old age, to adopt an orphan, a ten-year-old girl. In fact I was her godfather: we keep her like a daughter and raise her.

– What prevents you, in that case, from applying the rules of the life of St. Philip to your adopted daughter? Raise your adopted daughter in the true Christian faith and instill in her good pious morals and it will be a blessing to both you and her and you will receive praise from God.

– Somehow it is said, Father, that an adopted child is not the same as one's own!

– Now, as you heard, St. Philip was kind to widows and orphans; you too can imitate this! You also heard how St. Philip propagated and spread the faith of Christ. This activity, too, you can imitate. Wherever you can and should invite, persuade, entreat, and through the example of your life teach others to live by the law of Christ and not to break His commandments. Your word and especially your life, as an old and experienced person, can carry great weight and significance in righting those whom you notice deviating from true faith and Christian piety.

"May the Lord strengthen you in every blessed work," I said, taking my leave of the old man. The old man was visibly touched by my sincere words. He was not able to say a word to me and merely bowed down low and accepted a blessing. And the lesson for me was this: in my homilies, I need to more often lay out the life and deeds of the saints.

Friday. How easily, freely, with some humility one chants the akathist to the Protection of the Most Holy Mother of God. Again the church is full of people. It's clear that the people too are moved in their hearts when they hear this akathist before the start of the liturgy. Truly this is a good practice – to chant an akathist every day before the beginning of the liturgy. The priest himself, too, as he chants it, disposes his soul to the reverential celebration of the rites, since a certain warmth and heightened Christian feeling remain in the heart and, indeed, sustain among the people themselves a feeling of reverence, of Christian piety. In my homily to the people I continued with yesterday's discussion because I felt that yesterday's talk was not quite finished. In particular, I hadn't fully explained how to imitate in life the saint whose name each of us bears. And so I briefly recounted the lives of Prov, Tarakh, and Andronik (whose memory is honored on this day) [12 October], and showed that in one's own life one can imitate the life of these saints too. In conclusion I reminded my listeners that those who distance themselves from the names of such saints as, for example, Prov, Tarakh, and Andronik and others, and ask, when their child is being named, that they be called Ivan or Petr or Anna or Mariia or something like that, are not doing the right thing. At the end of the liturgy a child was brought for naming and baptism. The child turned out to be ill, premature. We had to hurry with the baptism. I asked the advice of the senior priest who comes every day to the church during the service, even though it isn't his week, and inquired what he does in such circumstances. He referred to his predecessor at this church saying that he had followed his practice in these cases. After that, I said the prayer for the naming of a child, followed by the prayer "Praise God every person who wishes to be saved" and another, "Sovereign, Lord, Our God, call your servant to your holy enlightenment" and so on. Right away then the Epiphany water was brought and I used it to baptize the baby by pouring it over him, after singing Alleluia and making the sign of the cross three times over the water with the mote and anointing oil.[7] Then I said all the prayers appointed in the prayer book for baptism and finally the ill baby was chrismated along with the prayers appointed for that sacrament. My first experience of administering a baptism! By necessity, I performed it by pouring the water. It didn't seem hard to me. But it will be another thing when I have to baptize healthy children by immersion! It seems quite terrifying if you think about it, but in fact something will happen! By the way, I've never heard of a case and, they say, there has never been a case where the child, while being immersed during baptism, choked on the water and died. And indeed, after all, it's the all-powerful Lord who administers the sacrament and we are only His servants: and would He allow the death of an innocent child during the celebration of the sacrament that is the door to entering the Church of Christ!

Saturday.

I didn't give a homily today because I was extremely tired from reading the list of prayers for the dead and also because after the Great Entrance, I was told that I needed to counsel an ill person. The service ended; I headed to the ill person's house. I will never forget this striking incident in my pastoral work. I went into the shack, which was full of drafts; cracks everywhere, and broken windows stuffed with some sort of rags – the poverty in the home was horrendous. In a corner by the stove was a dilapidated bed on which the sick person lay. Imagine a skeleton not yet cleaned of its skin; eyes so deeply sunken that you can hardly see anything at the bottom of the hollows under the eyes; hands that are skin and bones.

– "How do you [ty – the informal form of address] feel?"

– "Pretty bad, Father, my death is before me, would you [vy – the formal form of address] be so kind as to confess me and give me the holy sacraments," the sick man said to me with difficulty, barely getting the words out. It was completely evident that the sick man was suffering from consumption and was in the final battle of life with death. By trade he was a tailor. Tailoring is a murderous life! I speak, however, of the poor who don't have assistants, who try by their efforts to feed a family. It's no wonder they get consumption when they are constantly in a half-bent position and have little rest day or night. The prayers "when soon it will be time to give a sick person communion" were read. Then I got to the confession. With great detail, clarity, and precision the patient confessed his sins: the sins of youth, the sins of impudence, sins of commission and omission. "What a fortunate illness consumption is," I thought to myself. "It takes away neither the memory, nor the intellect from the patient. But because of this, what suffering!" However, there appeared in my heart such a gratifying feeling from what I saw, how even in a very ill state, people so candidly and sincerely confess their sins. "May God make you rest with the saints, good toiler." This is what I was thinking as I left the shack, after giving the sick man his final admonishment through the holy gifts – for it was clearly visible that my patient had but a few hours left among the living. I was offered some pay for my labor. But I refused such payment and advised his wife to take care of the life of her profoundly ill husband. In addition to the wife, there are two children in the family as well.

Archpriest I. G.

NOTES

1. Prot. I. G., "Dnevnik sviashchennika," *Rukovodstvo dlia sel'skikh pastyrei* no. 45 (871): 305–12; no. 49 (1871): 438–49; no. 52 (1871): 569–78 (excerpted).
2. Ps. 70:1. This well-known psalm is used in the service of Compline.
3. The author cites a Russian translation of the Oration on the priesthood of St. Gregory the Theologian (St. Gregory of Nazianz).
4. In the weekly cycle, Mondays are devoted to the Mother of God and the heavenly host. See http://www.krugosvet.ru/enc/kultura_i_obrazovanie/religiya/BOGOSLUZHEBNIE_KNIGI.html (accessed 9 September 2013).
5. His feast day is October 11.
6. *Voskresnoe chtenie* (Sunday Reading) was a weekly journal aimed at a popular audience published by the Kiev Theological Academy.
7. Baptismal water was used for special occasions and believed to still be effective after death. In contrast to the usual Orthodox method, baptism by pouring water over the head is performed when the candidate is too ill to be immersed.

SUGGESTED READINGS

Kizenko, Nadieszda. *A Prodigal Saint: Father John of Kronstadt and the Russian People.* University Park: Penn State University Press, 2000.

Manchester, Laurie. *Holy Fathers, Secular Sons: Clergy, Intelligentsia and the Modern Self in Revolutionary Russia.* DeKalb: Northern Illinois University Press, 2008.

Shevzov, Vera. *Russian Orthodoxy on the Eve of the Revolution.* New York: Oxford University Press, 2004.

SEVEN

"Another Voice from the Lord": An Orthodox Sermon on Chriſtianity, Science, and Natural Disaſter

Nicholas Breyfogle

MULTIPLE EARTHQUAKES SHOOK THE LAKE BAIKAL REGION OF Russian Siberia for several consecutive days beginning on New Year's Eve 1861/62.¹ In the province's capital city of Irkutsk, buildings wobbled violently, cracked, and collapsed (especially churches and other stone structures). Church bells rang uncontrollably and an organ in someone's house suddenly started playing on its own – an eerie, discordant music to accompany the screams of residents and the crashing of household items that tumbled to the ground. Barrels of fish weighing over seven hundred pounds went flying across courtyards; animals howled and ran in panic. Across the lake, on the eastern shore on the Tsagan Steppe, the shock of the earthquake unleashed a tsunami that rolled rapidly over the steppe and then retreated as quickly as it came. It left behind a "mincemeat" landscape and piles of ice blocks more than two kilometers inland. More ominously, water began to gush from widespread fractures in the land created by the seismic shaking and the ground began sinking. More than two hundred square kilometers of the Tsagan steppe, along with the villages on it, sank permanently underwater – Atlantis-style.

Both during and after the 1861/62 earthquakes, the people of the region struggled to explain and make sense of these horrifying, life-changing events. The Orthodox sermon translated here – delivered in Irkutsk in the days after the major earthquakes struck but still in the midst of the violent aftershocks (during a time when people slept, if they slept at all, with their clothes and shoes on in constant fear of another major seismic event) – represents one way in which the people around Baikal strove to make sense of the earthquakes. "Another Voice from

God" offers us insight into how Orthodox priests and their parishioners understood their place in the universe, their relationship to nature and God, their understandings of causation, and a Christian explanation for nature's all-too-often destructive powers. It also attempts to critique and confront head-on the efforts of the more secular and scientific community to explain the earthquakes through the natural sciences.

The tension highlighted here between religious and scientific explanatory systems – between different understandings of how the universe functioned (and God's role in the universe), what defined proof and evidence, and the relationship between faith, scripture, and observation – represents one example of a pan-European intellectual debate that had been boiling over since the Scientific Revolution of the seventeenth century and the Enlightenment of the eighteenth century. By the nineteenth century, three main strands of interpreting nature existed in Europe: a Judeo-Christian explanation that saw God's hand at work directly in all natural events; a Deist approach that argued that while God had created the machine that was the universe and set it in motion, He could not tinker with it and overturn the laws of nature He had created; and finally, a scientific approach that saw nature as a great machine (and not necessarily created by God), which humans could understand through sustained and rational investigation. Natural disasters played a very important role in the development and debate of these different intellectual viewpoints, particularly the great Lisbon earthquake of 1755, which the prominent Enlightenment thinker Voltaire wrote about at length.

In the Baikal case, for the majority, the earthquake was a religious event saturated with moral significance: "a special sign of God's punishment for their sins and for their forgetfulness before God." Indeed, Orthodox priests and parishioners understood nature and the environment around them as a tool through which God could act on human communities. Here, they manifested a Providential view of the natural world as a space controlled by an activist God whose power sustained and controlled human activity, and who often acted vindictively to show his displeasure with human activity and to entice the survivors back into the proper way of God and the church. In this explanatory system, humans (as the sinners) were ultimately the cause of the earthquakes, prompting God to act. The human and natural worlds were inextricably linked, with the environment a mirror reflecting the status of human behavior. As they looked to the future, this approach to the environment led Orthodox leaders to argue that the best way to avoid future earthquakes – the best form of disaster preparedness – was to ensure that all people in the region lived godly and moral lives.

The Providential approach was by no means the only way of confronting the catastrophe, however. The efforts of the people around Lake Baikal to explain the earthquakes unveil two other distinct understandings of "nature." First, scientists and local intellectuals approached the earthquakes as a physical, morally neutral event subject to rational, predictable rules that could be known through scientific methods of observation and analysis. For this group, scientific knowledge could then be applied to mitigate and perhaps control or prevent nature's threats.[2] Second, those who found the activist-God understanding of nature unsatisfying explained the earthquakes as a manifestation of a "living earth" – in some ways similar to the current Gaia understanding of the planet. Here, nature was a powerful, living entity (albeit lacking consciousness) – one that acted by its own rules and thus stood outside of humanity's and God's direct power.

In the aftermath of the Baikal disaster, the Orthodox Providential understandings of the earthquake affected the religious beliefs and practices of the people in the region. Orthodox clerics reported that their congregations became more fervent in their prayer, regular in their attendance, more willing to share their little material wealth, and more devout in their efforts to repent of their sins and thereby prevent future disasters. To mollify God, and exhorting Mary to help them, a vast crowd set off on a religious procession through town on 1 January, carrying aloft two icons: the wonder-working Kazan Mother of God and the icon of the town patron St. Innokentii. Moreover, as the crowds thronged the churches in search of answers, comfort, and aid, they looked everywhere for signs that their penitence and impassioned prayers had convinced God to forgive them. They found the Lord's "astonishing mercy" in the rapid rate of, and passionate devotion to, church repair. For parishioners, the stakes for rebuilding were high – the possibility of again unleashing God's wrath was all too real and frightening if they did not properly make amends.

Before turning to the translated document, a word should be said about sermons as a genre of communication and their changing social and religious role in late tsarist Russia. As part of a much larger process of reform in the Orthodox Church aimed at ministering to the laity more actively and efficaciously, the church took much greater interest in the form and content of preaching from the mid-nineteenth century on. In the hope of enhancing communication with the mass of the laity, the church leadership transformed the format of the sermon from a rigid speech to a more informal talk, which could be given with greater frequency. At the same time, sermons began to appear in published form with much greater regularity (for example in the newly created diocesan newspapers, like this sermon). Here, sermons were to be read as well as listened to (and there was, of course, a substantial difference in the experience of the sermon whether one read it or listened to the priest speak it). Finally, the content of sermons shifted along with the format. In an effort to bring the word of God into the daily lives of the parishioners and to have their say in contemporary events, priests increasingly came to include topics of social and cultural interest (such as earthquakes) in their preaching along with more abstract scriptural analysis.

Another Voice from the Lord[3]

On that day [1 January 1862], under the dome of this holy church and in filial fear and awe at the prophesying of the voice of the Lord that was shaking our hearing and heart in the great temple of nature, when you and I tried to make sense for ourselves of the meaning of this voice, the divinely inspired words of the Apostle Paul offered this warning to all of us: "See to it that no one makes a prey of you by philosophy and empty deceit, according to human tradition, according to the elemental spirits of the universe, and not according to Christ" [Col. 2:8].[4]

The warning of the apostle was clearly a warning of the Lord Himself, Whose prophesying we all made out. And judging from the circumstances of the time, it was necessary because the voice of the Lord, although it was strong, was not articulate; although it was obviously from heaven, it manifested itself in a phenomenon of the elemental world. And therefore, it could seem to people whose hearing is not opened by faith that this was not the voice of the Lord, shaking the wilderness, but simply a resounding rumble in the void. So it seemed to some people.

We also heard comforting stories, of the great reverence with which many of the inhabitants of the town accepted the visitation of God and of the great filial awe with which, at the time of the shaking of the earth and the wavering of our buildings, some knelt to the ground; others raised their hands to the sky, thereby revealing that their heart understood where that terrible voice rang out from.

We were still under the active impression of that gratifying sight, when, in response to our appeal, an unusually large number of people from all sides thronged together and gathered under the banner of the cross of the Lord, with which we walked around the shaken boulevards and streets of our city.

We had only just begun to taste the consolation of the splendid surge of people into the temples of God, as a result of which God's temples became manifestly fuller, and the places where we provoke the wrath of the Lord, emptier. The path to the dwelling place of God's Saints was enlivened, and the paths to the common places of holiday merriment were already not as audacious.

We still found ourselves, I say, under the influence of these sensations, which are comforting to the heart, when we heard a voice resounding around the town. It was a voice entirely unexpected after the complete shaking of the town and one that penetrated even into the midst of the people who are simple of heart and faith – with its interpretation, as if in defiance of the apostolic warning, that the terrible events that had occurred in our town were not some sort of religious-moral event but a simple manifestation of nature, which by its own powers brought about the unpleasant effect on the people. Such a surprise became all the more unpleasant in that it acted very harmfully on the good mood that had formed in the spirit of the people, and all the more dangerous in that the explanatory rumors about the earthquake emerged from the lips of those who have mastered the knowledge of the new scientific discoveries about nature.

If these opinions of natural reason regarding the terrible events in the town restricted themselves to the scope of the scholar's study, if these explanations of the earthquakes were proclaimed within the walls of some chemistry laboratory, or if these efforts to shock the convictions of the people concerning the causes of the earthquakes were intended for the people's education, then we would consider all of this simply an external matter for us. But, quite the opposite, when the explanatory rumors about how to comprehend the earthquake in our town begin to take on a direction directly in opposition to spreading the word of God about the right hand of the Almighty that governs the world; and when, as a result, those rumors begin to act scandalously on the penitent, moral mood of the people, can we leave without a reminder to each and every one about the warning of the apostle that we heard on the first day of the new year: "See to it that no one makes a prey of you by philosophy and empty deceit, according to human tradition, according to the elemental spirits of the universe, and not according to Christ."

I love nature when it opens the great book of the revelation of God before the eyes of my reason and heart. I get lost in contemplation of the phenomena of visible nature, when in these manifestations, as in some mirror, although dimly but tangibly portrayed: "Ever since the creation of the world his invisible nature, namely, his eternal power and deity, has been clearly perceived in the things that have been made" [Rom. 1:20]. I listen with delight, exulting in my heart to the highest heavens, when together with the prophet Psalmist I begin to heed, how: "The heavens are telling the glory of God; and the firmament proclaims his handiwork" [Ps. 19:1].[5] As there in heaven, "Praise [the Creator and Almighty], sun and moon, praise him, all you shining stars! Praise him, you highest heavens, and you waters above the heavens!" [Ps. 148:3–4]. Here, in the vale – on the earth – "Praise the LORD," in a mellifluent, harmonious choir, "fire and hail, and snow and frost, and stormy wind fulfilling his command! Mountains and all hills, fruit trees and all cedars! Beasts and all cattle, creeping things and flying birds!" [Ps. 148:8–10].

I love science about nature when the toiler of science – human reason – entering into the sublime cathedral of nature, contemplates its beauty with veneration and, delving down into the deep, into its innermost hiding-places, takes the light of God's revelation for illumination, and in that light disassembles its structures and tries to discern the function of the parts and the whole. But when that toiler permits himself, in that Godly cathedral, to treat its features in a way that no passerby would permit himself even in a neglected and abandoned home; when he does not consider it rapaciousness to analyze and dismantle it and build from it his caprice in the manner of people like Epicurus, Descartes, Schelling, and others, without any attention to the plan of the wise creator that is revealed to all; and when, removed from the light – "The true light that enlightens every man was coming into the world" [John 1:9] – he builds his own somber theories, in which he himself becomes perplexed and confuses others; then what can we show you in that science that is not that ancient pagan philosophy, overthrown by Christianity, about which, in his time, the apostle cautioned, saying: "[Brothers] see to it that no one takes you captive through philosophy."

Those interpreters of the earthquake who explain it as a purely natural manifestation of nature present themselves as champions in the name of science and of all its great discoveries for the benefit of humanity. But would it really be against the rights of science to contest a monopoly over the education of humanity that does not belong to it? For, can it really be human science that formed that best part of humanity that the Christian state visibly represents? And in the science of nature itself, is it really the case that only one view of nature and its phenomena exists, that is, the view from earth – a purely physical perspective? Is it really the case that the interests of that science are only material? Would the [scientific] view on the phenomena of nature really abase itself, if we were to look at them from heaven – from the perspective of divine revelation? Really, does true science lose something when the phenomena of nature are explained by the instruction of Him who calls himself the *God of reason* or science? No, it is *vain flattery* – to fight for the inviolability of human science while neglecting, or worse, belittling the science of divine revelation! And for this reason I again repeat to you the warning of the apostle: "See to it [Brothers] that no one takes you captive through philosophy" and vain flattery.

No one indeed! Those who get carried away with new discoveries in the arena of natural sciences generally try to raise their fame to such heights that, in their opinion, every mind should bow down before this eminence. But who are all these former and expected celebrities? True, they are educated men, investigators of nature who are deserving of respect. But in addition to this, who are they? They are people, and here is the true judgment of the God-inspired judge, the prophet David, about each of them individually: "Everyone utters lies" [Ps. 12:2]. And is it disagreeable to someone to take upon himself the burden to show which among all these ideas – before which our ancestors, in their time, bowed their intellects – were not lies? Let their consciences say whether in all today's discoveries of science there is not the holy and heavenly truth? And most importantly, whether the current nineteenth century will see the end of all new discoveries in the secrets of nature? And those theories that will appear as a result of the new discoveries, will they, in future centuries, completely overturn the theories of today? For, all these theories of science, like human legends, are always changeable and unsteady. Is it fair for that reason to neglect the eternal truth of God's revelation because of human legends? No, Brothers, "see to it that no one takes you captive through philosophy and empty deceit, according to human tradition."

Ever since the discovery, in the area of visible nature, of [nature's] own agents or forces, since her laws have become known, there always were and are people with narrow viewpoints on nature, who do not want to allow for another actor in nature other than the force of nature itself. There is no argument that, through the study of the forces of nature, the innumerable phenomena of nature are explained; that, through the application of the laws of these forces to the needs of human life, useful structures have been created for the earthly prosperity of humanity. But is it fair to give such magnitude to nature, so that the Creator of nature himself becomes hidden? Is it fair to assign such an extensive sphere of action to the strength of nature, so that in this arena there no longer remains a place for the actions of Him Who is the beginning and end of all activity, both on the earth and in heaven, and Who said about Himself: "My Father is working still, and I am working" [John 5:17]. Is it fair to consider the right of nature to its independence inviolable by any outside activity? But look more closely – are these forces of nature not subordinated, to a certain extent, to humanity itself, which is called, in the well-known phrase, the sovereign over nature? They are obviously subordinated. And serving as proof of that fact are the many different uses of natural science for the needs of humanity that have been carried out by science: in steams and gases, in electricity and galvanism, and so on. How is this so? To the vain command of humanity, and for the sake of humanity's earthly profits, the forces of nature with their laws are subordinated so that humanity can dispose of them freely, but the Almighty Creator of these forces and Ruler of the heavens and earth cannot dare touch these powers and use them for the attainment of his goals – for the moral improvement of humanity and its eternal salvation! No, such an *elemental* wisdom looks too unworthily on the Creator and the Sovereign of the world – completely in the Epicurean way! No, you will lose your way, brothers, may not one of you be tempted by philosophy and vain flattery, by human legend, about the elements of the earth.

No one should think (although from all that we have said there is no occasion to think), that in pointing to Another Actor in the appearance of the earthquake that has taken place, we had in mind to reject the action of the power of nature in this natural phenomenon, and thereby to present it as a supernatural, miraculous phenomenon. No, our goal is singular – to inspire those who experienced this terrible phenomenon to look on it not only with human reason, but with faith, and judge it not only from the perspective of science but also from the view of Christ's Gospel. And how does Our Lord Jesus Christ teach us to look on the phenomena of nature, even the most mundane? He teaches that we should see in them the actions of that graceful, that righteous right hand of our Heavenly Father. And how pleasing for the heart to listen to these lessons of the Heavenly Teacher, when your ears begin to ring with, for example, such instructions: "Look at the birds of the air: they neither sow nor reap nor gather into barns, and yet your heavenly Father feeds them.... And why are you anxious about clothing? Consider the lilies of the field, how they grow; they neither toil nor spin.... But if God so clothes the grass of the field, which today is alive and tomorrow is thrown into the oven, will he not much more clothe you, O men of little faith?" [Matt. 6:25–30]. Or: "But I say to you, Love your enemies, ... so that you may be sons of your Father who is in heaven; for he makes his sun rise on the evil and on the good, and sends rain on the just and on the unjust" [Matt. 5:44, 45]. Or: "And do not fear those who kill the body but cannot kill the soul ... Are not two sparrows sold for a penny? And not one of them will fall to the ground without your Father's will. But even the hairs of your head are all numbered" [Matt. 10:29–30]. And with these explanations of natural phenomena, in which you do not look at anything except the necessary laws of the forces of nature and their actions, what do you arrive at if not a dismal fate, prophesied by Mohammed? No, brothers, watch out so that none of you will be enticed by philosophy and vain flattery, by human legends, by elements of the earth, *and not by Christ.*

If in the end, and after the warning of the apostle, someone finds himself in difficulty to expose the falsehood of the vain flattery, by human legends and by elements of the earth, then here is another very simple means of unmasking the lie – the very same that in his time the Savior proposed against the false prophets and teachers of lies. Which one? "Thus you will know them by their fruits ... So, every sound tree bears good fruit, but the bad tree bears evil fruit" [Matt. 12:20 and 17]. Now look, what fruits are promised us and what fruits have already been borne by the spreading of rumors among the people that the terrible events of the earthquake that befell us were not actions of the hand of God, but simply were the actions of the forces of nature? That is, to which thoughts and feelings should this explanation lead and already be leading? Obviously to [the thoughts and feelings] that if the earthquake was nothing more than a manifestation of the powers of nature, then that means that they who at the time of the shaking of the earth and the shaking of the houses bent on their knees before God, or raised their hands up to the heavens, found themselves in quite a delusion! If the earthquake was simply a natural phenomenon, then how absurd and incompatible with the progress of science was the instruction to begin the religious procession around the town following the earthquake! If this terrible event had no other meaning beyond the natural, then what would all these religious movements in the population, appearing in our town as a result of the earthquake, all these penitential feelings, all these pious vows be found to be in the eyes of this science other than the fear of superstition! Look, what fruits! You will know the tree by its fruit!

Brothers, do not be carried away, like the original mother in paradise, by the external appearance of the tree, with the beauty of its fruit and smooth-tongued promise that your "eyes will be opened" [Gen. 3:5] through tasting of that tree, for the infiltration of the innermost secrets of nature. Let no one entice you with *vain adulation*. God's judgment was long ago pronounced on trees with similar fruits: "So, every sound tree bears good fruit, but the bad tree bears evil fruit" [Matt. 7:17]. Amen.
Sermon delivered 6 January 1862.

NOTES

1. Research for this article was supported by funding from the National Council for Eurasian and East European Research (NCEEER), under authority of a Title VIII grant from the U.S. Department of State, American Philosophical Society, American Council of Learned Societies/Social Science Research Council/National Endowment for the Humanities Area Studies Fellowship, Davis Center for Russian and Eurasian Studies, Kennan Institute for Advanced Russian Studies, Mershon Center for International Security Studies, and the Ohio State University. None of these organizations is responsible for the views expressed within this text. I offer special thanks to Mark Soderstrom for his research assistance and to Heather Coleman, Irina Paert, and Vera Shevzov for their very helpful translation suggestions.

2. Since our current understanding of earthquakes as caused by the movements of plate tectonics did not come into prominence around the globe until the 1960s, the explanatory models put forward by Russian scientists in the nineteenth century are no longer scientifically accepted. However, their approaches, discourses, and endeavors regarding nature were decidedly scientific, seeing the non-human world as rational, non-moral, mechanistic, ordered, and knowable through human reason and the application of the scientific method.

3. "Inoi Golos ot Gospoda," *Irkutskiia eparkhial'nyia viedomosti*, pribavlenie k no. 6 (2 February 1863): 59–67.

4. A footnote in the original indicates that this was one of the appointed readings for 1 January.

5. Ps. 18:2 in the Russian Bible.

SUGGESTED READINGS

Bouteneff, Peter. "The Two Wills of God: Providence in St. John of Damascus." *Studia Patristica* 42 (2006): 291–96.

Johns, Alessa, ed. *Dreadful Visitations: Confronting Natural Catastrophe in the Age of Enlightenment.* New York: Routledge, 1999.

Steinberg, Ted. *Acts of God: The Unnatural History of Natural Disaster in America*. New York: Cambridge University Press, 2000.

Walker, Charles F. *Shaky Colonialism: The 1746 Earthquake-Tsunami in Lima, Peru, and its Long Aftermath*. Durham, NC: Duke University Press, 2008.

Ware, Bishop Kallistos. "God Immanent Yet Transcendent: The Divine Energies According to Saint Gregory Palamas." In *In Whom We Live and Move and Have Our Being: Pantheistic Reflections on God's Presence in a Scientific World*, ed. Philip Clayton and Arthur Peacocke, 157–68. Grand Rapids, MI: Eerdmans, 2004.

EIGHT

A Ukrainian Priest's Son Remembers His Father's Life and Ministry

Heather J. Coleman

THIS MEMOIR TAKES US INTO THE WORLD OF THE VILLAGE priest in Kiev diocese between the 1830s and 1850s – a time when Kiev province was a relatively new addition to the Russian Empire. Although the city of Kiev itself had been ruled by Russia since 1667, it was only with the Partitions of Poland of 1793–95 that the provinces of Right-Bank Ukraine (Kiev, Volynia, and Podolia) were incorporated into the Russian Empire. It was an often violent process, but St. Petersburg characterized the annexation as a repatriation of Orthodox, Russian lands that rightfully belonged to Russia.

Situated on the frontier between the Austrian and Russian empires, between the Polish Catholic and Russian Orthodox religious worlds, the Southwest Region (as Right-Bank Ukraine was called after 1832) remained a volatile borderland right until 1917. In 1800, only official Kiev spoke Russian. Poles continued to dominate the regional nobility and rose in rebellion in 1830–31 and again in 1863 against Russian attempts to change the traditional political and social patterns of the region. Most urban residents were Yiddish-speaking Jews; they also frequently served as the leaseholders who ran the Polish estates and mills. The villages remained the preserve of the Ukrainian-speaking peasantry and the Orthodox clergy that emerged from their ranks. Relations between these groups bore the scars of the great religious and political struggles that had accompanied the collapse of the Polish-Lithuanian Commonwealth in the late eighteenth century. In particular, the struggle between the Orthodox Church and the Uniate (Greek Catholic) Church (which had agreed in 1596 to a union with Rome, recognizing the supremacy of the

Pope in exchange for the preservation of eastern Christian liturgical practice in the Polish-Lithuanian Commonwealth) for the allegiance of the Ukrainian population had left its mark. Although most Uniates in Kiev Province had converted to Orthodoxy, whether voluntarily or forcibly, in the mid-1790s, only in 1839 did St. Petersburg "reunite" the Uniate Church with Orthodoxy and in effect suppress the Uniate faith in the region. Yet social and political tensions would continue to take on important religious and ethnic colorings. During the nineteenth century, Right-Bank Ukraine was increasingly incorporated into the Russian social, administrative, religious, and cultural world. By the 1880s, when this article was written, all official business and education took place in Russian; and, indeed, publications in Ukrainian had been outlawed in 1863 and again in 1876 in an effort to combat the emerging nationalist movement in the region and to ensure that the cultural orientation of the increasingly literate common folk was Russian.

This anonymous article appeared in the journal *Kievskaia starina* (Kievan Antiquity) in 1882. Founded by Ukrainophile cultural activists, *Kievskaia starina* was an important Russian-language journal of Ukrainian historical studies. It published scholarly articles and reviews, historical documents, belles lettres, and memoirs relating to Ukrainian history at a time when other forms of organized Ukrainian nationalist activity were impossible.

The author of this memoir was Evfimii Mikhailovich Kryzhanovskii (1831–88), who spent most of his career in the Kingdom of Poland as a zealous russifier, heading the Sedletskii (Siedlce) school district. He would go on, from 1883 until his death in 1888, to serve as a bureaucrat of the Holy Synod, active on its schools committee, and an advisor to Konstantin Pobedonostsev on western borderland issues. Everything about Kryzhanovskii's career could lead the reader to be surprised by his article's defense of the value and authenticity of things Ukrainian. Yet Kryzhanovskii was also the son of a Kiev province priest and a devout local patriot. Due to his poor health but also his academic gifts, Kryzhanovskii did not follow his father into the priesthood. Rather, he pursued a degree at the Kiev Theological Academy, graduating in 1857. As a student, he developed "a love for studying Russian history, especially that of south Rus'," and a particular interest in "the fate of church ritual in the past of southern Rus', the particularities of which are still expressed in current south-Russian church ritual practice," wrote the editor of his collected works in 1890. Thus, Kryzhanovskii concluded his studies with a thesis on the 1646 Book of Needs (*Trebnik*) published by Kiev Metropolitan Petr Mogila in an effort to standardize and purify Orthodox ritual practice in the Polish-Lithuanian Commonwealth, a service book that remained much favored by local priests in Kryzhanovskii's own day (ironically often in Uniate editions), despite the Russian Orthodox Church's official insistence on its own version.[1]

Although written for a secular journal, this text is both a description of clerical and religious life in mid-nineteenth-century Kiev diocese and a narrative written in a religious key, telling the story of Ukraine as a suffering Christ. While asserting the essential and ancient Orthodoxy of "southern Rus" (Right-Bank Ukraine), Kryzhanovskii reveals, through the story of his father's career as a priest, that the "return" of this region to Russia and the Russian Orthodox Church was no simple homecoming. Kryzhanovskii concurred with the official view that blamed the Poles and the Jews for the sufferings of the Ukrainian village. But contrary to the official line, Great Russia appears not so much as a savior in Kryzhanovskii's telling as another alien force, one that brings the standardization of the impersonal modern state with its bureaucratized church and educational system, a standardization that dismisses the local and the authentic and the truly Christian. Like the Russian priests' sons whom Laurie Manchester has studied, Kryzhanovskii traces his own secular career of service to the people to the village and his father's values as a priest. And when he speaks of Ukraine, he means Kiev province, for that area was known as Ukraine in the Polish period and remained so in local parlance; his broader regional unit is not all of present-day Ukraine, but the Right-Bank provinces west of the Dnieper River, which he and others like him called "southern Rus." This reminds us that *Kievskaia starina*'s contributors held a wide range of political views, from left to right, and from those whose Ukraine spanned the right and left banks of the Dnieper and might one day have an autonomous or even independent future, to others who combined a strong local or regional attachment with a commitment to the Russian imperial state.[2] Kryzhanosvkii shared many of the views of the Russian "native soil" conservative nationalists, the *pochvenniki* such as Fedor Dostoevskii, who were interested not so much in looking back to an idealized pre-Petrine past as in seeking the national sources of Russian cultural life as a basis for moving into a future built on truly Russian principles. For Kryzhanovskii, true Russianness could – indeed, in the southwest, should – speak with a Ukrainian accent. Suffering Ukraine would be resurrected through education, leading to a reanimation of its faith and true culture.

---

*Childhood Memories of the Ukrainian Village in the Second Quarter of the Present Century*³

I was born in 1831 in one of the southwestern provinces, in a village where my father served as priest for twenty-six years. For exactly half of my life up to now, that is until the end of my education, I was connected with the village. From age seven to twenty-five, I was at school and thus spent three quarters of the year in town, but I felt with my whole soul that I lived in the village, around the family hearth....

It would have been one thing if the Ukrainian village of the day had in fact been a free space, yet it was heavily enslaved, enserfed by the Poles and Jews (*zhidam*),⁴ an oppressed, drunken, naked and barefoot village! At home, it was poverty: you lived mostly on moistened bread rusks; Father worked to exhaustion and drove us out into the fields to work ... All the common people around were worn out, – sullen and *downcast* on weekdays, drunken on holidays; huts on wobbly stumps (*na kur'ikh nozhkakh*), around the majority of which there was neither a fence nor a yard; my childhood companions were hungry like puppies; the air always smelled of the Polish lord's lash, the Jew's slipper (*patynkom*), and the policeman's steamed birch rods, – and the words, "A dog's faith! A dog's race!" ("*Psia wiara! Psia krew!*") [P], "Hey, you peasant, pig, Havrilo..." ("*nu, ty, myzyk, shvinia, Hav-rilo*")⁵ ... Yes, a dreary, oppressive environment! And yet somewhere, at a level invisible to the landlord-Jew (*zhid*)-policeman was concealed the most delicate, healthy, and life-giving breath of life, which you used to feel on yourself at each step and which, once experienced, you'll never forget!

It used to be that the very nearing of the date for heading "home" changed our entire ordinary, boring, and sleepy mood. At that time, day by day we literally awakened from a long hibernation, grew up, became strong, "reckless." . . .

Wretched orphans who, for the first time, at age seven or eight, were taken 200–300 versts on foot to the church school (*bursa*) by their mothers, mourned up and down by them all the way, flooded with that special feeling that the wretched widow of the time breathed in her whole being, these orphan-church-schoolboys (*bursachki*) now happily sewed sacks from begged rags, prepared long walking sticks and thrilled at the thought of the long trip, barefoot, without a penny to their names, sleeping in the fields and meadows, in inclement weather in peasant huts or shanties (*kureniam*) [U] for a hunk of bread which, at another hut, a tender-hearted old lady offered, asking, "Are you from the church school? An orphan? There, my little kiddy, eat a little, so that's why your belly's so tight . . ." [U] A sort of frenzy comes over you when you drive out of the city and find yourself among the ripe, golden fields, when you see nearby the first village and the church with three green domes in a row. Away with hat, shoes, little frock coat – jump from the cart! Bare feet drown in the warm, downy dust of the black earth . . . What a treat! In the fields the sunburned, sweaty, dust-covered faces move limply; on the boundary strip stands the boy with his two-tined pitchfork (*s blyzniukami*) [U], free of his hat, boots, and so on, who grins at us and shouts: "The priests' sons! . . ." [U]; along the road, an old woman holding the band of her scythe (*s ban'koiu*) [U] stops and shades her eyes with her hand, good-naturedly greeting us: "Now it's as if the sacks had been untied! . . . strewing yourselves around like crows . . ." [U] And you shout to all of them happily, "Good day," "May God help you" (*pomohaibi*),[6] "Good luck" . . . [U] The long road stretches out – familiar villages, fields, woods, meadows, dykes [local dialect], bridges . . . How life-giving the burning rays of the midday sun seem here, how honorable are these mute laborers in the fields, angrily keeping an eye on the landlord's son hanging around nearby with the lash! How despondent the village is in daytime, everything is as if deserted, everyone is out working the landlord's fields![7] With what reverence you cross yourself when, among the fields, flooded with the quiet golden light of the setting sun, warm waves of air bring from afar the ringing of church bells summoning all to vespers!

> The author continues the description of coming home through the familiar countryside.

And here's the very last village, here's the forest beyond which our native fields open up and beyond them the tops of the domes of our home church. Both the driver [U] and we carefully and ceremonially get ourselves ready, dress ourselves up, tidy up the wagon, quietly drive through the woods, having first removed our hats and directed our eyes ahead of us. "To the Lord Jesus Christ..." piously whispers the driver [U] and he crosses himself, for he sees even before we do the cherished domes through a glade in a thicket of the forest.[8] The prayer freezes on our lips! Here is "our" village, all the familiar huts, even more subsided and swaying, but painstakingly whitewashed. There is the old, high roadside cross (*figura*) [U] in the middle of the village, from which it always has seemed to me that the suffering Savior looks at the people who suffer in such heavy slavery as if he himself suffered along with them and inspired them with his example.[9] How appropriate is this holy image here!...

Here is our farm, there is Father standing on the little porch, watching us arrive, heading to the gate, barefoot, not dressed up, worn out, – our little sister who lives alone with our widowed father runs to the gates, beyond the wicker fence Ivan'ko, the old soldier and church sexton, hangs around, visibly preparing to call out to us, "Greetings to you ... what can I do for you..." We look around, – the very same wretched little house, the same storehouse [U], barnyard [U], fences, cattle sheds, the little cherry orchard, the same dogs... Everything is where it should be, nothing has changed and everyone looks so welcomingly at us, and there is such a feeling of grace in the soul, such a warmth and joy in the heart!...

And life continues on, a life that you can't compare with anything. You feel that you are growing and strengthening, that you live a full life, like a luxuriant ear of corn on a sturdy stalk, like that young oak tree with its metallic leaves, like that strong and lush grass in the oak forest. The horizons of your thoughts stretch broader and broader, everywhere something invisible wanders behind you and whispers daring ideas and projects, inspires secret aspirations, holy vows and love – endless love for everything that is suffering and burdened, for every poor soul, for one's benighted and warm-hearted people, for one's naked, barefoot, and sometimes drunken mother – Ukraine...

> The author goes on to address his reader, saying that he is talking about the time of his childhood, long ago, when the village was crushed by the "Polish-Jewish yoke" and there existed two states – a Russian one in the city and a Polish-Jewish one in the countryside. After the unsuccessful 1831 uprising, he asserts, the Poles retreated to the countryside and oppressed the peasantry even worse.

No, reader, do not accuse us of naïveté. It is not without reason that we remember with such love the village that nursed and raised us, that implanted in us the first lessons of life. We love her for her suffering, her patience, and her sighs in the name of love for the native principles of life, for our strong faith in the saving qualities of these principles, for all those good qualities that grew in the soil of suffering together with that love and faith. And the closer we get to the time of our childhood, the deeper and more distinctly we are aware in ourselves of the beating of the people's pulse and of boundless civic strength, and the fuller and more alive become our social and civil ideals and our faith in great Rus.

Under the influence of new conditions, the Ukrainian village is changing its former appearance; processes taking place there would seem to cool our sympathy for her, to shake our faith in her. City life is encroaching upon her, is percolating into the former serfs' huts. Peasant men, women, girls, and boys buy themselves outfits in the city, often spending their last penny on them, – they drink tea, sweet Santorini wine, they smoke cigarettes, learn to dance the polka and the quadrille... Seminarians with walking sticks promenade around the village and say to the maidens: "My compliments." Cantors read novels, sing sentimental romances, sometimes even a couplet from an operetta. The priests worry about the latest issue of *The Herald of Europe* or the lead article in *The Voice*....[10] There are many signs that point to the fact that now, for the first time since the division of Rus into two halves, the south-Russian village is beginning real, lively participation in all-Russian life. Disorder, mayhem, the chaos of Babel! Coldness instead of warmth, drunken gaiety instead of drunken sorrow, extravagance instead of poverty, unruliness rather than disenfranchisement, shtundism instead of quiet devotion to the statutes of the church!....[11] Publicists just passing through clamor! But we are not confused. At first, after a long period of isolation and slavery, this picture in the villages is inevitable. That force which bore on its shoulders the alien ancient yoke and saved nationality and faith will not betray, will not bend, will not cause the region to collapse; allow it just to look around, become familiar with the new conditions of life, to introduce schools everywhere, to raise up a new generation....

> In the meantime, he says, he wants to describe the Ukrainian village of the 1830s and '40s and its key figures, the priest, the sacristan, the Polish landlord, and the people. He then recounts his father's family history. His father, a priest, was the son of a priest. This grandfather was the first priest in the family, however, and a former Cossack. He then moves on to focus on his father's life and views.

My father was born in 1798 and was the "little finger" in the family, that is the youngest, the last child. A few years after his birth, his mother died and the "little finger" received the bitter fate of the general family "drudge" [U], and no one gave a thought to his needs. His sisters one by one got married and took with them as dowries the best things on the farm; finally, the whole farm went to the hands of the eldest brother, a deacon. My father grew up sort of a burden on his brother and he lived in the family, as he liked to say, "like a lonely bird on the housetop."[12] His father didn't have any money left to send him to schools and get him up to at least the "rhetoric" class, like his older brother. And so he was sent for schooling to the cantor [U] Ian, who was then famous over quite a wide area. This Ian was considered a celebrity in a large district of parishes, a genius-cantor [U]. He educated entire generations of priests and cantors [U] in a large number of parishes; his method was renowned for its special spirit, tone, and self-possession. Even in my time people still talked about a particular priest whose reading and serving were exemplary and say, "Ah, yes, he studied with Ian!" In the days of my early youth, among the clergy Ian was like a sort of myth, an ideal cantor [U], a god of the choir [of the church building – klirosa]. They used to tell how even priests who were experienced in serving the liturgy, former pupils of his, shook with fear when during the service Ian suddenly appeared in the choir of the church, come for the service or just to call on his former pupil. Heaven help the priest who made an error in reading or serving or who behaved in a sluggish way, who violated the "Ian" tone and tact, – Ian could unceremoniously and loudly observe on the spot, "Hey hey, I didn't grab your ears enough!" [U] – or else just call him a "fool" [U]. It never crossed anyone's mind to appeal Ian's criticism, everyone thought it best to submit, to take his opinion as a joke, or else the judgment would stick to you like a brand. My father knew all the local tunes, had a wonderful tenor voice, had the reputation as an outstanding singer locally at the time, loved and knew well the church service; during the liturgy, he held himself with great confidence and freedom of movement and always asserted that he owed all his accomplishments to Ian. . . .

> Kryzhanovskii goes on to describe in detail Ian's teaching principles and the broader pattern of teaching by cantors in Right-Bank Ukraine in the eighteenth and early nineteenth centuries.

One day, Ian said to my father, "Now go off and seek your fate, you'll make a good cantor" [U]. It was for the young man an attestation of maturity.

> His father heads out into the world, to the city with its many golden-domed churches, presumably Kiev. He is penniless and, while the consistory takes its time over his appeal for a position, he is starving.

One day he sat out on the grass at the consistory until evening; the cathedral bells rang out the call to vespers . . . My father suddenly had the urge to sneak into the bishop's home church. He went in . . . and began to move closer and closer to the choir, to join more and more boldly in the singing; finally he found himself next to the cantors and began to sing is his full, sonorous, and supple voice. He chanted the Psalter section, the canticles . . . He liked it there and so the next day he headed back for the liturgy, read the hours, sang and asked permission to chant the epistle. "And I let her rip with that epistle" [very colloquial U], as my father would put it in his simple way, when he often recalled this incident that would have a decisive influence on his future career. From the time of Empress Catherine II's visit to Kiev, in the south of Rus, in diocesan seats, the practice of chanting the apostles and Gospel in a bass voice, beginning with a low bass and gradually rising to the very last bass note, began to be implanted. This tradition, which developed exclusively in the north of Rus, undoubtedly due to the harsh climate, to this day exists nowhere but in Russia. At the time we're describing, in the south of Russia too it had become practically the law that the archdeacon be the most ferocious bass, the kind that would make the walls shake. Local deacons and even cantors had already become keen on this sham grandeur and, buttered up by the Great Russian merchants who had migrated to the south Russian cities, tried to copy their archdeacon. But in the villages the ancient tradition, taken from the Greeks, of chanting the epistle and the Gospel remained in all its inviolability. The Greek particularities of this chant (nasal, with trills and runs), remain the way it is done today in the churches of Greece, Syria, Bulgaria, and Serbia; thus in the south of Rus both the common people's spirit and its beloved tunes have been betrayed. Chanting was done here at the middle tenor "C," rising in places by no more than one note and descending by no more than three notes; the whole artistry consists in moving from one note to another; the sounds should be measured, flowing. Even since I became familiar with different methods of church singing and with church chants and harmonies, it has always seemed to me that there was something painful, pleading, lamenting in this chanting, just like in south-Russian singing. The entire history of southern Rus is reflected in it. Those of our zealots for the purity of Orthodoxy who trace south-Russian church chanting and singing to Catholic churches are crudely mistaken. My father, in deciding to show off in this particular case in front of the bishop's cantors, drew on all his art, remembered all Ian's instructions; his young, sonorous voice flowed like a river beneath the arches of the cozy church. When he finishing chanting and, having closed the book, looked up "to God," as he sang the last word, suddenly, behind the glass door to the right of the altar, the curtain was raised and the face of the bishop appeared... [13] My father glanced at the door and stopped suddenly and barely made it to the choir out of fear. The then archbishop was a Little Russian [Ukrainian] and, although he had an archdeacon who was famous across all south Russia at the time for his bass voice, he nevertheless very much loved the ancient village chanting and singing. When the liturgy ended, the glass door swung open and the bishop appeared on the threshold: as was the custom everyone went up to him for a blessing.

My father too went up and fell at his feet. "Who are you and where are you from?" asked the bishop. And so he answered, as my father told it, beside himself with fear. "You chant and sing well; robe up for my next service," said the bishop and added, turning to a monk standing right there, "Tell them to prepare everything for him . . ." Usually, when my father recalled this event, at this point his voice would break and tears would well up in his eyes . . .

My father's career went swimmingly after that. He immediately found himself a position as a high-rank cantor and lived in clover. He liked to recall the golden years of his youth as a cantor [U] in a surplice.[14] The cantor [U] in a surplice, young and a singer, was truly lionized in the Russian village community of the time. At that time the plan to completely transform the position of the south Russian clergy was barely contemplated. In 1819 the Kiev-Mogila Academy, which had up to then been an institution for all social estates and covering what was considered the full range of education at the time, was transformed into an estate institution for the clerical estate and broken down into three educational institutions, making up the three levels of clerical education: the *bursa* or elementary school to prepare sacristans (*prichetnikami*) and candidates for further education; the seminary to prepare priests; and the academy for higher theological education. The Reform aimed to abolish the old everyday relationships among the clergy and to provide all parishes with educated priests, better-versed deacons, and sacristans, allowing the bishops to appoint them as they saw fit and not in accordance with the choice of the ignorant village community (*hromada*) [U]. Under the influence of the ideas of the eighteenth century about the absolute power of enlightenment and the absolute danger of ignorance, which was embodied by the "uneducated rabble," forgotten was the necessity of a moral connection between the priest and his parish, forgotten were the historical, popular principles the violation of which leads to dislocation and the moral impotence of the education itself; it was not known how radicalism in particular has a harmful influence on religious morality. But at the time that we're describing here the plan had only been proposed, no one knew anything about it in the villages, and there old relations continued to reign with full authority. Cantors did not yet have competitors in the form of "theologians. . . ."

As suitors, the *cantors* [U] had no competitors among the other ranks of society either. It was a strange, long-ago era. In the Russian land, in the Russian village, the Russian people were governed, judged, and managed directly and in a virtually unchecked manner by newcomers of a particular tribe that was inimical to everything Russian. The Polish magnates, noblemen, petty nobles, and would-be nobles made up the ruling class in the region; all educated society and officialdom kept itself strictly separate from the rest of the population, with which it had nothing in common. As a result, both of what were then the two Russian classes of the population, the clergy and the peasantry, drew ever more strongly together, representing a particular world in the region, a self-sufficient society. Priests and the most honored property-owners of the parish and their wives and daughters set the main tone in this society, and the salt of this social world, the flower of its youth, were the cantors [U] and the priests' sons, the inheritors of the parishes, the best grooms....

> In 1821, the author's father married the daughter of a priest, as was typical within the clerical milieu.

The young couple was lively, happy, loved society, and were both singers, but they were poor managers. Children came along; my father became a deacon in 1824. The new community liked him, he lived in peace with the priest, and he threw himself into making money, indeed he worked a lot, but there was never enough.[15] Never to the day of his death did my father drink a glass of vodka while alone, and he hated those people who drank "for the sake of their stomachs." But he didn't shy away from company and was ready to give his last penny to a friend. My mother loved society – to chat, to drink, to dance, to treat visitors to the *varenukha* that she made so well.[16] The reason for the lack of money in the house was clear, then, but not to the householders themselves, who continued alternately to give themselves over to worldly poetry and to worry, to strain every nerve as they awaited the cherished day of my father's thirtieth birthday as the escape from all troubles. According to the church canons, no one could be ordained a priest before the age of thirty; in our country, we make an exception for those who have completed theological education. Happiness smiled on the unfortunate pair: Father had hardly turned thirty when a priest, a close neighbor of his father-in-law, died without an heir to his parish. The father-in-law, who was well-known in that parish, immediately summoned his son-in-law and appeared with him before the *hromada* [peasant community]. The hromada at that time was making stacks of the landlord's hay. At the haymaking, the first recommendation took place. In order to show more vividly the virtues of his son-in-law and candidate, the father-in-law asked the hromada for permission to serve vespers, matins, and the liturgy with him in their parish church. These services put my father in an excellent light before the village hromada. There was no competition, since the hoarse and languid neighboring deacon could not be considered as such and the other candidate was a priest who was famous in the neighborhood for his restless character. After the liturgy, the hromada was invited to the yard of the late priest to make the final decision. Here, of course, the community expected to be offered a treat at the expense of the applicant. In this way they could also test the day-to-day virtues of the candidate: was he able to respect the householders, to have a heart-to-heart talk, was he inclined to get combative when drunk and so on. After this came the negotiations over fees for rites. At this point, my father made a blunder: "Whatever you like, hromada – each person as he is able" [U], he answered to the question about the level of pay. The hromada really liked his response, but later my father often regretted it because the lack of precision led to quite a few misunderstandings on both sides, and the parishioners themselves were burdened by not knowing what to give the priest for his labor in order to offend neither him nor themselves. Be that as it may, a *letter of approval* was drawn up and my father, together with a few local householders, set off with it to see the local landlord. An old man and a simpleton, the Polish squire received my father kindly: he came out on the porch along with the Jew [*evrei*] Azril, the owner of the tavern and mill on his estate and his business agent, took the letter of approval, signed it, and handed it to my father, saying, "If you are good, so I'll be good to you" [P], and then he even sent my father a shot glass of vodka, which the latter respectfully drank to the health of the landlord.

With his *letter of approval* in his pocket, witnessed by the dean as well, Father gladly sold his last belongings and headed to the diocesan city. There everything worked out successfully. . . .

My father was ordained on 4 August 1828, a day that he held sacred every year, and by the parish festival (8 September), he was already in his parish. The community really liked how he led services in church....

> The author ends this section by discussing setting up housekeeping in the parish. He then moves on to a detailed discussion of the 1830–31 Polish uprising and its aftermath. The author asserts that the south-Russian village was in some ways worse off after it, since the Poles were thrown out of power in the cities and refocused their energies on the countryside. He notes that his father adored Nicholas I and believed all the rumors about his superhuman exploits and thought that if only he knew about what the Poles and Jews were up to in the region, he would come and deal with them once and for all.

At the time when he first came to his parish, in the whole deanery of eighteen parishes there was only one *scholarly* priest, and a *theologian* at that, who had graduated from the newly opened theological seminary. All the other priests of the deanery were of one school with my father, "psalterists" (*psaltyrniki*), "cantor-trained theologians," as my father called himself. The following year, another "theologian" appeared. It was only later, in the 1840s, as the "psalterists" died off, that they were all replaced by "theologians" such that by the early 1850s my father remained the only representative of the old ways in the entire district. I remember almost all of my father's "psalterist" neighbors. All of them appeared in smoke-colored robes with a button-up cincture, in squat downy hats with broad brims and with an oilcloth cover. The rich Jews wore the very same costume at the time and, as a result, the new generation of priests who already dressed in the prescribed way and who would throw themselves into the mazurka, the waltz, the polka, and the quadrille in their cassocks disdainfully called their elderly fellow priests the "Chaldeans." At home, my father preferred to wear a shirt, in the winter a sheepskin coat; he went out into the village in some sort of long frock coat that he called a *shpenser* [a loose-fitting jacket]; walking to the church for the liturgy he put on a caftan, and he wore his cassock only for his representations to the dean or for trips to the city and for some reason always considered this part of the clerical costume to be something "thought up by scholars," which, in his way of speaking, meant a stupid pretense, an empty vanity. Almost all the "cantors" whom I remember already felt subject to the inexorable force of the new and with a distressed heart made concessions. All of them educated their sons in seminaries, or at the very least in the district school, and dreamed of marrying their daughters off to "theologians," served visiting seminarians tea and not *varenukha,* and indulgently listened to them singing "I look without a word at the black shawl..." accompanied by a guitar and all the myriad silly sentimental trios that even in my time consumed all the musical feeling of seminarians.... After 1839 in our deanery there appeared two former Uniate priests, converted to Orthodoxy by Bibikov's method.[17] They avoided all contact with the other clergy, made friends only with the Polish nobility, and spoke Polish. My father was radically different from all these old and new types of clergymen. He recognized the decisive need to educate his children and passionately wanted to see us become "theologians." Sometimes he would walk along and dream aloud, "The father's a Psalterist, but the sons will be theologians!... and maybe one of them will even graduate from the academy!..." [U]. Alas, these dreams were strongly darkened and lost their sweetness for Father when he compared the new with the old. Instead of a person of a respectable age who knew well and respected the popular spirit, the head of the parish became a beardless youth in a silk cassock, with aspirations to be a Polish petty noble or would-be noble, whose hand it was shameful for the peasant to kiss. Earlier priests had received the parishioner in their "chambers"; they seated respected householders next to them and offered them bread-and-salt [a sign of welcome] and heart-to-heart talks; the new generation of priests saw in their parishioners only "peasants" and received them in the kitchen, standing, or set up, at their expense, a special room in their houses called the "office" in which to receive them and in which they performed for them the domestic church rites, even the sacrament of baptism.... He could not exactly say what it was that sickened him in the spirit of the new pastors and in his own way explained his antipathy to them. "They don't know the regulations, don't know how to sing the chants – oh, just don't ask me about people like *them* – they often don't know how to choose the canticles and canons – the cantors [U] laugh at them ... They disdain the peasant, associate with the landlords. Yet it's better to drink with the peasant than with the squire ... Another, may the Lord forgive him, on Wednesdays or Fridays eats non-fast-day food at the Pole's [U] – does he really believe in God? ... It's not just that he can't drink in a godly way with the peasant, but he can't stand with him, nor eat with him, nor talk to him, nor even give him a good dressing down as he should, but instead it's 'What?' 'How,' the peasant is a 'fool' ... In church they officiate woodenly, 'mumbling', sing either like soldiers (courtly singing) or like pigs in the rain...."[18]

To the very end of his career in 1853, my father himself never changed a thing either in the way things were done in church or in his relations with his parishioners: everything was like in the olden days. Luckily, the dean was exactly the same way, himself imbued with the old ways and, thanks to the location of the parish away from the big road, not one bishop visited it during my father's time there.

The parish church was not big, made of wood, with the three cupolas that were well-known all over the south-Russian region at the time. From Uniate visitation records preserved at the church it is clear that the church was built in the middle of the last century at the expense of the parishioners. It is not known whether it was Orthodoxy or the Uniate faith that gave the then-small settlement the inspiration to build the church....

> He goes on to discuss his theories of why it might have been an Orthodox initiative rather than a Uniate one, based on the character of the iconostasis and the alleged enthusiasm with which parishioners got rid of their Uniate priest in 1792.

The church was not cross-shaped but oblong (in the shape of a ship). In my childhood this was the usual shape of all village churches in south Russia. Later on, when they were expanding churches, they began to build wings and as a result the churches acquired the look of a cross and not a boat inside. On the roofs they built domes and the churches became five-domed. Young priests, "theologians," who brought from the seminaries of the day wild views about the relics of Orthodoxy and Russian nationality in south Russia and who saw in everything that was original the remnants of the Union and Polonism, asserted that the practice of three domes on a church had a Catholic origin and expressed the idea of the supremacy of the pope over church and state. Some of them claimed that five domes also expressed a Catholic idea, specifically about the supremacy of the pope over the four eastern patriarchs. After the diocesan consistory started to issue plans for building new churches with one dome with a bell tower above the church-porch, plans which were obviously approved with a view to saving money, they began to assert that the Russian Orthodox form of the church is one-domed. As for the three-domed form, which was the most disdained in Catholicism, its antiquity and originality to south Rus is indubitable....

In the celebration of rituals and the liturgy, my father stood out for his great simplicity and independence. Now they wouldn't even find him a place for penance in a monastery for such independence – even then, under the "theologian" priests who flaunted the new forms of reverence and respect for the service, he would have gone straight to "sowing the fields" had it not been for the old dean who loved him.

At home, Father always and invariably prayed by the book, morning and evening, and often also throughout the day. He recited prayers, sometimes standing before an image, sometimes walking around the room, the yard, or the village common pasture. Sometimes he whispered the words, sometimes he shouted out phrases loudly. It was nothing for him, in the middle of a prayer, to address various questions, comments, even admonishments to passers-by. "Forgive me, God, by Your great mercy"... he would recite movingly, sighing...: "Hey, where are you running to?" he'd suddenly ask a servant hurrying by and, when he got a reassuring answer, he'd continue: "... and in Your great benevolence wash away my lawlessness..." For an interesting incident, he could stop his prayer, chat for a long time, pass judgment if needed, and then continue on with his prayer. The "theologian" priests laughed at this custom of the "psalterists." But I saw the same practice in the great bishop of the Russian church, the Metropolitan of Kiev Filaret (1837–57), when I was a chorister in his choir. It is well known that he was quite literally constantly at prayer, that the Psalter never left his lips....

There's no doubt that my father never gave a sermon in the current sense of the word. He gave homilies or brief hagiographies appointed in the church cycle or got me (when I was already a "theologian") to read them. In special cases his own *ex prompto* homilies of the following nature would also occur to him: "What's up with you, good people, you forget the holy church. Yet again your church is not full! Vasyl... Stepan ... Ivan ... yet again I don't see them in church! Tell them that this is a sin, it's shameful. Come the time for confession, I'll catch them, give them what they deserve..." [U]. If there was some sort of disorder arising in the village, a scandal over evening and overnight parties of young people (*vechernitsakh i dosvitkakh*) [U], drunkenness, men beating their wives, theft and such, Father would give a homily: "Why is there strange behavior here in our village? Have the people gone crazy or something? So have you already stopped fearing God? Have you forgotten that he [sic] who is in heaven watches what is done on earth? Do you really want him to come from heaven to you with a lash?..." [U], and so on. But his most impressive sermons took place during the fasting before communion [*goven'e*]. At that time Father was always in a state of excitement. Someone came up to the little table with a cross and an icon, knelt, and bowed his head; Father, sitting on a chair, covered him with his stole and, bowing toward him, talked to him in a half-whisper. Then the discussion became louder and louder and you could easily hear: "So it is good that your children are not wild, they obey their elders and it's peaceful at home, with your neighbors... The Lord will not leave you..." There followed the prayer after confession. The person who had confessed stood up, kissed the cross and the icon, and walked away, and Father called out after him, "Bow down deeply ten times and recite the Lord's Prayer and the Hail Mary" [U]. Another one approached: the quiet discussion again turned into a loud one: "What's this all about, are you really a saint, you don't have a single sin? Go away and change your mind, lazybones... Tell him, good people, how to confess his sins," he said to the person standing before him. That person went away ashamed and reappeared an hour or two later. But he seemed somehow sullen, visibly confused; he bowed and a murmur went through the crowd. Father looked at him without covering him with his stole: "Hey, my pigeon, you come like this to the Lord God," Father loudly said, "you will not escape from God..." "It is we who brought him," a voice quietly came from the crowd. "So," continued Father, "you can't escape from God, God will find you everywhere... So, what will happen to us? What do you yourself think?..." The sinner knelt down, completely lost. "What will we do with him, good people?" Father asked the onlookers. "Take him and tie him to the apple tree for a little while and let him atone for his sin there..." [U]. *The good people* had expected this. The elder, the cantor, the respected householders grabbed the sinner, took him from the church and tied him with a rope to the apple tree at the entrance to the church. Passers-by looked silently at him, no one was surprised, no one asked why he was there. Only some peasant woman expressed some pity: "Oh, a heavy sin, what a misfortune!" No one asked about the reason for the punishment because everyone in the village had known his guilt for a long time, had long talked about it and had long ago decided how to deal with him at confession. He was a son who had beaten his father, a drinker, a trouble-maker at home, who obeyed no one and had not been to church for a long time. To beat your father or your mother was considered the very worst sin. Besides penance assigned to the penitent, besides private or personal penance, there was also a general penance for everyone that required the penitent to perform some sort of work at the church and on Father's land, such as digging a trench around the garden, enclosing the yard with a wicker fence, fixing the roof on the house or on the farm buildings, and the intelligent and knowledgeable ones would fix or move the fence around the church graveyard, fix the wood paneling on the exterior walls of the church, and so on. This was an old custom and Father never changed the tradition, even after the "inventories" were introduced that made the peasants responsible for building and repairing the clergy's house and outbuildings at their own expense – a requirement that my father never recognized, preferring the penance method or the "*toloka*," which is to say work in exchange for a party.[19]

In private rituals, my father piously observed the old ways, paying no attention at all to decrees and prohibitions. As is well known, the "Moscow Book of Needs," which was given its final form under Patriarch Nikon, accepted a very insignificant number of rituals for various events in the daily life of the Christian – from among the great number of them that existed up to that time in the various editions of the Book of Needs in Greece, Serbia, Moldavia, and at Athos, in the south Russian church, and in Great Russia itself.[20] In Petr Mogila's 1646 Book of Needs alone there are forty-eight rituals that are not accepted by the Nikonian one. After the unification of the Belarusian Uniates with the Orthodox Church in 1839, a decree of the Holy Synod ordered that old local editions of service books be removed from all churches and replaced by the Muscovite versions. My father did not obey this decree with respect to the Book of Needs. He carefully preserved some sort of ancient edition of the Book of Needs with no title page and, in addition, handwritten prayers for various occasions. Some little beetle appeared in the fields – there was a ritual for that: Father would head out to the fields and hold a prayer service for getting rid of beetles. A plague hit the cattle in the village – there was a ritual for that too: they herded all the cattle from all over the village, father led a prayer service for deliverance from pestilence and sprinkled the cattle with holy water. Cholera appeared in the village and there was the following ritual: Father led a procession around the edges of the entire village and in each of the four directions he stopped for a prayer service and sprinkled the whole route with holy water. There were orders of prayer for "a person suffering from fever [local U dialect]," "against fire" (during a house fire) and so on. In a word, for every conceivable need there was a ritual or a prayer. I remember how once, when I was reading to my father the Uniate church visitation records that were preserved at the church, I encountered in them a reference to the tradition of ringing the bell every evening so that the parishioners in every house stopped to pray the Hail Mary... – a custom first instituted in the parish by the Uniate authorities following the example of Roman Catholic churches. My father, who very much valued this custom that had been preserved in the parish but who hated the Uniates, reacted with consternation, but then decided that the Uniate visitor was lying and likely the Uniate priest, whom the visitation record described as a drunkard, insouciant of the good customs of the parish, had omitted this custom too – after all, in his father's parish the bell had been rung, from time immemorial the bell had been rung in all Orthodox parishes ... And the ringing remained as before... His reasoning was similar with regards to baptism by pouring water over the candidate, and he baptized by the pouring method, "in the old way and not the new way" (through full immersion), as he expressed it....

And so my father remained faithful to the precepts of the past to the very end. New ways, new trends came at him like waves from all sides but he steadfastly and stubbornly defended himself against them with all his strength. He was not an enemy of new requirements; on the contrary, he blessed the name of the Emperor Nicholas [Nicholas I, r. 1825–55], attributing to him personally the initiative for all of these demands, since, after all, every order began with "By decree of His Imperial Majesty the —— spiritual consistory *heard* . . ." But "heard" and "ordered" for the most part didn't follow one from the other, to his mind, and it always seemed to him that "the tsar did not want that which they *ordered*." He greeted us with tears of joy when we arrived home for holidays and showed him our certificates as proof that we had been "promoted to theology," but he could in almost no way identify with "theologian" priests and was alien to their way of life. He rejoiced when "inventories" were instituted but always firmly asserted that with the introduction of inventories everything got ever worse for the people and became unbearable for everyone. The old was not able to understand the new, just as the new regarded the old with disdain. That is the historical sin of our reforms! The new relations created by the introduction of the inventories were the last blow for my father. The embittered Polish landlords made mountains out of molehills, expected peasant uprisings, the slaughter of Poles, disobedience, disputes over the boundaries of the estate; moreover, in frivolous talk they saw rebellion, asked for the troops to be sent in, and the peasants paid harshly for their half-freedom. Priests aroused against themselves the strong discontent of their parishioners for avoiding all explanations of the inventory rules and from all appeals relating to them to the landowner and the authorities. The peasants could not believe that the priests were forbidden to give any explanations in these matters because, as they saw it, it was in church that they were given the inventory rules by the district police officer and at the time it was announced that any questions should be addressed to the priest. Some priests bowed to pressure from the peasants but the peasants achieved nothing out of this, and the bold-spirited priests were arrested, sent for penance, removed from their parishes. The new race of priests wanted to live according to the standards of "the educated person" . . . and, taking advantage of the inventory rules, which required that the peasants, at their [own] expense, build the priest a house and outbuildings, work the land, and gather the grain, demanded the building of houses at least no worse than those in which the Polish landlords' estate managers lived: that there be an entryway, a reception room, family rooms, an office for receiving the "common folk"; they demanded the peasants work for them and, if they refused, they told the estate manager or the landlord who, through their agents, ordered in the village that people "do corvée for the priest." In the minds of the peasants, the priest became a beggar of the people along with the landowner! Instead of one serfdom, there were now two! There were cases when peasants were thrashed in the landowner's yard, sometimes even with the policeman present, for refusing to do corvée for the priest. My father, who had never turned to corvée and settled for the same old little house with a clay floor, was more and more discouraged by the turmoil in relations between priests and parishioners and in the village as a whole. He remained alone, surrounded by new priests who cheerfully bore the new spirit, the demands of the time, and completely isolated himself in his parish – yet even here, he found no peace. The sounds of construction from the neighboring parishes reached his parish too and sometimes created misunderstandings. The new priests criticized him for his fraternization with "the folk," his views about his responsibilities, for everything by which he had lived and breathed his whole life, and his own children too seemed to adhere more to the side of the "theologian" priests ... He began to lose confidence in himself, quickly began to lose energy and physical strength, considered himself useless on this earth, and just waited for a groom for his daughter so that he could hand over his parish to him. ... In 1853, Father relinquished his parish to his son-in-law and two years later, he died.

NOTES

1. *Sobranie sochinenii E. M. Kryzhanovskago*, tom 1 (Kiev: Tipografiia S. V. Kul'zhenko, 1890), viii–ix. N., "Ukrainskaia derevnia vtoroi chetverti nyneshniago stolietiia, po vospominaniam dietstva (Prodolzhenie)," *Kievskaia starina* no. 4 (October 1882): 59.

2. For a brief discussion of this social type, see: Andreas Kappeler, "Mazepintsy, Malorossy, Khokhly: Ukrainians in the Ethnic Hierarchy of the Russian Empire," in *Culture, Nation and Identity: The Ukrainian-Russian Encounter, 1600–1945*, ed. Andreas Kappeler, Zenon E. Kohut, Frank E. Sysyn, and Mark von Hagen (Edmonton: Canadian Institute of Ukrainian Studies Press, 2003), 174–75.

3. N., "Ukrainskaia derevnia vtoroi chetverti nynieshniago stolietiia, po vospominaniiam dietstva," *Kievskaia starina* no. 9 (1882): 457–85 and no. 10 (October 1882): 39–65. Although the article was written in Russian, the author makes extensive use of Ukrainian (and also some Polish and transliterations of a

Yiddish accent in Ukrainian); I have indicated this in the translation by the letters [U] and [P] to give the reader a sense of the hybrid character of the language.

4. A neutral term for describing a Jew in Russian until the early nineteenth century, the word *zhid* had acquired a definite pejorative connotation by the time Kryzhanovskii was writing in the 1880s. There is strong evidence that it remained a neutral term in Ukrainian (*zhyd*) for much longer. See: John D. Klier, "'Zhid': Biography of a Russian Epithet," *Slavonic and East European Review* 60, no. 1 (January 1982): 1–15.

5. The birch rod was made more "effective" by steaming it for twenty-four hours.

6. This was the typical greeting in the dialect of the region. The response is "*Zdorov' bud'*" (be healthy). D. P. de lia Fliz, *Al'bomy* (Kyïv: Instytut ukraïns'koi arkheohrafii ta dzhereloznavstva im. M. Hrushevs'koho NAN Ukrainy, 1996), 28.

7. The author uses the word *panshchina*, the Ukrainian term for labor obligations (*barshchina* in Russian).

8. A typical greeting in the region. The answer was "for ever and ever, Amen." De lia Fliz, *Al'bomy*, 28.

9. "Figura" was the local term for a roadside cross depicting the crucified Christ, deemed to be very typical of the region. There was considerable controversy in the mid-nineteenth century over whether this feature constituted a Roman Catholic "remnant" on the landscape.

10. *Viestnik Evropy* (the Herald of Europe) and *Golos* (the Voice) were a leading liberal journal and newspaper, respectively, in the early 1880s when this article was written.

11. Shtundism was a widely used term for an evangelical, Baptist-like movement that spread rapidly among the Ukrainian peasantry from the 1860s onward.

12. He quotes Ps. 103:7 in Church Slavonic.

13. In a section not translated here, the author emphasized that Ian's instructions were to look up "to God."

14. It was a privilege to wear a surplice, one usually reserved for ordained clergy.

15. As was typical, upon marrying, he moved into his father-in-law's parish.

16. A Ukrainian drink made from vodka stewed with dried fruit, honey, and spices.

17. General Dmitrii Bibikov served as governor general of the Southwest Region from 1837–52. In 1839 he oversaw a renewed campaign to force remaining adherents of the Uniate (Greek Catholic) church to convert to the Russian Orthodox Church. Orest Subtelny, *Ukraine: A History*, 3rd ed. (Toronto: University of Toronto Press, 2000), 211.

18. This is the only place where his father is quoted in Russian, perhaps because it is such a long speech?

19. In 1847, Governor General Bibikov, in a bid to reduce the power of the Polish nobility over the "Russian" peasantry of the Southwest Region, introduced the Inventory Regulations, which were supposed to stipulate exactly the amount of land a peasant had at his disposal and the dues he owed his landlord. These were designed to limit the landlords' ability to interfere in the private affairs of the peasants and to regulate serfdom in the region, but in the end they merely complicated relationships and led to a series of minor revolts. Subtelny, *Ukraine*, 209–10.

20. Here the author added a lengthy footnote where he pointed out that there was still a lot of variety in the prayer books being used, most often Uniate ones but also various manuscript collections of prayers, and argued that it was time to resolve the question of whether if a prayer was not in the Moscow Book of Needs, it was forbidden. N., "Ukrainskaia derevnia," 59.

SUGGESTED READINGS

Manchester, Laurie. *Holy Fathers, Secular Sons: Clergy, Intelligentsia, and the Modern Self in Revolutionary Russia.* DeKalb: Northern Illinois University Press, 2008.

Senyk, Sophia. "Becoming a Priest: The Appointment and Ordination of Priests in the Orthodox Church in Ukraine in the Eighteenth Century." *Orientalia Christiana Periodica* 69 (2003): 125–51.

Skinner, Barbara. "Borderlands of Faith: Reconsidering the Origins of a Ukrainian Tragedy." *Slavic Review* 64, no. 1 (Spring 2005): 88–116.

Thaden, Edward C. *Conservative Nationalism in Nineteenth-Century Russia.* Seattle: University of Washington Press, 1964.

Weeks, Theodore R. *Nation and State in Late Imperial Russia: Nationalism and Russification on the Western Frontier, 1863–1914.* DeKalb: Northern Illinois University Press, 1996.

NINE

Akathist to the Most Holy Birth-Giver of God in Honor of Her Miracle-Working Icon Named "Kazan"

Vera Shevzov

IN THE STUDY OF MODERN RUSSIAN ORTHODOXY OVER THE past two decades, perhaps the least studied and appreciated topics – socially, culturally, politically, and religiously – remain liturgy and prayer. The complexity of the Orthodox liturgical calendar and the trove of its liturgical texts, combined with the fact that believers' voices – especially those of lay men and women – describing liturgical and prayer experiences are difficult to unearth, often contribute to the scholar relegating this area of Orthodoxy to the arcane and archaic aspects of its tradition.

The excerpt below offers students of modern Russian Orthodoxy the opportunity to consider the creative role and various functions of liturgy and prayer in Orthodoxy's sacred storytelling culture. The excerpt is from a specific genre of communal and private prayer – the akathist hymn – that enjoyed enormous popularity among all strata of believers in the nineteenth and early twentieth centuries. The Russian term *akafist* originates from the Greek *akathistos,* meaning "not sitting," implying that the hymn is to be chanted while standing. Akathist hymns in honor of Christ, the Mother of God, and saints were chanted in Russia privately and collectively, in churches, chapels, private homes, and monastic cells. Part of their appeal lay in the fact that the chanting could be entirely initiated by laity; the presence of clergy was not necessary.

While a modern phenomenon, Russia's nineteenth- and early twentieth-century akathist hymns historically stemmed from a Byzantine liturgical poem composed in honor of Mary, the Mother of God, that is usually dated to the sixth century. Having begun as a hymn celebrated only locally, the original akathist to the Mother of God eventually became a part of the annual Byzantine liturgical cycle, celebrated during the fifth Saturday of Great Lent. Several more centuries passed before its establishment in Byzantium as the prototype of an entire genre of hymnody composed in honor of saints as well as in honor of events in the life of Christ and the Mother of God.

Although the translation of the original akathist in honor of the Mother of God made its way to Russia perhaps as early as the tenth century, the akathist as a genre of hymnody became established later, by way of what would later become Russia's southern and western regions, first appearing in prayer books published in Kiev. Prior to the eighteenth century, only some seventeen to twenty-five akathist hymns in honor of such saints as St. Nicholas, John the Baptist, the Archangel Michael, the Great Martyr Barbara, and St. Sergius of Radonezh circulated in Russia, some of which were translations of Greek hymns, while others were authored locally by Orthodox and Uniate believers.

A golden age for akathist hymns – the nineteenth and early twentieth centuries – saw the official approval of approximately 130 new hymns, the vast majority of which honored male saints. Twelve were penned in honor of Byzantine and Russian female saints, while only five were composed in honor of Christ, including his passion, resurrection, and Holy Communion. The Synod denied publication of some three hundred more hymns, usually for lack of poetic quality or for historical, theological, and grammatical inaccuracies. As a consequence, saints such as Boris and Gleb had no officially approved akathist in their honor in the nineteenth century. These ongoing compositional efforts, combined with the fact that countless more akathist hymns were composed and circulated in manuscript form on the local level, testify to what one Russian scholar has termed an "everyday-ization" (*bytovizatsiia*) of the akathist in modern Orthodoxy.[1]

The variety of authors who penned these hymns also underscores the genre's widespread appeal. Authors were noblemen and women; peasants and merchants; government bureaucrats and professors of theological academies; bishops, priests, and deacons; monks and nuns – all highly literate to be sure, since akathist hymns were composed and published in Church Slavonic. For instance, the akathist in honor

Akathist to the Most Holy Birth-Giver of God

9.1. Kazan icon of the Mother of God. *Prazdniki v chest' chudotvornykh ikon Presviatoi Bogoroditsy* (Moscow, 1905), 73.

of Russia's famous Vladimir icon of the Mother of God was composed by a lay woman. Like Russia's icons, akathist hymns remained unsigned by their authors.

Despite the appeal of such hymns and the support of such spiritual luminaries as Theofan the Recluse who spoke of the spiritual benefit of their composition, some clergymen remained ambivalent about their widespread use. On the one hand, they believed such hymns to be inferior to the established order of church services and already known traditional prayers. On the other hand, as the well-known priest and dissident, Father Sergei Zheludkov (1909–84), remarked concerning what he termed "akathist-mania" among Orthodox believers, it was difficult to deny the power of the akathist hymn in drawing Orthodox believers into the communal liturgical life of the church.[2]

The excerpt below is taken from an akathist in honor of the most widely revered icon in late imperial Russia, the Kazan icon of the Mother of God. One of seventeen akathist hymns composed in honor of miracle-working icons of the Mother of God during the synodal period, it recounts key events from the *life* of this icon, from its foundational story in sixteenth-century Kazan through the construction of the Kazan Cathedral in its honor in the early nineteenth century. Memories of Mary's dispensation toward Russia by means of her icon are interspersed with lauds and thanksgiving. The author of this hymn, the writer of devotional literature and censor Nikolai Vasilievich Elagin (1817–91), followed the compositional structure that typified this genre: twenty-four stanzas alternating between shorter, narrative verses that describe episodes from the hagiographic life of the subject of the hymn (*kondak*) and a longer set of praises in honor of that person or event, often inspired by and drawn from more traditional Orthodox liturgical texts (*ikos*).

Beginning with general praise of and gratitude to the Mother of God for her protection of Russia through her icon, Kondak 2 and Ikos 2 recount the story of the icon's discovery in 1579 by a young girl, Matrona, some twenty-five years following Russia's siege of Kazan. Kondak 4 and Ikos 4 recount the second major episode in the icon's *life*, namely the icon's perceived role in Russia's victory over the Poles during the Time of Troubles in the early seventeenth century. Today, the celebration of this victory lies at the foundation of Russia's National Day of Unity, a civic holiday instituted in 2005 in order to correspond with the church's celebration of the Kazan icon of the Mother of God on 4 November (22 October, Old Style).

Akathist to the Most-Holy Birth-Giver of God in Honor of Her Miracle-Working Icon named "Kazan" (Excerpt)[3]

KONDAK 1

To You, the Birth-Giver of God, chosen from all generations and Protectress of Christians, who blankets our Orthodox land with the mantle of Your goodness, we bring our hymns of thanksgiving for the appearance of Your wondrous icon. As You are All-Merciful, the Helper of all those who hasten to You, comfort us in all of our sorrows and needs, calamities and afflictions, so that we may exclaim: Rejoice, fervent Protectress of Christians.

IKOS 1

The Archangel was sent to the Birth-Giver of God saying "Rejoice" when God the Word became incarnate in Her womb: and we, sinners, glorifying the appearance of the wondrous icon of Her and the divine infant Christ, the Savior, with compunction cry out to the One filled with grace:

> Rejoice, God-chosen maiden;
> Rejoice, Mother of God;
> Rejoice, Queen of heaven and earth;
> Rejoice, radiant adornment of the heavenly and earthly church;
> Rejoice, you who are honored by angels;
> Rejoice, you who are hymned by the Seraphim;
> Rejoice, joyful prophetic fulfillment;
> Rejoice, praise of the apostles;
> Rejoice, the confession of the martyrs;
> Rejoice, crown of the saints;
> Rejoice, joy of the righteous;
> Rejoice, hope of the sinners;
> Rejoice, fervent Protectress of Christians.

KONDAK 2

From the heights of your heavenly abode, where you reside in glory with your Son, O All-Pure One, having seen the afflictions of your servants in the newly enlightened city, where because of the visitation of God's wrath Christ's faith was ridiculed by the Hagarian heresy, you mercifully willed your icon to appear, glorifying it with miracles so that strengthened by the signs of your grace, the Christ-loving people faithfully cry out to God, Alleluia.

IKOS 2

Seeking to fathom the three appearances of the Mother of God, the wise maiden ran to the authorities to recount to them the wondrous occurrence and the dreadful threat. Marveling at the revelation given from on high for the maiden's edification, we reverently cry out to the Most-Blessed One:

> Rejoice, you who through the mouths of children praise God;
> Rejoice, you who reveal the mysteries of God's grace to the youthful;
> Rejoice, doubtful rumor to the unfaithful;
> Rejoice, known praise of the faithful;
> Rejoice, lightning that frightens the unfaithful;
> Rejoice, you who enlighten the thoughts of the faithful through the glory of your miracles;
> Rejoice, you who exposes the Hagarian heresy;
> Rejoice, bane of their pride;
> Rejoice, affirmation of the Christian faith;
> Rejoice, confirmation of the veneration of holy icons;
> Rejoice, O one who transforms our sorrow into joy;
> Rejoice, O one who gladdens us with unwavering hope;
> Rejoice, fervent Protectress of Christians.

KONDAK 4

The blessed Germogen tried to quell the storm of confusion and insurgence stirred by enemies in our land.[4] Having recorded the miracles from your icon, O Mother of God, he prayed with tears before it and seeing that your icon was given as a shield and sign of victory to the Orthodox regiments, was fortified with faith until the end of his life, and cried out to God: Alleluia!

IKOS 4

Hearing of the secret revealed by Saint Sergius to Bishop Arsenii about how the judgment of our homeland was transformed into mercy thanks to the intercession of the Mother of God, the Orthodox warriors embraced the icon of the Mother of God as a banner of victory and rescued the mother of Russian cities from the hands of the adversaries, crying out to the Protectress of Christians:[5]

> Rejoice, Mother of the Most-High God;
> Rejoice, you who entreat your son, Christ, our God, for everyone;
> Rejoice, you who enable the salvation of those who seek your mighty protection;
> Rejoice, Protectress of all the sorrowful and the sick;
> Rejoice, you who grant beneficial things to all those who pray before your most pure image with a contrite heart;
> Rejoice, deliverance from evil for all those who have irrevocable hope in you;
> Rejoice, peaceful and kind refuge;
> Rejoice, quick Helper;
> Rejoice, ready and warm cloak of salvation;
> Rejoice, you who pour forth abundant mercy;
> Rejoice, you who anticipate needed help;
> Rejoice, deliverance from all calamities;
> Rejoice, fervent Protectress of Christians.

NOTES

1. Churkin, A. A. "Russkii akafist serediny XIX–nachala XX v., kak zhanr massovoi literatury," http://churckin.narod.ru/akafist.htm [stet] (accessed 9 May 2012).

2. Sergei Zheludkov, "Liturgicheskie zametki," http://krotov.info/library/07_zh/zhel/udkov_23.htm (accessed 11 September 2013).

3. Translated from "Akafist Presviatei Bogoroditse v chest' chudotvornyia Eia ikony Kazanskiia," *Akafisty presviatoi Bogoroditsy chtomye v razlichnykh nuzhdakh* (Moscow: Danilovskii blagovestnik, 1999), 73–83. An earlier English translation of this text is also available. See Isaac E. Lambertsen, trans., *The Kazan' Icon of the Mother of God: History, Service and Akathist Hymn*. Liberty, Tenn.: The St. John of Kronstadt Press, 1988, 38–47.

4. "The blessed Germogen" refers to the patriarch of Moscow and all Russia (1606–12), Germogen (or Hermogen) who at the time of the Kazan icon's reported finding in 1579 was a priest in Kazan. In 1594, he authored the first *Life* and liturgical service in honor of the Kazan icon of the Mother of God. Patriarch Germogen played a pivotal role in rallying Russian forces to help liberate Russia in 1612 from the occupation

of Polish-Lithuanian forces. Germogen died of starvation in a prison cell earlier that year.

5. Saint Sergius refers to Sergius of Radonezh (d. 1392), a renowned saint, spiritual leader, and founder of Russia's Trinity–St. Sergius Lavra. Arsenii refers to Arsenii Elassonskii, the eventual archbishop of Suzdal and Tarusa (1615–25). Born in Greece, Arsenii, as the representative of Moscow's clergy, played an active role in talks with the King of Poland, Sigismund III. In 1612, Arsenii reportedly had a vision of St. Sergius, who predicted the end to Russia's Time of Troubles.

SUGGESTED READINGS

"Akafist." *Pravoslavnaia entsiklopediia.* Moscow: Nauchnyi tsentr "Pravoslavnaia entsiklopediia," 2000. I: 371–81.

Churkin, A. A. "Russkii akafist serediny XIX–nachala XX v., kak zhanr massovoi literatury." At *http://churckin.narod.ru/akafist.htm.*

Liudogovskii, F. B. "O prichinakh populiarnosti akafistov." Bogoslov.ru, 16 January 2009. At *http://www.bogoslov.ru/text/372613.html.*

Popov, Aleksei. *Pravoslavnye russkie akafisty, izdannye s blagosloveniia Sviateishago Sinoda. Istoriia ikh proiskhozhdeniia i tsenzury, osobennosti soderzhaniia i postroeniia.* Kazan, 1903.

Shevzov, Vera. "Between 'Popular' and 'Official': Akafisty Hymns and Marian Icons in Late Imperial Russia." In *Letters from Heaven: Popular Religion in Russia and Ukraine,* ed. John-Paul Himka and Andriy Zayarnyuk, 251–77. Toronto: University of Toronto Press, 2006.

———. "Scripting the Gaze: Liturgy, Homilies, and the Kazan Icon of the Mother of God in Late Imperial Russia." In *Sacred Stories: Religion and Spirituality in Modern Russia,* ed. Mark D. Steinberg and Heather J. Coleman, 61–92. Bloomington: Indiana University Press, 2007.

TEN

A Nineteenth-Century Life of St. Stefan of Perm (c. 1340–96)

Robert H. Greene

LIVES OF THE SAINTS (*ZHITIIA SVIATYKH*) WERE AMONG THE most popular reading material for Orthodox Russians in the nineteenth and early twentieth centuries. As part of its efforts to improve religious knowledge and catechize the laity, the Russian Orthodox Church promoted the popularization of saints' lives in church newspapers, devotional pamphlets, and occasional publications, in the hope that men, women, and children could learn from the example of "God's Beloved" and imitate the Christian virtues of faith, love, and good works that the saints embodied in life. Diocesan newspapers and Orthodox journals from the latter half of the nineteenth century encouraged priests to incorporate examples from saints' lives into their sermons and to hold informal discussions (*besedy*) with their parishioners on the moral lessons that the faithful could glean from the lives of the holy dead. Literate parishioners were enjoined to borrow copies of saints' lives from the church library and familiarize themselves in their free time with these texts. Although a saint's written life was seldom lengthy, Orthodox publishing houses also issued condensed and easy-to-read versions of the lives, often with a helpful paragraph at the end summarizing the valuable lessons that believers might learn from the saint in question. In 1895, for example, the religious journal *Kormchii* [The Helmsman] ran a year-long series called "Lessons from the Lives of the Saints," in which readers were given succinct and pointed instruction on such various moral and religious topics as the preservation of chastity, the importance of visiting the sick, the existence of miracles, how to live in Christian harmony with one's spouse, how to avoid both gossip and flattery, and the significance of confession and communion for an Orthodox Christian.

The translation that follows is a life of the fourteenth-century saint Stefan of Perm, best known for the three decades he spent in missionary work among the Zyrians and other Finnic peoples of the Perm region, a land rich in furs and much coveted by Moscow's chief rival, Novgorod. Through his efforts, Stefan succeeding in spreading Orthodox Christianity (and the authority of the Muscovite principality) eastward into the Ural Mountains of European Russia. Stefan died in 1396, and was eulogized shortly thereafter by the Orthodox panegyrist and hagiographer, Epifanii the Wise, in a celebratory address regarded as one of the classics of early Russian literature.[1] In the years after his death, Stefan acquired a posthumous reputation for sanctity among the local laity and clergy, which prompted the Orthodox Church's decision to elevate him to the ranks of the saints sometime in the late sixteenth or early seventeenth century.[2]

Numerous reprints and retellings of Stefan's life appeared throughout the nineteenth century, particularly as the five-hundredth anniversary of the saint's death approached. This particular edition was written by Nikolai Nikolaevich Filippov, a prolific author of religious, historical, and patriotic texts, as well as retellings of classic works of Russian literature abridged for young audiences. Filippov's account of the life of St. Stefan was published by the St. Petersburg house of M. V. Kliukin in 1893 as part of a special series of twelve short, illustrated booklets titled "Reading for Children and the Folk." Priced at a mere five kopeks and written in the accessible style that was Filippov's trademark, this fifteen-page, large-print pamphlet was aimed at a broad readership. The bulk of the narrative concerns Stefan's efforts to spread Orthodoxy among the Zyrians, recounting the many hardships and tribulations that the saint endured in order to bring the gospel and the church's teachings to the native peoples in their own language and in an alphabet of his own creation. The details follow the accepted narrative of Stefan's life, though Filippov elaborates on the themes of persistent effort, hard work, and humble submission to the will of God. A pious and studious man by nature, Stefan accepts the hazardous mission for which God has se-

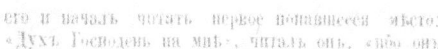

10.1. Image of Saint Stefan of Perm from His *Life* (1893). N. N. Filippov, *Sviatoi Stefan, episkop Permskii. Istoricheskii razskaz* (St. Petersburg: Izdanie M. V. Kliukina, 1893), 5.

lected him, and despite the numerous obstacles he encounters, Stefan is shown to persevere and remain steadfast, ultimately winning over the Zyrians not by force or compulsion, but through his kindness and love. The Zyrians respond to Stefan's Christian "tenderness" with wonderment and surprise; experience has led them to expect their Russian neighbors to greet them with swords and warhorses, not sermons and Bibles. Similarly, as newly appointed bishop of Perm, Stefan succeeds in winning the confidence of the local population by relieving them of the tyranny of unscrupulous tax collectors and corrupt officials sent from Moscow. Considering that Filippov's life of St. Stefan appeared at a time when the imperial government of Alexander III was pursuing a vigorous policy of Russification, these points represent a strikingly candid commentary on the Russian state's often strained relations with national minority groups and non-Orthodox confessions, as well as serving as an endorsement for young readers of proper Christian governance cast in an Orthodox key. Although Filippov portrays Stefan as an extraordinary figure who smashes idols, faces off against angry pagan mobs, and is prepared (literally) to walk through fire for the Christian faith, the author suggests throughout the story that the values of love, compassion, and a faith made manifest in both word and deed are not restricted to medieval saints alone, but are virtues that all Orthodox men, women, and children can and should strive to emulate in their own lives and in the modern age.

N. N. Filippov, Saint Stefan, Bishop of Perm'. Historical Story[3]

> "Men of God, penetrating
> the remote and wild places,
> planted in the people's soul
> the image of the pure Christ."
>
> A. MAIKOV[4]

I.

St. Stefan was born around 1340, in the town of Ustiug in Vologda province. His father, Simeon, was a deacon at the Ustiug cathedral. When Stefan grew up, he became cantor of the very same church. His mother and father wanted him to marry and thought that Stefan would spend his whole life with them, eventually taking his father's place. But the Lord deemed otherwise.

From his earliest years, Stefan was drawn to the secluded life of a monk. At the age of twenty, he surrendered to this desire. He bowed down before his father and mother, took his leave of them, and set off for the faraway town of Rostov Velikii to seek out a life that suited him.

When he arrived in Rostov, he entered the monastery as a simple novice, and there he led a most observant religious life.

How long he remained a novice, we do not know. But the brothers loved him very much, and so, with the hegumen's blessing, he became hierodeacon.

While living in the monastery, Stefan remembered well his days in Ustiug, when strange people would come to town, dressed in animal skins and speaking some sort of savage language. There were some Russian people who understood this tongue. Hierodeacon Stefan understood it, as well. He knew that these people were called Zyrians, that they lived in the deep, impenetrable forests of Vologda and in the wild mountain regions of Perm, that they venerated wooden logs and women carved of stone, and did not know the faith of Christ.

And so Stefan began to think more and more about these people and their pagan ways and he desired to help them leave behind this savage life. He began to pray to the Lord God: "Lord! Help me to enlighten these ignorant people with the light of thy truth! Teach me how I may serve Thy Holy Name, not in word alone, but in deed."

He began to think about this more and more often, and finally he resolved to perform a great deed of the spirit.

When he was not working or praying, he very much loved to read and study sacred texts. One evening he was sitting alone in his cell, and having taken the Gospels from the shelf he opened them and began to read the first passage he came across: "The Spirit of the Lord is upon me," he read, "for he has anointed me to proclaim the good news to the nations . . ."[5] He shut the book at once and opened it again to another place. And again his eyes fell upon the words: "Go forth, teach all pagans, baptizing them in the name of the Father, the Son, and the Holy Spirit."[6] Taking all of this as a sign of his own future, Stefan grew ever more resolved to go and preach the word of God to the pagans of Perm. From that very day he took upon himself the great task of compiling an alphabet for the Zyrian language, for they had none, nor had they any books. He labored over this for a long time, translating all the sacred books into their language. Finally, his task completed, he set off for Moscow to ask the metropolitan's permission for his endeavor.

The metropolitan sent him to the bishop of Kolomenskoe, the blessed elder Gerasim. The bishop received him with great tenderness, ordained him a priest, and sent him forth to do God's work in Perm.

II.

How long it took Stefan to reach the Perm lands we do not know. We only know that as soon as he reached the first Zyrian village, Pyras (or Kotlas, as it is known today), he called together all the villagers at once and began to preach to them. As it happened, that day was one of their festival days and a great number of people had come together. They were curious why such a strange person had appeared among them! No Russians had ever come among them so peacefully – more often they came on horseback and with swords, for which the Zyrians feared them. Yet here was a lone man who appeared all by himself and without any fear. He looked calm and gentle; he spoke with such tenderness that it was obvious he meant no wickedness and saw only the good in people. A completely unusual person...

The Zyrians began to listen to him, but as soon as he told them of the Russian God, the people took fright. "He's trying to trick us," the crowd cried, "We know his kind! They always talk about their God, but look at what they do! Our gods are better – we do no evil to anyone!" And so the people walked away from him, but some of the more wicked among them decided they would kill Stefan. But Stefan gave no sign that he was afraid of them. He lifted up his eyes to heaven and sang "Lord of strength, be with us!" and then he began to pray in Christ's own words for those who would do him harm. At this their resolve faltered and not a single one of them laid a hand on him!

Though Stefan saw that his words had had but little effect on the inhabitants of the village, he remained to live among them. The people grew accustomed to him. They saw that he would not harm a soul, that he was gentle and good and kind. They began to come to him to talk and to bring him food. And so some time passed, and almost the entire village accepted the Christian faith. Stefan rejoiced at this his first success and so he set forth once more to teach the people, giving thanks to Christ for having helped him in his difficult work. But there were still many wicked people who did not believe the words of Christ, of which Stefan spoke. These people succeeded in stirring up the local residents and meant to do harm to Stefan. Everywhere he went he had cause to fear an ambush purposefully set for him, but he went forth boldly and firmly, fearing nothing and taking faith in Christ's words – that unless God our Father so wills it, not a single hair should fall from a person's head.[7]

And so Stefan reached the village of Gam, some two hundred versts from the village of Pyras. In this village there stood a little hut, deep in the thick forests, with various wooden idols in whom the Zyrians believed. These idols were brightly painted and adorned with much finery; it was the superstition among the Zyrians that these idols would neither sink in water nor burn in fire. Stefan knew of this. And so he entered this little place of worship and began to smash the idols and then set the hut on fire. The residents saw the flames and ran toward the fire. They saw a man with an axe in his hands, pointing toward the flames, who said to them: "It seems these gods of yours cannot defend themselves. As I was smashing them, not a single one of them called for help." The people cried out: "He must be killed!" But Stefan threw aside his axe, laid his hands upon his breast, and his face shone and he smiled as he said, "Do not be afraid, brothers, I will not touch anyone! You may kill me!" Whereupon a great clamor arose from the crowd, some saying, "He must be killed!" and others trying to stop them: "Don't touch him. If he were a wicked man, he would not have thrown aside his axe, but would have defended himself, and if he says, 'Kill me!' then that means he is not afraid of dying! He must be a righteous man!" Then the old people spoke out: "Can he be killed when he has come to us as a guest? Let him go in peace!" And while all this commotion was taking place, the women and children came forward to get a closer look at Stefan and to see what kind of a man he was. Stefan stroked the children's heads and gave them berries that he had gathered in the nearby forests to feed himself, and then began to talk with them and preach about God. The women and children listened to him and gradually the rest of the people drew closer, little by little, and they forgot all about their debate. They saw a gentle, friendly man, who caressed the children and treated them to the only food he had, and so they decided to leave him in peace. He stayed there among them for some time, and then set forth once more for the village of Ust-Vym. Many of those who had come to believe in the words of Christ followed him along the way.

III.

He arrived in Ust-Vym. There the inhabitants greeted him joyously, listened to him, and asked him to stay with them. Stefan agreed and built for himself a little hut on top of the mountain, and there he lived, feeding himself by the work of his own two hands. He started his own garden, digging it himself and planting vegetables, and he asked nothing of anyone, for he said that it was a great sin to beg of others when you could work yourself. And the people of Perm listened to him, marveled at him, and soon came to love him. They loved him so much that they did not want to see him go. Nor did he want to take his leave of them. He remained there and built a small chapel atop the mountain where he lived. He consecrated it to the memory of the Annunciation of the Blessed Mother of God and performed the liturgy there himself. He also built a school adjoining the church, where the Zyrians, with great joy, sent their children to study the Gospels and listen to Stefan's good teachings. Stefan taught them that it was bad to be lazy and that God loves when people work, that it was bad to believe in many gods and to carve them out of stone or wood, and that it was bad to take one's gods from the world of nature that surrounds man, for there is only one God who lives forever and reigns over the entire world, and there is no need to seek out this God around you, for He dwells in each person.

Stefan taught the Zyrians many other things, as well, and the Zyrians listened to him with love. And he built a second church here, dedicated to the Holy Archangels, Gabriel and Michael.

There lived in the town an old man named Pama. He had a reputation among the Zyrians as a powerful sorcerer. Pama heard that among the Zyrians there had appeared a certain man, a Russian, who was teaching them to believe in some sort of Christ and in some sort of God. The old man flew into a furious rage against Stefan. "I will teach him," he said, "how to respect our gods." He went to Ust-Vym, summoned Stefan, gathered the people together, and sought to expose Stefan before the people as a liar. But no matter how hard he tried, he could not! And so he decided upon the following: "You say that you are right, and I say that I am right. Let us settle this. Tomorrow we will go before all the people and leap through a lighted bonfire. Whoever lives and is unharmed – he is right. Agreed?" "Agreed!" replied Stefan. On the following day, early in the morning, a great bonfire was set alight, and when the wood was burning and the flames rose high, Pama and Stefan approached the fire. The people watched them with great trembling and wondered what would happen. And Stefan turned to the people and said: "People of Perm! Are your lives better with Christ or without Him? If it is better with Christ, then hold on to Him, for I go now to die for His sake, just as He died for the truth!" And he strode toward the bonfire. The old man Pama dug in his heels and stood fixed.

"What's the matter with you?" Stefan asked him. But the old man had suddenly gone out of his mind with fear. "I won't go!" he said, "I'm afraid!"

"You see, it is you who lied!" Stefan said. "You yourself do not believe in your gods. What say you, people of Perm, who is right – he or I? Answer!" And from the crowd there came a great hum: "We want to live with Christ." And Stefan sent Pama home and forbade him henceforth to disturb the people with superstitions and false teachings.

The number of people who had come to believe in Christ grew larger and larger, and so it became necessary to establish a diocese in Perm to oversee all sorts of matters. Stefan traveled to Moscow to ask the metropolitan for permission. The metropolitan and all the clergy decided to appoint Stefan himself bishop. "You know these borderlands well, and the local priests, too. You'll have no problems administering the diocese with them!" they told him, and finally Stefan consented to accept the bishopric, and the grand prince even designated special funds for the support of the churches and clergy of Perm. On his return to Perm, Stefan stopped in his hometown and there he chose several wise and honest people as his helpers and set out with them for his diocese. But much disorder had transpired there while he was gone: taking advantage of his absence, the tsar's men had robbed the local population. All of this misfortune had to be set right, and Stefan took it upon himself to do so. He treated everyone with great kindness and gave work and provisions to everyone! Not a single tax collector was able to oppress the people with unjust extortions, as they had before, because they knew well that the bishop would not fail to defend his people and would certainly denounce their illegal acts. The Zyrians could not praise Stefan enough! For no sooner had Stefan resolved one misfortune, then another befell the people.

Beyond the Urals there lived a mighty and restless people – the Vogulichi, a tribe similar to the Zyrians. They live there even to this day, only now they are no longer a warlike people, but support themselves by hunting and trapping.

The old man Pama, who had quarreled with Stefan about the faith, appeared among the Vogulichi and incited them to march against the Zyrians. The Vogulichi soon conquered all of the Zyrians' land and gave it over to fire and the sword. Finally, they reached the town of Ust-Vym and threatened to burn it and destroy all of the inhabitants. Stefan was not afraid of them. He put on his best chasuble and set out alone on foot to meet the Vogulichi. He found them on the move, in their wooden longships. The Vogulichi were amazed when they spied this unarmed man who had come to parley with them. They bowed before this venerable old man – for the Vogulichi had great respect for elders – and left the Zyrians' land for good. And since that time they have not set foot in the region!

* * *

Stefan thus spent twenty years among the Zyrians. Finally, in 1396, he was summoned to Moscow to decide some important matters. Stefan felt that he would be saying farewell to Perm for the last time, and he wept bitterly as he took his leave of the people: "Brothers, fathers, and children – friends!" he said to the people. "Men of the Perm lands! We must give thanks to our Lord God, who has enlightened us by the light of faith. Having formerly dwelt in darkness and the shadow of death, we have now left this darkness and have been made not into slaves of God, for He knows no slaves, but His children, for we know that we are doing the will of our Father and Creator, that we are called to freedom and to the glory of Christ, the Son of God. For, in the words of the Apostle Paul, we are not wanderers and strangers here on earth, but the children of God who dwell with the saints.[8] And so, strive to understand the will of God, Your Father, and his commandments on love. He Himself said, in the words of the Apostle John: 'Whosoever says that he loves God, but loves not his brother, he is a liar, for how can he love God and not love his brother, if God dwells in the spirit of this brother?'[9] Do good on the basis of your faith in God, remember that faith alone without good works will not save you, for it is dead. Do not be like the whited sepulchers which appear beautiful on the outside, but are filled with bones and decay within.[10] Do not call out to God: 'O Lord! O Lord!' for He will not save you if through your deeds you do not show your faith in Him and your obedience to His will. Do not quarrel, do not give in to anger, do not fight – be helpers and partners to each other. And the final words I will say unto you: Henceforth, brothers, I commend you to God and to His Word of grace, which has the power to save you, for He is our Savior, glory to him forever, amen!" The old man wept bitterly as he spoke these words. It pained him to know that he was to die in a strange land. And the sobbing of the people, as they said farewell to their champion and father, often interrupted his words.

Stefan's premonition of his coming death came to pass. No sooner had he arrived in Moscow than he fell ill, and after taking to his bed for a short time he died peacefully. The fifty-seven years spent in ceaseless labors and deprivation and in traveling among his flock had taken their toll on his health. Just as he had lived his life for the good of the people of Perm, so too he died with his final thoughts fixed on them. "Praise to God in Everything!" were his last words.

His memory is celebrated on 26 April.

To this day, "Stepa the monk" lives in the memory of the Permiaks, Vogulichi, Votiaks, Zyrians, and Cheremis.[11] It is possible that the light of Christianity reached even to them all in the time of Stefan of Perm. The body of the great and glorious preacher of God's word was buried in Moscow, in the Church of the Savior in the Pines in the Kremlin, where it lies to this day.

"Hark, ye heavens, for I am a river,
Hear, o earth, the words of my mouth;
Let my words pour forth like the rain,
And my teachings sound down to the valleys,
Like dewdrops to the flower."

V. K. TRED'IAKOVSKII[12]

NOTES

1. Epifanii the Wise, "Panegyric to St. Stephen of Perm," in *Medieval Russia's Epics, Chronicles, and Tales*, ed. Serge A. Zenkovsky, rev. ed. (New York: Meridian, 1974), 259–62.

2. Archpriest Evgenii Popov, *Sviatitel' Stefan Velikopermskii (Zhizn' ego s litografirovannym izobrazheniem)*, (Perm: Tipografiia gubernskogo pravleniia, 1885), 91–92; and Paul Bushkovitch, *Religion and Society in Russia: The Sixteenth and Seventeenth Centuries* (Oxford: Oxford University Press, 1992), 83–84. On the political motivations for Stefan's canonization, see Jukka Korpela, "Stefan von Perm': Heiliger Täufer im politischen Kontext," *Jahrbücher für Geschichte Osteuropas* 49 (2001): 481–99.

3. N. N. Filippov, *Sviatoi Stefan, episkop Permskii. Istoricheskii razskaz* (St. Petersburg: Izdanie M. V. Kliukina, 1893). Series "Chtenie dlia detei i dlia naroda" (No. 12).

4. Apollon Nikolaevich Maikov (1821–97), a lyrical poet whose work often addressed themes of Russian nature and sacred history.

5. A slight variation on Luke 4:18. The original reads "to the poor."

6. Based on Matt. 28:19, though the original substitutes "nations" for "pagans."

7. A reference to Acts 27:34.

8. A gloss on Heb. 11:13.

9. See 1 John 4:20.

10. A reference to Matt. 23:27.

11. Stepa is a diminutive form of Stefan, used to imply both familiarity and friendship.

12. The son of a village priest, Vasilii Kirillovich Tred'iakovskii (1703–69) was one of the great stylists of eighteenth-century Russian letters. This excerpt is from the opening lines of his Ode XVIII, a paraphrase of the Second Song of Moses (Deut. 32).

SUGGESTED READINGS

Brooks, Jeffrey. *When Russia Learned to Read: Literacy and Popular Literature, 1861–1917*. Princeton, NJ: Princeton University Press, 1985.

Chernetsov, A. V. "The Crosier of St. Stefan of Perm." In *Picturing Russia: Explorations in Visual Culture*, ed. Valerie A. Kivelson and Joan Neuberger, 21–27. New Haven, CT: Yale University Press, 2008.

Freeze, Gregory L. "Institutionalizing Piety: The Church and Popular Religion, 1750–1850." In *Imperial Russia: New Histories for the Empire*, ed. Jane Burbank and David L. Ransel, 210–49. Bloomington: Indiana University Press, 1998.

Khodarkovsky, Michael. "The Conversion of Non-Christians in Early Modern Russia." In *Of Religion and Empire: Missions, Conversion, and Tolerance in Tsarist Russia*, ed. Robert P. Geraci and Michael Khodarkovsky, 115–43. Ithaca, NY: Cornell University Press, 2001.

Martin, Janet. *Treasure of the Land of Darkness: The Fur Trade and Its Significance for Medieval Russia*. Cambridge: Cambridge University Press, 1986.

ELEVEN

Written Confessions to Father John of Kronstadt, 1898–1908

Nadieszda Kizenko

AT THE TURN OF THE TWENTIETH CENTURY, WHEN THESE confessions were written, Orthodox Christians in the Russian empire learned how to confess their sins from a variety of sources. Children going to their first confession at the age of seven learned from their mothers, older siblings, church school, and even children's story-books. A daily confession at the end of the evening prayers in the standard prayer-book kept fresh the main categories of sin and a general sense of compunction. Before and during Great Lent, when most people went to their annual confession, priests delivered sermons on the sacrament's importance. Lenten church services fostered the themes of sinfulness and repentance. Published guides grouped by sins pertaining to the ten commandments contained helpful questions meant to aid in soul-searching, and concrete models of what to say. Fictional accounts, such as those written by Tolstoi and Dostoevskii, illustrated how literary heroes like Konstantin Levin and Natasha Rostov went to confession. Although such models dealt with conventional spoken, or auricular, confessions, the confessions presented here show how successfully they could be adapted to written form.

This is all the more remarkable because written confessions like these were not supposed to exist. Most Orthodox Christians in the Russian empire went to confession once a year as part of a days-long process called *govenie*. Govenie took several steps. First, the penitent had to attend church services for several days before going to confession (usually during the first, fourth, or last weeks of Great Lent), and read or listen to special prayers before confession. On the day of confession, at the end of a church service, one stood in line with other penitents, bringing a candle as an offering. When one's turn came, one told one's sins to the priest without the privacy of the Roman Catholic confessional, as priest and penitent stood next to one another at a slight distance from those waiting their turn. Either before or after confessing, one told one's name to the sacristan, who would mark it off in the church register: annual confession was a legal requirement in the Russian empire for Orthodox Christians, and priests had to send in confessional records every year to the Holy Synod. One then fasted until Divine Liturgy the next day, when one partook of the Eucharist. The only people encouraged to bring a written list of sins to the priest were literate deaf mutes, who then saw the priest burn their written confession in front of them. This precaution reflected the emphasis on the secrecy of the confessional constantly reiterated in canon law and pastoral advice manuals.[1]

But written confessions such as the ones that follow were more widespread in imperial Russia than one might think. They stem from early nineteenth-century Russian letters between spiritual fathers and their children. People dedicated to pursuing spiritual growth often sought out guides along the path to salvation. Although spiritual fathers and children could discuss a variety of religious topics in their letters, as Irina Paert's contribution to this volume illustrates, confession figured prominently.[2] The confession of Anna translated here resembles them.

Most written confessions have remained largely unknown. One reason is that they were private documents not meant for publication, but as tools to aid in one's spiritual growth. Another reason lies in the kinds of sins or dilemmas they describe. Most of the writers of the confessions presented here thought their sins to be scandalous, and had no intention of making them public. Indeed, some noted that they were too ashamed to confess such sins to their parish priest. Why, then, did they write them to another priest? And how did the letters survive?

These confessions have survived because they were addressed to Father John Sergiev of Kronstadt (1829–1908), a priest celebrated for his holiness. When Father John died, the contents of his office were sealed and removed by representatives of the Holy Synod. These confessions and others like them now form part of his archive in the Central State Historical Archive of St. Petersburg.[3] They were written by Russians of different social and educational backgrounds: a barely literate peasant woman; a young male schoolteacher; a young, unmarried, materially comfortable woman who lives in her family home; an educated Jewish woman; and a garrulous old cook.

These confessions are remarkable for many reasons. They show how Orthodox Christians in the Russian empire at the beginning of the twentieth century understood right and wrong. They share some ideas about sin – pride, envy, anger, cursing, illicit sex – with members of other religions. But some themes, such as their intense relationship to icons, the observance of holidays, proper fasting (abstinence from sexual activity as well as from meat, fish, and dairy products) and the Eucharist, are specific to the Orthodox. Modern urban dwellers may notice how often animals appear in the lives – and the sins – of rural people. Men and women, and educated and uneducated people, remark on different things. Particularly striking to contemporary Christians may be the persistence of Biblical bans, such as traveling on Sundays for any purpose other than attending a service, or women's observing ritual purity. Such Old Testament prohibitions may have been technically no longer sins in the New, and yet Orthodox Christians still regarded them as sinful. As we read these confessions, we vividly see every detail of people's lives.

As interesting as *what* people say is *how* they say it. It is clear from these confessions that the people who wrote them knew the familiar script they were supposed to follow. Liturgical language appears alongside everyday speech; even barely literate people seem steeped in religious texts. The writers interweave their own words with those from the Psalms, the Gospels, the lives of the saints, and the rituals of the Orthodox Church. The schoolteacher Iakov, for example, draws upon priestly language when he admits that he approached the Communion chalice with an impure heart, writing, "I partook of the Holy Mysteries with the kiss of Judas." In the next line, he continues, "And then I drank vodka." For Iakov and other Orthodox believers, the religious and the secular, the sacred and the profane, did not exist as two separate languages or two separate worlds. At the same time, even as people followed a ritual that might most seem to signal their submission to the authority of the Orthodox Church, they used the template to fit their own purposes, and to tell their own stories. Educated women like Anna, for example, seek to minimize their sins, qualifying them with such expressions as "sometimes" and "not always." Less educated people like Faina, by contrast, simply write down their actions. In all cases, the urgency and immediacy of these confessions shows that the practice offered a vivid, living way for people to make sense of their lives.

As a contrast to the others, the confession of a secular Jewish woman shows how educated, worldly Russian society understood confession in a broader, non-sacramental sense. In her mind, the essential elements are not the naming of sins, repentance, or a request for absolution, as they are for the Orthodox. Instead, the purpose of her "confession" is to describe the seemingly impossible situation in which she finds herself – a choice between romantic love and familial duty – and to ask for guidance in making a decision. These elements – the unburdening of a soul and the sought-for resolution (rather than absolution) – occur in other examples of people seeking the relief they imagine confession to a priest will bring.[4]

But written confessions like these are not only relics of late Imperial Russia. In present-day Russia and Ukraine, priests now encourage believers to prepare for their spoken confession in writing. Worldwide, the Orthodox Church may follow the lead of the Roman Catholic Church, which has given its seal of approval to a confession "app," in which the believer texts himself as part of his preparation for confession.[5] Confession has mutated more than any other sacrament in response to changing circumstances: written confession may only have begun its golden age.

Confession No. 1 (Faina, a Peasant Woman)[6]

Father I confess my sins to you, I repent dear Father accept and
    absolve [me].[7]
I was proud
and slandered and judged my neighbors
and was dejected
and deceived
took what belonged to others and stole

and accepted what belonged to others
and over-ate
and got drunk
and sang obscene songs
and swore
and used bad language
and kissed men
was lazy about working
and was lazy about praying to God
and flattered
and painted my face
and played cards
and smoked tobacco
swore at babies
and ate fish during Great Lent
and ate in secret
I committed adultery, and committed adultery with priests
and talked idle talk
and laughed witlessly[8]
and blamed my parents
and was cruel
and was unmerciful to my neighbor
and on New Year's eve I told fortunes using cards
and complained and was discontented with life
and quarreled
and fell asleep in church during services
and at prayer there were foul and blasphemous thoughts
and was crafty
and got furious
and got annoyed
and did not keep the fasts
and extorted money[9]
and there were lecherous thoughts
and I exalted myself
I bore grudges
and drank wine

and envied
and went to weddings[10]
and ate non-Lenten food on fasting days
and listened to music
was lazy about going to church
was lazy about doing prostrations[11]
told untruths
and went dancing
and cursed the wind
and beat animals
and went dirty to church[12]
Father and I also had mortal sins, I fornicated with my female friends and my own sisters and little girls and with myself and with babies and taught them to do the same thing and committed adultery and committed adultery in my heart[13]
and at confession was ashamed to say my sins I did not admit them to the priest
Having eaten, I then ate a prosphora[14]
Father, forgive me my great sins, Father, how I fear for my mortal sins
and I was perfidious
and hurt birds
and beat animals
and was greedy about money
the sinful Faina
forgive [me] Father

Confession No. 2 (Iakov, a Schoolteacher)[15]

I do not venerate God with sincere faith, hope, and love. The Most Holy Mother of God, the holy Angels, and those pleasing to God I also do not venerate in a Christian way. I neglect to pray to God at home and to go to church for Divine services. And if I do pray, then it is inattentively and distractedly. Sometimes during prayer I will ask for something I should not ask for. Sometimes I call out to the Savior and the Most Holy Mother of God with mixed-up words.[16] While in church I look round on all sides, I laugh, I talk, and have every promiscuous thought possible, not only as concerns people, but also the saints, as I gaze upon their most bright images. So I leave church with more sins than when I entered. I put my trust in myself and in other people rather than in God, the Mother of God, and all the saints. I believe in fortune-telling, I had my fortune told in cards, and I believe in various unfounded signs.

Horrible sins: overweening pride, vainglory, excessive miserliness, gluttony, drunkenness. I took the name of the Lord in vain, I cursed using the name of God, was in a desperate state, treated sacred objects disrespectfully. I did not fulfill the promises I made to God.[17] On ordinary working days I was lazy, and I worked on holy days. I did my job not in good faith, but out of fear, or for the sake of praise. On holy days I spent my time not in pious readings or conversations, but in those repugnant to God. I did not help poor and unfortunate people, but rejoiced all the more at their misfortune. And, even if I did help people in some way, then, because of various self-satisfied and prideful thoughts about this help, I ultimately sinned more than I did good. I did not observe fasting days, and, even if I do fast, then it is not with love and joy, but out of a sense of compulsion.

Always and in all ways I did not honor my parents, I did not listen to them, and did not carry out their bidding. I scolded them, swore at them, laughed at them, envied them. I buried my father not as one's own son should, but as a Judas betrayer teeming with infernal pride, self-esteem, and vainglory.[18] My funerals are not pleasing to God. When I bade my father farewell for the last time, it was not as a son, with love and weeping, but as a damned and unfaithful servant toward his lord.[19] Neither did I respect those older than I, nor those placed in authority over me; I did not obey them, and I did not conscientiously carry out the obligations entrusted to me. I am especially culpable against persons of the black and white clergy, cursing them with foul language and shaming them with vile thoughts. When I was a schoolboy I was constantly lazy and did not honor my teachers and supervisors. Several times I quarreled with the teachers and even with the priest in charge. And thought foul thoughts against them. Not only as regards all people [in general], but even as regards my relatives and parents I do not have truly-Christian love, honor, and obedience.

I treated cattle inhumanely: I beat them unmercifully, I over-burdened them with heavy loads, and I swore at them with various words.[20] Almost every person that I know, have seen, or even heard about from others, I killed with my words.[21] I am hateful, I am envious, I quarreled, I fought, I tempted my neighbors toward bad and sinful acts in every possible way. I did not sleep at night, but went around looking for a fight, holding sharp sticks and other objects. Around people I am sullen, gloomy, ungracious, unloving, and arrogant.

I had illicit love with a woman. I attended immodest shows and events and myself played various games with my tongue, I had foul thoughts, went dancing, used foul language, and engaged in masturbation. I had every possible fantasy and adulterous thought about married and unmarried women, whether upon seeing them or alone – and not only as regards grownups, but even as regards small, innocent children. I even had such thoughts toward members of my family and relatives. With my hands I touched women in indecent places.

Knowing full well that someone was guilty of something, I said that he was not guilty. I stole at every possible opportunity. I did not pay my debts; knowing that something belonged to someone else, I did not return it. I treated everyone with no respect, and, if I did treat them with respect, then it was only outwardly, like Judas the betrayer. I almost always spoke untruth to the harm of my neighbor, and taught others to say lies. I was very careless with my words always and in all ways. I was frequently displeased with my lot, and even with my life itself. There is a fearful envy in me. I did, wished, and thought harm to my neighbor. I smoked. I tore out pages from books and gave them to others to use to roll cigarettes. I made the sign of the cross the wrong way.[22] If I saw any flaw in anyone, I did not try to correct him, but let it go, and indeed sometimes joined him, and together we did even deeper and greater evil.

Sometimes while reading holy books I became consumed with infernal rage at the Savior and all the saints, thinking, why am I not like the others who are pleasing to God? When I start reading impious books, I feel high spirits, gaiety, and desire; whereas when I turn to pious books, then it is dejection, despondency, sleepiness, unbelief, and for the most part resentment.

I taught children carelessly and punished them angrily, sometimes when they were innocent of any wrongdoing. I was lazy about coming to classes. I cursed students with every vile word imaginable, which it is shameful and frightening to even think of. In classes my laziness drove students to sleep. I went to lessons without preparing for them. I did not feel the truly Christian love a teacher ought to feel for my pupils. My innocent girl pupils I tempted to fornication by using various signs. I touched them with my hands in indecent places. I laid them down next to me on a bed. I laid her on top of me, and myself lay on her. In class, when I looked at them, I had infernal sexual passions. I ripped pages out of class catalogues and journals. I took books that were school property out of the school library and did not return them. I am more of a corrupter of young people than I am their teacher. About religious education I concern myself but little. I even had thoughts and passions about fornicating with animals.[23]

During meals I talked and laughed.[24] When I saw or heard that evil was being done, I did not walk away from it, but peered at it even more closely. I wore gold-rimmed glasses because I wanted to look fashionable. Sometimes, knowing what a good deed would be, I don't want to do it, and sometimes, knowing that something is bad, I do it anyway. I composed letters of recommendation in other peoples' names deceptively interceding on my own behalf.

How many times I went to confession but did not really confess, but just took my turn and got checked off. And during those confessions I sinned all the more: I kept quiet about all the big sins. And partook of the Holy Mysteries with the kiss of Judas.[25] After partaking of the Holy Mysteries I drank vodka. In my room, I hung pictures depicting the Savior, the Mother of God, and the faces of the saints next to worldly pictures, for decoration. Often I got others, even my late father, horribly drunk with alcohol. It often happens that, when I read holy or sacred books or conduct discussions on such subjects with whomever, then I get various horrible sexual thoughts not only about God's saints, but even about the Savior and the Most Pure Mother of God.[26]

I adorned my appearance for the sake of getting fleshly love. Often I ate not to maintain my bodily strength, but just for the pleasure of it, just to devour voraciously. On Sundays I traveled, riding and driving on the road.[27] I keep fearing being called up for military service, even to the point of being willing to bribe people if I have to. Many times I reached a desperate state when I cursed not only sinful people with foul language, but also the Savior, the Mother of God, and the saints of God. I am especially sinful in all possible internal thoughts and words. I am greatly sinful in all my feelings: sight, hearing, taste, touch, smell, and especially with my tongue, always and in all ways.

I destroyed birds' nests. I went to bed without praying, and I ate without first praying. I whistled using my tongue.[28] I prayed without any faith, hope, love, inclination, or zeal. I have the greatest sins: once for a long time I could not find money I had hidden in the ground and then in desperation cursed the Savior and God with the name of the devil. While standing in church as people were partaking of Communion, I thought obscene thoughts against the Holy Gifts. In the Zhirovitskii Monastery, I mentally compared the Most Pure Face of their wonderworking icon of the Mother God to an animal's rear end. Then I compared the heads of the Savior and the Mother of God and other holy people to the head of a snake and other similar objects.

Besides these sins, I have innumerable other sins which I have forgotten but which I committed. So sinful am I, Father, that I can't even cry open-heartedly and sigh from the depths of my soul to the Savior and the Most Holy Mother of God for mercy and salvation and to God's saints for intercession for me, a sinner. I never prepared for all my previous confessions and [even] for this one, too, I have not prepared in a Christian way. I am sinful always and in all ways. While traveling here, I swore using bad language at my own brother and got angry at him. In Kronstadt at the cemeteries I commemorated the souls of my parents, Father, and yours, too. But this commemoration felt somehow coerced and a fearful miserliness appeared in me.[29] Father, accept my money and distribute it among the poor in Christ's name, so that by their prayers the Savior and the Most Holy Mother of God might have mercy upon me, save me, make me a true Christian, and in the life to come not deprive me, a profound sinner, of the Heavenly Kingdom.

I have barely performed one good deed of true Christian love. In me are the most awful pride, hot temper, miserliness, stupid garrulousness, and other countless inadequacies. Father, pray to the Savior and the

Most Holy Mother of God for my wavering and doubting faithlessness to end, and instead for me to have true, firm faith, hope in Christ the Savior, the Mother of God, all the saints, and in the future eternal imperishable life beyond the grave. Father, forgive me for having doubted you. Father, give me your blessing to visit you and to partake of the Holy Mysteries from your pastoral hands, and to receive a blessing from you, along with some consoling words for the affirmation of my wavering, much-sinful life.

r. B. Iakov.[30]

Confession No. 3 (Anna, a Young, Educated, Unmarried Woman).[31]

Dear Father!

Asking your blessing, I warmly kiss your hand.[32] Forgive me for writing my confession with your blessing: I beg you to read it.[33] Forgive me, Father: I was lazy about praying to God; I was distracted and inattentive in church; in prayer I often tended toward quantity rather than quality; I was vain and conceited, I rarely engaged in self-examination; in my thoughts I sometimes had spiritual pride and did not always struggle against it, but I grieve at this and beg you to pray for me. I was not always sympathetic to the poor and to my neighbors; in sicknesses and sorrows[34] was impatient; I humbled myself but little; I judged others; I envied; I deceived; sometimes I lusted after money; was sometimes intemperate in food and drink; on occasion it would happen that I broke the fasts; I laughed; I broke the commandments; I was swept away by music and earthly delights; I was both disobedient and insubordinate; I offended people, and I took offense; I fulfilled my whims; I was not always fair to the servants; I was rancorous; I am not submissive to my parent, I treated him with distaste, mentally recalling his misdeeds; and, forgive me, Father, I do not feel the love for him which I ought to feel as a daughter.

Forgive me, I often wept from vexation and at being hurt by others; even on Easter[35] I cried about the illness and death of the dear elder Father Aleksei; I went to him several times for confession, and, through his holy prayers and yours, came to know spiritual sweetness and sincerely wish to improve and to obtain[36] at least a little love of wisdom; pray [for this], Father. Forgive me, I rarely weep for my transgressions, and I feel the meagerness of my tears, which stems from the hardness of my heart; but, believe me, Father, I recognize myself to be a great sinner and sincerely wish to improve. Forgive me, Father, I grieve; I sinned through outward piety. I unintentionally captivated a good man, who, they say, even wanted to propose to me, but, having learned that I would not marry, proposed instead to Mania on St. Thomas week, but she, not feeling disposed to him, refused. He sometimes visited us at home and, forgive me, without any ulterior motive I got carried away and listened with pleasure to him [talk] about Father Aleksei, to whom he was quite close. True, he also brought me presents which I did not know how to decline, and now my conscience torments me because of it, though I did already repent of this [at confession] to the reposed Father Aleksei, and long wanted to tell you personally about this and to repent, but it kept not working out, and I cried several times. I repent for all of it – forgive me, Father, and absolve me.

Forgive me – I entered church at an inappropriate time, sometimes even venerated icons [in that state].[37] When you celebrate church services, I feel compunction for my sins more acutely and feel more reverence than I do whenever anyone else is serving. I mentally bow down before your feet, and repent for all these transgressions and of all those committed by me, willingly or unwillingly, in knowledge or in ignorance, in word, in deed, in thought, and with all my feelings,[38] and for the transgressions I have forgotten I earnestly repent and ask your forgiveness and absolution. Forgive me, I who have sinned much, and pray for me, your unworthy, spiritually disposed toward you, and sincerely loving spiritual daughter, Anna ... L ... [ellipses in the original].

Bless me, Father, to approach [the Communion chalice]. Forgive me for burdening you – I wrote too much here. Forgive me, I may have offended you and Father Aleksei – I repent, and forgive me for [my] disobedience.

Confession No. 4 (Ekaterina, a Middle-Aged Cook).[39]

Lord, bless. My merciful Master of Heaven and earth, accept my great transgression from me, the sinful slave [of God] Ekaterina. As a girl I loved to dance and worried about devils, I kept them in my mind day and night but forgot to pray and repent to the Lord. I fornicated every minute of every day when I lived in Yaroslavl, I judged everybody and fought with one manservant and hated him and kept slandering him to the masters and constantly stole food from the masters and ate in secret and slandered the neighbors and the salesmen. I also lived in Kostroma, there too I cursed with the nannies and committed adultery and fornicated with the coachman and how I fought with the cook, day and night we snarled at each other like dogs. Forgive her, Lord; her name is Vasilisa. I concocted pastries and would lick up half the dough secretly, all I said to the masters was lies. When I lived at the Mazaevs', I stole all the sweets from the shop and secretly baked myself good, rich pies. I constantly lied to the masters and ate and drank in secret and did not repent to you, my Lord. Then I lived at the Andronovs' and kept swearing how hard life was and murmured and all day and night the maid and I talked about fornication and gossiped about everybody and stole from the masters and ate to satiety in secret. Then we slandered the Archbishop that he went visiting the widow Trofimova and laughed at how often he rode around with her and fornicated with her and I did not repent to you, Lord, and did not realize that you have to repent for everything. Lord, my sins are greater than the sands of the sea and in the winter I committed adultery with a teacher, forgive me, Lord. Also I worked as a nanny at the Petrovs' and we cooked a lot there and ate to satiety day and night, both secretly and in plain view. Beneath us there was a pub and I would go there for a good time, listen to the music, the dancing, and the songs, this was a great consolation to me, and not what should have been. I fought with everyone, swore, and when I would come home my heart would hurt.

And I denounced the priest for fornicating with a widow, I denounced the widower–community elder also for fornication, and I denounced all the neighbors, teenage boys and girls, and slandered them. There is no counting my sins. Then I lived in Rybinsk where I sinned greatly in the apartment next door, I fornicated in my thoughts and in my deeds. Then every hour and every day I fought with the master's daughter and the chambermaid I cursed the delivery-man and ate and drank secretly, I concealed the food I ate in the pantry and did not pray to God, neither morning nor evening.

Then when I lived at the Chernyshevs' there too I stole and ate everything and blamed the masters every minute, as I worked I kept cursing, I swore at the manservant with foul language and envied all the cooks and my heart kept breaking about my son. He lived on their ship there and started disobeying me, started drinking, got involved with one hussy in matters of fornication and I thought about knifing her, shooting her, or for their house to burn down with everyone in it – all this evil was in my heart, Lord. I kept envying others' wealth and went to a psychic to ask who would die first. And when I lived at the Il'tekovs I constantly quarreled and fought and blamed the masters and censured the masters' relatives and stole from the cook, I stole from the provisions I bought for the household and hid it. Then when I lived at Mukhin's I stole and stole anything I cooked. When I lived at the colonel's I constantly insulted the manservants, godlessly slandering them, also the scriveners and the laundry-maid and the nanny. I stole wine out of all the bottles and drank it and fornicated and ate meat on Wednesdays and Fridays and never fasted and drank milk and stuffed myself with food every day. When I lived at the train station I fought with everyone, swearing that it was hard to live, and did not pray and did not repent to you, Lord. When I lived in Rostov I kept trying to fornicate and envied the wealth of others. And when I went to the Iakovlev monastery I tempted a priest serving before the altar of God and then tempted the station master. On Holy Saturday before the late liturgy I went to the neighbor's for milk and went stone-deaf and remembered that I had sinned – that people don't even eat bread on a day like this. At that very minute the bells started ringing for liturgy and only then I realized how heavily I had sinned then on three holidays, Sunday and St. Nicholas and St. Isaiah, there were three holidays on one day and before early liturgy I fornicated and climbed through a window to an officer and went around with a lot of soldiers and blamed and cursed everybody and gathered bread and sold scarves and constantly swore and took the name of the Lord in vain . . . Lord my sins are greater than all the stars in the Heavens and the sea, then when I lived at the Lavrovs' I masturbated with sticks and a spindle and a knife and I stole sour cream and butter then blamed the masters. When I worked at my in-laws' I blamed them and slandered them and lied and stole and did many things not in a godlike way, I kept fornicating with my husband, and [then] he was dead. When I lived at my aunt's there too I took offense and swore and stole and ate and drank in secret. When a widower courted me, I did not marry but fornicated with him in my thoughts. I was hurt that they wouldn't let me go to church, on every holiday we had to go to the woods to work. I slandered my mother-in-law and sister-in-law and all the neighbors and kept wanting to get married [again]. See, Lord, what a great sinner I am. I led all the neighbors and my acquaintances into sin and they all started to slander my mother-in-law and me....

When I decided to go to Kronstadt to visit you, Lord, I went to St. Sergii and made a vow to give the poor three dresses a year and did not fulfill it. I promised to fast and in no way did that. I promised to pray, to read a thousand akathists, and did not do that. I go to the cathedral and promise to stay in one place and pray fervently but I never do that; I run around the whole cathedral, and then fall asleep.... Cleanse me, Lord, and accept my sins.

Confession No. 5 (An Educated, Secular Woman).[40]

Dear Father! Before you stands a great woman sinner. Pray for me and hear out my brief confession. I am Jewish. I got married at the age of sixteen; I won't say it was out of love, particularly; but was attached to my husband and treated him very warmly and with great sympathy. He too was young, twenty-three years old – someone not yet able to govern himself, let alone a wife, let alone a wife who was just a girl, as I was. As someone without any education or upbringing, from childhood all he could think about was only where to get his next piece of daily bread.[41] Therefore he reasoned that, since I was his wife, that meant that I was one of his things, his property, and no one could train him to think any other way.

In short, we were both to blame for getting married without first giving it some serious thought. As a result it turned out that I was constantly home alone; during the day my husband was at work; in the evenings he was out playing cards with friends. At my requests to put an end to this way of life he would laugh at me, deeply convinced that, since I was his property, that meant he could treat me as he saw fit. I cried, I entreated him, and, finally, after four years of life like this, I grew completely indifferent to him, I started to regard my marital obligations much more lightly, and during all this the birth of a child every year sapped my already weak health. I didn't live in the sense of living, but aged rapidly because of the tears and the sleepless nights. It went on like this for eight and a half years. Meanwhile my husband, seeing my growing coldness toward him, started to treat me foully, making jealous scenes – sometimes deservedly so – but for the most part they were outrageous and degrading for me, both as a woman and as the mother of his children.

As a result, after such a brutish life, without a bit of spiritual connection with my husband, during one of my convalescent trips for *kumys* treatment,[42] I met a man who treated me with such kindness and warmth. That, along with all the misery of the life I had endured thus far, compelled me to love this man despite myself – and to love him so much that, for the sake of this love, I abandoned my husband, left my four children in the hands of my aged (though materially comfortable) parents, and left Siberia, where I was born, for Kazan, to be with the man I loved. This year he will take his state certifying medical exams, he knows you well, and he is deeply grateful to you for your goodwill toward him.

Now, having been with him for four months, I have been tormented so much that it is hard to imagine one could suffer so much even in Hell. The causes of these torments are the gnawing pangs of my conscience, anguish at missing my children, pity for my old parents and for my husband, who only now has realized how dear I am to him. Nonetheless, to abandon the man I love is more than my weak abilities can bear.

All this taken together, when my heart is being ripped to pieces, when I suffer for all those near to me, has reduced me to such a state that I have gone nearly mad. I have not spent one peaceful night; I will soon go blind from tears. My nervous attacks combined with my anemia verge on insanity. I often do not recognize or do not remember what is happening to me, or what has happened, and even suffer from hallucinations. Last night at the very worst moment, suddenly, like a bright flicker of light, I thought of turning to you, dear Father. Instruct me, teach me, advise me what to do. Maybe you will say that I should listen to what my heart tells me.[43] But, dear Father, my heart is so sick that I myself cannot make out its echoes.

I am so sorry for my husband it hurts, but to live with him once again, deceiving him with the falseness of my caresses, is beyond my strength – I have not yet learned how to lie. But I cannot leave where I am, either – yet there my father grieves and weeps, my mother wastes away with grief, my children miss me... all this is ripping my heart to pieces! So please guide me, my kind Father! This howl escapes from the depths of my shredded heart. As you command me, so I will do. I swear to you that I will not murmur any more, nor will I resort to suicide, which so attracts me that only the thought of my poor family holds me back from such folly. I await your response as something filled with grace. Write me: should I leave for Siberia and go back to my parents, my husband, my children, or should I convert to Orthodoxy and marry the man I love? As you advise me, so I will act. Just one thing, believe me, kind, good, Father, that my desire to receive your blessing is so sincere, so frank...
[last page missing]

NOTES

1. S. V. Bulgakov, *Nastol'naia kniga dlia sviashchenno-tserkovno sluzhitelei*, tom 2, (Khar'kov: tip. Gubernskago Pravleniia, 1900), 985–1076.

2. *Pis'ma vysokopreosviashchennago Filareta, Mitropolita Moskovskago, k Ekaterine Vladimirovne Novosil'tsevoi* (Moscow: Russkaia Pechatnia, 1911); For the confessions of Nataliia Kireevskaia, see Sergii Chetverikov, *Optina Pustyn': istoricheskii ocherk i lichnye vospominaniia* (Paris: YMCA Press, 1926), 125–27.

3. TsGIA SPb, f. 2219 (personal fund of Father John of Kronstadt), op. 1, d. 31 (confessions).

4. See, for example, Hilda's confession in Nathaniel Hawthorne, *The Marble Faun* (New York: Oxford University Press, 2009), 275–81.

5. See 148 Apps, App Detail – Confession: A Roman Catholic App, at http://www.148apps.com/app/416019676, which includes the "ability to add sins not listed in standard examination of conscience," and a "confession walkthrough including time of last confession in days, weeks, months, and years."

6. TsGIA SPb, f. 2219, op. 1, d. 31, ll. 121–220b.

7. Scholars of Roman Catholicism maintain that only an explicit request for absolution makes a written confession a proper confession, as opposed to simply a letter of repentance. This confession would thus qualify. Alphonse Michel, "Confessions et absolutions données par écrit," *Revue d'histoire et de littérature religieuses*, t. VII, no. 1 (Mars 1921), 58–72.

8. This is a reference from one of the recitations of the day's sins in the evening prayers. For an edition contemporary with these confessions, see *Molitvoslov* (Kiev: tip. Kievo-Pecherskoi Uspenskoi Lavry, 1884).

9. This archaic phrase retained by the Orthodox Church, *likhoimstvo*, may mean simply "lent money with interest."

10. Orthodox Church Fathers regarded wedding feasts as occasions of drunken revelry and dancing; Faina has internalized this teaching.

11. Orthodox Christians were expected to prostrate themselves to the ground during some church services and as part of their penance.

12. Although Faina uses the word "dirty" and not "unclean," this was usually code for to going to church while menstruating, that is, in a state of ritual impurity.

13. Although the word "sexual" may sound neutral to the modern ear, in the mental world of these confessions, sexuality does not exist as a neutral area: anything sexual is *bludnyi*, or fornicatory.

14. A prosphora, or sacred bread blessed at Divine Liturgy, was meant to be eaten only before one consumed other, non-consecrated, food.

15. TsGIA SPb, f. 2219, op. 1, d. 31, ll. 180a–83.

16. This suggests that Iakov has been trained to pray in a certain way, using specific texts. This illustrates the perceived importance of doing religious things in the right way.

17. Iakov's relation with God may be difficult, but he is still in a vital, palpable relationship: he makes promises, and feels guilty about breaking them. Here he also paraphrases the prokeimenon in the 8th tone: Pray and make your vows before the Lord our God (cf. Ps. 75:11).

18. Note that self-esteem was regarded as something to root out rather than to build up.

19. This is an allusion to the unfaithful servant in Luke 12:41–48 and Matt. 24:45.

20. Swearing at animals and hurting them appeared in guides to confession and priests were instructed to ask about those acts. See Platon (Fiveiskii), *Napominanie sviashchenniku ob obiazannostiakh ego pri sovershenii tainstva pokaianiia*, 4th ed. (St. Petersburg, 1859, repr. Saint Petersburg: Voskreseniie, 2004), 216 (Questions on the sixth commandment).

21. Killing with words was a staple in guides to confession in the section under the sixth commandment: "You may not have killed someone physically, but maybe you killed them with words, a look."

22. Making the sign of the cross the right way was emphasized in peasant culture and in Orthodox education, as Roy Robson's text in this volume confirms.

23. Bestiality in thought and deed was not unusual for people of rural background, and priests inquired about it. See Platon (Questions on the seventh commandment), 217.

24. This indicates that meals were to be taken in silence, as in monastery refectories; with respect, and not gaiety.

25. The prayer read by the priest before Communion warns people not "to give Thee a kiss, as did Judas."

26. This "blasphemy" is actually a sign of the living presence, importance of the holy in people's lives: they defile what is sacred because they share the same life, because the earthly is not compartmentalized from the heavenly.

27. Note the Biblical ban against travel on the Sabbath, Exod. 16:29.

28. Peasants regarded whistling in general as taboo, as they believed it summoned demons, but it is interesting that Iakov specifically mentions his tongue.

29. Such commemoration would have involved a sum of money, hence Iakov's miserliness at doing it.

30. This abbreviation for "slave of God" was the standard Orthodox phrase by which Orthodox Christians described themselves on commemorative notes, and by which they were named by the priest as they partook of Communion ("The slave of God, Iakov, communicates...").

31. TsGIA SPb, f. 2219, op. 1, d. 31, ll. 95–96.

32. This is a formulaic opening for a pious person's letter to a priest, and refers to the usual form for a layperson's greeting a priest by kissing his hand.

33. The writer is schooled enough in the practices of pious Orthodoxy to note that she is not taking the initiative of writing a confession on her own, but has sought and obtained a blessing to do so beforehand.

34. This phrase comes from the troparion hymn to the Kazan icon of the Mother of God.

35. People considered it sinful both to rejoice or make merry on sad holidays (for example, Good Friday or the Beheading of John the Baptist) and to mourn on joyous ones (as here, on Easter).

36. Such incorporation of Church Slavonic words – here, *stiazhat'* – is characteristic of people who became "churched": they use church language as their own. By contrast, non-religious people rarely use Church Slavonic in their writing or speech.

37. She is referring to the belief that menstruating women should not only not partake of Communion, but also not venerate icons, kiss the cross, or indeed even enter church (as being in a state of ritual impurity). See Lev. 15:19–24.

38. This phrase combines sections of the prayer read by the priest before Communion followed by one from the daily confession of sins.

39. TsGIA SPb, f. 2219, op. 1, d. 31, ll. 69–70.

40. TsGIA SPb, f. 2219, op. 1, d. 31, ll. 133–360b

41. The phrase is the same wording as in the Lord's Prayer, suggesting that this expression was used by Russian-speaking non-Christians as well as Christians.

42. *Kumys,* or fermented mare's milk, was a common treatment for various women's diseases, and rest cures to the Caucasus to drink it are a staple of memoirs and literature. As mare's milk would not have been acceptably kosher, this suggests that the writer's family were not particularly observant Jews.

43. The writings of the early church fathers normally urged people *not* to trust their own hearts.

SUGGESTED READINGS

Kizenko, Nadieszda. *A Prodigal Saint: Father John of Kronstadt and the Russian People.* University Park: Pennsylvania State University Press, 2000.

———. "Written Confessions and the Construction of Sacred Narrative." In *Sacred Stories: Religion and Spirituality in Modern Russia,* ed. Mark D. Steinberg and Heather J. Coleman, 93–118. Bloomington: Indiana University Press, 2007.

Tentler, Thomas N. *Sin and Confession on the Eve of the Reformation.* Princeton, NJ: Princeton University Press, 1977.

Examples of websites containing contemporary Orthodox Christian guides to confession in English:

St. Nicholas Russian Orthodox Church, McKinney (Dallas area) Texas, at *http://www.orthodox.net/confess/index.html.*

Orthodox Christian Information Center, at http://orthodoxinfo.com/praxis/pr_confession.aspx.

TWELVE

An Obituary of Priest Ioann Mikhailovich Orlovskii

Laurie Manchester

BEFORE THE FIRST DIOCESAN NEWSPAPER BEGAN PUBLICATION in 1860, very few obituaries of clergymen were printed. As such newspapers gradually began to open in every diocese, it became standard for priests' obituaries – usually several pages long – to be published. The obituaries of rural priests, who comprised approximately ninety percent of all priests, were written by either their fellow clergymen or their sons. Since they almost always discuss the lives, both personal and professional, of the deceased from cradle to grave, these obituaries provide rich biographical information about village priests. Similar to hagiography, they also provide an outline of what the author revered in the values he invokes when he praises the deceased, thereby also affording a window into the ideals of the parish clergy. Lastly, because clergymen and their families were supposed to adhere to a "model piety" that parishioners could strive to emulate, the values described in obituaries shed light on how Russian Orthodox Christians were ideally to live their lives.

The following obituary of a village priest was written by his son, Ivan Orlovskii (1869–1909), and was published in 1905. Prior to 1869, the parish clergy was a caste-like estate, and clergymen's sons were required to receive permission from ecclesiastical authorities to obtain secular employment. Ivan's generation, given secular status at birth, were technically not members of the clerical estate. Yet because most clergymen's sons continued to receive their education in theological schools, which reserved admission for clergymen's sons, and because the vast majority of clergymen's families intermarried and very few individuals from other social estates entered the clerical estate, they received a traditional clerical estate upbringing and education. An ethnographer of his native Smolensk province and a member of the Moscow Archeological Society, Ivan was also employed as a teacher at a women's diocesan school that educated primarily girls from the clerical estate. Politically, he was a conservative nationalist. Because he was a clergyman's son, and because he was employed by the clerical domain and published his obituary of his father in a diocesan newspaper, Ivan's text can be considered part of the clerical obituary genre.

Russian priests' obituaries generally fit two flexible types, which espouse the same values but apply them to different spheres. These archetypes can be traced back to the contradictory attitude toward the world first evident in early Christianity, a tension manifest in many religious traditions, between participation in political ecclesiastical activities versus a contemplative inner life of holiness. These two archetypes are rooted in popular Russian saints' "lives." The existence of multiple, flexible hagiographical models allowed authors of obituaries to accommodate the particularities of the deceased's individual experiences. Their modifications render these obituaries texts for modern Christian self-fashioning, as opposed to traditional Christian self-fashioning, which is purely imitative. As the century unfolded, and more and more priests grew up reading these obituaries – diocesan newspapers were often distributed to village clergy for free – priests' obituaries became prescriptive models crafted by average priests themselves. Because they were grounded in nineteenth-century clergymen's lives, these obituaries offered contemporary role models that Saints' Lives could not.

The first type of clergyman is characterized by being meek and modest, and by his withdrawal from temporal affairs. The higher glory he seeks is not measured by worldly accomplishments. He is even-tempered, exhibiting a gentle calmness and kindness. He never complains, even when unjustly persecuted. He is exacting of himself, but incredibly tolerant of others' weaknesses. Jokes and empty words are foreign to him. He adores books but reads only theological texts.

The second type is epitomized by Ivan's father. Committed to pastoral care, a movement that first gained momentum among the Russian parish clergy in the 1860s and has been characterized as "Reformation-like," the senior Orlovskii displayed a zeal to transform the temporal world. He organized informal theological discussion groups with parishioners, gave original sermons, founded a parish library, attempted to eradicate peasant superstition, and combated illiteracy – roughly 6 percent of rural residents were literate in the 1860s – by opening a school in his home. He also engaged extensively in charity, and in keeping with Orthodox prescriptions about modesty, this charity was distributed anonymously. While Ivan acknowledges that his father's material welfare improved considerably over the course of his career – which allowed him to be such a generous benefactor – he goes out of his way to emphasize his father working the fields early on in his career, and he recalls early childhood memories of his entire family eating with wooden spoons. Arguing that the clergy shared the lifestyle of the peasant masses was widespread among clerical offspring. In an age of widespread populism, they employed this alleged kinship to bolster their claims of moral superiority. This populism is also evident in Ivan's contention that his father preferred the company of his poor parishioners.

Pastoral care included clergymen enlightening themselves as well as their parishioners. Ivan's father is the opposite of the stereotypical barely literate Orthodox priest caricatured in Russian literature and radical propaganda. Despite the fact that he was a rural priest, the senior Orlovskii kept a diary, wrote a lengthy chronicle of the history of his village, possessed an immense library, and read avidly on a wide variety of subjects, including science. Because Russian Orthodox theologians understood faith and reason as entirely separate, his father's attachment to his telescope and Leyden jar did not betray the senior Orlovskii's faith. In fact, his father approached religion with the same inquisitiveness that he devoted to science. Despite being a stickler for adherence to every detail during church services, he loved debating theological questions. When it came to the temporal world, he was not adverse to change; after all, one of the historical figures he most revered was Peter the Great. The senior Orlovskii's overtly judgmental personality no doubt did not endear him to all of his superiors or subordinates, nor to all of his parishioners, especially the sinners he dealt with harshly, nor the enemies to whom his son alluded. Either censorship or Ivan's conservative pro-Church politics may explain why he devotes less than a sentence to a denunciation that derailed his father's career and undermined his health. Ivan's politics may also explain his overly enthusiastic description of his father's seminary years, an experience the clerical press was not loath to criticize and which few clergymen remembered fondly. Lastly, like many clergymen's sons, he worshipped his father, as he states below, and thus contradicts himself by claiming his "steadfast and stern" father was actually well liked by everyone who knew him. Given these contradictions, Ivan's obituary can thus be read as much as a portrait of an ideal Russian Orthodox priest as an actual biography.

Priest Ioann Mikhailovich Orlovskii (Obituary)[1]

On 25 January 1905 in the village of Danilovichi, Elninskii district, the retired priest Ioann Mikhailovich Orlovskii died.

The deceased was born on 25 February 1833 into the family of the priest who served the village of Belovost, Mikhail Grigor'evich Orlovskii (subsequently Arkhimandrite Mitrofan of the Kolochskii monastery). When he was six years old he lost his mother and was left alone with two younger sisters in the care of his eight-year-old sister and an elderly peasant nanny. Devastated by grief, Father Mikhail wanted to join a monastery, but the Right Reverend Bishop Timofei in a fatherly way talked him out of this and transferred him to the village of Kokhany in Elninskii district.

A landowner there, General A.I. Kiprianov, quickly appreciated this intelligent and educated priest who passionately performed his work and lived his life austerely. A veteran of the war of 1812, a former member of a mason's lodge, Kiprianov owned a large library, from which he allowed Fr. Mikhail to borrow. Socializing with the family of Kiprianov had the most beneficial influence on the development and upbringing of the children of Fr. Mikhail. Fr. Mikhail himself, who taught in his home school the children of peasants and landless household serfs, nevertheless found time to teach his own children. In the church school Ivan Mikhailovich was among the top pupils, and in 1847 he successfully enrolled in the seminary.

The deceased retained the most pleasant memories of the seminary. His favorite themes of conversation were stories about his professors, comrades, and seminary life: its festivities, recreation, examinations, and so on ... How many talented minds, intelligent, sincere people, lovers of art, eloquent preachers and singers there were there! They were the pride of the seminary, or, as they used to say then, "the splendor of the seminary." There were legends about them, and the seminary administration held them in high esteem.

The deceased especially warmly recalled rector Fotii, whose dogmatic theology lectures took place in the theology auditorium for both upper grades; the students listened to his two-hour lectures holding their breath. He also warmly recalled inspectors (!) Pavel (Bobrov) and Dmitrii, scholarly men with independent views, as well as professors Karchevskii, Kunitsin, V. I. Dobrotvorskii and Solov'ev. But his very favorite was rector Iosif (Pozdnyshev), whose sensible mind, kindness, and firmness of character he respected, as well as his talent and his wholehearted love of singing. He was prepared to talk about Iosif endlessly, reproducing his sedate manner of speaking and demeanor. The deceased kept his writings, which he had accurately copied. He distributed them throughout the countryside, and taught a rural choir how to sing them. In his old age, distraught by the tedium of loneliness and unused to retirement, he constantly remembered favorite chants learned from Iosif.

In 1853 Ivan Mikhailovich graduated from the seminary in the top third of his class, and on 25 September he was hired as a teacher at Smolensk district church school, where he taught Russian grammar to all six of the grades, church regulations to grades three through six, and Russian history to the last two grades, grades five and six.

In addition to his teaching responsibilities, Ivan Mikhailovich was also the organizer at that time of an informal catechism and sermon discussion group, talks which, with the approval of the rector (Fotii, and then Moisei), he gave in the cathedral and in urban churches, with the permission of Archbishop Timofei.

On 4 December 1858, I. M. was ordained a priest in the church of the village of Sychev.

Exemplary and revered service, friendliness, and sociability attracted parishioners from every social standing to the new priest.

In Sychev Fr. Ivan continued his pastoral care activity. Following the example of his father, he started a school in his home and in 1862 earned gratitude from the Right Reverend Antonii "for his attention to the spreading of literacy." In the same year he was appointed the inspector of rural schools, and he filled that position until May 5, 1864. He was awarded a *nabedrennik*[2] in 1863 for the zeal with which he carried out his responsibilities and for his good behavior. In 1864, following a denouncement, Father Ivan was moved ten versts from Sychev to the village of Pesochnia. This move was of no benefit to his work, but the destruction of his household and the moral blow were substantial.

A year after moving to Pesochnia Fr. Ivan was struck by another sorrow: on 18 October his four-year-old first-born, Mikhail, died of scarlet fever. At that same time he was already preparing to move to the village of Kamenets, where he had been transferred, by request, on 15 October. He took his dead son with him and buried him in Kamenets (ten versts from Pesochnia). He had not succeeded in unpacking in Kamenets before his younger daughter Mariia came down with croup, and on the first of November she died. Seized by grief over the loss of his beloved children, Father Ivan asked to be transferred, regardless of where, just so he could leave Kamenets. He received an appointment in Danilovichi.

With his ill five-year-old daughter he moved to Danilovichi on the first of December, and on the twenty-third this last child of his died. Thus in the span half a year he had to endure three moves from village to village and within two months lose all three of his children. These blows strongly reverberated in his soul and left on it the stamp of anxiety, of excessive nervousness and sensitivity.

In Danilovichi it became possible for him to improve his material welfare, which had been disrupted by all these transfers. In fifteen years of service here he was able to build a new house to replace the old and cramped house he had bought from his predecessor. During that time his children were born and grew up. Fr. Ivan himself prepared them for school at home, even teaching them ancient languages. When each turned nine years old, he took them to board at school. A new and long period of uninterrupted expenses and worries about his children, and bleak thoughts concerning their failures, which he always let worry him too much, began.

Meanwhile, his health began to deteriorate. A sickness (cataracts) of the eyes, from which he at least was healed, especially affected his health and his mood. One would have to have seen him to understand what he endured during this time. His deteriorating health forced Fr. Ioann more and more to think about retiring. Only the organic need – instilled in him by forty-five years of service – to serve God at His altar and the thought of sadly stagnating without that service gave him the determination to continue to serve. In 1902 he finally retired his position. As was to be expected, left without the holy work to which he was accustomed, he quickly passed away.

Fr. Ioann died at the age of seventy-two. Of the forty-seven years he had been a priest, thirty-seven of those years he served in Danilovichi and two years he lived there in retirement. He was the last of the Danilovichi elders, the last representative of that tenor of local church-parish life that took shape in the second half of the nineteenth century, and which was shaped by, especially in the last years, his influence and personality. Fr. Ioann himself imparted the impression of a priest and person of the "old stock," but without the negative traits of that type. He was a sincere and firm believer, devoid of saccharine pietism and somber old belief. He loved to read and discuss theological questions, many of which actively interested and worried him. Half of his library consisted almost entirely of religious-theological titles, which he had inherited from his father or purchased personally. He also founded a parish library, acquiring books for it and subscribing to theological journals such as *Bogoslovskii Vestnik* [Theological Herald]. His religious proclivity left a particular mark on his services in church. He possessed favorable natural gifts: a sensitive heart, aesthetic taste, a pleasant sounding voice and a dignified appearance. His services in church, devoid of any affectation or artificiality, were distinguished by lofty beauty, earnestness, and poignancy. Fr. Ioann loved church services. He derived from them sincere spiritual delight and performed them strictly according to regulations, not considering any part of them to be trifling. At the altar he was completely imbued with this love and reverence, and his disposition was involuntarily communicated to worshippers. Everyone loved to attend Father Ioann's services, and the parishioners of Danilovichi will long remember specific moments during them, such as the reading of prayers, the Gospels, and his exclamations. His services during Holy and Easter weeks made an especially strong impression. They were conducted strictly according to regulations, without any omissions, with all singing appointed for two choirs. Because of the heartfelt and complete feeling of their leader, parishioners could not for a minute lessen their religious mood, and thus the duration of these services didn't tire them. At several moments, for example during the reading of the Gospels of the Holy Passion, Father Ioann became so agitated that his voice was interrupted by tears. In the church, a deep silence ensued, and an impression of grave sorrow and grief seized his parishioners. The bringing out of the shroud of Christ, the burial on Holy Saturday – all of this occurred so serenely, with such grandeur and sincerity, without a tinge of any kind of abrupt, unnecessary features, that it created a completely real and unusually moving effect.

Father Ioann's parishioners loved and respected him. And not just habit, but also his personal traits drew them to him. The care and strict order with which he carried out church services and ceremonies, the fact that he always kept his word, his common sense, his consistency, his true sincerity and the ability to actively sympathize (as opposed to being simply well-mannered), the straightforwardness of his character, and his pastoral authoritativeness – all of this made the pastor, as the leader of the parish, completely appealing in the eyes of the people. Many parishioners turned to Father Ioann for advice and directions concerning their affairs, particularly regarding their families and intimate matters, knowing that he would judge the matter wisely and conscientiously and would not betray their secrets to anyone. The peasants said of Father Ioann that he had a "strict character," and they liked that strictness, which was understood by them in the broadest possible sense. They understood by it the seriousness with which he approached his work, his sense of duty, which obliged him to treat himself and others sternly; independence and steadfastness of views, with no fear of being known as an eccentric; honesty and straightforwardness, connected to a sincere aversion to any hypocrisy and deception, exaltation, and artificiality. He displayed this "strictness" both in his home and in the parish. In relation to those with weak characters, which the majority of "sinners" turn out to possess, it was more useful than sluggish placidity and indulgence.

Those who were the recipient of his severity, despite their pride being injured, recognized that Father Ioann acted without a hidden agenda, and only desired to help them. People made their peace with this strictness also because he was alien to giving anyone special treatment, and without embarrassment rendered to everyone what they deserved. His highly developed sense of righteous justice and self-worth did not allow him to curry favor with and grovel before some, and behave haughtily toward others. At his table one would simultaneously find a land-owning noble, the cantor who was subordinate to him, and a peasant whom he respected. And in the village he received with great pleasure the hospitality of a poor peasant, who was closer to his heart than an unlikable wealthy kulak. He acted this way everywhere. For example, he reacted with tears to the news of the death of his colleague Father Nikandor Ivanov, whom he had cherished since their early days of acquaintance. But while Father Nikandor was alive, he never allowed himself to turn to him for backing or patronage in work matters, although he happily responded to greetings sent from him. In general, what he said never differed from what he did. Several people considered him prideful, which they explained by citing his rather stern appearance. But his parishioners, and anyone who got to know him better, understood that he was a sociable, approachable, and simple man.[3] He was an irreplaceable interlocutor for a serious discussion but also for an amusing one as well. This is why he was a coveted guest in peasants' homes as well as in landowners'. His erudition and refinement allowed him to feel equal to and sometimes even superior to many rural landowners-noblemen, who eagerly socialized with him.

Love of books and reading was his passion. A careful spender in his domestic life, Father Ioann did not economize when it came to books and journals. His library, which comprised up to 1,500 volumes, was renowned in the region. (He donated part of it for the founding of the Pushkin Public Library in Danilovichi.) Its contents were as diverse as could be, though it was predominantly comprised of theology, sermons, scripture, and liturgical books (among them were more than a few rare and valuable volumes). It also included books on his beloved subjects of history, geography, science, and *belles lettres*. To provide an idea of his views, we should note that the historical personalities he respected the most included Peter I, Nicholas I, Skobolev, and among poets, Pushkin. He always passionately defended them against any attacks, and he acquired almost every new edition of Pushkin. Interested in history in general, he compiled a chronicle of our village, kept a diary and notes, and it would be easy to compose a history of the village over the last forty years based on his papers. He also loved science, and in his office, besides books, one could also catch sight of a telescope, and home-made instruments – a Leyden jar, barometers and various instruments for forecasting the weather, mechanical devices, and so on . . . Folk life, customs, manners, and language also attracted his attention, and he could convey all sorts of interesting information about these themes. But he was an unmerciful opponent of coarse superstition, and there were no shriekers in his parish. The peasants, having crossed themselves, had to dig up the wheat they had "bewitched" in their grain fields. Those fortune-tellers and psychics who tried to exploit their fellow peasants, after the first public reprimand, ceased their practice, fearing severe penance.

But regardless of his strictness and sternness on the surface, Father Ioann had a kind heart. By nature quick-tempered, he could not stay angry for long. His parishioners with whom he found fault knew this. He couldn't bear tears or persistent pleading, and usually the guilty or offender, after a stern rebuking, received forgiveness from him and departed having reconciled with him. In his relations with his co-workers, he was an attentive colleague, avoiding quarrels, and was prepared to make any concessions; similarly, he treated his fellow villagers simply and kindly, in spite of his sternness. Disliking trials and complaints, he did not offend anyone at work. His kindness was expressed through his widespread charity. Many instances of his assistance were revealed only after his death. Not to mention the assistance he gave to his relatives, even the most distant, whom he tracked down zealously. He always enthusiastically gave when asked by charitable societies and institutions. He never refused even the organizers of reading groups in the countryside, fire departments, or libraries, which does not correspond to the image of him as a man of the old order. Stinginess was completely alien to his character and all of his resources he spent on charity, books, and the education of his children.

In this last respect he was true to himself. Reasonable severity, discipline, religiosity and churchliness, development of the mind and heart – these were the fundamentals of his upbringing of his children. From childhood he accustomed us children to be in church, to sing and read there, to strictly follow church regulations, and so on... This strictness did not hamper him from expressing love and concern for his children. However, his love for his children never brought Father Ioann to the point of spoiling them. He was implacable not only toward improper behavior, but also to trepidations of the soul, and he did not hesitate to offend one's pride in order to correct a deviation from righteous truth. As a result, a conscious respect developed toward him, similar to the esteem in which he always held his deceased father, of whom he was reminiscent in many aspects.

His children, his parishioners, and all who knew him well, schooled by the severe experience of life, will forget, we firmly believe, the human weaknesses and feebleness of the deceased. They will remember his direct, maybe at times even harsh, but incorruptible and honest speeches given in various circumstances and instances, and not only once will repeat to themselves: "The late Father Ivan spoke the righteous truth" and will remember him with a prayer and a kind word.

NOTES

1. Ivan Orlovskii, "Sviashch. Ioann Mikhailovich Orlovskii (Nekrolog)" *Smolenskie eparkhial'nye vedomosti* no. 10 (1905): 533–41.

2. A thigh-shield usually given as the first vestment award a priest receives.

3. Footnote in the original text: Without a doubt, the conditions in which he lived made this possible. While he was physically able, he himself always worked in the field, in the meadow, on the threshing floor along with his family and hired workers. Scarcity forced him to live a simple type of life: we still remember how twenty-five years ago Father Ioann's entire family ate in the kitchen, and not in the "dining room." At the table, we used wooden spoons and such.

SUGGESTED READINGS

Hedda, Jennifer. *His Kingdom Come: Orthodox Pastorship and Social Activism in Revolutionary Russia*. DeKalb: Northern Illinois University Press, 2008.

Fedotov, G. P. *The Russian Religious Mind*. 2 volumes. Cambridge, MA: Harvard University Press, 1966.

Fowler, Bridget. *The Obituary as Collective Memory*. New York: Routledge, 2007.

Freeze, Gregory L. *The Russian Levites: Parish Clergy in the Eighteenth Century*. Cambridge, MA: Harvard University Press, 1977.

Manchester, Laurie. *Holy Fathers, Secular Sons; Clergy, Intelligentsia and the Modern Self in Revolutionary Russia*. DeKalb: Northern Illinois University Press, 2008.

Ziolkowski, Margaret. *Hagiography and Modern Russian Literature*. Princeton, NJ: Princeton University Press, 1988.

13.1. A Word of Saint John Chrysostom on the Fear of God, and on How to Stand in the Holy Church of God in Awe and Good Order, and How to Make the Sign of the Cross over One's Person.

THIRTEEN

Not Something Ordinary, but a Great Mystery: Old Believer Ritual in the Late Imperial Period

Roy R. Robson

TAKE A LOOK AT THE TWO MEN ON THIS POSTER: ONE PRAYS with an angel defending him, while devils sneak up on the other one. Other than that, it is very difficult to tell the two men apart. In fact, both are Old Believers, the most traditional segment of imperial Russian Orthodox culture. Though long persecuted by the state-sponsored Russian Orthodox Church, the Old Believers did not stray from Orthodoxy so much as intensify it, doggedly adhering primarily to the rituals, texts, and art of the generation before Peter the Great.

The term "Old Believer" encompasses dozens of smaller groups. Though differing in ideology, they bonded through their shared desire to follow the "ancient piety" of seventeenth-century Russia, crystallized in practices before the reforms introduced by Patriarch Nikon and accepted by a church council in 1666. Of all the rituals, the most important was how to make the sign of the cross. For Old Believers, this was no empty movement of a hand "waving in front of their faces." Instead, the sign of the cross brought a symbol to life, physically realizing the mystery of Christ's existence on earth, his divinity, and the power of God to shield, help, and transform Christians.

In October 1905, Emperor Nicholas II promulgated the October Manifesto, dramatically broadening Russian people's rights to assembly, political participation, and religious freedom. Though leaders of the Russian Orthodox Church wept at its loss of legal supremacy in Russia, minority Christians rejoiced at their first opportunity to meet legally, to build churches, to publish their own literature, and to accept converts from the long-dominant Russian Orthodox Church. The Old Believers,

13.2. A Word of Saint John Chrysostom on the Fear of God, and on How to Stand in the Holy Church of God in Awe and Good Order, and How to Make the Sign of the Cross over One's Person. Image detail.

often also called the "Old Ritualists," may have gained the most from the October Manifesto, as they could take advantage of their new freedoms to link an extensive network of communities across the empire. In fact, some scholars estimate that Old Believers numbered as many as one-sixth of all ethnic Russians, and perhaps 10 percent of all subjects of the Empire. Countless millions more sympathized with Old Believer ideals and traditions.

After 1905, the publishing firm of G. K. Gorbunov in Moscow published dozens of works for Old Believers. The firm concentrated on liturgical books that Old Believers needed to celebrate correctly the many services of Orthodox Christianity according to the "pre-Nikonian" (that is, pre-1652) ritual. The firm also published liturgical guides and educational volumes from the Holy Transfiguration Almshouse, an umbrella organization for ultra-traditionalist Old Believers called the Theodosian Concord.

Gorbunov also printed posters like the one shown here. It was a remarkable illustration of new technology – commercial lithography – put to the service of centuries-old rituals. Looking closely, we can learn much about Old Believer religious ideals and behavior in the late imperial period. Most Old Believers would have first noticed the top half of the broadside, which shows the effects of making the sign of the cross correctly and incorrectly. On the left side of the picture, an Old Believer prays as he should: shoulders back, standing straight, holding his right hand correctly and touching fingertips to the very top of his forehead. He looks toward the icons and the holy book arrayed in front of him on a stand draped with a traditional cross-embroidered cloth. An angel defends the man with both a sword (such as Archangel Michael used to defeat Satan) and a cross, held in a distinctively Old-Believer style. Above the Old Believer, another angel writes the words that inspire the prayerful person (and that appear again in the text below): "If any man comes to church and stands before the image of God, he will receive the forgiveness of his sins and the mercy of God." Because of all this, tiny demons run away.

On the other side of the picture, though, another Old Believer succumbs to liturgical laziness. At first glance, the two men appear nearly identical – they have similar beards, haircuts, cassocks, and general hand positions. Yet the man on the right hunches his shoulders a bit and slothfully lets his *lestovka* (an Old Believer prayer-rope similar to a rosary) drop below the waist. He bows his head, face creased with fatigue, and his right hand does not make it all the way to the top of his shoulder. Though the differences from the man on the left might be small, they illustrate disrespect and carelessness in this man's prayer. And thus angels stay away and devils approach the Old Believer. A bold demon – with a silly look and bulbous nose – taps the man on the shoulder. To an outsider, even a pious Russian Orthodox Christian, the man on the right would seem to be following the ritual zealously. But the devils know differently.

Now study the architectural elements on each side of the poster. The room on the left has a slightly more Russian feel than that of the right, due to the ornamentation on the columns and the tapering arch. The room on the right has a vaguely Greek or Renaissance (that is, non-Russian) style with its broad arch. Most importantly, though, look at the floor. On the left, the floor tiles go straight back from the front, with no attempt at perspective. On the right, they move toward a vanishing-point perspective. While it might seem more realistic, perspective also reinforces worldliness (how things look on earth) instead of the iconographic otherworldliness of the room on the left.

At the top center of the picture we see St. John Chrysostom writing the homily that appears on the bottom half of the poster. This creates a bridge between the picture and the text, a visual corroboration of their truth. By quoting one of the great fourth-century Christian theologians, Old Believers used an unassailably Christian text to defend and to legitimize their ritual practices.

On the bottom half of the poster, Old Church Slavonic text explains what we're seeing. The poster quotes from two sources, *A Son of the Church* and *The Great Catechism*. The former book, first popularized in the early seventeenth century, was a great Old Believer favorite as it precisely described the rituals of Russian Orthodoxy using easily understood language. By tradition, it included the sermon attributed to St. John Chrysostom on the sign of the cross and, in the *Prologue,* a compendium of texts organized for reading each day of the year. Text from the Great Catechism, also of seventeenth-century origin, complemented *A Son of the Church*.

The pictures and text, taken together, create an intriguing portrait of traditional Christianity in the late imperial period. The publisher chose to print the text in Old Church Slavonic, use an icon-like graphic design, and include text that merged ritual action, theology, and an implicit defense of the "ancient piety" against innovation. Likewise, the text celebrated a highly physical form of Christianity, exhorting Old Believers to confess the faith "so that your body feels it, and not only in your clothing." In these ways, the poster both reminded Old Believers of their duties while intrinsically contrasting Old Believers to other Russian Christians, who had lost interest in Old Russia's holy rituals.

A Word of Saint John Chrysostom on the Fear of God, and on How to Stand in the Holy Church of God in Awe and Good Order, and How to Make the Sign of the Cross over One's Person[1]

Many ignorant people pretend to make the sign of the Cross by waving their hands over their face. In vain do they labor; they do not draw the Cross on themselves correctly, and their hand-waving gives joy to the demons, but if you cross yourself properly, placing the hand on the forehead, on the belly, on the right shoulder and then on the left shoulder, the angels watch and rejoice to see the true Cross traced over your person. An angel of the Lord also writes down the names of those who enter the church of the Lord with fear and faith. If any man comes to church and stands before the image of God, he will receive the forgiveness of his sins and the mercy of God, but if he stands there without fear, he will go out having committed a greater sin. Thus, when we come to church, let us stand there with fear, awaiting the great mercy of God in this age and in the next. To Him be glory, now and ever, and unto the ages of ages (from the *Prologue* for 18 April).

THE CROSS WHICH YOU MAKE WITH YOUR HAND

Pay attention to the Cross whose protective sign you make over yourself with your hand. It is not something ordinary; it contains great mystery. When you join the large finger, called the thumb, together with the two smaller fingers, which are the last on your hand, this forms a sign of the mystery of the beginningless being of the indivisible Trinity, the Father and the Son and the Holy Spirit. When you have thus joined these fingers together, incline your middle finger together with your index finger. This is a sign of the two natures, the Divinity and the Humanity, in the one Person of Christ. These fingers are placed upon the forehead, and then brought downward to the breast and the navel, indicating that God the Word came down from heaven to earth, and was incarnate of the most pure Virgin Mary, and lived on the earth among men, and freely suffered His Passion in the flesh for our sake and for our salvation, and ascended into heaven, and sat at the right hand of the Father. Placing the hand on the right shoulder indicates and signifies that He sits at the right hand of the Father, and will come to the earth again to judge the living and the dead, and to give every man a recompense for his deeds, and to those on His right He will show the kingdom of heaven. Bringing the hand over to the left shoulder shows that sinners will take their places at His left, and will be sent away into everlasting punishment. After you have made the sign of the Cross, spread your hand out into its usual position, and then make a bow.

IF THE SIGN OF THE CROSS IS MADE INCORRECTLY

Be careful that all these things are performed correctly, because they concern, first of all, the Trinity, and second, the economy of the two natures. If you do not make the sign of the Cross properly, you do not confess your faith in the indivisible Trinity, and you do not confess your faith in the economy of the two natures in the one Person of Christ. The same applies to placing your hand on your forehead and bringing it down as far as the navel. The body represents the image of God, and the navel is taken to mean the footstool of the Lord, the head of Adam. If you do not make the sign of the Cross correctly, you do not confess faith in the Incarnation of God the Word. Likewise, if you are careless and lazy, and do not bring your hand to the right shoulder and to the left, you do not confess Him to be the judge of the living and the dead. Take care, therefore, and do not be too lazy to move your hand to your right shoulder and to your left shoulder. Furthermore, I shall tell you this about the sign of the Cross. Remember to make the Cross not merely over your clothing, but on your body. Thus, when you cross yourself touch yourself with your hand solidly, so that your body feels it, and not only in your clothing.

HOW THE DEMONS TREMBLE BEFORE THE TRUE SIGN OF THE CROSS

If you draw the proper sign of the Cross over yourself, according to the testament of the holy Apostles and the holy Fathers, then the demons greatly fear him; they tremble, and they flee far from him, but if anyone forms the Cross incorrectly, the demons rejoice over him and tempt him with all kinds of deceptions. Such is the significance of the life-bearing Cross of the Lord (from *Son of the Church*, chapters 65–67, folios 83–87 reverse).

And now, in our day, we see many people who do not take Christ's Sign upon themselves: that is, they do not raise their right hand to make the sign on their forehead, then their stomach, then the right shoulder and then the left. If they do not take this sign upon themselves, it means they have already taken – on their head and right hand – the seal of Antichrist. For, as it is written, where there is deprivation of light, the darkness has already arrived (*Great Catechism*, folio 102).

NOTE

1. Adapted in part, with permission, from *A Son of the Church*, trans. German Ciuba (Erie, PA: Russian Orthodox Church of the Nativity, 2001), 25–26.

SUGGESTED READINGS

Crummey, Robert O. "Old Belief as Popular Religion: New Approaches." *Slavic Review* 52, no. 4 (Winter, 1993), 700–12.

Michels, Georg B., and Robert L. Nichols, eds. *Russia's Dissident Old Believers: 1650–1950*. Minneapolis: Minnesota Mediterranean and East European Monographs, 2009.

Robson, Roy R. *Old Believers in Modern Russia*. DeKalb: Northern Illinois University Press, 1995.

Rogers, Douglas. *The Old Faith and the Russian Land: A Historical Ethnography of Ethics in the Urals*. Ithaca, NY: Cornell University Press, 2009.

Rosenfeld, Alla, ed. *Defining Russian Graphic Arts: 1898–1934*. New Brunswick, NJ: Rutgers University Press, 1999.

FOURTEEN

Orthodox Petitions for the Transfer of the Holy Relics of St. Stefan of Perm, 1909

Robert H. Greene

IN BOTH THEOLOGY AND PRACTICE, RUSSIAN ORTHODOXY places great stock in the belief that the saints in heaven are willing and able to work miracles for the benefit of the living faithful on earth. Imperial-era sources reveal the manifold ways in which Russian Orthodox laypeople and clerics alike stressed and celebrated the tangible, sensory presence of the sacred in their everyday lives. While Orthodox theologians maintained that the "spiritual hearing" of the saints was so keen that they could discern and heed the prayers of the faithful anywhere on earth, believers felt that the shrines and reliquaries that housed the holy relics of the saints were the most direct conduits through which the miraculous intercession of the holy dead might be obtained. Orthodox miracle stories and devotional literature emphasized that physical contact with the saints (through touching or kissing their relics and shrines) was the most immediate way for believers to procure the miracles and healing cures they so desired.

The documents below recount the efforts of the Orthodox community in Perm to acquire the holy relics of their saintly protector, Stefan of Perm, the Orthodox missionary and bishop who brought Christianity to the native peoples of the region in the fourteenth century. Over the course of the nineteenth century, believers in Perm had presented at least half a dozen petitions to the Holy Synod requesting that St. Stefan's relics be transferred to Perm from their presumed place of burial in the Moscow Kremlin. Each of these grassroots campaigns, however, had met with failure, most recently in 1896, on the occasion of the five-hundredth anniversary of the saint's death. Their nearest success had come in 1849, when the Synod granted permission that St. Stefan's staff be delivered to the city cathedral of Perm from a monastery in the diocese of Lithuania.[1]

By the turn of the twentieth century, however, prospects for the realization of this long cherished dream must have seemed brighter. Emperor Nicholas II (r. 1894–1917) had sanctioned the canonizations of three new saints in the first fifteen years of his reign (compared with only four in the preceding two centuries), and Stefan's devotees in Perm were doubtless aware that this emperor was more disposed than most to grant requests that might have a salutary effect on the spiritual well-being of his subjects. The campaign of 1909 began on 26 April, the 513th anniversary of St. Stefan's death, with a telegram to the Holy Synod signed by some of the most prominent citizens in Perm society. Throughout the spring and summer, the bishop of Perm, the provincial governor, city and district officials, noble landowners, merchants, and industrialists continued the letter-writing campaign, appealing to well-placed Petersburg patrons to exert what influence they could to assist in their cause. The coordinated efforts of the local organizers culminated in September 1909 with a formal petition to the Holy Synod signed by 12,019 of the nearly 100,000 citizens of Perm. While they framed their arguments in the rhetoric of pious devotion and the language of humble supplication, the petitioners also intimated that by returning St. Stefan's holy relics to the site of his great missionary work the Orthodox Church could reestablish an outpost of faith in the distant Urals region and strengthen the spiritual stamina of a body politic weakened by the recent upheavals of the revolution of 1905.

Tempting though those prospects might be, the validity and provenance of St. Stefan's remains would first have to be confirmed before the Synod could grant any requests regarding the relocation of his relics. The Synod solicited the opinion of Archpriest Ioann Ianyshev, father confessor to the imperial family and superintendent of the Kremlin churches, who concluded that while there was certainly no theological impediment to relic transfer, a practice common in the Orthodox world for centuries, "several complications of no small importance" made it difficult to proceed. For one, there was some confusion as to the actual location and condition of St. Stefan's relics. Tradition held (and the petitioners insisted) that the saint was buried beneath the floorboards of the

Church of the Savior in the Pines, an ancient chapel in the Kremlin, but as Ianyshev reported, "There is no way of ascertaining the condition of the prelate's supposed coffin beneath the cathedral floors, nor whether his sainted relics are in fact preserved therein."[2] Still smarting from the recent scandal of 1903, when the allegedly uncorrupted relics of St. Serafim of Sarov were discovered to be anything but, the Synod instructed a select team headed by Metropolitan Vladimir of Moscow to investigate Stefan's putative gravesite. The dismal condition of the broken and scattered bones discovered therein cast doubts on the authenticity of Stefan's relics and prompted the Synod to reject the petitions in a resolution of December 1909. The Prelate Stefan would not make one last excursion to the Urals, but would remain instead in Moscow.

The efforts of the Perm faithful ended once again in failure, but their labors speak to a larger set of issues and concerns in Orthodox life at the turn of the twentieth century, principally, popular notions of what constituted holy relics and the powerful localized dimension of sanctity. Orthodox tradition maintained that the bodies of the saints could be preserved against the inevitable processes of decay and decomposition by the power of the Holy Spirit. Although incorruptibility was not a prerequisite for sainthood, theologians and lay believers alike held that it was particularly vivid and striking evidence of God's favor for the deceased and therefore strong, though inconclusive, proof of sanctity.[3] Had the investigators been able to conclude that the bones in the Kremlin cathedral were in fact those of St. Stefan, the Synod need not have fretted over the condition of the relics themselves; evidence from miracle stories demonstrates that Orthodox believers sought the assistance of saints with proven track records of miracles and healing cures, even those whose bodies and bones were incomplete, charred by fire, or otherwise corrupted. The saints whom the faithful treasured most were those with exemplary résumés of miracles, not necessarily those whose relics had been preserved uncorrupted. Ultimately, incorruptibility mattered less to Orthodox believers than efficacy.

The documents below suggest also that Orthodox communities treated seriously the question of where their saints were buried. While they already had possession of the saint's staff, the faithful of Perm wanted their bishop's body, too. So did rival claimants from the town of Ust-

Sysolsk in Vologda province, some five hundred kilometers northwest of Perm, who lodged their own petitions for the transfer of St. Stefan's relics in that same summer of 1909. Stefan's past missionary successes in the region had made his relics into bones of contention, with competing Orthodox communities claiming ownership of the peripatetic prelate's earthly remains. Though St. Stefan had been absent from the region for more than five hundred years, Orthodox communities across the distant Urals felt that the saint's presence among them was of vital importance, particularly in the recent context of social unrest and spiritual uncertainty. While the petitioners framed their arguments broadly, seeking to strike the proper chord that would motivate the Synod to grant their request, obtaining regular, permanent access to the saint's miraculous powers through possession of his holy relics was of paramount concern to the ordinary men and women who joined their voices to the campaign. Orthodox communities in Perm and Ust-Sysolsk hoped to bring Stefan back home, where the Orthodox faithful believed he belonged and where they felt they needed his body to be.

Telegram from citizens of Perm to S. M. Lukianov,
Over-Procurator of the Holy Synod, 26 April 1909[4]

We, the undersigned, most humbly beg Your Most High Excellency to rest assured that the petition from the people of Perm, presented to you by Prince L'vov, requesting the transfer of the holy relics of our great prelate and first bishop and enlightener of our region, Saint Stefan of the Great Perm Region, represents our most warmly cherished desire, passed down from one generation to the next. It is our deep faith and hope that in accordance with the intentions you conveyed to Prince L'vov you will find it possible to present this matter to His Imperial Majesty and to determine whether it should be His most merciful pleasure to grant this request to us, the people of Perm. If the Great Tsar's mercy should not see fit, then we would consider it our sacred duty to postpone our intention and pass on to the generation that succeeds us the desires and aspirations we received from our forefathers, bequeathing to them the task of petitioning once more, at a later date, for the resettlement of our great prelate at the site of his original deeds so that new service may be rendered for the great joy and happiness of our northern region and neighboring Siberia. We propose to limit our petition to a request that the Holy Synod first give its blessing to the ceremonial opening of the holy relics of the Prelate Stefan, which were open for veneration in Moscow prior to the invasion of the Poles at the beginning of the seventeenth century and thereafter sealed, in light of the depredations of the enemy. Be our patron in this our good and great cause. May it please Your Most High Excellency to favor us with a gracious response and to address your reply to Pavel Stepanovich Zhirnov in the city of Perm. Citizens of the city of Perm: Pavel Zhirnov, Nikolai Pesochenskii, Efim Permiakov, Nikolai Cheremisinov, Fedor Kruglov, Petr Starikov, Vladimir Sudoplatov, Nikolai Mikhailov, Pavel Korolev, Dmitrii Zhirnov, Prince Sergei L'vov.

Bishop Palladii of Perm to S. M. Lukianov,
Over-Procurator of the Holy Synod, 19 June 1909[5]

Your Most High Excellency, Sergei Mikhailovich,
Dear Sir,

In response to your letter no. 73,[6] dated 13 May of this year, I have the honor of reporting the following to Your Most High Excellency.

For my part, I wholeheartedly support the petition from the citizens of Perm concerning the translation from Moscow to Perm of the holy relics of the Prelate Stefan, Bishop of Perm, and I believe that such a translation would be both beneficial and timely, not only for the city of Perm but for the entire Perm region. The neighboring dioceses (Viatka, Vologda, Ekaterinburg) are rich in the relics of God's Saints, and each Orthodox Christian living there has the full opportunity and happiness of rushing forth to their healing shrines, of pouring out before them their sorrows and their joys. The vast Perm diocese is deprived of such great Christian comfort. Moreover, the city of Perm is now a major cultural and economic center, one to which residents from across the breadth of the

Perm region might readily travel to venerate a great sacred object. Furthermore, in these troubled times, the ceremonial transfer of the holy relics of the Prelate Stefan might serve to inspire a tremendous upsurge in religious spirit, not only among the inhabitants of the Perm region, not only among the inhabitants of those localities and dioceses through which such a rare and wondrous religious procession would pass, but in the hearts of the countless multitudes of the faithful children of the Holy Russian Orthodox Church. The entire Perm region awaits this ceremony with hearts atremble, from imperial administrators to the most recent settlers in the region, all of whom hold sacred the memory of the Prelate Stefan, Enlightener of Perm. All of Orthodox Rus will rejoice at this ceremony, for this will truly be an all-Russian ceremony.

Calling for God's blessing upon You, with full reverence and sincerity, I have the honor of being Your Most High Excellency's humblest and most prayerful servant, Palladii, Bishop of Perm and Solikamsk.

---

*A. V. Bolotov, governor of Perm, to P. A. Stolypin,
prime minister and minister of the interior, 15 May 1909;
forwarded by Stolypin to Lukianov, 30 May 1909*[7]

Your Most High Excellency, Petr Arkadievich,

In the Moscow Kremlin, in the Church of the Savior in the Pines, the relics of the Prelate Stefan of Great Perm lie buried in oblivion. For a considerable period of time following the Prelate's canonization, his relics lay open for veneration but were concealed when the Poles devastated Moscow as a precaution against their profanation.

The Prelate Stefan of Great Perm, who passed to his rest in 1396, was the apostle and enlightener of the Zyrians and Permiaks, who settled the broad region between the basins of the Kama and Northern Dvina Rivers, a region that today comprises a large part of the provinces of Perm, Viatka, and Vologda, and is known under the general designation of Great Perm. Properly speaking, the preaching and missionary work of the Prelate Stefan occurred primarily within the borders of what is now Vologda province, presently the center of the Zyrian settlements, as well as in the northern districts of Perm province, which are populated almost entirely by Permiaks, and thus it can be said that the preacher's influence was felt throughout the entire region of Great Perm. At that time, settlements in these impassable forests were clustered together only along the banks of the rivers, which served as the sole means of transportation. Thanks to this, the mighty Kama River, with its numerous tributaries, could not help but become the principal center for the Zyrians and Permiaks of the region in question. Having initiated the spread of Christianity in the Perm lands, the Prelate Stefan became the first Bishop of the diocese of Great Perm, which encompassed the entire territory mentioned above. This is why his memory is especially honored here in Perm, not only as a great holy man and prayerful intercessor before the Lord God the Most High, but also as the intimate protector of the local region.

Upon assuming the governorship of Perm province and acquainting myself with the mood of the local population, it occurred to me to raise the issue of transferring the Prelate Stefan's relics from Moscow to Perm, but so long as His Grace Bishop Nikanor held the diocese I did not consider it possible to broach the question. Recently, however, at the initiative of Prince S. E. L'vov and the most well-intentioned elements of the population, the notion has been put forward most insistently of petitioning for the transfer of the relics of the Prelate Stefan to Perm, for which purpose a deputation has already been appointed, consisting, in addition to Prince L'vov, of the following individuals: the merchants P. S. Zhirnov, F. G. Kruglov, and E. F. Permiakov; Senior State Councilor A. A. Malleev; State Councilor N. I. Pesochenskii; Archpriest A. A. Voskresenskii of the city cathedral; and the peasant A. V. Perevoshchikov. All of these individuals are held in high esteem, occupy prominent positions in society, and are undoubtedly deserving of full confidence: the first three are prominent members of the Perm City Duma and Perevoshchikov is the elected chair of the Kungurskii district zemstvo administration. Thus, they are all representatives of the very best elements of the local population. The present bishop of Perm, His Grace Palladii, is also in complete sympathy with the sentiments expressed above.

The deputation intends to deliver its petition in person to His Eminence Metropolitan Antonii, senior member of the Holy Synod, and to the Over-Procurator of the Synod.

The presence of the Prelate Stefan's relics in Moscow, where his great deeds of the spirit are but little known to the public at large and where there are so many other sacred objects besides, cannot possess the same significance that their presence would in Perm, which is connected with the name of the Prelate and where the great services he has rendered and the prayers he has passed on to God are so popular. Given the decline in the belief in God observed among certain strata of the population, the translation to Perm of the holy relics of this prominent champion and spreader of Orthodoxy would now be of particular importance and timeliness – as a means for the strengthening of the Orthodox faith in the hearts of the wavering and the indifferent, and for setting deluded sectarians and those of other faiths along the path of truth. With regard to this particular point, it bears mentioning that the deputation includes the merchant E. F. Permiakov, an Old Believer from birth who seeks only the true path to salvation. Permiakov enjoys great influence among the Old Believers and expresses his firm conviction that the transfer of the relics of the Prelate Stefan to Perm would be of tremendous value to the cause of converting the Old Believers to the Orthodox faith.

I consider it my duty to inform Your Most High Excellency of the above, with the most respectful request that Your Most High Excellency may see fit to render assistance toward a favorable resolution of the question of transferring the holy relics of the Prelate Stefan to the city of Perm.

I ask that Your Most High Excellency remain assured of my deep respect and devotion to You,

Your humble servant,

A. Bolotov

A Most Humble Petition, from 12,019 residents of the city of Perm and Perm province to the Most Holy Governing Synod[8]

After he arrived in Moscow on church business in the winter of 1396, the Prelate Stefan, Enlightener of the Perm lands and Bishop of Great

Perm, fell ill, exhausted from his lengthy labors and trials, and there he died peacefully on 26 April of that same year. The Prelate Stefan was buried in the Church of the Savior in the Pines, inside the holy Moscow Kremlin, where the Prelate's holy relics now lie in repose, along the north wall of the church.

From the very first days following the blessed passing of the Prelate Stefan, the grief of the orphaned children of the Perm lands was indescribable. Across the years and centuries that followed, moved by deep reverence for the great Prelate, who cast the light of Christian faith upon the pagan inhabitants of the Perm region who had hitherto wandered in darkness, the church of Perm had always desired to possess for itself the saintly remains of its heavenly protector and prayerful intercessor. But, to the continued great sorrow of the people, the pious wishes of the faithful have not yet come to pass. Only in 1849, by order of the Holy Synod, was the crozier alone of the Prelate Stefan transferred from the Supral'skii monastery in the Diocese of Lithuania to be housed in the cathedral church of Perm.

The Prelate Stefan is famed as one of the preeminent local apostles of the Christian faith, and therefore it is natural and fully understandable that the residents of the Perm lands should desire to be in close proximity to the Prelate through the pious veneration of his saintly relics. As the city of Perm is the heart of the region, it is most proper, right, and fitting that the precious relics of the Prelate Stefan be housed here, for though Perm is a relatively young city, it has already been deemed worthy by the supreme church authorities to serve as the repository of the Prelate Stefan's episcopal crozier.

Especially now in this present day, amidst the widespread wavering of minds and the breakdown of morals, it is of the utmost importance to desire, strive, and pray that the apostolic spirit be strong in the pastors of the Perm lands, that they fortify themselves, and thereby the entire flock of the Prelate Stefan, with the same faith, the same zeal for the Lord God, and the same courage by which the Prelate himself was known. May the shepherds and their figurative sheep alike emulate the model of virtues set by their glorious First Teacher and receive his timely assistance as they strive to achieve them. If it be God's will to grant the desires of the citizens of Perm and the entire Perm nation, then pastors for all of the vast Perm lands will be nurtured here at the relics of this first teacher; pastors will prepare themselves at his saintly shrine to take up the great cause of continuing the service of Saint Stefan; the suffering and the burdened will flood here to this shrine for mercy, help, and comfort. Even today, with modern modes of rapid transportation, Moscow, the repository of the Prelate Stefan's sainted relics, lies far distant from the site of his legacy and the apostolic deeds that he and his close circle of saintly imitators performed. Thus, only a relatively few fortunate ones from the Perm region are afforded the opportunity to venerate the Prelate at the site of his earthly repose.

Glory to God, wondrous in His saints, that now the inhabitants of the Perm lands, moved since ancient times by the one immutable desire to venerate the Prelate's relics on their native soil, piously, openly, and with full ceremony, have, through their representatives, most humbly petitioned the Most Holy Governing Synod for permission to transfer the holy relics of Saint Stefan of Great Perm from the city of Moscow to the city of Perm, with the full honor and glory due to Sacred Objects.

Therefore we now commend to the pastoral care of the Holy Synod our new and humble petition for the most speedy resolution of this our cherished request, in full faith and steadfast hope that granting this request will result in great joy and happiness for the one million inhabitants of the northern Perm region and neighboring Siberia and in blessing and prayerful comfort for our God-protected city that bears the name by which the entire vast region was known in the Prelate's day and where the Prelate performed his apostolic deeds. May his holy relics shine forth in the cathedral church of Perm, whose main winter chapel is consecrated in the name of the Prelate Stefan.

[230 pages follow with 12,019 signatures]

---

*Excerpt from the decision of the Holy Synod
of 3 December 1909, no. 9785*[9]

At the order of HIS IMPERIAL MAJESTY, the Holy Governing Synod heard the case of the petition from the citizens of Perm and Ust-

Sysol'sk concerning the transfer of the holy relics of the Prelate Stefan of Great Perm from the Church of the Savior in the Pines in the Moscow Kremlin.

SO ORDERED: On 26 April of this year, Prince Sergei L'vov, Pavel Zhirnov, and others, eleven individuals in all, requested by telegram that the Over-Procurator of the Holy Synod relay to HIS IMPERIAL MAJESTY AND SOVEREIGN EMPEROR the "warm and cherished desire" of the people of Perm to transfer the holy relics of Saint Stefan, the enlightener and first bishop of the Perm region, from their present site in the Church of the Savior in the Pines in the Moscow Kremlin to Perm. On 1 May of this year, the contents of this telegram were brought to the attention of the SOVEREIGN EMPEROR by the Over-Procurator, whereupon HIS IMPERIAL MAJESTY saw fit to regard the petition favorably, though without any final decision on the matter. On 13 May of this year, the Over-Procurator wrote in confidence to His Grace the Metropolitan of Moscow (letter no. 73) and His Grace the Bishop of Perm (letter no. 74), and on 23 May of this year to Archpriest Ianyshev, Father Confessor to THEIR IMPERIAL MAJESTIES (letter no. 77), requesting their opinions on the aforementioned petition from the citizens of Perm. Upon receipt of these opinions, the petition in question was once again relayed to the SOVEREIGN EMPEROR, whereupon it pleased HIS IMPERIAL MAJESTY to command most graciously that the Holy Synod convene and discuss, on the basis of the opinions received and other materials, the proposal to transfer the saintly remains of the Prelate Stefan of Great Perm from Moscow to Perm, and most humbly submit an official memorandum on this present matter for the consideration of HIS HIGHNESS at the upcoming winter session of the Holy Synod.

On 6 July of this year, in fulfillment of HIS HIGHNESS's will and judging it necessary to have accurate information concerning the question at hand prior to making a final decision in the matter of this present petition, the Holy Synod instructed (resolution no. 5514) His Grace the Metropolitan of Moscow to conduct a full investigation at the Church of the Savior in the Pines, with the participation of Archpriest Ivantsov, ecclesiastical superintendent of the Moscow palace churches and cathedrals; Archpriest Aleksandr Voskresenskii of the Cathedral of the Transfigured Savior in Perm; and Prince Sergei L'vov, proprietor of the

Pozhevskii ironworks in Solikamskii district, and charged the commission to present a report on their findings to the Holy Synod.

On 29 July of this year, in fulfillment of these instructions, His Grace Metropolitan Vladimir submitted to the Holy Synod a report on the investigation performed (no. 298). From this report it was ascertained that the investigation consisted of removing the gravestone and examining the earth beneath to a depth of more than seven feet. There, near the southwestern corner of the excavation, human bones and portions of a shattered skull were discovered; although the bones had been laid there in a certain order, they did not constitute a human skeleton, but rather a "pile of bones in the shape of a square." Alongside this pile of bones lay some rusted iron clamps, four small human bones, and tiny pieces of rotted wood so decayed that it "crumbled into dust at the first touch." Further examination of the aforementioned "pile of bones and the entire area beneath the gravestone at bone-level and somewhat below revealed that several other burials had been performed here as well, and that aside from the pile in question no discernible order could be ascertained. In all, within a space no greater than the dimensions of the gravestone above, there were discovered: 2 complete skulls, 5 incomplete skulls and as many as 40 skull fragments, 25 rib fragments, 36 arm and leg bones, of which only two leg bones were complete, 9 incomplete jawbones, some of which still contained teeth, 17 scapulas and hip-bones, more than 100 various small bone fragments, and a great number of bone fragments so small that they proved difficult to count. Despite such an abundance of bones, there is no basis to conclude that they constitute a complete skeleton, since, for example, the number of vertebrae and other vertebral bones discovered were too few." Moreover, it bears mention that "no cross was found, nor a gospel, nor any sort of icon, nor anything at all which might belong to a set of clerical vestments." Upon conclusion of the examination, all the bones discovered were laid in a small wooden coffin covered in white brocade and sealed with the wax seal of the High Savior Cathedral of the Moscow palace; the coffin was lowered into the very site where the aforementioned bones had lain prior to the investigation.

Before the Synod received the report submitted by His Grace the Metropolitan of Moscow, and especially afterwards, the Holy Synod began receiving petitions from the residents of Perm concerning the transfer of the saintly relics of the Prelate Stefan to Perm. Similar petitions continued to be submitted to the Over-Procurator of the Synod. Thus, on 15 June of this year, a petition was presented to the Holy Synod on behalf of the "people of Perm," signed by the aforementioned Prince L'vov, honored hereditary citizen Zhirnov, and others, eight signatures in all. On 1 September, the chairman of the Perm city duma presented to the Holy Synod a petition on behalf of the "residents of the city of Perm and Perm province," to which were appended 12,019 signatures. On 5 September, the Perm provincial zemstvo administration submitted for the Holy Synod's consideration a resolution approved by the Perm provincial zemstvo, dated 13 August of this year, with the same request. In a letter to the Over-Procurator dated 31 August (no. 793), the governor of Perm reported on the especially deep reverence that the masses of the Perm region feel for the Prelate Stefan and the general rejoicing with which they would greet news of the proposed transfer of his holy relics to Perm. The governor asked that the abovementioned petition from the residents of Perm receive favorable attention. Furthermore, in a letter of 30 May of this year (no. 11,736) Minister of the Interior P. A. Stolypin, also judging this petition worthy of full attention, requested that the Over-Procurator assist in the favorable resolution of this matter in the Holy Synod and inform him of the outcome.

In addition to those from the residents of Perm province, a series of petitions was received from the residents of Ust-Sysolsk, Vologda province, concerning the transfer of the Prelate Stefan's saintly relics to their city, in view of the fact that the Prelate Stefan was the enlightener of the Zyrians who inhabit Ustsysolskii and Iarenskii districts in Vologda province, which districts constituted ancient Perm and from whence the Prelate Stefan received the appellation "Stefan of Perm." These petitions maintained that the present city of Perm has no ties whatsoever to the apostolic acts of the Prelate Stefan and, furthermore, that the Prelate Stefan had never even set foot within the borders of what is today Perm province. The governor of Vologda presented the Over-Procurator with a resolution from the Ust-Sysolsk city duma dated 29 July of this year concerning the transfer of the relics of the Prelate Stefan, Enlightener of the Zyrians, to the city of Ust-Sysolsk. For his part, the governor of Vologda considers that this transfer would undoubtedly elevate the religious spirit of the region, which has wavered in recent times, owing to the presence of a large contingent of political exiles banished from the central provinces of the Empire. On the basis of similar petitions that he has received, His Grace the Bishop of Vologda reports that if, following the examination of the relics, the Holy Synod should see fit to allow their transfer, then in all fairness and in accordance with the wishes of God's Saint himself, they ought to be transferred to the site of ancient Perm, the very place where the Prelate carried out his labors, and not to the present-day city of Perm, which lies beyond the Kama River, a region in which the Prelate himself never set foot. Thereafter, on 4 November of this year, the Over-Procurator forwarded to the Holy Synod a letter passed on to him by the Chair of the Council of Ministers on behalf of Stefan Klochkov, a Member of the State Duma, petitioning also for the transfer of the relics of the Prelate Stefan of Perm from Moscow to the city of Ust-Sysolsk.

Having discussed the circumstances of this present case, the Holy Synod finds that according to the chronicle accounts and the details in the life of the Prelate Stefan compiled by the monk Epifanii, a contemporary of the Prelate and an eyewitness to his final moments, Saint Stefan passed away on 26 April 1396 in Moscow, whereupon his body was buried "in the monastery of the Holy Savior, along the left wall of the stone church." (Life of Stefan published by the Archeographical Commission, 1897, p. 86) – that is, inside the present-day Church of the Savior in the Pines, in the Kremlin, close to the northern wall. Following the Prelate Stefan's elevation to the ranks of the saints by the Moscow Church Council of 1549, tradition holds that his saintly relics remained open for veneration until the beginning of the seventeenth century, at which time they were concealed. As far as the circumstances surrounding this subsequent interment and where precisely the holy relics were buried this second time (whether in the place mentioned by the monk Epifanii or in another part of the church), no historical evidence survives.

In view of this, and since the city of Moscow and its cathedrals and churches have suffered such terrible misfortunes over the past three centuries (for example, the onslaught of the French in 1812), and since the Church of the Savior in the Pines has itself undergone numerous repairs and renovations over the course of its centuries-old existence, it is difficult to determine with certainty the actual site of the Prelate Stefan's interment. Further, since the report of the examination reveals the presence of bones from the skeletons of numerous individuals, the Holy Synod cannot ascertain with firm conviction whether the human bones found during the examination of the Prelate Stefan's supposed burial site are in fact the saintly remains of the Prelate Stefan of Perm, Enlightener of the Zyrians. Therefore, the Holy Synod does not consider it possible to grant its blessing to the translation of these bones to Ust-Sysolsk, the site of the Prelate Stefan's apostolic deeds, nor to the city of Perm, as requested by the residents of that city. Consequently, the Holy Synod resolves: that the Over-Procurator most humbly relay this conclusion to HIS IMPERIAL MAJESTY AND SOVEREIGN EMPEROR, that a copy of this decision be delivered to the Chancellery of the Over-Procurator, and that the case be remanded to the Chancellery.

21 December 1909
P. I. Ispolatov, over-secretary of the Holy Synod
N. V. Numerov, secretary of the Holy Synod

NOTES

1. RGIA, f. 797, op. 79, otd. 2, st. 3, d. 173, ll. 25–27 (A. Nikol'skii, archivist of the Holy Synod, to S. M. Lukianov, over-procurator of the Holy Synod, 24 June 1909).

2. RGIA, f. 797, op. 79, otd. 2, st. 3, d. 173, ll. 28–30 (Archpriest I. L. Ianyshev to S. M. Lukianov, 31 May 1909).

3. Gail Lenhoff, "The Notion of 'Uncorrupted Relics' in Early Russian Culture," in *Slavic Cultures in the Middle Ages*, ed. Boris Gasparov and Olga Raevsky-Hughes. *California Slavic Studies* 16 (Berkeley: University of California Press, 1993), 252–75.

4. RGIA, f. 797, op. 79, otd. 2, st. 3, g. 1909, d. 173, ll. 8–10.

5. RGIA, f. 797, op. 79, otd. 2, st. 3, g. 1909, d. 173, ll. 24–25.

6. These references to specific letters and resolutions are present in the archival documents.

7. RGIA, f. 797, op. 79, otd. 2, st. 3, d. 173, ll. 19–20.

8. RGIA, f. 796, op. 190, otd. 6, st. 3, d. 282, ll. 1–10b.

9. RGIA, f. 797, op. 79, otd. 2, st. 3, d. 173, ll. 46–49.

SUGGESTED READINGS

Brown, Peter. *The Cult of the Saints: Its Rise and Function in Latin Christianity*. Chicago: University of Chicago Press, 1982.

Freeze, Gregory L. "Subversive Piety: Religion and the Political Crisis in Late Imperial Russia." *The Journal of Modern History* 68 (1996): 308–50.

Greene, Robert H. *Bodies like Bright Stars: Saints and Relics in Orthodox Russia*. DeKalb: Northern Illinois University Press, 2010.

Shevzov, Vera. *Russian Orthodoxy on the Eve of Revolution*. Oxford: Oxford University Press, 2003.

Worobec, Christine D. "Miraculous Healings." In *Sacred Stories: Religion and Spirituality in Modern Russian Culture*, ed. Mark D. Steinberg and Heather J. Coleman, 22–43. Bloomington: Indiana University Press, 2007.

FIFTEEN

Dechristianization in Holy Rus? Religious Observance in Vladimir Diocese, 1900–1913

Gregory L. Freeze

COMPARED TO FRENCH AND ENGLISH HISTORIOGRAPHY, scholarship on Russian religious life has yet to map out the patterns of religious observance. The fundamental question concerns the scale of "dechristianization" before the 1917 revolution: did believers abandon the faith, cease attending church, and omit rituals and sacraments (such as confession and communion)? Did literacy and secular mass culture, industrialization and migrant labor, and radical propaganda undermine religious life? Did proselytizing by other confessions (especially after 1905) lead to large-scale "apostasy"? One place to look for answers is the documentation amassed by the church – the reports and statistics on religious observance that the church compiled each year. From the church's perspective, was religious life waning on the eve of the 1917 revolution?

Given the heterogeneity of this vast empire and the sheer volume of the data, it is essential to focus on a single diocese – in this case, Vladimir. An old religious heartland, Vladimir remained a bastion of Orthodoxy, claiming 1.6 million adherents (98 percent of the province in 1901).[1] Here the church had a strong institutional base: the bishop had two vicar-bishops and 69 local deans (*blagochinnye*) to help govern the dense network of monasteries, clergy, and parishes. But the church faced growing challenges in Vladimir – rapid industrialization, cultural change, revolutionary agitation, and proselytization by other confessions (especially Old Believers and sectarians).

The diocese was unquestionably undergoing religious change: the annual report (*otchet*)[2] for 1900 expressed confidence about popular religiosity, but expressed growing anxiety during the revolution of 1905–1907 and afterward. Such fears pervaded the bishop's private correspondence and found its way into the official report for 1906. Even after the regime suppressed the revolution, the bishop complained that "the spirit of the time of 1905–1907" had left a lasting imprint. The reports emphasized the growth of indifference (especially among the young) and, simultaneously, rising demands from parishioners (especially, for control of parish finances). Gone was the myth of the "pious, simple" folk: the clergy now stressed the differences in generation and gender (with piety stronger among the elderly and women) and variations across the diocese. The data on confession and communion map this heterogeneity, showing the gender gap and observance rates in different parts of the diocese. Although observance far exceeded that in Western Europe,[3] the clergy nonetheless had cause for concern, especially in areas subject to industrialization and to challenges from the Old Belief and sects.

Such concerns led diocesan authorities to establish a blue-ribbon commission to study the problem and make specific recommendations. The commission report in July 1913 provides a candid assessment of the status of Orthodoxy and describes the clergy's strategy on ways to combat indifference and proselytization by other confessions. Among other things, the commission supported parish reform as a way to revitalize popular piety and engagement in the church. The clergy were ambivalent about empowering parishioners (fearing that they would reduce support for the clergy and the seminary), but most wanted to reinvigorate the parish, partly by enhancing its power, partly by mobilizing the faithful (hence the proposal for "circles of zealots"). The diocesan congress endorsed the report but went further, suggesting that the clergy be funded by a state salary in lieu of the traditional land allotment and gratuities. The cautious Archbishop Nikolai was generally supportive, but ignored the salary proposal – given the anti-church sentiment in the Fourth State Duma (1912–17).

The reports, statistics, and commission report provide, from the clergy's perspective, a graphic portrait of religious life and how it changed after the revolution of 1905–1907. Blithe assumptions about the "simple, pious" folk were no more; the clergy recognized that, even if overwhelmingly observant, the flock now included a larger number of the indifferent unbelievers and disaffected believers. At the same time, these documents suggest a church that was anything but moribund; they reflect not only changes in popular religious life but also the clergy's determination to defend Orthodoxy and combat negative influences – even at the risk of empowering the laity and harming their own vital interests.

Annual Report for 1900[4]

The activities of the consistory, deans, and deans' councils were very successful.[5] Life in the monasteries was satisfactory. Insofar as their resources permit, monasteries have contributed to the cause of popular education; many of them have established parish-church schools at the monasteries' own expense.[6] Churches in the diocese, thanks to the efforts of the parishioners, in the overwhelming majority of cases are splendid, with sufficient church utensils and sacristy. Each year the libraries at the churches add books of a spiritual and edificatory content. In the current year the clergy were dutiful in performing their direct responsibilities and in providing spiritual guidance *(uchitel'stvo)* in all its forms; nor was their morality a cause for criticism. The clergy's material support, which drew on private contributions, was satisfactory. The conditions in parishes with extremely limited means for supporting the clergy have improved through the allocation of state assistance.[7] The clergy's relationship to their parishioners was proper and peaceful. The moral-religious condition of the flock was also satisfactory; that was mainly due to the fact that the population was gradually absorbing the moral principles transmitted in sermons from the pulpit of the church, in talks outside of church services, in schools, and so forth. Under the influence of these factors, there were signs of weakening of the schism *(raskol)*,[8] which in time could ease the burden of the pastors in the cause of returning those who have strayed from the bosom of the Orthodox Church.

Letter from Bishop Nikon (Sofiiskii) of Vladimir to Metropolitan Flavian (Gorodetskii) of Kiev (21 December 1905)[9]

These are hard times. In the coming new year, may the Lord change things for the better! In Vladimir diocese, it is difficult to make sense of popular tendencies: some preach the most liberal teachings or become enthralled by those who preach such things; others firmly adhere to the old order and do not want to hear about freedom – even in the spirit of the manifesto of 17 October. In Orekhovo, a large factory village, the youth take off their crosses and shoot them; the deceased are buried with red flags and songs instead of the traditional church ceremony conducted by a priest. In some parts of the diocese, parishioners compile resolutions to reduce, to the most insignificant amounts, the gratuities paid to the local clergy [for performing religious rites];[10] they are also abolishing collections in kind from the parishioners. Significantly, as one priest reported to me on 16 December, in some places seminarians are inciting the parishioners to do this. In several parishes the church elders[11] have categorically refused to pay the deans the levies on parish churches to cover general diocesan needs – some on their own initiative, others under pressure from the parishioners. If the seminary is reformed and made into a general educational institution, especially if the [upper] theology level is removed,[12] then not a single church elder will give a kopek for a seminary reformed in that way. Then many children of the clergy will be deprived of that education the current seminary now provides.

Report of Vladimir Diocese for 1906[13]

After reiterating the traditional view that the situation in the diocese is generally satisfactory, the Archbishop Nikolai (Nalimov)[14] adds this critical caveat:

It is impossible to conceal the fact that various shortcomings are evident in the moral life of the flock in Vladimir. These include, for example, the indifference of some Orthodox (especially in factory areas) to attending the divine churches and to performing the Christian duty of confession and holy communion; instead, they spend this time on Sundays and holidays on debauchery and the excessive use of alcohol; [there is also] the use of foul language; discord in families. . . . [sic] In general, the people treat the clergy with due respect and, very often, with true devotion and obedience; however, during the upheavals of late (thanks to the influence of some newspapers, various brochures, and proclamations – especially among the factory youth), a disdainful attitude toward the clergy has become evident.

Annual Report for 1908[15]

Faith and piety among the population have, in general, remained firm; the older generation and women unfailingly observe the mandates behest of their forebears and show a love for church prayers. The flock expresses its religious-moral attitude by zealously attending divine churches and homilies given outside of church services; it is also manifested in the endeavors to support special holiday services and in donations to meet the needs of churches, parish staffs, and schools. . . .

In times of public calamity or joy, at the request of the parishioners, the clergy take the holy icons from the churches to the villages and to the fields, where they perform prayer services with the consecration of water; they walk around the fields and settlements, sprinkling holy water on homes, fields, and livestock. In general, the religious character of the life of the population gives one the right to conclude that the people have a clear consciousness of the need to live in the closest possible unity with the Orthodox Church; that Orthodoxy remains for the people its foundation and the official state religion. There were no striking instances of apostasy from the Orthodox faith in 1908. The schism, which did not increase numerically, has not been so stubborn of late. It is mainly the older generation that adheres to the schism; the young generation shows an indifference to the faith of their forefathers. . . .

According to the testimony of some deans in the diocese, however, the spirit of 1905–1907 – which disturbed the public and popular life of our fatherland – has even had an impact on parish church life. The waves of a liberal character (which easily infect all who are prone to being mindlessly swept away by every novel teaching) have significantly shaken the foundations of parish church life established over the centuries. This is partly expressed in religious and political freethinking, in a disdainful attitude toward religion, the church, and its sacraments, and in total indifference. In some places the laity has exhibited dissatisfaction with the existing order of parish life and has begun to complain about the formalism and alienation of the clergy from the flock, but first and foremost about the laity's lack of rights in organizing parish-church life. Some (though not many) deans have noted a growing indifference to attending sacred churches, to ensuring the material splendor of the church, and to performing the Christian duty [of confession and communion]. Those [who neglect confession and communion] amount to 77,102 for the entire diocese. The violation of fasts, the time spent in drunkenness, the debauchery on holidays, foul language, and dissipation have become ordinary phenomena; much time and work is demanded of the pastors to counteract these foibles, if only partly. The young generation is especially guilty in this respect. Leading a libertine, uncontrolled life much of the year in factories, industrial plants, and other enterprises using migrant labor, often far removed from divine churches, the youth becomes alien to good behavior and does not live in accordance with the rules and norms of the church. Indicative of the degradation of the morality of the youth (especially in areas with factories and industrial plants) is an arrogant conceit, rudeness even in the relationship to their own parents, the consumption of spirits and gambling for money at cards (even during regular working hours), a fondness for fashion, and debauchery (fostered by the involuntary closeness of both sexes at the factories and their casual relations, especially in the cramped housing for workers). Returning home with such moral shortcomings, here too this [younger] generation infects their peers with highly undesirable qualities.

The population of the diocese in general treats the clergy with due respect and very often with true devotion, although some deans have noticed a cooling of parishioners toward the material needs of the clergy and an attempt to worsen the material condition of the clergy by violating the age-old order for collecting rye donations and by reducing the payments for rites. Such a negative disposition toward the clergy and their needs is particularly striking (from the entire diocese) in several villages in the fourth deanery of Iur'ev-Pol'skii district. The villages of this deanery (Chislovskie Gorodishcha, Iurkovo, Skomovo, and Belianitsina) have a significant number who belong to rationalist sects, as people familiar with the teachings of [Leo] Tolstoi[16] and harmful theological literature. On the one hand, the stern measures taken by civil authorities against the hooligan excesses of the youth vis-à-vis the clergy had a sobering effect on the population; on the other hand, this [hooliganism] gives rise to undesirable attitudes toward the clergy among that part of their flock that threatens to repudiate the traditional method of material support for the parish clergy. Therefore the clergy in some villages of this deanery, oppressed on the one hand by material need and on the other by the rudeness of the people, of late have demonstrated a strong urge to relocate to other parishes. Hence in the last two to three years fully half of the former staff of the clergy in this district has been replaced by new staff members.

Annual Report for 1910: Regional Variations[17]

1. The districts of Suzdal, Iurev-Polskii, Aleksandrov, Pereslavl-Zalesskii, and parts of Kovrov and Vladimir districts

The first group of the population is entirely Orthodox, zealously attends the divine churches on all holidays, exhibits a profound belief in God, and reveres the sacraments and institutions of the Orthodox Church. Everyone performs the Christian duty of confession and communion each year, while the elderly and especially women do so during all the fasts; some are so pious that they also make confession and receive communion several times during the year (as they say, "not going over six weeks" – i.e., they cleanse their conscience and receive holy communion every six weeks). Failure to perform the duty of confession and holy communion occurs only because of absence and because it is impossible to perform the Christian duty where they have gone.

2. Industrial areas: Pokrov and Shuia Districts

The zeal of the Orthodox population with respect to church services and the sacraments is not so high in those places where the population, while Orthodox, resides in a factory area. Amidst the inhabitants of factory areas there are many migrants who are alien to the indigenous population in terms of moral foundations and sometimes with respect to their faith. In the midst of the factory workers there are often agitators who have read some booklets that repudiate God, the civil and family order, and private property. Youth in the factories, who are not sufficiently developed and morally sound, constitute a fertile soil for the activity of such people. The dean of the town of Shuia, Archpriest Nesmeianov, in his report about the dark sides of recent years (1905–1906), reports – against a bright background of the religious-moral life of Orthodox parishioners – that "young people who work in factories, having given into the influence of propagandists and having read fashionable books and brochures with an atheist bent, have acquired a negative attitude toward the faith and the holy church, and in general have come to neglect their religious duties." The dean of the village of Orekho (a center of factory life), Feodor Zagorskii, points out that "among the young factory population the moral ills lead to indifference toward the holy church, disrespect for elders, indecent foul language, moral dissoluteness, and drunkenness." The dean of the first ward of Shuia district, the priest Nikolai Shirokogorov, in referring to such a moral condition of the factory youth, with deep regret notes that for purposes of exerting moral influence on the factory youth, for purposes of correcting it, it is difficult for the clergy to undertake things, for the youth reacts with distrust and sometimes even with hatred.

Given what is apparently the dismal situation described by deans Zagorskii, Nesmeianov, and Shirokogorov, some consolation is afforded by the reports from the deans of the cities of Murom, Melenki, and Iurev-Polskii. They write that "some of the instability in religious beliefs, which arose during the so-called revolutionary years of 1905–1906, is beginning like fumes to dissipate, and the student youth has begun to attend the divine churches more willingly" (Dean Bobrov); "the epidemic of social insanity has begun to weaken significantly" (Dean

Florinskii); "parishioners who experienced a political internal disorder show signs of a rise in piety" (Dean Znamenskii); "the piety of the parishioners, which weakened during the past popular disturbances, is now beginning to grow stronger" (Dean of the first ward in Vladimir district).

3. Areas with Old Believer and sectarian influences: the districts of Gorokhovets and Melenki, and parts of Vladimir and Pokrov districts

The Orthodox population, who live alongside the Old Believers and sectarians and who interact with them in secular matters, cannot always remain alien to the influence of either of these in matters pertaining to religion. Although instances of defection from Orthodoxy to the Old Belief and to sectarianism are very rare (declarations about leaving the church[18] come from those Orthodox believers who, for many years, were not really members of the Orthodox Church). But one cannot deny that Old Believers and sectarians (especially if they predominate) have an influence on the Orthodox population – in terms of undermining a zeal for the divine church, for church services, and for cleansing one's conscience through the sacraments of confession and communion. This is primarily seen in those areas where the majority of the population are schismatics who do not accept any sacraments or rites and who are fanatics with regard to the Orthodox Church.

Confession and Communion Statistics for 1910 (in percent)

AREA[1]	City/ Rural[2]	Both Confession & Communion		Communion Only[3]		Neither: Excused Absence[4]		Neither: Lack of Zeal[5]	
		M	F	M	F	M	F	M	F
Kirzhach	City	95.2	96.3	0.0	0.0	4.8	3.7	0.0	0.0
Pereslavl	Rural	94.3	97.4	0.0	0.0	5.5	2.5	0.2	0.0
Aleksandrov	Rural	93.6	95.8	0.0	0.0	5.6	4.1	0.8	0.1
Pokrov	City	93.5	96.6	0.0	0.0	5.8	3.3	0.8	0.1
Sudogda	City	92.7	95.2	0.0	0.0	5.5	3.3	1.8	1.5
Pokrov	Rural	90.0	96.4	0.0	0.0	8.9	3.3	1.1	0.3

Dechristianization in Holy Rus? 217

AREA[1]	City/Rural[2]	Both Confession & Communion		Communion Only[3]		Neither: Excused Absence[4]		Neither: Lack of Zeal[5]	
		M	F	M	F	M	F	M	F
Suzdal	Rural	89.4	93.2	0.0	0.0	8.4	6.1	2.2	0.7
Aleksandrov	City	89.2	89.9	0.0	0.0	10.7	10.1	0.1	0.0
Kovrov	City	87.6	91.5	0.0	0.0	12.4	8.5	0.0	0.0
Shuia	Rural	87.0	92.0	0.7	0.6	7.4	4.8	4.9	2.7
Ivanovo	City	87.0	91.9	0.2	0.2	5.1	3.3	7.7	4.6
Iurev-Polskii	Rural	86.8	91.6	0.0	0.2	12.2	8.0	1.1	0.2
Suzdal	City	86.3	94.3	0.0	0.0	10.6	5.1	3.1	0.6
Vladimir	Rural	84.5	91.8	0.1	0.0	12.2	6.5	3.3	1.7
Viazniki	Rural	81.9	90.9	0.0	0.0	13.6	6.4	4.5	2.7
Kovrov	Rural	81.8	89.9	1.3	1.3	12.1	6.3	4.8	2.5
Diocesan Average		81.0	88.1	0.2	0.2	11.8	6.5	7.1	5.3
Shuia	City	80.6	89.3	0.0	0.0	8.2	4.3	11.2	6.4
Vladimir	City	80.2	86.5	0.0	0.0	13.4	8.6	6.4	4.9
Melenki	City	78.7	86.2	0.0	0.8	9.1	5.0	12.1	8.0
Murom	Rural	78.0	88.1	0.0	0.0	15.2	6.8	6.8	5.1
Sudogda	Rural	75.8	84.6	0.1	0.1	12.5	6.9	11.6	8.4
Iurev-Polskii	City	75.3	84.0	0.0	0.0	24.0	15.8	0.8	0.3
Murom	City	74.7	86.9	0.0	0.0	23.8	12.4	1.5	0.7
Viazniki	City	73.1	83.8	0.0	0.0	26.6	16.2	0.3	0.1
Gorokhovets	Rural	62.1	72.6	0.1	0.1	17.8	9.1	20.1	18.2
Melenki	Rural	60.8	70.2	0.1	0.3	13.2	7.4	25.8	22.1
Gorokhovets	City	57.6	66.3	0.0	0.0	16.0	9.5	26.5	24.2
Pereslavl	City	40.9	51.9	0.0	0.0	54.0	46.9	5.0	1.2

Source: RGIA, f. 797, op. 72, otd. 2, st. 3, d. 403, ll. 97–100.
Notes:
The data apply only to those over age 7; children under that age were not expected to observe these sacraments.
1. Ranked by male percentage for performing both confession and communion.
2. The report mirrored secular administration, dividing units into "cities" (*goroda*) and rural districts (*uezda*).
3. Believers who had committed great mortal sins or violated the rules of Lent might be denied Holy Communion; from the mid-nineteenth century, the Synod had strongly discouraged such semi-observance, emphasizing the salutary importance of communion.
4. Parishioners who were away or ill had a valid excuse for missing confession and communion.
5. Such negligence was deemed to be due to "lack of zeal" (*po neradeniiu*).

Report of the Commission on Raising the Religious and Moral Condition of the Population of Vladimir Diocese (1913)[19]

The waves of the "liberation movement" of 1905–1906 also reached the rural population, and life in the countryside then reflected a lot of the senseless willfulness and unbridled passion. To judge from the pastors' observations of popular life, one cannot say that these waves have now disappeared. To be sure, compared to the explosive times we experienced earlier, there is now tranquility. However, among the rural and factory population, periodically there still appear false teachers; they continue to incite people by disseminating illegal literature, by distributing free brochures and leaflets with anti-religious, socialist, sectarian, and even immoral content. All this plainly aims to undermine the foundations of faith and morality in popular life, to sunder the ties between parishioners and pastors and the trust in them. Our people, who have not been brought to reason by the sad lessons of the recent past, are not averse to reading the leaflets and brochures that promise to bestow every possible kind of blessing without the church. In particular, this is of interest to the contemporary peasant youth and especially those who leave to work in enterprises as migrant laborers; there, through direct contact with the false benefactors of popular well-being, they are naturally captivated by their errors. Having been infected by this alien culture, this semi-literate youth – upon their return home – begin to teach all this to the village. And now in many parishes, according to reports of our clergy, the people are becoming indifferent to the Holy Church; in their lives one sees a violation of the age-old foundations of the holy faith and piety – by failing to perform the Christian duty of confession and communion, to visit the divine church, to pray during workdays, to hold in some places prayer services in remembrance of the dead, and to show the earlier veneration of sacred images. On the contrary, one sometimes sees – especially among the young – a desecration of all that is holy, all that is precious to an Orthodox heart. With regard to the clergy, in some places the people are extremely coarse, insolent, and disrespectful; some behave in a provocative manner in the presence of priests. As for the moral life, one notes an extreme willfulness of the youth; a disrespectful attitude toward their elders and parents; a desire to get rich by easy, illegal means; an extreme hatred of the propertied classes; drunkenness (which of late has reached horrifying dimensions); licentiousness; and so forth.

Hence, migrant labor, illegal literature, the propaganda of rationalist sects (the Baptists, the Baptist faith, the main premise of which holds that "salvation [is] by faith – regardless of deeds"), drunkenness (with a large-scale distribution facilitated by a secret trade in vodka) – all this, to a significant degree, undermines the religious-moral condition of the population in this diocese.

On 27 July 1913 a special meeting of the members of this Commission (with those who met having signed below) convened on this matter in the offices of the Consistory. The only member of the Commission who did not attend was Father Nikolai Shirokogorov of Shuia, who did not come because of his pastoral duties. Having chosen from their midst the sacrist of the Cathedral, Archpriest Vladimir Valedinskii, as chairman and the diocesan missionary, Father Grigorii Orfeev as secretary, the Commission embarked on a comprehensive discussion of the religious-moral condition of the population, based on the materials compiled by the pre-congress commission representing localities in the diocese. The Commission also sought to explain the causes of the decline of faith and piety. Furthermore, the Commission made a serious attempt to devise measures that, at the present time, would be suitable for arresting a further decline in the foundations of faith and morality among the people. The Commission also focused on those means and measures of pastoral influence that were prepared at the deans' assemblies of the clergy of the diocese.[20] These were formulated into a coherent system by His Grace, Bishop Evgenii (Mertsalov) in 1911;[21] [the text] was then reviewed by the Diocesan Consistory, which on 3 August 1911 distributed this (in circular no. 13,457) to the clergy for implementation (in accordance with a resolution of His Eminence[22] dated 21 March 1911).

The Commission has recognized all the measures listed in the circular as highly desirable: (a) because they were prepared by the parish clergy itself (who knows well the contemporary ills of popular life) to revive the religious-moral life of the population of the diocese; and (b) because, to a significant degree, they make full use of the existing power of the church and the pastorate to heal the contemporary religious-moral shortcomings of parish life and because they are completely appropriate for this effort. But for its part, with the same goal of raising the religious and moral condition of the people of the diocese, the Commission finds the following measures necessary at the present time.

1. A turning of the entire Orthodox Russian people with a special prayerful appeal to the Lord God to strengthen it in the foundations of the Holy Faith and morality, as expressed in the prayer distributed by the Holy Synod (*Tserkovnye vedomosti*, 1905, no. 44).[23]

2. A model life (in all respects) of the Orthodox clergy as a necessary condition for an active religious-moral influence on the people; tireless religious-enlightenment pastoral activity among those preaching the Word of the Gospel truth, in both a timely and untimely manner, every pastor should vigilantly watch for spiritual needs that arise from time to time in his parish and act to satisfy them. Moreover, it is essential that the parishioners be as close as possible to their pastor and more frequently turn to him directly in all vital questions.

3. So that the pastors of the church are permeated by a certain spiritual attitude and transmit the healthy foundations of the Gospels and so that they can be "all things to everyone" to their contemporaries, the pastors must unfailingly rely on their spiritual experience and the strength of their lofty predecessors. In addition to a prayerful appeal to the Holy Fathers, it is necessary that they immerse themselves in the written instructions bequeathed by the church fathers.

4. One must bear in mind several things: (a) one of the barriers to the renewal of the church-social order in our people is the lack of cohesion seen everywhere among the pastors of the Orthodox Church, the dispersion [and] the lack of unified, planned religious-enlightenment work; and (b) given the varied, not-easily-resolved questions that church-social life has raised for the clergy, the Commission finds it substantially necessary and highly desirable – for an exchange of opinions about the questions of contemporary religious-philosophical thought, the religious-moral edification of the people, a good order in parish life, and so forth – to organize at the local level, on general legal foundations, pastoral assemblies [and] congresses, and thereby gradually to organize a closely unified corps of people toiling on behalf of Christ's domain.

5. Taking into account that the elementary school is the main factor in bringing religious-moral principles to the people, the Commission deems it quite necessary to petition, in the name of the Diocesan Congress, in the appropriate manner about giving the priests who teach religion a leading role in the religious-moral education of children not only in the parish church school, but also in the schools subordinate to the Ministry of Education and the zemstvo.[24] At the present, in the latter two schools the pastor teaching Orthodoxy is merely an ordinary instructor in religion.

6. In the opinion of the Commission, one of the most substantial factors in contemporary church life is the disjuncture between pastor and flock. Instead of being in close interaction and striving, under the canopy of the church, to achieve the supreme goal of our life – eternal salvation – the pastors and flock are quite far apart from one another and often appear alien to each other. The link between them often appears to be only a formality. The pastors appear only to be mere performers of church services and rites, not the spiritual leaders of their flock. The latter, for their part, are indifferent to the causes of the church and, if they do turn to the clergy, for the most part it is only because of purely external motives. Such an abnormality in the mutual relations of pastors and their flocks, which is accompanied by sad consequences for both parties, can be only overcome by a renewal of parish church life – and that is through a reorganization of the parish. It is necessary to recognize not only the parish as a territorial unit, but its significance as a church union. Only by opening broader access for parishioners to parish life is it possible to rejuvenate religious life; the participation of parishioners in parish life can bear the most diverse character and encompass its various dimensions – religious, moral, educational, and philanthropic. For this reason the Commission would send a petition, in the name of the Diocesan Congress, to the Supreme Church Authority about the earliest possible realization of the proposal to reorganize the Orthodox parishes. As a provisional measure to resuscitate parish life and to raise the religious-moral condition of the population of the diocese, the Commission finds it exceedingly useful and desirable to organize parish circles of zealots of the Holy Orthodox faith and piety. The priests should recruit the most religious, literate, and capable men and women to help

combat the various negative phenomena that are eroding the church organism. The priest should not only inform them regarding what is transpiring in the parish in its religious and moral life, but also counteract the dissemination of false ideas and beliefs and expose their groundlessness by holding conversations and by reading brochures and flysheets that the priest has approved. These aides of the priest should themselves be distinguished by devout behavior; they should assist him in the struggle against the vices that are corrupting the parish organism. Moreover, the Commission deems it timely to recommend that the diocesan clergy recruit the youthful forces from among the parishioners (i.e., young men and women) to join the parish circles; parish circles for youths led by the pastors should also be formed. The creation of such circles is a necessity at the present time; the parish circle should be in each church in the diocese.

In addition, the Commission resolved to ask the diocesan missionary, Father Grigorii Orfeev, to prepare a draft statute for the organization of a parish circle of adults as well as rules for youth circle leaders and to apprise the diocesan clergy of all this by publishing them in the diocesan gazette.

7. The Commission finds it highly useful to conduct church services on patron saint festivals in as grand and celebratory manner as possible. It is desirable that, on these days, the liturgy be conducted by the senior priest of the parish church, with the participation (if the holidays do not coincide) of neighboring priests, combined with an icon procession, so that the best preachers of the district deliver sermons at all the church services on this holiday. And, in general, the first concern of each pastor should be the majesty of church services and sacred rites, which have great importance for the Christian education of believers and for combating rationalist sectarianism (which denies external worship of God). It is necessary to encourage, in every possible way, the organization and improvement of church choirs, to introduce popular singing of church canticles, to invite parishioners who are very literate and of good morality to perform readings after church services (explaining in advance, in a comprehensible way, whatever is not easily understood).

8. Since one of the main causes of the decline of faith and morality is the alcoholism to which the peasant and factory populations (not only adults, but also children) are addicted, the Commission deems it vitally

necessary for their fellow pastors to pay attention to drunkenness (which has developed to a significant degree) and to the urgent need for an energetic struggle against this vice – through exhortations, through speaking to people known to be tipplers, and through the broad dissemination of anti-alcohol literature among the people.

9. To combat the growth of anti-religious and immoral publications, the Commission proposes to ask, in the name of the [Diocesan] Congress, the Publications Commission of the Holy Synod to provide popular parish libraries, as quickly as possible, with books and brochures of a religious-moral content that answer church and social questions of the present time. In the interim, before the works of the Publication Commission appear, the following publications are recommended to the clergy of the diocese for dissemination among the people:

> The Leaflets of the St. Petersburg Missionary Council (1,000 leaflets of 1–2 pages @ 1 ruble; 2–4 pages @ 2 rubles);
>
> publications of the Odessa St. Andrew Brotherhood (from 4 to 8 rubles per 100);
>
> publications of the journal *Kormchii* [The Helmsman] (1,000 leaflets @ 5 rubles);[25]
>
> publications of Nikol'skii, a teacher at the Tambov Ecclesiastical Seminary (100 leaflets @ 5 to 10 rubles);[26]
>
> publications of the editorial board of *Missionerskoe obozrenie* [Missionary Review] (100 leaflets for 80 kopeks; 1,000 leaflets for 7.50 rubles);
>
> the works of Archpriest Skubachevskii of Kharkov (from 3 to 5 rubles for 100 brochures).[27]

10. The Commission, finally, recognized the urgent need to petition in the appropriate manner (in the name of the Diocesan Congress) for the closing of bazaars which, in many places, are organized on Sundays; for the elimination of popular entertainment and events in electrified cinemas, circuses, etc., on the eve of Sundays and holidays in cities; and to petition for the absolute ban on work in factories and plants on holidays, since all this distracts the people, especially the young generation, from attending the churches of God.

The Commission has the honor to present these considerations, together with a circular of the Diocesan Consistory from 13 August 1911 (no. 13,457) to the Vladimir Diocesan Congress on 31 July 1913.

Chairman of the Commission: *Archpriest and Sacrist, Vladimir Valedinskii*

Members: *Priest Nikolai Preobrazhenskii (Feodorovskaia Church, city of Kovrov)*

Priest Ioann Sakharov (Blagoveshchenskii Cathedral, city of Gorokhovets)

Priest Aleksii Rozhdestvenskii (Village of Strunino)

Priest Mikhail Tikhonravov (Village of Serbilovo)

Priest Aleksandr Akipetrov, diocesan missionary

Secretary: *Priest G. Orfeev*

Resolution of the Vladimir Diocesan Congress[28]

The Congress has heard the report of the Commission on the question of raising the religious and moral condition of the population of Vladimir diocese and has judged it to have a completely solid foundation and to encompass comprehensive measures for pastoral action (aimed at healing the contemporary religious and moral ills of parish life). The Congress has ordered that these measures be fully implemented and expressed its gratitude to the members of the Commission for their work at indicating measures to raise the religious and moral condition of the population of the diocese.

["Agreed." – Archbishop Nikolai]

Deeming the material dependence of the clergy on the parish to be a cause of the conflict and antipathy between the pastors and their flocks (and thereby paralyzing the good activity of the former), the Congress unanimously expressed a wish for the earliest possible support of the clergy with a state salary.

To counteract antireligious and sectarian propaganda, the Congress deems it necessary to distribute brochures and leaflets of a religious and moral content in the largest possible quantity, and to ask the St. Alexander Nevskii Brotherhood for assistance in this matter.

["Inform the Council of the Brotherhood" – A. N. (Archbishop Nikolai)]

NOTES

1. RGIA, f. 796, op. 442, d. 2442, l. 38. Old Believers and sectarians thus constituted, at least officially, a minuscule part of the diocese: just 36,714 Old Believers and only 2,000 sectarians before 1905. RGIA f. 442, op. 442, d. 1825, l. 27, and d. 2016, ll. 48 ob.–49 ob.

2. In the mid-1840s the Synod began to require an annual report on local administration, local monasteries and clergy, and religious state of the flock. The reports improved in quality, especially in the late imperial period, becoming more detailed and incorporating the biannual reports from lower-level deans.

3. The statistics on European churches is complex but generally shows a sharp decline in observance, even to single digits in some cities. See Hugh McLeod, *Secularization in Western Europe, 1848–1914* (New York: St. Martin's Press, 2000), and the literature cited therein.

4. RGIA, f. 796, op. 442, d. 1825, ll. 49 ob.–50 ob.

5. The consistory, established by in the early eighteenth century, was an administrative board of monastic and parish clergy appointed by the bishop; it processed all cases and adopted a resolution for review and approval (or revision) by the bishop. In 1900 it consisted entirely of five members of the parish clergy (five senior archpriests); it processed 16,000 documents and adopted 3,654 resolutions (RGIA, f. 796, op. 442, d. 1825, ll. 1 ob.–2). The dean *(blagochinnyi)* was a member of the secular clergy appointed by the bishop to function as his local overseer (for ten to fifteen churches); after the mid-nineteenth century some dioceses, including Vladimir, created "deanery councils" with several local priests to advise the dean on critical matters.

6. Practical activities, such as the establishment of schools and homes for the elderly, represented a response to criticism, widespread since the 1860s, about the "parasitic uselessness" of monastic institutions.

7. Beginning in 1829, the state began to allocate small supplemental stipends to extremely poor parishes and gradually expanded such subsidies to include more and more parishes in the empire.

8. The official term for the Orthodox dissent whose adherents rejected the seventeenth-century reforms by Patriarch Nikon was *raskol* (schism); adherents were *raskol'niki* (schismatics); the dissenters themselves preferred the terms *staroobriadchestvo (old ritual)* and *staroobriadtsy* (old ritualists), often rendered as Old Belief and Old Believers in English. Note that in 1900 the bishop used the pejorative *raskol*, but by 1913 that had given way to *staroobriadchestvo*.

9. RGIA, f. 796, op. 205, d. 731, l. 1. Because of its sensitivity, the Synod placed this letter (and others) in the "secret section" of its archive.

10. The gratuities, voluntary donations for performing baptism, weddings, burials, and sundry other rites, were entirely voluntary; they constituted, however, a key part of the clergy's income – hence the concern about the decision of parishioners to reduce or even eliminate the gratuities.

11. The church elder (*tserkovnyi starosta*), established by a statute in 1808, was responsible for managing church finances and making annual payments to support diocesan institutions (above all, the system of church schools and seminaries to train the clergy's sons to become future priests).

12. The seminarians in Vladimir were at the forefront of the radical seminarian movement in 1905–1907; one of their key demands was to transform the seminary (where the curriculum was narrowly devised to train future pastors) into a general secondary school, which would give them greater opportunities for a lay career – a goal that growing numbers of them shared. Theology was the main subject in the last two years of the seminary; reformers proposed to eliminate this level and reconstitute it as a separate, specialized training for those who actually planned to enter the priesthood. See their collective petition in GAVO, f. 454, op. 3, d. 48, l. 9–9 ob. They were hardly alone in making this demand. When the Education Committee of the Synod discussed seminary reform in June 1906, one member was vociferous about the need to eliminate barriers to admission to the university: "The principal cause of disorders in the seminaries is the lack of access for seminary students to secular higher educational institutions: the protest against this usually constitutes the basis of the seminary petitions, in which everything else bears a significance that is only supplementary, often accidental and insubstantial." RGIA, f. 796, op. 187, g. 1906, d. 509, l. 21.

13. RGIA, f. 796, op. 442, d. 2136, ll. 24 ob.–25.

14. Archbishop Nikolai (Nalimov) replaced Nikon (Sofiiskii) in June 1906; he remained archbishop here until his death in July 1914. Like his predecessor, he was a widowed priest – who had taken monastic vows to rise in the hierarchy – and therefore had an intimate knowledge of parish life. He submitted this report on 1906 – his first as the archbishop of Vladimir – in early 1907.

15. RGIA, f. 796, op. 442, d. 2261, ll. 62–65 ob.

16. Count Leo Tolstoy (1828–1910), famous in world literature for classics like *Anna Karenina* and *War and Peace*, underwent a spiritual crisis in the late 1870s and came to preach a kind of Christian anarchism (which rejected the Russian Orthodox Church in favor of ascetic morality, sexual abstinence, the abolition of marriage and property rights, and pacifism). In February 1901 the church anathematized Tolstoy for his heretical teachings and has continued to spurn requests to rescind the excommunication.

17. RGIA, f. 796, op. 442, d. 2398, ll. 43 ob.–45 ob.

18. Such formal declarations only became possible after the manifesto of 17 April 1905; the overwhelming mass of declarations came from Catholics, and to a lesser extent, Muslims and Protestants.

19. GAVO, f. 556, op. 1, d. 4856, ll. 3–6 ob.

20. Deanery assemblies (*Blagochinnicheskie s"ezdy*) were meetings convened at the level of the deanery, affording parish clergy an opportunity to consult and exchange views on pastoral priorities and problems.

21. Evgenii (born Evgenii Aleksandrovich Mertsalov 1857–1920), in December 1907, was consecrated as the bishop of Murom (the second vicar-bishop in Vladimir diocese). In 1912 Bishop Evgenii was promoted to become the Iur'ev-Pol'skii bishop (the first vicar-bishop in the same diocese); he continued to serve in that position until 1917. *Pravoslavnaia entsiklopediia* 17 (Moscow: Pravoslavno-nauchnyi tsentr "Pravoslavnaia entsiklopediia," 2008): 81–82.

22. Nikolai (Nalimov), archbishop of Vladimir (1906–14).

23. *Tserkovnye vedomosti* [Church News], the official weekly published by the Synod (1888–1918), consisted of an official part (with resolutions and other decisions of the Synod and central church organs) and a supplement (*Pribavleniia*) with articles and other "unofficial" materials. The Synodal resolution and appeal, adopted in the wake of the October Manifesto of 17 October 1905, appeared in issue no. 44 (29 October 1905).

24. The Great Reforms allowed for three types of elementary schools: (a) parish-church schools, funded by the local parish (later with state subsidies) and subordinate to the church; (b) state schools, funded and supervised by the Ministry of Education; and (c) zemstvo schools, funded and supervised by the zemstvo – the new organ of self-government created in 1864. The Commission proposes that the priest have authority over not only parish-church schools, but also those operated by the Ministry of Education and the provincial zemstvo.

25. *Kormchii*, which bore the subtitle *religiozno-nravstvennyi narodnyi zhurnal* (religious-moral popular journal), appeared weekly in Moscow from 1888 to 1917.

26. Most likely, the Commission had in mind Pavel Andreevich Nikol'skii, who did publish "moral-religious" tracts (including a tract on Serafim Sarovskii, canonized in 1903), with press runs of up to 3,000 copies, which he distributed gratis; he was a senior instructor at the Tambov Ecclesiastical School (the four-year elementary level, not the seminar) and active in the right-wing Union of Russian People (see biography on website Khronos: vsemirnaia istoriia v internete, at http://hrono.ru/biograf/bio_n/nikolski_pa.html). Another potential "Nikol'skii" was N. Nikol'skii, who coauthored a short, twenty-two-page pamphlet with the more famous missionary V. M. Skvortsov in 1911: *Kaiushchaisia khlystovka* (The Penitent Female Flagellant), which appeared in the *narodno-missionerskaia biblioteka* (popular missionary library).

27. Petr Nikolaevich Skubachevskii (1864–1917) was a priest and missionary in Khar'kov diocese; he was also a founding member of the local branch of the right-wing Union of Russian People (see biography on website Khronos: vsemirnaia istoriia v internete, at http://www.hrono.ru/biograf/bio_s/skubachevski_pn.html).

28. GAVO, f. 556, op. 1, d. 4856, l. 2.

SUGGESTED READINGS

Chulos, Chris J. *Converging Worlds: Religion and Community in Peasant Russia, 1861–1917.* DeKalb: Northern Illinois University Press, 2003.

Freeze, Gregory L. "Russian Orthodoxy on the Periphery: Decoding the *Raporty blagochinnykh* in Lithuania Diocese." In *Problemy vsemirnoi istorii,* ed. Boris V. Anan'ich et al., 124–31. St. Petersburg: D. Bulanin, 1999.

——— . "All Power to the Parish? The Problem and Politics of Church Reform in Late Imperial Russia." In *Social Identities in Revolutionary Russia,* ed. Madhavan K. Palat, 174–208. London: Macmillan, 2001.

——— . "A Pious Folk? Religious Observance in Vladimir Diocese, 1900–1914." *Jahrbücher für Geschichte Osteuropas* 52 (2004): 323–40.

——— . "Priests and Revolution: The Parish Clergy of Vladimir in 1905." *Rethinking the Russian Revolution of 1905,* edited by Franziska Schedewie et al., 19–38. Bloomington, IN.: Slavica, 2013.

SIXTEEN

Petitions to the Holy Synod Regarding Miracle-Working Icons

Vera Shevzov

ICONS HISTORICALLY PLAYED AN EXTRAORDINARILY IMPORTANT role in the lives of Orthodox believers in imperial Russia. Officially linked since the eighth century with the church's teachings regarding Jesus' identity as both human and divine, icons found their justification in the Orthodox Christian understanding of the incarnation and the nature of humanity. Moreover, as quintessential symbols of religious and national identity, icons were as often bearers of political and social meaning as they were of the spiritual and theological.

While the prominence of icons in imperial Russia is well known, the complexities and nuances associated with their use and veneration are much less appreciated. The two cases that follow offer first-hand insights into the often entangled world of iconic piety from the perspective of two lay believers, both male peasants, writing at the beginning of the twentieth century. Lay men and women frequently petitioned diocesan officials and even central church authorities in the capital, St. Petersburg, testifying to their active engagement in church life. Their letters concerned a broad array of issues, including parish administration and management, the construction of churches and chapels, fund raising, and icons, to name a few. Their numbers rose and took on a particularly sharp, candid tone at the end of the nineteenth century, and especially in the wake of the revolutionary events of 1905, when many lay believers seemed to awaken to their roles and responsibilities as members of the church.

Cases concerning perceived miracle-working icons were common to all dioceses in Russia and represented a small yet nonetheless significant minority of all the petitions church officials annually received from lay men and women throughout the Russian empire. Ultimately what was at stake in most such petitions, regardless of the regions from which they were received, was simply the veneration of a particular image – believers' access to an icon in order to be able to establish and cultivate, through prayer, their relationship with the holy figures depicted on it. Through this connection believers hoped to nurture a closer relationship with God. The hope for healing or other forms of divine mercy was usually not far behind.

While the initial starting point for each case is somewhat different – a familial icon of Christ in a private home in the first case and a well-known and highly revered icon of the Mother of God for a parish community in the second – each offers insights into the rich culture that iconic piety generated and sustained. This culture included: the "writing" or painting of an icon and its blessing once it had been completed; caring for an image and the intricate decoration and gifts left before it; visitations of icons to believers and believers' journeys to venerate icons; the more private, familial ritual of entrusting an icon from one generation to the next and the more public communal celebration of perceived divine grace in their midst as signaled by the icon. Similarly each petition emphasizes the significance of space. According to believers' devotional sensibilities, icons could not simply be kept anywhere. In order to realize their full potential, icons had to be ensured a proper and fertile environment – namely, one steeped in active prayer and one in which the icon was visually accessible to the devotional gaze. At the same time, such a fertile environment was not necessarily limited in lay believers' eyes to the monasteries and cathedrals designated as the most appropriate by church authorities.

As these petitions illustrate, church officials were no less concerned with the proper veneration of icons and attempted to monitor believers' activities associated with them. In particular, they were concerned with sudden and unexpected displays of intensified devotion to a particular image on account of reported miracles. Although miracles were integral to the Orthodox world view, historically church officials adopted a deeply nuanced approach to them. In order to protect the integrity of the church and the Orthodox faith in modern times, church officials sought to prevent fraud, profiteering, and other improprieties that might be associated with proclaimed miracle-working icons. The Orthodox Church in imperial Russia had no official mechanism for officially and systematically ruling on the authenticity of miracle-working icons. Instead, after receiving reports of miracle-working images, in many instances church officials resorted to a law implemented in 1722, during the reign of Peter the Great, directing that newly surfaced miracle-working icons be investigated and taken from private homes and placed in provincial cathedrals and monastery churches for "safekeeping" and further monitoring. By transferring an icon from a private home, and in some cases from a remote parish church, to a diocesan cathedral or a monastery, church officials expected to have full control over the culture that developed around the image. This was the institutional logic behind the actions of church officials in the Chernigov diocese in the first case below.

In the second case, involving the veneration of an icon of the Mother of God named "Multiplier of Grains," church officials expressed a different, but nonetheless related, concern. The icon of the Mother of God named "Multiplier of Grains" was a new iconographic type that surfaced in 1890. Associated with the highly revered elder of the well-known monastery Optina Pustyn, Amvrosii (1812–91), and the abbess of the Bolkhovskii convent in the Orel diocese, Ilariia, the icon quickly gained popularity and was disseminated widely without official approval. As this case shows, church officials were unsettled by an icon that had no prototypic precedent. Iconography was an ancient vocation in the Eastern Christian tradition that had its own canon. Icons were generally painted according to long-established prototypes. Consequently, icons with new depictions and new names put church officials on guard for potential improprieties and unacceptable innovations.

In both cases, church officials disturbed or obstructed the veneration of an icon and the culture that such veneration spontaneously bred. This obstruction positioned the icon in a different field of discourse, which was driven by competing understandings of religious authority, sacred power, and the notion of ownership with respect to the sacred. Behind the fierce determination believers displayed with respect to what they considered to be "their" icons lay deep religious sensibilities concerning hierarchies and self-identity within the Orthodox Church. In both cases, the broader social and political processes underway in Russia during the revolutionary period of 1904–1905, when Nikolai Zelenyi

16.1. Print of the specially revered icon of the Mother of God named "Multiplier of Grains." RGIA, f. 796, op. 173, d. 2670a, l. 5a. Reproduced with permission.

wrote, and in 1916, when Vasilii Novoselov wrote, informed their thinking and response. The allusion to lay "rights" in the letter of Nikolai Zelenyi and the equation of "the church" with the "assembly of faithful" or laity in the letters of Vasilii Novoselov gave ancient-sounding religious concerns an unmistakably modern pitch.

The case concerning the petition of Nikolai Zelenyi, a peasant from the village of Zelenyi, near the village of Kuznichi, Gorodnia district, Chernigov diocese, regarding an old image of the Savior, which was purportedly miraculously renewed in his mother's home.[1]

On 13 August 1904, the Holy Synod received the following petition from the peasant Nikolai Antonov Zelenyi, from the village of Zelenyi, near the village of Kuznichi, in the Gorodnia district in the Chernigov province:

During his lifetime, my mother's [now] deceased father-in-law, Iakov, received an icon of the Savior as a blessing from his father, Artem. This was about eighty years ago. Because of the passage of time, the face of the Lord [on the icon] was indiscernible, but on 9 May of this year, in my mother's home, the icon was renewed ... and she informed the parish priest, Spasskii, of this event.[2] Having learned of this occurrence, large numbers of pious people come to my mother's home to venerate the image, but it is cramped for the faithful in this home. For this reason, my mother donated the icon – her own property which had been handed down from generation to generation – to the church in the village of Kuznichi so as not to deprive herself, her family, and other faithful of eternal prayer before the renewed image of the Savior. The local priest, Spasskii, informed His Eminence, Bishop Antonii of Chernigov and Nezhin, about this important event, after which the Chernigov consistory issued a directive to the dean of the first district of the Gorodnia district to transfer the image to the Domnitskii monastery. In implementing this directive, the dean, accompanied by police, arrived in my home, while the icon was located in my mother's home and not mine. Finding the consistory's directive offensive, I humbly request the Most Holy Ruling Synod to rescind it and to leave the icon in the parish church in the village of Kuznichi, which was constructed in memory of the martyr-like death of His Imperial Majesty Alexander II.

1904, August 8.
Signed, Peasant Nikolai Antonov Zelenyi

On November 14, the Holy Synod received a report from Antonii, the bishop of Chernigov and Nezhin, in which he describes the following:

On 5 June, Vasilii Spasskii, the priest of the village of Khotivlia, Gorodnia district, reported that a renewal of an icon of the Savior occurred in the home of the honest and God-fearing peasant woman, Elena Iakovleva Zelenaia, in the village of Zelenyi, which is about .25 versts from the village of Kuznichi. On 17 May, the priest Vasilii Spasskii was conducting a liturgical service at the Kuznichi church. Following the service, Elena Zelenaia invited the priest to her home to rest and fortify himself, but because an exam had been scheduled at the Khotivlia parish-church school, the priest Spasskii turned down the invitation. At that point, the cantor from the village of Khotivilia, Pavel Kovalkovskii, Zelenaia's relative, explained to the priest the purpose of Zelenaia's invitation – namely, to view the icon and to offer advice on what she should do. On the next day, 18 May, the priest Vasilii Spasskii traveled to the village of Nikolskoe-Zelennoe and learned the following at the home of Elena Zelenaia. On 6 May, she returned home from Chernigov, where she had traveled to venerate the relics of St. Feodosii.[3] On the night of 8–9 May 1904, the icon of the Savior in her home was renewed. One of her sons had cleaned the covering on the icon of St. Nicholas, which was located near the icon of the Savior, which occupied the central place among the icons. The icon of St. Nicholas with its gleam made the icon of the Savior, which had no covering and was covered with a thin layer of dust, appear even darker. Zelenaia noted this and scolded her son for not taking care of the icon of the Savior as well. But on the morning of 9 May, everyone saw the icon of the Savior renewed without any external aid.

The circumstances that preceded and followed the renewal of the icon were the following. On 8 May, Elena's twenty-year-old son, Daniil, was getting ready to drive the horses to the field for the night. At around 10 PM, he came in from the outdoors ... there was no light in the house. When he began putting on his boots, he was suddenly frightened by the brilliance of a flame, which appeared in the form of lighting on the icon of the Savior.... From within the flame Daniil clearly saw the face of the Savior. The flame appeared on the icon for about a minute, then gradually subsided and disappeared toward the middle of the icon. Asleep on the couch located below the icons, Elena Iakovleva's married daughter also saw traces of light on the icon of the Savior. The next morning it became clear that the icon of the Savior, which had appeared old, now appeared like new: the face was surrounded by a radiance.... The Savior's vestments and his left hand, which held an orb with a cross on top, came into relief, his cheeks now appeared slightly flushed, his formerly dark eyes were now blue.[4] The widow Zelenaia could notice such a change with the icon of the Savior since she prayed before the image every day, morning and evening. Moreover, before the feast of the Resurrection, she [annually] washed and cleaned all of the icons. When this year she did so, the image was not recognizable from the entrance to the cottage. Attributing all of this to divine mercy, the priest Spasskii directed to light a *lampada* before the icon.[5] News of the icon began to spread; on occasion, people from other villages came to venerate the icon. Those who were unfavorably predisposed to the Zelenyi family, on the other hand, began to claim that the entire history with the icon was fabricated and an exploitation of a holy object. In view of this, Elena Iakovleva requested the priest Spasskii to place the icon in the church. Reluctant to do anything with the icon on his own, he requested my directions with respect to the issue.

In the meantime, on 16 July, the dean of the first district of the Gorodnia district, the priest Vasilii Petrovskii, reported to me that the warden of the first district of the Gorodnia district informed him that numerous believers gathered in the home of the peasant Nikolai Antonov Zelenyi, the son of Elena Zelenaia, in order to venerate the reportedly renewed icon. In view of this, on June 15, the dean, Father Vasilii Petrovskii, arrived in the village of Zelenyi in order to investigate the case and to examine the icon. He composed a directive to curtail the gathering of faithful in the private home and to uphold proper respect toward the icon. He also directed the priest Spasskii to move the icon from Zelenyi's home to the local cemetery church in the village of Kuznichi, to which the icon's owner, Zelenyi, agreed. In learning, however, that the icon was to be transferred without a procession, which he apparently desired, the priest Vasilii Spasskii declined to move it, citing my verbal directive to leave icons alone until receiving special directives from diocesan authorities. In view of this, Dean Petrovskii did not dare to elicit the help of the police in moving the icon before I issued my directive.

According to the report of Dean Vasilii Petrovskii, composed in the presence of the priests Pavel Lobov and Vladimir Kartel', the following is established. 1) An icon of the Savior was located in one of the two rooms in the home of Nikolai Zelenyi. Painted with oil paints on a board, the icon was encased in an old *kiot* behind a glass cover.[6] A wax candle and a lampada burned before the icon. A metal container with metal and silver coins left by the faithful stood on the table. By its looks, the icon in question cannot be considered ancient; it is written correctly by the hand of a skilled artist. Its face is quite lucid and there are no particular signs of restoration. On 15 June at 8 o'clock in the evening, there were no faithful in this home; on 16 June, several people from distant villages arrived to venerate the icon. According to Zelenyi's family and residents of the village of Kuznichi, the faithful continue to come daily, sometimes in large numbers, and rumors of numerous miracles from the icon are spreading. According to the local clergy and the local church elder, the twenty-two rubles that have been left as donations were given to the church in the village of Kuznichi. . . . On the basis of the Synod rulings of 21 February 1722 and 8 February 1895 . . . the [Chernigov] consistory directed the dean Vasilii Petrovskii to take the icon and give it to the nearest Domnitskii monastery and, in the case of non-compliance on the part of the Zelenyi family, to seek the aid of police authorities. . . . In a telegram dated 5 August, Zelenyi requested to donate the icon of the Savior to the church in the village of Kuznichi since neither he nor his mother agreed to give it to the monastery.

Following this, a police report was received on 9 August from the Gorodnia District Police Administration, which stated the following. On 5 August, the warden journeyed to the village of Nikolskoe-Zelennoe in order to aid the dean, the priest Vasilii Petrovskii, in taking the icon of the Savior from the home of Nikolai Zelenyi. Nikolai's mother announced that she "would not agree to give her blessed image of the Savior to anyone." She hung it on her chest and when the warden wanted to take it off of her, all the members of Zelenyi's family surrounded her and announced that they would allow the icon to be taken only to the Kuznichi church. Having discussed the report of the police administration, on 19/20 August diocesan authorities decided the following: to deny the peasant Nikolai Zelenyi's request to give the renewed icon of the Savior to the church in the village of Kuznichi. On 25 August I requested help from the governor of the Chernigov province in getting the icon located in the home of Zelenyi placed in the Domnitskii monastery. Regarding the petition of the peasant Zelenyi to the Holy Synod about leaving the reportedly miraculously renewed icon of the Savior in the church in the village of Kuznichi, on 18 August the diocesan authorities decided to leave the icon in the Kuznichi village church until the resolution of Zelenyi's appeal to the Synod – a decision released in my name to the Governor of the Chernigov province.

Signed by Antonii, Bishop of Chernigov and Nezhin.

> Having reviewed the petition of the peasant Nikolai Zelenyi about leaving the icon of the Savior that belongs to his family in the local parish church, as well as the report of the diocesan authorities and the diocesan bishop of Chernigov, on 1 December 1904 the Holy Synod decided the following: "Taking into account the pious devotion" of the members of the Zelenyi family, to place the icon into the church in the village of Kuznichi, of which the diocesan bishop was to be informed.
>
> On 6 January 1905, the Holy Synod received via the office of the Over-Procurator of the Holy Synod two requests from peasants of the village of Kuznichi. One of the petitions from the peasants Tikhon Lushchii and Foma Sidorenko, dated 12 October 1904, states:

With great effort and with our own funds ... we constructed a church in our village in memory of the late Sovereign and Liberator Alexander II. We were very happy that, although infrequently, we were still able to pray with the priest in our village, and thereby not deny our children the Orthodox faith. But now everything has changed. We have a church, but we have nowhere to pray. The problem is that in August of this year, one local peasant woman, Elena Iakovleva Zelenaia, donated to the church an ancient icon of the Savior that had been blessed by her parents. The icon had been glorified by various miracles, and by the mercy of God our peasant Aleksandr Martynenko and others received healing. When the authorities were notified of the miracles, they directed the icon to be transferred to the Domnitskii monastery and to close the church until the icon was transferred. We do not desire to part with such an icon, and did not agree to give it away; on 6 September of this year, we requested His Eminence Antonii, the bishop of Chernigov and Nezhin, to inform us of the legal reasons for denying us the icon, and to open the church and to leave the icon in it. But instead of a response, the police arrived to take our icon from the church and announced that they were acting on the directives of His Excellency, the Governor, and the Chernigov consistory. It became clear to us that the consistory decreed to take the icon from the home of the resident of the village of Zelenyi, Nikolai Antonov Zelenyi, while the police set about taking the icon from the Kuznichi village church. In view of this, and on the basis of the fact that the donated icon belonged to the widow Elena Zelenaia, and as is evident from the directive, the aim was to take the icon from the home of Nikolai Zelenyi and not from the church of God, we petitioned Your Excellency in September to rescind the consistory's directive and . . . to leave the icon in its place in our church, as obtained by us and in view of the fact that every Orthodox peasant has the right to obtain icons according to his desire, and to open the church for communal prayer. Notwithstanding our petition, the Gorodnia police are trying to take the icon from our church . . . without any legal reason, despite the words of the Sovereign, given in Moscow during his holy coronation, that one is not to enrich oneself by the appropriation of another's goods, but from honest labor. . . . Because of this, we are emboldened to bother Your Excellency a second time and to humbly request you . . . to issue a directive about opening the church building in which there has been no service since 1 August . . . and to leave the icon with which we cannot part and which was donated by Elena Zelenaia to our church. We also ask that you suggest to His Eminence Antonii, the bishop of Chernigov and Nezhin, that he inform us of the legal reasons for the closing of our church for liturgical celebration, and if it turns out that liturgical services have been curtailed without any legal reason, then do not leave those responsible without punishment. . . .

Signed by fifty persons.

On 14 December 1904 Bishop Antonii notified the Over-Procurator of the Holy Synod that on October 12, the Chernigov consistory had decided and (and ratified): 1) to leave the icon in the church in the village of Kuznichi until Zelenyi's petition had been decided by the Holy Synod; 2) to explain to the dean, Vasilii Petrovskii, that the icon could not serve as an obstacle to the performance of liturgical services in this church.

On 4 February 1905, the Synod confirmed the decision to leave the icon in the church and to resume liturgical services. With this decision, it left the petitions of the villagers without further action.

The case regarding the request of the peasant Vasilii Novoselov for permission of church veneration of the icon of the Mother of God named "Multiplier of Grains" (Sporitel'nitsa khlebov).[7]

12 July 1916, the Holy Synod received a petition from the peasant Vasilii Konstantinov Novoselov, who writes on behalf of himself and what he calls "the assembly of the faithful." He identifies himself as a reserve bombardier in the First Battery of His Royal Highness Grand Prince Mikhail Pavlovich ... in the city of Petrograd.

I have the honor of humbly requesting that the Most Holy Ruling Synod not ignore my request but devote a part of your esteemed attention to reading the several lines of my petition. Christ is in our midst, was, and always shall be. Incidentally, as part of my service and responsibility to His Imperial Highness, I have annually had to accompany the following holy miracle-working icons on the territory of the Birsk district: 1) the Kazan icon of the Mother of God located in the diocesan cathedral in Ufa; 2) the icon of the hierarch and miracle-worker Nicholas "Zakamskii-Berezovskii" in the Birsk district.[8] Because of this, during the greeting and departure of the icons, I frequently had the opportunity to see in villages and chapels, especially during its greeting and leave-taking, the special veneration of the icon of the Mother of God "Multiplier of Grains." Peasant farmers, who support you and me, especially revere this icon. They relate to it with special devotion.... I have long had the thought and pressing desire ... to obtain such a holy icon of the Mother of God "Multiplier of Grains" and to send it to my homeland in the Viatka diocese, as I was born in the village and volost of Kichma in the Urzhumsk district in the Viatka province.... But since I am a very poor person and not in a position to acquire it, an assembly of faithful has gathered with me and decided to obtain the above-mentioned icon and to send it to the Viatka province, to the village of Kichma, my homeland. At first I had the desire to obtain an icon of the Entry of the Mother of God into the Temple ... but then things transpired differently, as God desired it.... On the night of 1 January 1916, after I returned from a prayer service, I fell fast asleep and had a dream in which I was in my homeland in Viatka, walking in the old fields that I had planted and harvested. The fields were so impoverished; the land was virtually barren, foreshadowing a terrible famine. My heart was very pained and I wondered why in the Ufa diocese the harvest was plentiful, and I became sad. A strong wind began to blow and raised the dust into columns, and in the storm I heard a voice that explained: "In the Ufa province, as you saw, there was an icon of the Mother of God named 'Multiplier of Grains;' but you don't have the Bread-Multiplier, the petitioner before the Lord God All-Mighty, Creator of a harvest of grains...." From that moment, I vowed, with the help of the faithful, to have an icon of the Multiplier of Grains written and to send it to my homeland instead of an icon of the Entry of the Mother of God into the Temple. Despite the expense of the Great War, God is not without mercy and the land is not without kind people. With God, all is possible. The assembly of the faithful related with great reverence to the acquisition of the holy object. A period of prayer and fasting was announced and the icon was ordered; during its writing, the faithful chanted the akathist to the Mother of God day and night.[9] It was written by an old pious elder, the seventy-five-year-old Feofil Pavlovich, who was living out his last days.... When the faithful [saw the completed] God-pleasing image of the Mother of God, the entire assembly of the faithful was surprised and glorified this icon. By the desire of the faithful, the holy icon was carried to the holy monastery, where, with the gathering of the monastery's brothers, it was ceremoniously blessed with the participation of the assembly of the faithful.... By the desire of the faithful, an inextinguishable icon-lamp was lit before the icon and the assembly of the faithful constructed a magnificent casing for the icon and placed a crown on the Mother of God's head. Three episcopal medallions (*panagii*), decorated with diamonds and amber beads, a pectoral cross also decorated with beads, many ribbons, flowers, crosses, and so forth, were placed around the icon as testimony to the grace and mercy of the Heavenly Queen and her honorable icon and as signs of thanksgiving and special devotion. Before its departure, the icon stood in the monastery and the faithful continually read akathist hymns before it. Incidentally, a remarkable miracle occurred with this icon. During the sixth week of Great Lent, I was preparing for Confession and Communion at the monastery and on the night of 29–30 March, during the Vigil service, I was reading an akathist before the newly glorified icon of the Mother of God named "Multiplier of Grains." ... Two streams of tears appeared from the eyes of the Mother of God. The Heavenly Queen wept, tears streamed down her image, and I began to weep and lost my head. I cannot explain it. I composed a testimonial about the incident and together with the icon sent [the report] to Viatka. Why such an event took place no one could understand, but I began to anticipate some sort of misfortune or grief....

Given the circumstances, the assembly of the faithful had requested the bishop of Viatka to greet the icon as it arrived by boat at the settlement of Kukarka. But the bishop declined. Then the faithful and I turned to the clergy of the village of Kichma, Urzhum district, to greet the sacred object, at least at the boundary of their parish. But here Satan-devil arose ... and gave the sacred object over for profanation and insult....

The clergy of the village of Kichma received my request and informed me of the following, which has neither been heard nor seen and would never come to the mind of an Orthodox believer. A history that could not be. I was informed that the Holy Synod had forbidden the icon "Multiplier of Grains" in 1896.... Such news was woeful, like a mortal wound.... In the meantime, the icon "Multiplier of Grains" has not ceased being made, either in monasteries or artist studios, and is printed everywhere without hindrance. It has become venerated throughout Russia, and many [of these icons] have been glorified as miracle-working. It is impossible at this time to forbid their veneration.... It is clear that it was pleasing to God that the icon of the Mother of God be glorified and God glorified it through the faithful. Otherwise, a second iconoclasm could erupt and the faithful would sooner lay down their lives for this icon and none of the faithful will allow profanation and insult to the icon....

Incidentally, the assembly of the faithful objects that spiritual authorities play with sacred objects as with dolls. This is not good. For the faithful, the appearance of the Mother of God did not take place to a witless person, but to a person revered by the whole world since he was sagacious. Optina Pustyn, moreover, is known to all pilgrims. Everyone also remembers the year of the famine and how the icon was revered by simple farmers.... The schemamonk Amvrosii was a man of prayer for harvests of grains and that is why he experienced a sign in the appearance of the Mother of God, which has been confirmed, and he was permitted to make holy icons.[10] No one up to the present knows why persecution [over it] followed....

The holy and miracle-working icon of the Mother of God "Multiplier of Grains" arrived safely. The benefactor, Peter Vasil'evich, brought it to the village of his parish. The assembly and the entire parish had requested the clergy of the parish in Kichma to greet it. But the clergy denied the request, citing the circulars of 1896 ... and directed that the icon not be unpacked, and everyone remained terribly unhappy. Not being able to contain their sadness, they unpacked the icon and saw the Mother of God as if alive, and they bowed to the ground and requested that they be able to carry the icon in their hands to the village, but they were not allowed to do so. Instead, the icon was wrapped in sackcloth and placed on a cart, like a deceased person or a drunken man, and [they] drove her away. The entire assembly of the faithful followed behind in tears instead of joyous greeting, that is what happened. The holy revered object suffered profanation, insult, and depravity....

The icon was brought to the village of Zaretskoe and brought into a home.... For two days, the faithful prayed before it. On the third day, believers accompanied it ceremoniously to the chapel, as it is not fitting to keep such a holy item in the home. But when the clergy of the village of Kichma saw it, they insisted they would not serve before the icon, that there existed no [special hymnography] in its honor ... and they ordered the icon taken from the chapel. Not one of the faithful raised a hand, however, to the miracle-working image of the Mother of God; they remained very unhappy and became terribly angry, hoping for the mercy of God, the protection of the Heavenly Queen, and the holy fathers of the Most-Holy Synod. The priests directed that the icon be packed up, but the faithful did not let this happen; then the priests directed that the icon be covered, so that no one would pray before it or see the holy God-pleasing image of the Mother of God.... To prevent disorder the priests covered it themselves, and so the icon of the Mother of God "Multiplier of Grains" remains covered up to the present. She does not receive her due honor and veneration. In view of this and everything else I have described, I humbly ask the Holy Synod to curtail the persecution and the insult and other things that have taken place with this icon of the Mother of God. I humbly request permission for the veneration of this icon such as is allowed other icons of the Mother of God.... And together with this I announce that if my request is not respected, I will never allow this sacred item to be given over for persecution or destruction. Let them first cut off my head and then do what they want with the holy object, if defenders of the truth can't be found.

Signed Vasilii Konstantinov Novoselov. 6 July 1916

> An inquiry into this case as compiled in a report of the Holy Synod dated 7 September 1916 showed the following: In April 1892, the Holy Synod upheld a decision by the Moscow Spiritual Censorship Committee to deny a request from Moscow merchant Perlov to print chromolithographic images of the Mother of God named "Multiplier of Grains." The censorship committee was concerned about the dissemination of an image of the Mother of God with this unusual name since it could incite "incorrect and undesirable interpretations among the people." It later became known that the example of the chromolithographic image of the Mother of God named "Multiplier of Grains" presented by Perlov was made by Fesenko in Odessa, at the request of Optina Pustyn and with the permission of the censor of the Kherson diocesan newspaper. In 1896, in response to the question posed by the bishop of Viatka about whether this icon should be allowed for veneration, the Holy Synod directed the Over-Procurator to contact the Ministry of Internal Affairs. The Ministry of Internal Affairs informed the Over-Procurator that it had directed print shops not to print this image. Such an instruction was officially issued by the Holy Synod in July 1896. In view of this past history with the icon, the Holy Synod decided on 29 September 1916 to take no action on Novoselov's case.
>
> Vasilii Novoselov received news of the Synod's decision on 28 October 1916. On 26 November 1916, the Over-Procurator of the Holy Synod received the following letter from Vasilii Novoselov and "the assembly of the faithful":

I have the honor of humbly requesting that Your Excellency reactivate my petition before the Holy All-Russia Synod, which was submitted from the Holy Orthodox Church, that is, the assembly of the faithful... which, according to a directive dated 20 September 1916, the Holy Synod left without action.... Since the assembly of believers found the decision incorrect... the assembly of the faithful humbly requests you, Your Excellency, in light of your great zeal toward the glory of God and toward the Orthodox faith, and in view of the current decline in faith and dissatisfaction, we humbly request that you introduce legislation about curtailing the insult and persecution of the holy icon of the Mother of God named "Multiplier of Grains" ... Incidentally, the directive stated that the Holy Synod also did not give a blessing for the honoring and veneration of the holy icon of the Mother of God named "Multiplier of Grains." This is not in accordance with the Gospel and the commandments of the Savior ... or with the Mother of God, who blessed the veneration of her icons.... The assembly of faithful, that is, the Orthodox Church, has venerated this icon for some time. Many religious faithful have petitioned about the veneration of this icon ... but the Holy Synod only insists on one thing, and does not pay attention to the Holy Orthodox Church and to the decline in faith and various sects, and despite the number of petitions submitted to the Holy Synod, always the same is heard: "Without action."... Incidentally, it almost came to bloodshed in the Viatka diocese, Urzhum district, village of Kichma, where the priests did not greet the icon and would not allow prayer before it. Now it [the icon] stands covered and profaned. And the Holy Synod will pay no attention to this case.... But incidentally, Your Excellency, after all, the Holy Synod is established and called not for the purpose of ruining the church and leaving petitions and requests "without action," as is accepted as the rule with our Holy Synod. The Holy Church desires to know from the Holy Synod why it does not allow the veneration of the icon of the Mother of God "Multiplier of Grains" and to explain the reason. Perhaps there are some shortcomings and irregularities.... If the Holy Synod does not recognize it as the Mother of God, then let it indicate another image and believers won't revere [this one]. But if the Holy Synod does recognize it as the Mother of God, then why don't they revere [the icon] and why do they forbid others to do so. Incidentally, let the Holy Synod not revere the icon, but let them not forbid others to do so; whosoever has the desire, let them pray, and whoever does not have the desire, let them not pray.... The Holy Church desires to learn from the Most Holy Synod a full explanation and directives about the icon ... Incidentally, why does the assembly of faithful, that is the Holy Orthodox Church, so earnestly revere the icon of the Mother of God named "Multiplier of Grains" and not some other icon, since there are more than two hundred types – that is the question. Despite the prohibition and insult and so forth from the Holy Synod, this icon is glorified and revered, and all workshops are filled with so many orders that they cannot keep up ... The Holy Synod in its pride, however, does not want to accede to the faithful in a unified body but moves against them. But who exists for whom – the Holy Church for the Synod, or the Holy Synod for the Church? He who has ears, let him hear and understand.... The members of the Most Holy Synod serve at God's altar and have lived to an old age, but they do not recognize the Mother of God; this is what is taking place in our Orthodox faith.... Incidentally, in almost every home where there is belief in God, there is an icon of the "Multiplier of Grains." I myself have personally seen and venerated these images ... it is impossible to enumerate all the villages, chapels, and monasteries where this icon of the Mother of God "Multiplier of Grains" exists, where the church and faithful revere it and earnestly pray before it in the fields and in all places, requesting from her help and protection ... In this current petition, the Orthodox Church, the assembly of the faithful, desires definitive results about what they are to do with the icon of the Mother of God named "Multiplier of Grains" that is in their possession in the event that the holy fathers leave this petition without action as well. In this case, it will mean that the holy fathers desire to throw out the holy object from churches, and to chop them for firewood or give them over for use as covers, shovels, and other objects. ... But the faithful will never allow this ... In view of all of this, Your Excellency, if the Holy Synod will not take into consideration [this petition] and will not present a full explanation and clarification and a final decision – how and where to proceed – then the holy Orthodox Church, that is, the assembly of faithful, will definitely petition for the view of His Most Royal Highness. Then they will end this case. Amen.

Signed Vasilii Konstantinov Novoselov.

> On 9 January 1917, the metropolitan of Petrograd and Ladoga, Pitirim, received the following petition from Vasilii Novoselov:

I have the honor of humbly requesting you, Your Eminence ... for your blessing; I humbly ask you to make an effort to read several lines of my petition about the following circumstances.... I submitted a petition on 6 July 1916 to the Holy Synod about the veneration of a holy, even miracle-working, icon of the Mother of God, "Multiplier of Grains." But the Holy Synod left my request without action.... This [response] saddened me, leaving me not knowing what to do or where to turn. That is why I am turning to you for advice and for an archpastoral blessing: 1) to revisit the issue about the veneration of the icon and to curtail persecution of this icon and to locate my petition and to review it once again. In it everything is clearly spelled out and explained, all of the circumstances which I cannot present in this petition; 2) this icon is located in the village of Kichma, Urzhum district, Viatka province . . . the assembly of the faithful, that is, the Orthodox Church, acquired this icon and glorified it. Incidentally, the faithful had wanted to greet the icon ceremoniously and had vowed to serve many prayer services. But the clergy of Kichma would not greet the icon and would not allow it to be carried openly; instead, the Mother Heavenly Queen was placed in a cart and taken away like a drunken Tatar woman. Old Believers and Baptists and other schismatics laughed at this. . . . But the faithful paid no attention and ceremoniously placed the icon in a chapel. When the clergy saw the icon in the chapel, they ordered that the icon be taken out of there; the faithful in turn arose, and turmoil followed that almost ended in bloodshed. The clergy calmed things down by agreeing to revere the icon if I would petition the Synod for permission to do so, and they covered the icon with a shroud. Everyone is attracted to the image of the Mother of God; whoever sees it falls to his or her knees. The icon cost two hundred rubles and the faithful have decorated it with flowers and gifts of silver, gold, and diamonds. And here is the question: all the faithful revere and all display some sort of zeal, especially the most religious of the people, who travel to holy places, but the Holy Synod does not understand how to proceed; they cannot determine and resolve this case. I have become so upset I am ready to leave the Orthodox faith; I ask your Grace to help me in my grief.

I had wanted to drop everything, to give up, but, again, I read in the Gospel text that states, ask and you shall receive, seek and you will find, and about the Canaanite woman who finally shouted her way to the Lord and became tiresome to the disciples. Now throw away the icon as a cover – but it is frightening to consider this since it was blessed ceremoniously in the Vladimir monastery. Everyone reads akathist hymns before it day and night. And on 29–30 March of this year, during Vigil service, I was reading the akathist and the image of the Mother of God began to weep. The tears flowed in two streams. Not knowing what would happen in the future, I thought that I would be chased to war and killed. But fate decided otherwise, since I did not know that this icon was under persecution and not revered. But I recorded the miracle anyway for memory's sake.... I very much ask that you, Your Eminence, turn your attention to me, a little person.... Incidentally, I want to rewrite the icon into an image of the Pokrov, but again the faithful do not desire this; they wish to leave the icon as it is. Incidentally, why does the Holy Synod forbid and not offer any reasons or explanation. I humbly request His Grace to be a defender and protector in this case, not for my sake, but for the sake of the Orthodox Church and the faithful and to stand up for the above-named holy icon. In addition, send me comfort in my grief in this situation regarding the holy faith and the above-mentioned sacred object, along with a complete explanation and decision about what to do with the image of the Heavenly Queen in view of the fact that she is located some 1,500 versts away. What grief. If she were with me, then I would not begin to go to such efforts; I would begin to pray and chant akathist hymns....

Signed Vasilii Konstantinov Novoselov.

> 1 February 1917, the Holy Synod, taking into account 1) that no action was taken on Novoselov's first petition on the basis of the fact that the Holy Synod until this time has not given blessing for the church veneration of the icon of the Mother of God "Multiplier of Grains," since the Orthodox Church does not recognize this title as one applied to the Mother of God; 2) that in Novoselov's current requests there is no new information that would serve to rescind or change the former decision, the Holy Synod decided to leave Novoselov's current request without action.

NOTES

1. RGIA, f. 796, op. 185, d. 3031. The phenomenon of so-called renewed icons (*obnovlennye ikony*) involved icons that had become darkened with time, often on account of soot and grime, and then, according to believers, inexplicably lightened.

2. An image "not-made-by-human-hands" (Greek *acheiropoieta;* Russian *nerukotvornyi*) referred to icons, particularly of Christ, that were believed not to have been humanly painted.

3. Feodosii (1630s–1696), Archbishop of Chernigov, was canonized by the Russian Orthodox Church in 1896.

4. An orb traditionally was a symbol of sovereign authority.

5. A lampada is a small oil lamp traditionally placed in front of icons.

6. A kiot is an encasing for an icon, usually made of wood with a glass cover.

7. RGIA, f. 796, op. 203, 6 ot., 3 st., d. 155a (1916).

8. One of the most revered saints in Russia, Nicholas of Myra was a fourth-century bishop in Lycia. The icon of St. Nicholas "Zakamskii-Berezovskii" refers to an image of St. Nicholas reportedly found in the sixteenth century in the village Nikolo-Berezovskoe located on the Kama River in today's Bashkiristan.

9. Dating back to the sixth century, the akathist hymn refers to a genre of hymnography in honor of Christ, Mary (or her icons), or the saints in the Eastern Christian tradition that can be chanted by laymen or clergy. The original akathist was a hymn to Mary, the Mother of God, which became one of the most well-known hymns in honor of the Virgin.

10. Optina Pustyn, or the Optina Hermitage, was a well-known spiritual center in nineteenth-century Russia located in the Kaluga province. The elder Amvrosii (Aleksandr Mikhailovich Grenkov, 1812–91) was widely known in late nineteenth-century Russia as a spiritual guide.

SUGGESTED READINGS

Greenfield, Douglas, and Jefferson Gatrall, eds. *Alter Icons: The Russian Icon and Modernity.* University Park: Pennsylvania State University Press, 2010.

Ouspensky, Leonid, and Vladimir Lossky. *The Meaning of Icons.* 2nd ed. Crestwood, NY: St. Vladimir's Seminary Press, 1999.

Shevzov, Vera. *Russian Orthodoxy on the Eve of Revolution.* New York: Oxford University Press, 2004.

———. "Iconic Piety in Modern Russia." In *Modern Christianity to 1900.* Vol. 6, *People's History of Christianity,* ed. Amanda Porterfield, 178–208. Minneapolis, MN: Augsburg Fortress Press, 2007.

Tarasov, Oleg. *Icon and Devotion: Sacred Spaces in Imperial Russia.* London: Reaktion Books, 2004.

SEVENTEEN

Missionary Priests' Reports from Siberia

Aileen Friesen

SIBERIA OCCUPIED A CONTRADICTORY PLACE IN THE RUSSIAN imagination. It simultaneously evoked the image of a cold, inhospitable place of exile, of a land populated by native groups considered outside of civilization, and of a geographically wondrous and diverse region, rich in natural resources. By the late nineteenth century, with the building of the Trans-Siberian Railway, Siberia also became Russia's hope for solving its agrarian crisis caused by population increases and land shortages in European Russia. Populating this vast territory beyond the Urals with "civilized" Russian settlers preoccupied the state; looking after the religious needs of these settlers preoccupied the Russian Orthodox Church.

This process of colonization created numerous opportunities and challenges for the Russian Orthodox Church. Millions of peasants relocated from Ukraine, Belarus, and central Russia among other places in the empire to take advantage of newly available lands in Siberia and Central Asia. Cities and towns also experienced growth during this period; however, these pioneering men, women, and children overwhelmingly settled in rural areas. New villages and settlements transformed Siberia's landscape, as colonists cleared the land, established farms, and built homes. New settlers also transformed preexisting villages established by waves of Russian settlement throughout the eighteenth and nineteenth centuries. These original colonists, who were called old residents (*starozhily*) or *Sibiriaki*, found their villages inundated by the new arrivals. Village life in Siberia, therefore, had to accommodate a variety of local traditions brought to the region by settlers from their homelands in

European Russia. Religion, on the surface, offered common ground for rebuilding community life: the majority of settlers to Siberia identified with the Russian Orthodox faith. Yet, conflicts arose among villagers, which demonstrated the heterodox nature of Orthodox rituals and the fragility of religious adherence in villages without access to churches and without a common interpretation of Orthodox practices.

While access to land motivated these settler-peasants to undertake the journey, the Russian state's support of colonization was motivated by visions of imperial grandeur. The imperial context of settlement shaped the religious life of the new settlers in both overt and subtle ways. The state associated adherence to the Orthodox faith with political loyalty and with the maintenance of social order. In a region where the institutional presence of the Russian state was less established, the church performed an indispensable role in providing education and addressing the social problems witnessed by parish priests and missionaries in the villages. To support the church in its work, the state provided funds for the building of churches and schools in Siberia and approved of the special training of priests to be deployed to the region. Despite this assistance, dioceses in Siberia struggled to keep pace with the flood of settlers who appeared every year. As the church liturgy stood at the heart of the Orthodox tradition, this inadequate supply of churches, priests, and decent roads for parishioners to travel the phenomenal distances to the nearest parish church affected the development of religious practice.

The timing of the colonization of Siberia – as the Russian empire experienced rapid social, economic, and political change – also held significance for how peasant-settlers understood and viewed their religious beliefs. The Trans-Siberian Railway, which the state began building in 1891, pulled peasants from their localized existence and comfortable community life into a world beyond their previous experiential boundaries. The 1905 recognition of religious diversity within the Slavic population by the Russian government also opened new possibilities for religious experimentation and conversion to other Christian faiths. Even before 1905, Siberia gained a reputation as being a hotbed of religious dissent. Sectarians such as Baptists, Molokans, Adventists, and other groups joined the settler movement to Siberia. The presence of sectarians added another element of religious diversity to a region that, for centuries, had been a sanctuary for dissenting religious groups like Old Believers who wished to create insular communities free from the interfering hands of state officials and representatives of the Russian Orthodox Church.

The following two articles were published in the *Omsk Diocesan Gazette* (*Omskie eparkhial'nye vedomosti*). Panteleimon Papshev, a diocesan missionary priest, wrote the first article as part of a series titled "Report on the Activities of the Omsk Diocesan Missionary Council for 1915," which appeared over the course of several issues. The missionary council helped to organize missionary activities in Orthodox dioceses, with the mandate of fortifying the faith of believers against the perceived threat of sectarian propaganda. In this series, Papshev discussed the duties of local missionaries, the characteristics of sectarian groups, and the conditions of religious life in Siberian parishes. Ioann Goloshubin, a native of Siberia and a graduate of Tobolsk seminary, wrote the second article, titled "From the Impressions of a Village Priest." This article, published as part of a series in 1911, illuminates the differences between the religious practices of new settlers and old residents in Siberia and the pastoral challenges posed by this environment for parish priests. It is based on Goloshubin's seventeen years of experience as a priest in the Tiukalinsk district of Tobolsk province.

Conditions Favoring Sectarian Propaganda[1]

All that directly or indirectly obstructs the correct flow of parish life, at the same time lays down very favorable conditions for sectarian propaganda.

To begin with, it is necessary to note the insufficient number of Orthodox churches and the consequences that result from this. Proper parish life, which developed in Russia over centuries of intense work, is closely and inseparably linked with churches and can proceed only under their beneficial and educational influence on the human soul.

The full satisfaction of the religious-moral requirements and the needs of believers and the spiritual consolation that people always need can only happen in the church. This is especially true for settlers to Siberia, who yearn for everything dear and familiar that they have left behind in their native villages. For a Russian, nothing can take the place of the church: not a school, not any other organization, and not books. Where there is no church, there is no proper parish life.

And in Siberia, there is not enough of this powerful tool, the church, which forms the basis of religious life. Omsk diocese, which is equal in territory to the whole of France, has only approximately 650 churches, including churches in cities. If we add merely the great distance in Siberia between parishes and how scattered these parishes are from each other, then the influence that these churches could have had in an area with a high density population is reduced to a great extent. The majority of the Orthodox flock lives far away from the church, without the satisfaction of their religious-moral needs in a full and familiar form. How can we discuss the correct form of parish life if in the majority of parishes the more or less minimum administration of rites is not available to the individual?

Indeed, Siberia has, so to speak, a local and particular parish life, with a more or less established system, but only in the parishes of old-time residents. In the parishes of new settlers, which are being formed as new lands are settled, parish life is in a period of very early development.

But in the life of old-time residents there is also something undesirable. It is true that old residents, or as they are called "Chaldons,"[2] are strong in faith and that they do not join sects. But at the same time they are very indifferent toward faith, and regard the whole church with a coldness that is incomprehensible to the Russian person.

Besides the fact that parishes are separated from each other and scattered, another reason preventing the early formation of parish life is the heterogeneity of parishioners. The settlers are drawn from all parts of Russia, with local and even regional dialects. They also have different mentalities and religious practices. This difference is sometimes so great that even simple affairs, like electing a village elder, appear to them a matter of insurmountable difficulty. And here are these settlers, who lived in Russia according to time-honored religious traditions and enjoyed in their homeland all the benefits of church life without any effort on their part, having received this life as an inheritance from previous generations and taking no part in creating it through personal participation.

Under new and unaccustomed conditions of resettlement life in Siberia, these settlers initially find themselves in a very difficult position.

They prove to be unable, through their own efforts, to create more or less reasonable conditions of religious life, because they do not know how this can be done. They, like children, need leadership, guidance, and support in positively everything. Having become accustomed from their birthplace to well-known customs, they cannot get used to new ones. They consider these new customs as something less holy and less worthy of veneration than their native practices. And here begins the discord over the religious customs. Settlers from twenty to twenty-five different provinces often move to the same village in Siberia. They all have different customs and religious rites, which sometimes seem to others not only ridiculous, but also reprehensible. On the basis of these disputes mutual ridicule and condemnation begin, resulting in terrible disorder. Both sides feel some sort of unpleasant, bitter aftertaste in their souls, and annoyance that what earlier seemed so pure and perfect to them is now condemned and ridiculed. Hence they begin to distance themselves from their customs, to feel embarrassed and ashamed of them. And so, after living from year to year away from the church, people begin gradually to get out of the habit of their old life and little by little lose their religious customs, until finally, after five or six years, they grow somewhat indifferent, or "grow uncivilized" in their religious life.

The younger generation does not have a conception of a true Christian upbringing. They have grown up without a strong or palpable connection with the church. This makes them completely unreliable for the Orthodox Church. This generation, as one can observe in settlements with sectarians, quickly and almost without any emotional hesitation, without the heavy torment and the kind of suffering usually linked with changing faiths, abandon the Orthodox faith. The youth do not value the Orthodox faith because they do not know it.

Among the Russian population, which is under the influence of socialist, atheist, and sectarian propaganda, a particular type of unhappy peasant emerges ever more clearly. This growing phenomenon is called "peasant nihilism," which is terrible because of its unrestrained denial of everything – negation for the sake of negation. Of course, these people are everywhere in great numbers: many of them are also in Russia.

But that is the very problem: they cannot bear staying at home. They long for somewhere, where they could without constraint come and find sympathy and support. Some of them begin to dream of Australia, America, and other overseas countries. A small portion of the boldest do indeed set off to the New World, where, for the most part, they perish in terrible servitude on plantations. But most of them fill the ranks of settlers to Siberia. Therefore, a large portion of this nihilistic rubbish gathers in our region. Siberia attracts them with its untrammeled, free life – free not only in the sense of economics, but also in religious attitudes. They find in Siberia not only a place to live, but also a new life and a new faith.

Settlers with this mood are a genuine calamity for Russian Orthodoxy in our diocese. Once they meet in Siberia with sectarians, they at once side with them, sensing them to be like-minded people and recognizing the sect as that very new "Siberian religion" that they have been looking for, a religion that they vaguely imagined back home. Without any verification, they gladly agree with all that is non-Orthodox. Almost without argument, they accept everything that is hostile to Orthodoxy, for the sole reason that it is hostile to Orthodoxy. To please such a person is impossible. He will always find reasons to feel dissatisfaction and to make fun of faith.

Finally, even if they themselves do not join a sect, often because they deny all religion in general, their poisonous criticism creates around them an environment that is very receptive to sectarian preaching. Their presence in the resettlement environment creates the basis for sectarian propaganda, preparing the inflammable material which at the slightest spark can catch fire.

Moreover, in the resettlement stream pouring into the boundaries of the diocese, there are a great number of ready, radical sectarians, propagating their sect everywhere: along the journey in the carriage, at transfer stations, and after settlement in new places.

Every year, the resettlement movement grows, increasing the general population of the diocese. At the same time, the number of sectarians increases through migration and there is no possibility to fight against this growth. No one can forbid them from arriving and settling in Siberia. And dissenters clearly understand all the benefits of life here and do not miss using them to their advantage.

Beside these external circumstances favoring sectarian propaganda, the organizational structure of sectarians significantly facilitates the harmful work of propagandists. In contrast to the difficulty and the countless troubles with observing the necessary and compulsory laws concerning the opening of Orthodox parishes, and even more, with the building of churches, sectarians accomplish this business very simply. As soon as two or three households of them have assembled, the congregation is already ready to go and is discussing building its prayer house, which soon appears. Even if it is bad, squalid, and plain – it performs its job, which is to satisfy the religious needs of sectarians and converting Orthodox believers to the sect.

Thus, these are the predominant and unusual conditions for a Russian diocese under which the activity of Orthodox missionaries and pastors takes place, and that should be taken into consideration when evaluating their work. And if the sectarians, despite their fervent aspiration to use the advantages of their own position as much as possible, remain unsuccessful in the overwhelming majority of cases and if their propaganda is futile, then this should be entirely attributed to the assistance of the right hand of God holding back militant sectarianism and blessing the work of the Orthodox mission and clergy. In spite of the obstacles, they have managed to give proper rebuff to the wicked leaders wherever possible and to the best of their abilities, thereby defending their congregations from any unjust action of seduction and evil.

From the Impressions of a Village Priest[3]

Settler marriages are, to a lesser extent, accompanied by strange customs. I don't know what customs accompany the wedding feast of settlers before and after the performance of the wedding ceremony, but I must admit that I have never had to deal with any absurd demands during the wedding ceremony in the church, with the exception of binding the hands of the couple with a kerchief or a piece of cloth.

Among those from Poltava province, I quite often enough encounter the following custom: after the wedding ceremony, the bride and groom return home to their own parents. A week later, they meet again and only then begin the wedding feast.

Brides at the church, almost without exception, wear flowers. The rule among the settlers is that the wreaths are held on the heads of the couple by someone in the wedding party. After the ceremony, the settlers often request prayers for the health of the newlyweds. One can't say anything against these customs, as they have only a positive side.

Because of various clashes during negotiations with settlers over certificates prior to performing a marriage, the priest should be extremely cautious and prudent. The most burning question is premarital documents. These documents are, for the most part, the source of unfortunate consequences. In most cases, a priest does not have any exact information about the settlers, with the exception of travel certificates, tax records collected by the district government, and ecclesiastical reports kept by the clergy of the parish to which they currently belong. In all these documents, the settlers give their own age. Since, upon leaving Russia, they intentionally give a younger age for their children in order to get a discounted rate on the tariff, naturally when they arrive in Siberia, they immediately face major obstacles when marrying off their children. Well done to those settlers who took their children's birth certificate; but one doesn't find this type of forward thinking in the majority of cases. Therefore, for many marriages it is necessary to order birth certificates from Russia, and this is inconvenient and causes long delays. Because of this, it is not uncommon for weddings to be disrupted. When there is a lack of accurate documents, Little Russian[4] settlers often produce certificates from some individual – one of their fellow villagers or in the name of the village elder. But those and other documents are too questionable to use, as they are acquired easily, sometimes even for a few glasses of horilka [Ukrainian for "vodka"]. . . .

In the religious sphere, the Sibiriaki to a greater extent than the Little Russian settlers follow the ascribed prayer services. This conclusion I make not only based on my work among old-time residents and settlers, but also based on the information I received from all over Omsk diocese for inclusion in the diocesan reference book.

During village celebrations, dedicated to the memory of any saints or events, settlers organize only one general prayer and two to three prayers in certain homes. In the summer time there are a few prayer services performed in the fields and at the wells of the village and very few prayer services performed at homes. At Easter, during the summer, and at village celebrations, the peasants from Riazan province request prayer services at every home. I can never forget the zeal that the villagers in Aleksandrovskoe (natives of Riazan) showed toward the prayer service. Upon the arrival of the priest in the village, almost everyone, old and young, gathers near the icon and turns out for a majestic procession through the village, during which the people sing. This procession continues until late in the evening and rarely does anyone go home from the icon. In the street, at every home the owner stands with bread, salt, and candles. He patiently waits for the icon from the house next door.

I haven't encountered anything like this among the Little Russian settlers. Many times, their events turn out like this: after two or three public prayers there's no one to carry the icons and it so happens that one person has to carry a lantern and a cross. But this is not the whole story. One comes across examples where the villagers during the procession divide into parties that engage each other in arguments. Because of the arguments, the prayers eventually have to stop. This happened, for example, in the village of Mikhailovskoe in the summer of 1910, where I was invited to perform a public service at the wells and in the fields. After the first prayer service was performed on the open steppe, the assembled villagers entered into a dispute over where to go with the icons and where to perform the next prayer service. One insists on going down one street and another insists on a different street. Naturally one party turned out to be stronger than the other and we went with the icons to the extreme left of the street, where I began to hold the service. At this time the settlers began to gather here, and on the two other streets. Behind me noises began, and I heard swear words. At the end of prayer, I addressed those present with a decent, didactic case. The quarrel that took place during the prayer service can be explained as follows: the settlers on each street wanted to have the icon before the settlers on the other, and they began to ask noisily, "Why not bring the icon here?" Because the settlers on the other two streets were so offended and angry with me that the service had been conducted on another street, they didn't want to continue to pray and all returned to their homes. And that concluded the prayer service in the village of Mikhailovskoe. Generally, during the public prayer services with Little Russians, there is never order as they do not arrange in advance where and how to perform the service. This is in contrast to the old-time Siberian residents, whose ceremonies are always performed in a strict and well-planned manner. In addition to processions with the holy cross at parish celebrations, Easter, Christmas, and the Epiphany, Little Russian settlers without fail demand a visit from the priest during the Advent and Easter fasts. For reading the prayers, parishioners award the priest baked bread and a slice of bacon, or two or three kopeks (rarely five kopeks) and a bucket of wheat or oats or their own sausage. Baked bread is given at every home. Little Russians attach greater importance to this procession with prayer than a pastoral visitation with a home blessing during celebrations.

On my first visit to parishioners with holy water during the celebration of the Epiphany, I also came across a special request to carry out a fairly strange custom.

We went with the cantor from house to house singing two hymns – the troparion and kontakion. I sprinkled holy water on the icons and all drew near to kiss the holy cross. At one cottage, the owner stopped me and said, "And what, Father, you won't draw us a sausage?"[5]

"What sausage?" I asked

"The same that is drawn at home in Russia."

This request was repeated at a few other peasant cottages. We were puzzled and tried to find out for ourselves the ritual of drawing a sausage, but we could not comprehend what it was from the inconsistent information the settlers provided.

We sat down to rest with one rather prominent settler from Chernigov. (He had recently married the widow of a priest.) It is here that we became acquainted with this custom of drawing "sausages."

At home in Russia during the festival of the Epiphany, the priest visits all homes with the holy cross and water and while singing the hymn [troparion], the cantor draws a cross on the wall and a spear and a sponge on its sides. At the top, he writes a shortened version of "Jesus Christ," and at the end of this drawing the cantor signs the bottom of the cross with the shape of Golgotha, and turning to the master or mistress of the house, he says, "And this here is your sausage." For this significant work of the cantor, the peasants give him either a sausage or two or three kopeks, on top of the compensation paid to the priest.

The settler T – ts, as he told me about this, personally drew the shape of the cross, which was drawn at home in Russia with coal, chalk, or some kind of special pencil depending, of course, on the color of the wall.

Some Russian priests have already adopted this peculiar custom in Siberian settler parishes among the populations from Poltava and Chernigov. One related to me an incident, closely connected with the custom of drawing "sausages" on the wall. He went through the parish with the holy cross and water. In place of the absent cantor, he took a young boy to help him sing and also to draw the "sausage" on the wall. They came to the home of a wealthy Little Russian originally from Chernigov. The priest began to sing the hymn and the boy stood on a bench and began to draw a cross on the wall. Seeing this, the homeowner, regardless of the fact that the priest had not yet finished singing, cried out:

"Where are you climbing and what are you dirtying there?"

After the priest finished kissing the cross and sprinkling the water, he turned to the peasant and said, "Why didn't you let him draw the cross? Isn't this your native custom?"

"No, Father, at home in Russia the cantor writes a prayer on the wall, not a cross."

"What prayer?"

"The same one that you were just singing," answered the peasant.

In any case, this is nothing but the pure invention of this settler. Just think about how much time would be required for the procession through the parish, if each cottage needed to have written on the wall the hymn for the celebration of the Epiphany.

Among Little Russian settlers, the procession with holy icons at Easter and with the holy cross at Christmas is accompanied by almost no special native customs. Here one can really only mention the custom of placing in the front corner of their homes some hay with baked bread on it, which is done during the Christmas celebration in remembrance of the baby Jesus in the cattle manger.

Speaking of walks about the parish with the holy cross or a pastoral visitation with a home blessing, I can't be silent on the issue of the income of the clergy that is received from these parishes with Little Russian settlers. Perhaps mentioning here the income of the clergy is not appropriate, but through this issue, it is possible to describe the attitudes of Little Russians toward their clergy. Compensation for visits with the holy cross in rare circumstances comes to a five-kopek coin and a small loaf of white bread, but more often they give two or three kopeks, and quite often nothing. Sometimes you feel ashamed when at the home of a wealthy settler, you are given in your hand a copper coin of three or five kopeks. But all things considered, of course, it is not necessary to distinguish between poor or rich – all need to be visited and equally thanked regardless of the value of the copper coin pressed into one's hand.

When speaking generally about the donations of Little Russian settlers in support of their parish clergy, their particular stinginess must be noted. In my first two years of service in Novosele, I went "for a collection" through the parish and from that day forward promised myself that I would not do so ever again. It turned into something indecent, humiliating, and even insulting. Many hid in their homes, and some, just for the sake of ridicule, gave a fistful of grain. There are also those who openly declared: "Why give him anything, he has a salary." What should I think about such crude pranks? I find it difficult to say. It is difficult to express in words the heavy state of my soul, which I have suffered as a result of my flock treating me this way. You understand right away that the person who addresses you with these words does not respect you and feels that he does not need you. I also cannot hide such cases (as in Novaia Rus) when my envoy during the "collection" was even showered with abuse. Where this Russian abuse originates, I can't say for certain; I only mention that it is a fact, and it needs to be noted that such behavior is only encountered among the Little Russians. As for the old-timer Sibiriaki, I never encountered anything of the kind among them. Who, for example, in the parish assembly shouts about establishing a set rate for the administration of rites? Without fail, it is a Little Russian settler who alone is able to grumble and find fault in all trifles of parish life and to point to laws and regulations and introduce his own ways of doing things.

NOTES

1. Panteleimon Papshev, "Usloviia, blagopriiatstvuiushchiia sektantskoi propagande," *Omskie eparkhial'nye vedomosti* 29 (1916): 17–21.
2. Term for native Russian inhabitants of Siberia.
3. Ioann Goloshubin, "Iz vpechatlenii sel'skago sviashchennika," *Omskie eparkhial'nye vedomosti* 15 (1911): 25–26, 30–35.
4. The phrase Little Russian was the standard term for describing Ukrainians in imperial Russia.
5. There are many Ukrainian words sprinkled through the reported speech of the settlers in this section, sometimes with a Russian translation in parentheses.

SUGGESTED READINGS

Clay, J. Eugene. "Orthodox Missionaries and 'Orthodox Heretics' in Russia, 1886–1917." In *Of Religion and Empire: Missions, Conversion, and Tolerance in Tsarist Russia*, ed. Robert P. Geraci and Michael Khodarkovsky, 38–69. Ithaca, NY: Cornell University Press, 2001.

Coleman, Heather J. *Russian Baptists and Spiritual Revolution, 1905–1929*. Bloomington: Indiana University Press, 2005.

Freeze, Gregory. "Institutionalizing Piety: The Church and Popular Religion, 1750–1850." In *Imperial Russia: New Histories for the Empire*, ed. Jane Burbank and David L. Ransel, 210–49. Bloomington: Indiana University Press, 1998.

Geraci, Robert P. "Going Abroad or Going to Russia? Orthodox Missionaries in the Kazakh Steppe, 1881–1917." In *Of Religion and Empire: Missions, Conversion, and Tolerance in Tsarist Russia*, ed. Robert P. Geraci and Michael Khodarkovsky, 274–310. Ithaca, NY: Cornell University Press, 2001.

Treadgold, Donald. *The Great Siberian Migration: Government and Peasant in Resettlement from Emancipation to the First World War*. Westport, CT: Greenwood Press, 1976.

EIGHTEEN

Petitions to "Brother Ioann" Churikov, 1914

Page Herrlinger

ON ANY GIVEN MONDAY IN 1914, EVEN ON THE COLDEST WINTER days, a line of as many as 1,500 people could be seen extending from the front door of 60 Troitskaia Street in Obukhovo, an industrialized village on the outskirts of St. Petersburg/Petrograd. The vast majority was working class, and many of them were, or recently had been, suffering from the debilitating physical and psychological effects of alcoholism, on account of either their own drinking or that of someone close to them. Others suffered from illness, or from the physical or mental infirmity of someone they loved; still others were impoverished, desperate for work, food, or a place to live. Some had stood in the line before (even many times), others did so for the very first time. Whatever the case, each individual came to the door with the singular purpose of petitioning for the prayers and counsel of the popular lay preacher, "Brother Ioann" Churikov, and each came with the hope that he could help them in a way no one else could.

By 1914, Churikov had lived and preached in the Russian capital for almost two decades. Originally from Samara province, he was raised by devout Orthodox parents but had lived a largely secular life until 1894, when a life-altering crisis led him to commit himself to his faith. Having quit his business pursuits and given away his material possessions, he turned first to the beloved Father John of Kronstadt for spiritual counsel and prayer, and then "wandered" the Russian countryside for two years in heavy iron chains. He also began to read the Bible, and upon returning to Petersburg, set out to share his love of Scripture with others, especially in the squalid working-class neighborhoods, where immorality and religious indifference and doubt were on the rise.

Petitions to "Brother Ioann" Churikov

18.1. "Brother Ioann" Churikov with followers. A. T. Mikhailov, *Koloniia narodnykh trezvennikov* (St. Petersburg, 1914).

Though inexperienced and lacking in official credentials, Churikov soon attracted large, enthusiastic crowds to his Sunday afternoon meetings. He preached a simple, uncompromising message of Scriptural hope, absolute sobriety, and self-help: embrace the Word of God, have faith and God will take care of you; free yourself from your sins, and you will no longer be punished because of them. To those who felt abandoned by God in the man-made urban environment, Churikov insisted that the city air was also "from the Lord": "Stay in Petersburg so that the Lord can show you how strong and powerful He is; put your hope in God, believe in His Words, and you will get healthy again, and you will be even better than before."[1]

By 1905, Churikov could claim hundreds if not thousands of devoted followers who testified that their lives had been transformed by his guidance and prayers. As news of his "miraculous" healing powers spread over the next few years, tens of thousands more turned to him with their problems, including debilitating addictions and all kinds of physical illnesses, from colds and "female problems" to cancer, paralysis, and other chronic or "incurable" conditions. Others sought his advice on how to overcome their struggles with relationships, poverty, unemployment, and all types of sin and vice.

In an era of increasing religious crisis and political radicalism, secular and religious observers alike praised Churikov as a unique and welcome spiritual leader among the working classes – a kind of urban "starets." Yet, even as Churikov repeatedly voiced his love of and devotion to the Orthodox Church, his unconventional popularity and the extreme devotion expressed by his followers concerned some Orthodox authorities. Consequently, Churikov's public meetings were periodically forbidden, and in 1905, he was forced to end private receptions with his followers and allowed to receive written petitions only.[2] Then, in 1914, after considerable debate, Church authorities made the decision to excommunicate Churikov, finding him guilty of a range of "sectarian-heretical" and "self-willed" behaviors. These included: freely interpreting Holy Scripture without direction from the Holy Fathers and Church; preaching a false understanding of the relationship between the Holy Sacraments and salvation; and "blasphemously" comparing himself to the "Evangelical Christ" and posing as a miracle-worker.[3]

Official efforts to lessen Brother Ioann's influence were largely ineffectual, however. In fact, even after his excommunication, many of his followers continued to believe in (and testify to) his "miraculous" powers and ability to predict the future. In fact, petitioners continued to write notes to Churikov not only until his arrest by Soviet authorities in 1929 and his death in 1933, but also throughout the Soviet period.[4]

The following represents a small sampling of the thousands of petitions that have survived, including some with Brother Ioann's responses. Most were written anonymously on small scraps of paper, some brief and to the point, others with a confession-like, cathartic quality; many contain grammatical mistakes, penned in haste or by a semi-literate person. Although the majority constituted requests for help of some kind, others expressed gratitude for past aid, while still others were intended to serve as written testimony of Churikov's "miraculous" abilities.

When read separately and together, the petitions offer an extraordinary window onto the varied needs, habits, and struggles of ordinary people, and help us to understand the petitioners' expectations of themselves as believers, as well as Brother Ioann's role as a spiritual healer and guide. With their focus on issues of everyday life – physical illness or injury, problems with alcohol or employment, and personal relationships – they resemble prayers made by modern Orthodox believers to their saints. The fact that many mention both physical and spiritual ailments reflects that petitioners assumed an interactive relationship between the body and soul and understood physical suffering as punishment for sin. That many petitioners consulted medical doctors before seeking Brother Ioann's prayer was typical behavior in a transitional age, when most people consulted practitioners of both science and faith in an effort to maximize their chances for recovery.

Sampling of Petitions to Brother Ioann in 1914[5]

[58] Dear Brother, pray for me, my eyes are hurting.

[61] Pray, Dear Brother, that the Lord humbles my son's heart to the Word of God.

[63] Pray, Dear Brother, that the Lord sends my wife a job.

[65] Pray, Dear Brother, my nose is sore, and [I have a] cold.

[68] Pray for me, Dear Brother, that I don't drink wine.

[72] Pray for me, Dear Brother, bless me that I get an apartment.

[75] Dear Brother, my mother is sick.

[77] Dear Brother, pray that I don't drink wine, and that I fear nothing.

[171] Dear Brother, don't turn your face from me. I am a great sinner. I have committed every sin, I'm ashamed to say. I lied to my husband and broke the law, and stole, and judged and was envious. Dear Brother, pray for my sins, so that I won't do them. My husband and I and (our) two daughters are being punished. [We've had] a rash and scabs on our bodies for three months already. And the teacher sent my daughter home from school, and forbade her to return until she has recovered and brings a doctor's note. I have been to the doctor, [he] gave me ointments. Pray, Dear Brother, that the Lord relieves me of the sickness without the medication.

[1930b.–94] Forgive me, Dear Brother, I am a great sinner, and a great harlot, soaked to the bone by playing the whore, and my mouth was desecrated. I am soaked in filth like a stinking dog; I danced to the church bells and sang street songs that mention the Lord and the Blessed Virgin Mary. I beg of you Dear Brother, pray for me, a great sinner; I believe I will be healed by your prayers. I used to suffer strong [asthma], [but] by thy prayers, I began to feel much better. For seven months now, I have had no doctor and have not been to a hospital, I do not breathe oxygen or inject morphine. I live with your prayers and breathe God's air. Forgive me, Dear Brother, that I disturbed you with my letter.

[200] Dear Brother, I sincerely ask you, would you be so good as to pray to the Lord God for my husband Vasilii (he has a great weakness for wine.) I hope, Dear Brother, that your prayers will be heard by the Lord God and my husband, God willing, will be saved from this dragon, for which I would be grateful to you. Your sinful slave, Elizaveta Zhukova.

[201] Dear Brother Ioann! Save my life! My life is completely destroyed; I am extremely bored, and I want to kill myself, because I have no hope in anything. And it's very difficult for me to live. Take me under your protection and pray for me that my life will work out, as it was in Petersburg. Right now I'm living in the country with my relatives.

[209] I thank the Lord God and you, Dear Brother, that the Lord by His great kindness and by your holy prayers helped me become sober, [and] that everything turned out well for me. I was sick in one eye, I put your holy and healing ointment on it at night, and it got better right away.

[210] Dear Brother! I wish to bring you gratitude for your prayer, by virtue of which I became a different person and quit drinking wine and now, thanks to your prayers, Dear Brother, I am happy and [so is] my family. We pray to the Lord God that he helps you to make many, many families happy, as I have become. I also want to ask you, Dear Brother, to pray for my sins, so that the Lord will free me of a nervous twitch. With deep love and belief in your great prayer, your slave Sergei.

[219] Dear Brother, I am sincerely grateful to you. By your prayers our boy was made better. More than we ever expected, his legs have been healed, and he has begun to walk.

[226] I am grateful to you, Dear Brother, that by your prayers the Lord healed me of venereal disease, corrected my wife's legs, and healed my daughter.

The following petitions include Brother Ioann's responses:

[5] Question: Pray for me, Dear Brother, I have become spiritually cold, [pray] that I [don't continue]. And my sides, and my chest are stuffed up, [I have a] cough, and I am freezing, [pray] that I don't suffer from the cold.

Answer: [If one] has cooled spiritually – [then one] can also become spiritually warm; read the word of the Gospel and listen to others who read it, and through faith in God's word the Lord will heal you spiritually and physically.

[6] Question: Dear Brother, pray for me, as I have been damned; I have betrayed you. For four years I was unable to write you and repent, and for that I suffer still, and am ruled by Satan. Dear Brother, you saved me from [my addiction to] wine, and from smoking, and from swearing, and I beg you to save me from the rest of my vices, [you know what they are], Brother.

Answer: If the Lord saved you from your former ailments, He is also strong enough to heal you by your faith from the rest of your habits.

[12] Question: Pray, Dear Brother, that I win at gambling.

Answer: Don't put your hopes in games, it won't be to your advantage. Believe in God, pray and work. You will be happy, like many other *trezvenniki*.[6]

[13] Question: Dear Brother, pray for my sinful self. The Lord was merciful – for a week I did not drink, thanks be to God. I beg you, Dear Brother, my leg hurts, it aches badly, when earlier I was lying drunk on a brick road, pray for [my sins].

Answer: God will heal you for the sake of your sober life. Because of your faith God will not refuse what you ask.

[14] Question: Pray for me, Dear Brother, my teeth ache.

Answer: The Lord ruins the teeth of sinners. Repent soon and you will recover soon.

NOTES

1. Davydov and Frolov, *Dukhovnyi partizan* (St. Petersburg, 1911), 40. This testimony was also published in *Novaia Rus'* no. 209 (2 August 1909).

2. Between 1905 and 1912, Churikov received petitioners bearing notes at his meeting place in Petrovskii park in Petersburg. Between 14 May 1912 and December 1918 receptions took place in Obukhovo.

3. RGIA, f. 821, op. 133, d. 212, ll. 329.

4. A series of petition notes written in the 1920s and 1930s can be found in GMIR, Koll. I, op. 4 "Materialy o trezvennikov," d. 19.

5. These petitions are located in GMIR, Koll. I, op. 4 "materialy o *trezvennikov*," d. 19. Page numbers are indicated in the text.

6. Literally trezvenniki means "teetotalers," but here it refers to the sober followers of Churikov.

SUGGESTED READINGS

Clay, J. Eugene. "Orthodox Missionaries and 'Orthodox Heretics' in Russia, 1886–1917." In *Of Religion and Empire*, ed. Robert Geraci and Michael Khodarkovsky, 38–69. Ithaca, NY: Cornell University Press, 2001.

Herrlinger, Page. *Working Souls: Russian Orthodoxy and Factory Labor in St. Petersburg 1881–1917*. Bloomington, IN: Slavica, 2007. Chapters 3 and 5.

McKee, W. Arthur. "Sobering Up the People: The Politics of Popular Temperance in Late Imperial Russia." *Russian Review* 58 (April 1999): 212–33.

Paert, Irina. *Spiritual Elders*. DeKalb: Northern Illinois University Press, 2010.

Steinberg, Mark D. *Proletarian Imagination: Self, Modernity, and the Sacred in Russia, 1910–1925*. Ithaca, NY: Cornell University Press, 2002.

NINETEEN

Archimandrite Toviia (Tysmbal), Prior of the Trinity-Sergius Lavra: Memoirs and Diaries (Selections)

Scott M. Kenworthy

THE CAREER OF ARCHIMANDRITE TOVIIA (TSYMBAL, 1836–1916) was a remarkable one: born a serf, he rose to become prior (*namestnik*) of Russia's most famous monastery, the Trinity–St. Sergius Lavra. In the mid-nineteenth century, about one quarter of monastic recruits came from the peasantry; after the Emancipation of the Serfs in 1861, the percentage of peasant recruits would rise steadily so that they constituted the vast majority by the early twentieth century. Toviia was born Trofim Tikhonovich Tsymbal in the settlement of Sheliakina, Alekseev volost in the province of Voronezh, on 23 July 1836. He first entered the Holy Mountain Monastery in Kharkov province at a young age in 1852; he took monastic vows and received the name Toviia (Tobias) in 1860 and was ordained deacon. In 1862 he transferred to the Trinity-Sergius Lavra. Because he had an exceptional voice and evident musical abilities, he became the Lavra's archdeacon, that is, the first deacon, who serves all the important liturgies with the prior of the monastery or visiting bishops and metropolitans (particularly the Metropolitan of Moscow). In Russian Orthodox liturgies a deacon is not requisite, but if one is serving, it adds to the grandeur of the service. Indeed, the deacon is in many ways more visible – and audible – than the priest, chanting all the litanies, the Gospel reading, and many other parts of the service. Therefore the archdeacon of a monastery like Trinity-Sergius – with its great number of pilgrims that periodically even included the royal family – was of paramount importance. Toviia served as deacon at Trinity-Sergius for over a quarter century until his voice began to lose its strength. In 1888 he was ordained to the priesthood, and he began to move up the monastery

19.1. Archimandrite Toviia (Tsymbal) in 1913. L. R. Vaintraub, *Khram v chest' Kazanskoi ikony Presviatoi Bogoroditsy v Podlipich'e v Dmitrove* (Dmitrov, 2005), 71. Reproduced with permission.

hierarchy. In 1893 he was appointed prior of the Chudov Monastery in the Kremlin, and in that capacity would participate in the coronation of Nicholas II in 1896. In 1903 he became abbot of the Znamenskii Monastery in Moscow, and the following year returned to Trinity-Sergius as its prior.

Monasticism therefore created opportunities in Russia for someone born a serf to rise to the position of head of the most important monastery in the empire, a position that involved receiving even the emperor himself. In 1915, Toviia took a somewhat unusual move for members of the church hierarchy and retired from his position as prior. As reflected in his diaries, there was evidently rumor that he had been forced to retire, although there is no paper trail in the archives to confirm this and Toviia explained that he wanted to retire to spend the end of his life in solitude and reflection. He spent part of his retirement at the Paraclete Hermitage, an isolated satellite community of the Trinity-Sergius Lavra; during this time composed his memoirs, which he based in part on diaries he had kept throughout his life (as he recalls in the passage translated below). He passed away on 7 March 1916. Because Toviia died shortly before the Russian Revolution, nothing was written about him (as was typical for important ecclesiastical figures) and his memory was largely forgotten even within the Trinity-Sergius community.[1]

Memoirs by monastics are rather unusual in the Orthodox tradition, in particular because the monastic path by its very nature was to focus on overcoming concern with oneself. Toviia's memoirs therefore allow a rare glimpse into the otherwise closed world of the monastery. Archbishop Nikon (Rozhdestvenskii), founder-editor of Trinity-Sergius's journal *Trinity Word*, published selections of Toviia's diaries in 1916 and began publishing the memoirs in 1917, but this project was cut short by the revolution and cessation of the journal after only four chapters (of thirty-nine) were printed. The remainder of the memoirs still remains unpublished.[2]

The selections from Toviia's memoirs translated here focus on his childhood and youth. Several aspects are worthy of note. For one, although he was a serf growing up in the 1830s and 1840s, before the advent of any system of formal education for peasants, Toviia reveals that members of his family, although receiving their education at home, enjoyed a surprisingly high degree of literacy – much higher than historians usually assume. Toviia never received any formal education, even in the monastery (although he did seek opportunities to learn from monks who did), yet his memoirs and diaries are exceptionally well written. Also of paramount importance, these passages reveal that peasants had a great deal of what we might call "church literacy." Virtually all accounts of peasant religiosity in the nineteenth century were recorded by elites – mostly ethnographers or Orthodox clergy – who tended to focus on peasant incomprehension of doctrine and therefore concluded that peasants were superstitious, virtually pagan, with only a superficial veneer of Christianity. In Toviia's account of his childhood and youth, theology certainly does not figure prominently, but this does not mean that the common people's lives were not profoundly shaped by Christianity. Rather, their Christianity was focused on the prayers, the church services, the liturgical calendar of feasts and fasts, on the veneration of saints (whose Lives were popular reading among the peasants), on pilgrimage, and on acts of piety (as evidenced by the rigorous fasting that Toviia's fellow pilgrims undertake). Although the young Trofim was no doubt particularly precocious, for a peasant boy to be able to "play church" by performing all the parts of the service – priest, deacon, and choir – suggests that many peasants were intimately familiar with the liturgy.

Nineteenth-century Russia witnessed a remarkable upsurge of pilgrimage as well as a resurgence of monasticism, two phenomena that are closely connected, as Toviia's story reveals. In his account we can see how important pilgrimage was for not only him personally, but for everyone in his extended family and village. Indeed, his family and neighbors in a sense participated in his pilgrimage vicariously, both by having him pray for them in the holy places and also by later gathering around to hear the stories that he recounted after his return. Finally, Toviia's memoirs point to the elements that attracted him to monastic life, thereby revealing some of what fueled the remarkable resurgence of monasticism in nineteenth-century Russia. Once again liturgy is central. Added to this, the spread of literacy meant that more people were reading saints' lives, and these saints became childhood heroes that inspired those like

Toviia to follow their example. A final element was pilgrimage: visits to monasteries inspired some to want to remain.[3]

Archimandrite Toviia, "Memoirs of My Past"

CHAPTER 1: CHILDHOOD[4]

Experienced people who follow the development of human nature confirm that in earliest childhood a child betrays tendencies that predict the future nature of his labors and activities to which he is called by God. Applying this observation to my own life, I can in part agree that, if not always, then in several instances it is just. According to the general law of nature, my infancy passed by unconsciously. I can recollect only my parents' stories that in the growth of both my body and my understanding I developed very quickly. Evidently I must have been quite mischievous, because I was often punished with the rod, that I remember very well....

When I became more aware of my environment, I remember particularly loving to be in church, which pleased my parents, and they endeavored to bring me to the temple of God. I must say that in our parish church the service was conducted devoutly, even with great solemnity during feast days, because in our church there were three priests, three deacons and three subdeacons, and three retired clergy in addition.

When I was in church, I loved to stand at the very ambo, in front of everyone else, so that I could see the clergy and the whole rite of the service. Out of the entire rite of the Divine Liturgy, I liked best of all the parts served by the deacon. Above all I liked the censing of the altar and the church. In imitation I made myself at home something like a censor, hanging a plate on three strings, placing on it a whetstone for weight and, when I was alone in the house, imagining myself a deacon, I would wave my censor at the icons, the windows, and the doors. Such censing I began to practice rather early, even before I could read.

When I was seven years old they began to teach me to read.[5] There were no schools for peasant children back then. I was taught at home, and my teachers included my father, who could handle reading Slavonic pretty well. Most of the time I was taught by my uncle Ivan Andreevich, the older brother of my father, who was renowned among the peasants as a great reader [*chtets*]. I got through the alphabet in one winter, and the next winter I already began to read the Psalter and the Book of the Hours. We had many books, but they did not give me anything other than Psalters and the Hours so I wouldn't get the books dirty or tear the pages. However I got tired of the Psalter and the Hours and therefore I (secretly) took the Menaion and Akathists, and I began to serve prayer services [*moleben*], during which I copied not only the deacon, but also the priest and the cantor. At that time I read and sang with my whole voice, in particular my favorite refrains of the Akathists and the Alleluias. My parents frequently stopped me at such exercises and punished me with the rod, finding such exercises inappropriate and a bit sinful.

Out of many such incidents I recall one: taking advantage of the fact that every member of the family was out, I, being alone, began to wave my whetstone censor so freely that the whetstone tore from the string and fell on the shelf where the pots stood, breaking one of them. At that moment my mother entered and, seeing the broken pot, grabbed the rod and mercilessly lashed me, then sat me at the table and put the Psalter in my hand, commanding me to read aloud and not leave the house under any circumstances. She hadn't even succeeded in letting the rod out of her hand when in walked my godmother, Zinoviia Grigor'evna Podgornaia, who lived only two houses away; she saw me at the Psalter, reading something incoherently and at the same time whimpering from the crying. Not understanding what was going on, she began to reproach my mother for such harsh treatment of her son, as I remember in such a way: "Why do you, *kuma*,[6] torture the boy with the Psalter? Are you preparing him to be a cantor or something? And in general what's it to us, poor people, to be especially literate? He can't be a cantor anyway.[7] Able to read prayers – well and thank God! We need literacy only to be able to pray to God." My mother answered her: "If only you had come an hour earlier and seen his pranks. He, left alone in the room, began to perform Vigil and a prayer service, where already he doesn't pretend to be just the cantor, but also the father deacon and even the father priest himself. But the deacon above all. Take a look (taking out the whetstone), he hung this stone on string and swings it with his whole arm, imagining himself a deacon. Finally he waved to the point that he broke dishes, the rascal. You are the one who got in my way, but after I see you off, I'll give him another whipping." My godmother heard this indictment and understood what was going on, laughed genially, then took the Psalter from my hand, kissed me, tossed some clothing on me, and let me outside to play, with the words, "Go, my future deacon, play with the kids."

I never got away with such pranks without punishment, but gradual exercise in literacy was not without fruit, and I began to read already with comprehension, so that it was possible for me to hear and understand what I read. At that time my parents (on feast days) set me to read the Lives of Saints, and themselves listened with attention; they liked it and it clearly comforted them. Subsequently I began to notice that I also liked reading, but this was mixed with a lining of vanity: I liked reading above all because the elders listened to and praised me. In spite of this tint of vanity, I nevertheless gradually took to reading, so that I frequently took books and read them to myself, and I especially liked the lives of the righteous hermits, the reading of which inspired in me thoughts of monasticism. In my imagination pictures of the hermit's life already began to be drawn: the thicket of woods, the little hut in which the monk kneels with hands lifted up to the heavens and praying to God. I really liked these scenes and although I was carried away by them, it did not yet occur to me to become a monk myself. But when I was ten years old my mother took me to Voronezh on foot to St. Mitrofan, where I saw monks and how each day they performed the liturgy in church and continually prayed to God, then the thought already appeared that it would be good for me too to be a monk. Subsequently that thought seized me so that after a year I conclusively decided to enter a monastery. But knowing that my parents wouldn't let me go, because I was their oldest, I decided to guard this intention in secret, looking out for a suitable opportunity or some sort of means to begin this matter. Sometimes monks appeared among us, at times those making collections, sometimes pilgrims, but I had not decided to reveal my thought to them because they would disclose it to others. Finally the Providence of God showed me in my sixteenth year the means to begin this cause that I desired.

CHAPTER 2: YOUTH; JOURNEY TO KIEV[8]

On 23 July 1851, I turned fifteen. Up to that time no one knew about my intention to leave the world and retire to a monastery, because a suitable opportunity to announce this to my parents and ask for their blessing had not yet appeared. But in the first days of September of that year, as God directed, the occasion for such a beginning appeared. My godfather, Ivan Ivanovich Rogozian, who lived four households away, came to us one day for some particular business and mentioned in passing that he was planning to make the journey to Kiev on pilgrimage any day now, and that three other adults, whom he named, were going with him. My parents wished him a good journey and safe return, asked holy prayers for themselves before the Saints of God, and let him go. At that time my heart beat in my chest with anxiety; I thought: here God has sent a suitable opportunity. At that moment I turned to my parents and began to ask their blessing to let me also go on pilgrimage to Kiev. Such a request didn't particularly surprise them because in our family all of the adult members without fail went to Kiev. However they didn't give me a complete promise, but said: "You are still young – you will get to Kiev later."

At that time I stopped talking about it, but a little later I repeated my request, pointing to the convenient opportunity to go with my godfather – which is like going with a parent. They taught us from childhood to honor our godfather and godmother equally with our parents. Hearing out my case, they agreed – but they couldn't give an affirmative answer until they asked their older brother Ivan Andreevich, who lived five versts away from us in the settlement of Sheliakino at the church. So as not to lose time, I volunteered to go to him by foot, to which they agreed. That very minute, nearly running, I left for my uncle's. On the road I nourished the complete hope in my soul that my uncle wouldn't hold me back, because he was very religious and had been to Kiev many times himself. My uncle, seeing me appear at an unexpected time and in an anxious state, became alarmed himself, wondering whether something bad had happened at home, but when I prostrated myself at his feet and began asking his blessing for me to go to Kiev on pilgrimage, he visibly rejoiced and asked with whom I intended to go; discovering that it was with my godfather, he blessed me with love. At that moment he remembered that I would need a monthly pass from the volost government, and he took me right then to the volost and asked the village elders to give me a pass; an hour later the pass was ready, and, running, I returned home to my parents. There was no longer any discussion of keeping me, because I already had the pass in my hands.

It was necessary to start getting ready for the road, which did not take long: my mother gave me some thick linen, from which I sewed myself a bag for the road with a contraption to carry it on my shoulders; I made a walking stick out of strong wood, and my mother prepared dried bread and put it in the bag and placed there two pairs of clean underwear and two towels. In this way the traveler was ready and the departure was set for two days hence. At that time I could no longer conceal from my parents my desire to leave the world and enter a monastery. When I informed my parents of this, it nearly ruined the whole matter, although such openness was unavoidable for me. My mother was in part afraid, and in part didn't understand my resolve, and my father was very alarmed and sharply stated that he would not let me go to Kiev, demanding that I stay home. Seeing such a turn of events, I began to ask forgiveness of my father, promising not to remain anywhere, but to return home. On such a promise my father, although he agreed to my journey, nevertheless took away the pass and money given to me for the road and gave them to my godfather, strictly instructing him not to leave me anywhere, but to bring me home.

When everything was ready, on the appointed day, the whole family gathered in the house, lit the icon lamps and candles, and prayed to God, during which I bowed to my parents' feet, and also to all the elders; all made the sign of the cross over me, wished me a good journey and safe return. They asked my prayers before God's Saints, and everyone accompanied me out of the yard. But uncle Ivan Andreevich escorted me to meet with my fellow-traveling elders. All together we entered the church, heard a parting prayer service, after which our priest Father Ivan blessed us with the cross and sprinkled us with holy water.

From there, with our knapsacks on our shoulders and our staffs in our hands we left on our path to Kiev. Our road went in the direction of Belgorod, Akhtyrka, Lubny, Pereiaslavl, Borispol, and on to Kiev. Getting ready for the journey, I stocked up on a whole notebook of paper and a pencil for taking travel notes. From the first days of our departure I began to keep a short diary. In the beginning I recorded only the names of locations, villages, and cities that we passed through, and I recorded also the number of versts between them. When my notebook was full, I placed it in the bag and then bought more paper and sewed a new notebook, in which I continued to write my diary. Here I began to write not just the names of the locations, but also events that we encountered, such as one Saturday evening [when] we arrived in the settlement named Ustinka (no more than forty versts from Belgorod) and came across a well with a chapel. This is the spot where the miracle-working image of St. Nicholas appeared, that icon which is now located in the cathedral church of the Trinity Monastery in Belgorod, in which are also resting the uncorrupted relics of St. Ioasaf.

A difficult, sandy road lay ahead to Belgorod, but we wanted to get to Belgorod the following day (Sunday) and venerate the holy things before having eaten anything. Notwithstanding the difficulty of the path and the old age of my fellow travelers, we awoke early and with the help of God arrived in Belgorod when the service had already finished and the brothers were having lunch in the refectory. On our earnest request, they opened the church and served for us a moleben [service] to St. Nicholas and a *panikhida* [requiem] at the tomb of St. Ioasaf; for that they took from us a "three-ruble," the silver money of that time, worth 2 rubles 62 kopeks. Reaching that goal was so comforting to us that we felt particularly healthy and happy that day. On leaving the church, we took shelter by the monastery well, soaked our bread rusks, salted them, and ate them with great appetite and drank the salted water. We rested there and went on our way. Already out of the city, passing by a melon patch, we bought a good watermelon and ate it like a delicacy.

The following circumstance is worthy of note: when we had lunch by the monastery well, which was located not far from the brothers' kitchen, a monk noticed that we ate only rusks and offered us some hot cabbage soup and kasha, but my old men, seeing such courtesy, stood and made a deep bow before the monk and politely thanked him for his offer, yet they refused the food on the basis that we had made a vow to go to Kiev observing a strict fast and not eating anything hot, so that in Kiev we

Archimandrite Toviia 279

could receive communion of the holy mysteries of Christ. Such an example of strong faith in God and pious Christian life is worthy of praise and imitation. In like manner in my diary I described the entire road to Kiev and back. On returning home, I read my diary for a long time to my mother, and she listened and cried from joy.

CHAPTER 3: CONTINUING THE ROAD TO KIEV;
THE AKHTYRSKII TRINITY MONASTERY[9]

Although I was obliged to fulfill the word I had given to my parents that I wouldn't remain in a monastery, nevertheless on the road I could not give up the thought that at some point I should live in a monastery. And therefore at each monastery we entered I tried to find out how the monks lived and whether or not I could enter it at least eventually. Coming to the town of Akhtyrka in Kharkov province, we prayed before the miraculous image of the Mother of God located in the city's cathedral. That was on the feast of the Elevation of the Pure Cross of the Lord, 14 September 1851. Then we went to the local Trinity Monastery, located two versts from the city on our way to Kiev. I liked this monastery tremendously. The round and high mountain on which the monastery was located simply charmed me. In addition to this I met there several monks who were fellow-countrymen (from Alekseev volost, who advised me to enter this monastery, praised their local cenobitic rule and the order of the monastery).[10] As I was charmed by the location of the monastery and the kindness of the local monks, I firmly decided not to choose another monastery, but, on returning home, earnestly ask my parents for their permission to enter that particular monastery. This thought and the firm decision possessed me so much that the further continuation of my road to Kiev had the sole goal only of venerating the holy relics of God's saints, for I didn't even think about choosing a different monastery for my life. Therefore the rest of the monasteries that I saw on the way, such as those in Lubny, in Pereiaslavl, and in Kiev itself, struck me only with their beauty and the grandeur of their buildings, but I didn't like a single one as a place to join.

For example, the Transfiguration Monastery near the city of Lubny seems even superior to the Trinity Akhtyrskii Monastery according to its internal good order and the beauty of the remote place where it is located. Moreover, there rest the holy relics of Patriarch Athanasius the Sitting.[11] The sum total of all this might have aroused in me the desire to live there and save my soul; however the internal disposition of my spirit didn't feel such a desire.

On the way to Kiev we encountered another monastery in the city of Pereiaslavl, but all of its spiritual beauty resided in the holy relics of the holy martyr Hegumen Makarii; the cathedral church is also very grand, but the monastery itself, as the residence of the bishop, didn't have the desired suitability for monastic quietude. Moreover, at that time it housed the Theological Seminary, which was later transferred to Poltava. We stayed there only a short time. Having heard the liturgy and moleben to St. Makarii, [and] venerated the holy relics, we ate, rested, and continued on our way.

CHAPTER 4: ARRIVAL IN KIEV[12]

From Pereiaslavl the main road to Kiev goes through Borispol and to the last station, Brovary, whence Kiev is already visible. But the shortest path is through the pine forest, only the road is sandy. However, we weren't afraid of the sand and went by that road. The pine forest goes to the bank of the Dnieper, hiding the view of the Lavra from the paths that approach it, so that we saw the Lavra only when we were leaving the forest, at the bank of the river itself. I must say that the best view of the Lavra is from this (eastern) side. I will never forget those stunning moments and the deep impression that suddenly overtook us as the majestic picture of the Lavra's churches and bell tower, with the golden cupolas and crosses, and also the whole mass of different buildings, which we had little seen in our lives. Seeing such beauty, we all stopped immediately and in silent reverence fell to the earth. Among all of us flowed tears of gratitude to God that we had finally reached the holy Lavra, the goal of our desires. Here each of us received a reward for all the labors undertaken on the journey. Arising, we made three prostrations to the Lavra and silently continued on our way, wiping away the tears and guarding ourselves with the sign of the cross. Going along the shore a quarter verst, we came to the bridge that was built on rafts and lay directly on the water. I had never in my life seen such a bridge, and therefore I was afraid to walk on it. Moreover the Dnieper was very wide and appeared rough at that time (from abundant rain). The waves rolled over the bridge.

We got to the Lavra's hotel after lunch, [and] they took us to a place with bunk beds. There, following our custom, we soaked our rusks, had lunch, and rested, then went to Vespers in the great church. The old men walked vigorously all the way to Kiev; evidently they were strengthened by the grace of God and the hope of seeing the holy things, but in Kiev they felt exhausted from the fasting and the labors, so that for the first three days they only went to the Lavra's churches and the caves. There we confessed and communed with the holy Mysteries of Christ in the Refectory Church. Twice we went to the caves and venerated the saints of God, and the rest of the time during those three days the old men rested. For me a rest of one day was enough, and therefore I left the old men in the hotel and went about Kiev with rapid strides. I was in the St. Michael's Monastery, venerated the relics of the holy martyr St. Barbara. I was in the Sophia cathedral, St. Andrew's Church, the Church of the Tithes, went to Podol to the Brothers' Monastery, walked around the bazaar, took a look at the Fountain of Strong Samson sitting on the lion with the pipe sticking out of his mouth, although there was no water coming from it. I even went to the embankment of the Dnieper where they were building the chain bridge. When the old men had rested and went to Podol, I was already able to serve as their guide, showing them the monasteries, churches, and public buildings. The old men were moreover surprised at my memory, how quickly I could get to know Kiev, just like a local resident. In the Lavra we attended two services in the cathedral, which were officiated by the local prior, Archimandrite Lavrentii, a starets already elderly and very good-looking, his voice was a rather strong and nice tenor.... In the Lavra God led me to see Metropolitan Filaret,[13] only not during the service, but at the holy gates, after lunch....

After looking around Kiev as we could, fulfilling our Christian duties of the sacraments of confession and communion, and venerating the saints of God who rest in the caves, we departed on our return journey, carrying away spiritual joy and gratitude to God, who granted us such mercy and grace.

CHAPTER 5: RETURN FROM KIEV; THE PROVIDENCE OF GOD, ARRANGING THE AGREEMENT OF MY PARENTS[14]

Returning home and harboring the hope of entering Akhtyrskii Monastery, the whole way I was anxious with the thought of how to approach my parents with the request to let me go and persuade them to agree to my request. This concern powerfully oppressed my soul, and therefore I fervently prayed to God as best I knew. On the road I tried to walk by myself, so as to give myself to prayer as much as possible. I called upon the help of the Mother of God, the Kievan saints and other saints that I could remember. And at the end of my journey the merciful God revealed to me His Providential miracle....

CHAPTER 6: AT MY PARENTS' HOME UPON RETURNING FROM KIEV[15]

My return from the distant journey brought joy not just to my parents, but to the whole family. The first day was like a holiday. Not only the members of my family, but even several of the neighbors left their work and came to take a look at me and hear stories about Kiev. There my diary, written in pencil, delivered a great service to me, and comfort to my family. Much I narrated from memory, and some I read from my diary, in order to strengthen the authenticity of my stories. My mother got me to read to her nearly every day (in the evenings) from my diary, hearing one and the same several times, always crying. My entire family experienced such a delight on the day of my return. What delighted me most of all was the mood of my parents, because I encountered a change that I did not expect. Now they not only supported my intention, but were ready and willing to let me go and blessed me to enter the monastery....

Archimandrite Toviia, Diaries

In addition to his memoirs, Toviia's diaries from 1914 to 1916 also survive. They focus on the end of his life looking back on his monastic career. While an element of self-justification is at work (defending his decision to retire), the diaries depict important dimensions of monastic life. To begin with, what attracted Toviia to monasticism was the pursuit of quietude (*hesychia* in Greek, *bezmolviia* in Russian), that is, contemplative prayer in solitude and silence. This approach to monasticism experienced a revival in nineteenth-century Russia and was one of the factors that fueled the larger resurgence of men's monasticism. But his own personal experience reveals the tensions in monastic life between the ideals of quietude and those of obedience and service. Finally, Toviia discusses his own daily routine and suggests a friction between the feeling of gratitude for the gifts he has received and his own sense of unworthiness for them. His dwelling on sin and death might strike the modern reader as morbid, but in monastic practice these were tools to impel the monk to repentance and to cultivate what matters most in the time one has in life.

7 MARCH 1915[16]

Even before I entered the monastery, a certain understanding of the image of monastic life had formed in my imagination. In my mind I pictured a monk, living alone in a narrow cell, carrying on a life of prayer and reading the word of God. In general, I imagined the ideal monk leading the spiritual, ascetic life. With such imaginings and spiritual longings of monasticism I began my monastic life. However, the very first experiences of monastic obedience convinced me that the life I had imagined was a long way from me as a beginning novice. Experienced elders explained to me that such a life could be led only by those monks who had lived in a monastery for decades, above all those who had meekly borne their monastic obediences their whole life. Beyond that, the life of stillness comes only to people who are advanced in years, and even then only under the strict supervision of other, more experienced elders. It is even dangerous for young people to begin such a life. For them, the most reliable path to salvation is holy obedience. From that time I began to watch myself, seeking opportunities to combine obedience with the solitude that my heart zealously sought. However, passing from one obedience to another, I became convinced that it is necessary to hold to the first path, that is, sincerely and meekly carrying out one's obedience, and that quietude would come of its own, according to God's command.

When the path of obedience led to positions of authority, then I frequently lost hope of achieving solitude, for the bustle of administrative matters swallowed up free time, took away health, and the years disappeared, and I grew closer to death. It frequently happened that I came to confusion and in part, as it were, to despair that I would have to die in the inconstancy of half-worldly bustle. However, my hope in the mercy of God did not leave me, on the basis that I always fulfilled holy obedience with great zeal. In recent years, seeing my declining strength, in particularly feeling weakness in my legs, I frequently asked God and St. Sergius to release me [from service] for quietude, but I did not know how to begin such a great change in my life. I did not want to begin this matter on my own initiative, but waited for a sign from above – from God. I saw such a divine sign in my illness, which developed into influenza and made me bed-ridden for two months, under the pressure of which I requested to be released from the post of prior in order to retire to solitude.

28 MAY 1915. HERMITAGE OF THE HOLY PARACLETE[17]

Lord bless the beginning and continuance of eremitical quietude!

Today I relocated for the summer to the cell I built in the Hermitage of the Holy Paraclete. 17 June of this year marks nineteen years since the death of my father, Schemamonk Tovit, whom I buried here.[18] At that time I bought for myself a burial place next to the grave of my father, where I dug myself a grave and laid a burial vault with brick.

That same year I requested permission of the Spiritual Council of the Lavra to build a special cell for myself and, receiving the blessing, began to build it, sustaining the hope that someday I would retire to it and pursue quietude. At that time I was prior of the Chudov Monastery in Moscow. But all these nineteen years I have not ceased thinking about the Paraclete Hermitage and my prepared burial vault, striving the sooner to retire there. In addition to this I prepared for myself, while still in Moscow, an oak coffin, which even now I keep in my cell, sustaining the hope that at death my sinful body would be put in the coffin and be buried next to the body of my father. This is also the point of my last will and testament.

Gratitude to the Providential God! My cherished desire has come true: I am in the hermitage and in my dear cell.

Through my whole life I loved solitude and quiet, and therefore (living in the Lavra) I often went to Gethsemane Skete to its elders: Filaret, Ilarion, and Aleksandr,[19] I admired the quiet of their solitary life, I expressed to them my desire for solitude, but obviously it was not yet the will of God to fulfill my desires. Even the elders with one voice said to me: "Labor in your obedience, to which St. Sergius himself has called you. Your solitude is ahead and it will not get away from you. The time will come when you will receive it, then treasure it and be faithful to it." At that time I obeyed the advice of the elders, for the inner voice of my heart told me the same. But the elders have died, their voices are no longer heard; the years have passed, bringing old age closer and reminding [me] of death. In particular since the time of my father's death, I have not parted from the thought of solitude. When the Lord placed on me the post of prior of the Lavra, then my soul not only strove toward solitude but, one could say, broke from the captivity of bustle into the freedom of the spirit. Finally the merciful Lord took from me the burden of these cares and granted me the possibility, by means of prayer, to purify my mind and heart – and ask remission of my sins.

Here I sit in my beloved cell, attuning my ears to the imperturbable silence of quietude. Quieting down a little, giving time for my mind and heart to dwell on one point, I take the Gospel into my hands (making the sign of the cross) [and] I begin to read it, then the Epistles of the Apostles, then the canons and prayers. Finishing my reading lesson, I take up the pen and write my daily notes. Finishing that, I take up the prayer rope and collect my wandering thoughts in the cage of my heart. After that I begin with the prayer to Jesus the Son of God and to God, then to the Most Pure Virgin Mother of God and the saints of God. There rings the bell, I go to the temple of God, listen to the prayerful doxology offered to the Almighty God. From the church I go to the cemetery to my grave and that of my father, reading there the litany for the departed, bowing before my father and blessing the place of my eternal rest. Sometimes I say to my grave, using the words of St. Dimitrii of Rostov: "My grave, my rest, in thee will I dwell in the flesh and await the trumpet of the Fearful Judgment. Receive me and give rest to the dust of my body." On the way back, I walk a bit along the path for a breath of fresh air. Coming to my cell, I sometimes lie down and rest a bit, and then again at the prayer rope and the daily canons. In the temple of God, during the liturgy, I try to bring to mind all my relatives and acquaintances, living and dead. Expressing my gratitude to God, I do not rejoice sufficiently in the sweet silence that surrounds me. Sometimes the thought occurs to me: is there a monk in the world happier than I am? At the end of it all, when I begin to remember my sins, then I see that my soul is like a dirty stagnant pool, filled with stinking water and teeming with repulsive worms and reptiles, then an inexpressible fear fills my mind and heart. Comparing that sinfulness of mine with the blessings of God that I have been given, I fear to appear at the Judgment of the True God, where it will be said to me: "I gave you all my blessings, as my vine, and waited for you to bring the bunches, instead you bring me thorns, therefore you are suitable only for burning, go then to the eternal fire!"

Bringing to consciousness my sins, I repent and tremble, and in the repentance of my soul, with tears I call to You, O God: "With Thy compassionate eye, O Lord, behold my humility, for little by little my life draws to a close, and I have no hope of salvation because of my deeds; because of this I beseech You: with Thy compassionate eye, O Lord, behold my humility and save me" (Ochtoechos).[20]

NOTES

1. One of the former monks, the elder Zakharii, later told his disciples that Toviia was hated by the monks, had been forced to retire, and even that Toviia had tried to kill him, although many portions of the source are fantastical and none of these claims can be corroborated by the archival evidence. See Jane Ellis, trans., *An Early Soviet Saint: The Life of Father Zachariah* (Springfield, IL: Templegate, 1977), esp. 42. For positive remembrances of Toviia, see *Blagodariu Boga moego: Vospominaniia Very Timofeevny i Natal'i Aleksandrovny Verkhovtsevykh* (Moscow: Pravilo Very, 2001), 75.

2. They are in, OR RGB, f. 771, k. 2, d. 4. Fond 771 contains other of Toviia's manuscripts, including diaries, sermons, and personal letters.

3. I am grateful to Vitaly Chernetsky and Lisa Priebe for help in translating a few difficult passages.

4. Skhiarkhmandrit Toviia, "Vospominaniia moego proshedshago," *Troitskoe slovo* nos. 376–77 (25 June–2 July 1917): 409–12.

5. My date of birth was 23 July 1836 [Toviia's note].

6. The term *kum* (fem. *kuma*) refers to non-blood relations established through baptism.

7. They assumed Trofim could not be a cantor because one could generally become a member of the parish clergy

only after going to a seminary, which was open only to sons of parish clergy.

8. *Troitskoe slovo* nos. 381–83 (1–15 August 1917): 436–39.

9. *Troitskoe slovo* nos. 384–86 (22 August–5 September 1917): 453–54.

10. In cenobitic monasteries, the brothers hold everything in common, take meals together, and worship together; it was considered stricter for large monasteries than the more prevalent idiorhythmic rule, which allowed for a great deal of independence.

11. Patriarch Athanasius III Patelaros, 1597–1654, was Patriarch of Constantinople for a brief period in 1634. He was a frequent visitor to Russia and on one return journey died in Lubny and was buried in an unusual sitting position.

12. *Troitskoe slovo* nos. 384–86 (22 August–5 September 1917): 454–56.

13. Filaret (Amfiteatrov, 1779–1857) was Metropolitan of Kiev, 1837–57, and one of the great bishops of nineteenth-century Russia.

14. OR RGB, f. 771, k. 2, d. 4, ll. 9 ob–10 ob.

15. OR RGB, f. 771, k. 2, d. 4, ll. 11–12 ob.

16. Skhiarkhimandrit Toviia, "Moi dnevnik," *Troitskoe slovo* no. 349 (1916): 650–53.

17. *Troitskoe slovo* no. 348 (1916): 758–60.

18. Toviia's biological father joined the monastery late in life; it was not unusual in Russian Orthodoxy to join a monastery after one's spouse had died and children were grown (see Kenworthy, *Heart of Russia*, chapter 4).

19. On Gethsemane Skete and its elders see Kenworthy, *Heart of Russia*, chapter 3.

20. The *Ochtoechos* is an Orthodox liturgical book containing collections of hymns used throughout the liturgical year.

SUGGESTED READINGS

Chulos, Chris J. "Religious and Secular Aspects of Pilgrimage in Modern Russia." *Byzantium and the North/Act Byzantina Fennica*, vol. 9 (1999): 21–58.

———. *Converging Worlds: Religion and Community in Peasant Russia, 1861–1917*. DeKalb: Northern Illinois University Press, 2003.

Kenworthy, Scott M. *The Heart of Russia: Trinity-Sergius, Monasticism and Society after 1825*. New York: Oxford University Press, 2010.

Robson, Roy R. "Transforming Solovki: Pilgrim Narratives, Modernization, and Late Imperial Monastic Life." In *Sacred Stories*, ed. Mark D. Steinberg and Heather J. Coleman, 44–60. Bloomington: Indiana University Press, 2007.

Thaisia, Abbess. *Abbess Thaisia of Leushino: An Autobiography of a Spiritual Daughter of St. John of Kronstadt*. Platina, CA: St. Herman Press, 1990.

TWENTY

"From Ignorance to Truth":
A Baptist Conversion Narrative

Heather J. Coleman

WHILE ACCOUNTS OF PERSONAL RELIGIOUS EXPERIENCE ARE common, the conversion narrative is a relatively rare form of Russian religious writing. The Orthodox Church, to which the vast majority of Russians, Ukrainians, and Belarusians belonged in the nineteenth century, teaches that salvation is a process. The purpose of the Christian life in Orthodox teaching is to restore, by grace, the union of God and humans, to become perfectly one with God. This is understood to be a long-term development, achieved through regular worship, prayer, reading, and adherence to the commandments. Because of this, and because most people remain within their ancestral faith, accounts of personal religious conversion in imperial Russia tended to come from the relatively small, but growing, number of believers who sought spiritual answers beyond the Orthodox Church among the various sects that populated the religious landscape. By the turn of the twentieth century, the fastest growing groups were evangelicals, in particular the Baptists. In contrast to the Orthodox, Baptist teaching on salvation emphasizes the need for an adult personal conversion. Attesting to such a conversion is the prerequisite for baptism by full immersion and membership in the church. It is not surprising, therefore, that tales of conversion emerged as a major form of Russian Baptist rhetoric and writing.

The Russian evangelical movement developed in the 1860s and 1870s, influenced by Baptist and Pietist ideas about intense personal religious experience, the importance of Bible study in small groups, and the priesthood of all believers that swept the many German-language communities in the Russian Empire. Particularly prominent were *shtundist* groups in southern Ukraine. Local Ukrainian or Russian peasants working for the German colonists who had settled in this region since the time of Catherine the Great began to attend the revivalist religious meetings occurring in their employers' communities. When they turned to organizing such Bible hours among their own people, the Slavic faithful were soon nicknamed *shtundisty,* after the German word for hour, *Stunde.* Although some shtundists would remain in purely local groups, most eventually found an identity for their movement in the Baptist faith. In 1894, the Committee of Ministers declared the shtundist sect to be especially harmful and prohibited its meetings (and those of any group, including the Baptists, who were deemed to be shtundists) on the grounds that it undermined the Orthodox faith and Russian national character. However, during the revolution of 1905, which brought a semi-constitutional order to formerly autocratic Russia, religious tolerance was declared and the Baptists enthusiastically began to organize publicly and to develop a lively press.

The conversion narrative that follows was published in 1914 in the Odessa-based Baptist weekly magazine, *Slovo istiny* (the Word of Truth). Its author, Vasilii Skaldin, was a forty-one-year-old missionary of the Russian Baptist Union. His article tells the story of his personal and spiritual journey from his birth as the son of poor Orthodox peasants in the village of Almazovo, Orel Province, to life as a worker in the big city of Odessa, where he finds the Baptist faith. In his story, we encounter well-known themes from the many worker autobiographies of the late imperial and early Soviet periods: the young peasant in his "bast" shoes of woven birch bark making his way in the modern world of the city, the factory, and military service, and wrestling with social injustice, moral questions, and new ideas about the self and society. Scholars have noted the important theme of conversion to revolutionary ideas in these workers' accounts. But peasants found other new identities in the city, too. Skaldin's tale illuminates recurring topics in many other Russian Baptist conversion narratives, both published and unpublished: the simple Russian person making his way in a changing world, the contest between political and religious answers to social problems, the search for salvation in Russian popular religion, the theological solution to these problems that the Baptist faith offered, the cultural conflict within oneself and in relation to others brought on by leaving the Orthodox Church, and the emergence of a Russian evangelical community. It thus shows the importance of the spiritual in the elaboration of new conceptions of the individual and community in the revolutionary era. Like all spiritual autobiographies, Skaldin's account aims to reinvigorate the community by reminding believers of their own conversions, while inviting prospective converts to reexamine their own lives and to join the community's collective story.

"From Ignorance to Truth."[1]

The goal of describing my conversion – may God give power to this story – is for His glory and for the conversion of many souls like me.

I was born to poor peasants in the village of Almazovo, Orel province. My parents were illiterate and didn't know anything beyond the prayer, "In the name of the Father and the Son and the Holy Spirit, Holy God, holy powerful, holy immortal, forgive us." Nevertheless, thanks to them, I received a primary education. After graduating from the village school, I became a shepherd in order, through my meager earnings, to contribute, however little, to the needs of our poor family.

When I turned sixteen, my father sent me to learn to be a blacksmith in the city of O., where I spent three years. Upon returning to my native village, I started working for the local blacksmith for twelve rubles per year. Heavy work with such low pay forced me to leave the village (*poiti na storonu*), [to find a place] where one can earn much more; and when I say "leave," I mean on foot, since there was nothing for me to ride on. My intention was realized. On a gloomy autumn day, family and friends got up early and gathered to see me off to "the foreign (*chuzhaia*) side." My father and mother took up icons and blessed me to go on my way. Having parted with them, I left behind my hovel, a chimneyless little hut, for several years. With my bag on my shoulders holding a couple of shirts, a couple of pairs of bast shoes and a few pounds of rye bread rusks and three rubles in my pocket, accompanied by my sister and a companion, I found myself outside the village. I had to make most of the journey to Kharkov on foot; only rarely was it possible to ride a few versts on horseback with passing travelers in exchange for a glass of vodka.

IN KHARKOV

On the advice of new comrades, in Kharkov I stopped at a tavern called Zabei-Rog.

Here, for the first time, I saw bad women. My heart flinched with fear and horror when I heard how they abused one another with the vulgar language of the streets. Remembering my father's admonition, I tried in every way to avoid bad company.

THE IUZOVKA MINES

From Kharkov I went to the mines, where I got a job as a coal miner. At first I earned little but then more and more, but nothing remained of either the low or the high wages – everything went to vodka and other alcoholic drinks. The mines, as is well known, are the breeding-ground of all evil and [people there] lead a barge-hauler's life;[2] and in two years there I acquired not money but only a full knowledge of evil and debauchery.

MILITARY SERVICE

I was enrolled in military service into a cavalry regiment. My predilection for wine even before military service developed in me extreme depravity and recklessness: the latter quality, by the way, helped me to get ahead in military service. The military leadership tries to develop a fighting spirit in every young soldier, and I turned out to have this ability. In a short time I landed on the training team and upon graduation was made a junior non-commissioned officer, then a senior one, and in my last year of active service I was promoted to cavalry sergeant-major. In that rank I remained for service in my regiment for three years beyond my compulsory period.

ARRIVAL IN ODESSA

Before I was discharged from military service, I married. I lived with my wife for a few months and then left her with her family in the town of Vasilkov, Kiev province, while I, by myself, on the advice of my former military superiors, headed for Tiflis in search of work.[3] When I arrived in Odessa, I stayed at a hotel with a comrade whom I'd picked up along the way. We walked together and admired the sea, and then stopped in a tavern where, to the sound of the barrel organ, we had a fair amount to drink. When we got back to our room, I immediately fell sound asleep and my comrade got to work cleaning out my pockets and did a wonderful job, leaving me, as they say, without a kopek. In an unknown city, with no acquaintances and not a penny in my pocket, what was I going to do? There was no point in going out to find some casual labor in full military uniform – no one would take me. This impossible situation plunged me into despair and I decided irrevocably to kill myself, where and how it didn't matter – whenever a convenient occasion presented itself: either to lay my head on the train tracks or throw myself in the sea. Having sold one pair of boots, I began bitterly to go on a spree with the money, bidding farewell to everyone I knew and this world; but, apparently, the Lord did not allow me to commit suicide. I was advised to go to the city governor and appeal for a job of some sort. The city governor, Count Shuvalov, ordered that I be given a position as a city policeman. I really didn't like police work: life in the barracks, everyone calling me "trigger," "bribe-taker" (*khabarnik*, the Ukrainian word), but extreme need forced me to make my peace with all of this.

By that time my conscience had awakened and I began to search for God with my whole heart; I began to re-read the prayer-books that I had brought from military service, and my main prayer was to the Angel Protector.

My post was at the gates of the Aleksandrovskii Park, and I became acquainted with people who tried to draw me into politics. One day I was chatting with a cabby about religious questions. He said to me:

"You know what is written in the twenty-third chapter of the Gospel of Matthew?"

"No," I answered, "I don't know."

"Well, read it, or listen, while I read it: 'But woe to you ... because you shut the kingdom of heaven against men; for you neither enter yourselves, nor allow those who would enter to go in.'[4] Who are they talking about here, who are these people?" he asked, and I wasn't able to give him an answer.

Back in the barracks, I thought about this question all the time. A few days later, he again started up a conversation with me on the topic, saying that it was addressed to the legalists – to which I strongly objected, asserting that they were the representatives of Christ; I had read that in the book *Enlightener in the Spirit of Orthodoxy*. Our dispute ended with my declaring his Gospel to be *incomplete,* and to prove the truth of my words, I promised him I would buy a *full* Gospel.

PURCHASING A FULL GOSPEL

For the purchase of a *complete* Gospel, I headed to the second-hand market.

"Give me a full Gospel," I asked the vendor; he handed me a big Gospel. I, with the air of an expert, looked at the cover, turned over a few pages, glanced at the censor's mark – all the while wondering how to know if it were a full version or not. After all, I had never read it.

"Your Gospel is incomplete," I said, at last, to the vendor.

"What do you mean – incomplete? Excuse me, Mr. Policeman, but it is the most complete Gospel with Revelations, the Psalms, look, all 150 psalms are there – how can you say it is incomplete?"

I became ashamed of my ignorance and without a word I went on to a different vendor. Here I already didn't ask for a *full* Gospel but simply said, "Give me the Gospel that has 150 psalms"; he handed it to me and I bought it. When I got home, I looked up Matthew 23 and started to read, and what do you know? In my Gospel was written word for word what was written in the cabby's one: "Woe to you ..." and so on.

DAILY READING OF THE BIBLE

I rejoiced that at last I had a full Gospel. When I got home from my post to the barracks, I always read one or two chapters, and although I didn't understand what I had read, all the same I started to think more of myself than I should have: "Here I read the Gospel, *The Preceptor* (*Vrazumitel'*), prayer books – this means I've become a pious person..."[5] My colleagues respected this religious feeling in me and began to gather around my bed to listen to the reading of *The Preceptor* and the Gospel. In the barracks there was a small iconostasis with icons before which I began to light an oil lamp every day, and when the oil was burned up, I gathered money for the purchase of new oil; I dusted the iconostasis too. Some of my comrades laughed at me:

"Look, we have a monk among us!" they said.

The reading of the Gospel took its normal course, and the sinful life took its course too.

MEETING WITH THE PIE SELLER

Without a tutor, reading the Gospel was not useful to me (Acts 8:30–31).[6] I became distracted by the spirit of revolution, and became its ardent supporter and enthusiastic propagandist. I read a book whose title I don't remember – nor do I remember the author – but whose contents I haven't forgotten; it talked about how they distributed land to the landowners and princes and gave the peasants to them as serfs and so on. All that got me so up in arms against everyone around me that I, a policeman, whose responsibility was to suppress such anti-Christian teaching, tried to spread it wherever possible.

One day, I was standing at my post, reading a forbidden book; the book's format was similar to a New Testament, which gave a pie seller the pretext to recognize me as "one of his." He came up to me and said,

"Hello!"

"Hello," I said, "what do you need?"

With frightened eyes, he looked at the book that I had in my hands and said,

"I thought that you were reading the Gospel and so I came over."

"I have read and continue to read the Gospel," I answered with dignity, "and do you read it?"

"Yes, I do."

"So, tell me then, who are these scribes and Pharisees who close the Kingdom of God to people?"

He avoided a direct answer and in turn asked me a question:

"Tell me, are you a Christian?"

This question embittered me.

"And who do you think I am, a Tatar or something?" Then I cussed him out with some choice swear words. "Here, want me to show you my cross?" I asked as I tried to get my baptismal cross out from under my overcoat and shirt in order to convince this doubting Thomas.

"And allow me to ask yet another question," the pie seller continued, "are you saved?"

"And who on earth can know that," I answered him.

"A Christian should know this," the pie seller answered softly.

"Do you pray the creed?"

"I do."

"And there it says, 'and was crucified for us under Pontius Pilate, and suffered and was buried' – what does that mean?"

I had never thought about these words and their meaning and so I calmed down and asked him to explain; he joyfully explained, as he was able, and I ended up happy with him, indignant with myself for my behavior.

"Come by more often, we'll chat," I said to him, "I don't know the Gospel well."

"Maybe you'd like to come to a meeting; there are people there who know Scripture, they could explain everything to you."

"Where is it held?"

"In Romanovka Slobodka."[7]

"Will you take me?"

"Sure, I'll take you."

He promised to pick me up that evening, at the end of my shift, to take me to the meeting.

FIRST TIME AT THE MEETING

My guide came to get me at the agreed time and we headed to the meeting. It was a dark evening and we had to go through slums and cliffs. The whole time, I was thinking, "Where is he taking me, who are these people, what do they do? . . ." Finally, we arrived at the house where "they" gathered to pray; the house still belongs to a family of believers, the M———vs, who are as hospitable as Gaius[8]. Even now, when I'm at that house, I always remember my first visit to a meeting and look on it with love as the cradle of my soul.

Coming into the front hall, I saw several men and women gathering, among whom I would later find my dear brothers and sisters. When I appeared in a police uniform, some became worried, but my guide calmed them, saying that I had come to listen to the Gospel and not to arrest or disperse them. I took off my hat and sat on one of the miserable benches that filled the meeting room. The brothers started to sing some sort of song; one even came over to me with a book, hoping I would sing with him, but I didn't feel like myself, I searched for something for my eyes and not for my heart. What they read, I don't remember. Among the participants at the meeting were brothers Kosho, Bubes (now in America), S. Avramenko, Norchenko, Nikolaev, sister Steblova and others. At the end of the meeting they chatted with me in a friendly manner. I found out when the next meeting would be and at whose house, then went home. When I got to the barracks, I thought over everything I had seen and heard; the only problem was that I couldn't seem to remember the name of the householder.

SECOND TIME AT A MEETING

On Saturday evening I headed out to find the meeting: I found the street, but the house wasn't there. I asked passers-by: "Is Ladyzhkin's house somewhere around here?"

"There is no Ladyzhkin here," people told me.

It turned out that I had gotten mixed up with the name and was asking for Ladyzhkin instead of Maklakov. With sorrow in my heart, I told myself that this misadventure had occurred because these were righteous, good people and I was a great sinner and therefore God was not allowing me to have contact with them – and so I had gotten lost: "Go, I say, to your comrades who are like you!"

My soul suffered. In my memory my whole past dirty, commonplace existence came to life in bright images. Before my eyes stood all those people whom I had offended to death, especially in military service where I had power over the soldiers. My conscience sat in the judge's seat in all the vestments of the incorruptible judge and mercilessly began to accuse me.

I admitted my guilt on all counts. The thunder of judgmental Sinai rumbled over my head. I sought help, protection, but I did not yet know the Protector. I literally didn't sleep on the night from Saturday to Sunday because I was going through hellish torture, if these words can begin to describe in words the suffering of my soul. When morning came, I thanked God. I went out in search of the meeting. I went to the street I now already knew and found the house. With a fearful, shy step I walked up and went in the door; in the hallway, my heart pounded; here at last was the meeting room, the quiet singing of spiritual songs, the dear faces... I thanked God that He had allowed me to see these people once again.

The songs were sung from the depth of the soul, and so they unwittingly entered into my soul. After the singing, they prayed, read the Gospel, then ended the meeting with a prayer and singing. After the meeting they came up to me, asking me who I was and where I was from. They didn't recognize me, since this time I was wearing civilian clothes. I explained that I was the same policeman of whom they had been scared at the meeting. They began to ask how my spiritual life was and I couldn't say a thing – I cried and my tears loudly told them the state of my spiritual life.

"Pray, friend, the Lord will forgive your sins," these kind people comforted me, and it seems that with their words, paradise entered my soul. Thank you for the good advice. "O, these people want me to be forgiven my sins," I told myself, and I began to love them even more strongly.

Not long before this, I was walking at the Panteleimon monastery. There I prayed so zealously and so long to all the saints, on my knees before the iconostasis, that when I got up, a monk came over to me and said,

"Get out of here, do you think you're better than everyone else or something, crawling right up to the very icons?"

I didn't think of considering myself better than everyone else – I considered myself an offender and had run to a place of refuge in the hope of finding a word of solace; and yet, I was judged a Pharisee, I was shamed for my tears, I was driven away. And I walked away with a chagrined heart, frustrated with people.

LIFE AND PRAYER IN THE BARRACKS

I wanted to pray to Him who could forgive me, but where and how? It seemed to me that everyone was following me and that everyone had already guessed that I was already a traitor to the traditions and beliefs of our fathers. In order to withdraw for prayer unnoticed I went to the tap and started to wash my sheets, handkerchiefs, and then with these wet things headed up the steps to the attic of the barracks to hang them up, so that everyone would think that I had gone to the attic with that goal in mind. But in fact I wanted to be as far as possible from people and be closer to God, to find a darker corner not in order to commit sin but to reveal sins already committed, for they were weighing on me. I knelt, prayed, asked the Lord to forgive me – but no answer! I then used a new mechanical technique: I lay down with my tear-stained face to the ground, I put my body against the dirty floorboards, thinking that in this way I would win over my Lord. Finally, I begged Him:

"O Savior! Tell me whether You have forgiven my sins, and for confirmation, tell me in a loud voice: 'Vasilii, all your sins are forgiven.' Or send one of the angels dressed in white whom I could see with my own eyes and from whom I could hear that my sins are forgiven . . ."

An exhausting hour or more went by, but no angel appeared to me and I did not hear the voice of the Savior. All around me it was quiet, except for in my heart where the rough sea had not calmed and the waves, each stronger than the last, were filling up my soul, threatening it with destruction.

Every day I seemed worse and more criminal in my own eyes – and life became unbearable. My only hope was to go to the meeting, pray, and perhaps receive forgiveness there.

At the meeting I heard neither the reading nor the prayers, for I was preoccupied by one single thought: to beg the Lord for forgiveness – to pray. During that time, as I sat on the bench, it was not only my soul that trembled but my greatcoat too, shaking as if feverish. The people sitting near me looked at me in amazement.

Impatiently, I awaited the end of the sermon – whatever it was about, whether or not it included a call to sinners like me to repent didn't matter to me; one way or another, I needed to ask God for forgiveness. The sermon ended, everyone knelt down and began to pray and I tried to pull out the word, "Amen," in order to get started on my prayer; but unfortunately my tongue wouldn't turn in my mouth, my lips wouldn't open, and someone else started praying instead of me, and then another person and then a third, and I remained unrepentant and unforgiven. I went through quite a few meetings like this, and after each one I felt really down.

THE DAY OF MY REPENTANCE – A DAY OF CELEBRATION FOR ME

Before this, I had an all-out battle between body and spirit. On Saturday I asked the supervisor to schedule me for the overnight shift so that I could have Sunday free. I was sent to guard the garden of the city head, Count Shuvalov. Upon arriving at my post, I immediately took off my service cap, fell on my knees, and began to recite the prayer of repentance that I planned to pray at the meeting the following day. An hour later, I again went to the bushes, again knelt and recited my prayer; indeed I repeated this several times that night. At one point I was on my knees when suddenly right in my ear I heard a shrill whistle; I leapt to my feet, put on my cap, and before me stood the supervisor on duty; I reported to him that everything was fine at my post...

"And where were you?" asked the supervisor. "You weren't sleeping in the bushes, were you?"

"Absolutely not," I replied.

The supervisor walked away and I went back into the bushes to memorize my prayer. After my shift, I headed back to the barracks. I put on civilian clothes and headed to the meeting, to the place of my repentance. Like the prodigal son, I hurried to meet my Father; but at the time I still didn't know that wonderful story of the prodigal son and God's love for him; no one in my whole life had told me about it. As a boy living in the village, I would await the day of repentance during Lent with joy because on that day I could treat myself to white *kalach* bread.[9] During military service, I looked forward to this day with joy, hoping to receive praise from the priest for verbosity in my confession, both for myself and for the soldiers whom I taught to make their confessions, and congratulations from my superiors for taking the holy sacraments.

I sat waiting for the meeting to start. This time I decided to start the prayer first, not waiting for any "Amen," knowing that I had the words for the prayer and wouldn't make a mistake, that I'd explain all my sins to the Lord. They began to sing and pray, but once again my mouth remained closed. "There's still time left," I told myself, "the sermon will end and then I will pray too." The sermon ended, prayer began, and I thought: "Now it's my turn," but once again I didn't have the strength to pray. The brothers were rising from their knees and I alone remained kneeling, quivering from an inexplicable terror, my memorized prayer forgotten.

"Oh Lord! I am a great sinner, forgive me!" These words finally tore themselves from my aching chest. "Brothers, pray for me!" I begged.

V. Bubes, N. Zarenba, Ia. Vil'khovskii, and others prayed that the Lord give me confidence in my salvation and the gift of the Holy Spirit. The prayers were said from the soul, with faith. When I got up from my knees, I cried with great joy. The brothers and sisters sang with tears in their eyes:

> O wonderful day, oh wonderful hour
> When the Savior first
> Answered my call and entered my soul
> And gave me peace in my heart.[10]

Leaving the meeting, I saw all nature as if renewed, like on the first day of creation. The caterpillar had turned into a butterfly: its cocoon had been burst, for it no longer wanted to sit on a cabbage leaf; spreading out its wings, it was carried upward, swimming in the warm rays of the spring sunshine; likewise, my soul burst toward the heavens on that day. How happy I would have been on that day to be at the feet of the Savior, at the feet of the One Who made ten lepers clean. Oh, I would have praised the Lord even louder than one of those lepers – his body was cleaned, made whole, but the Lord had cleaned my soul from the heaviest sins and given me eternal life. When I ran into acquaintances, I told them how the Lord had forgiven my sins. On that day the whole world was in my embrace: I wanted to tell all creation, the birds, the animals:

"Little birds, little horses, rejoice with me – my sins are forgiven."

Walking home, I was so consumed with new thoughts and feelings that I walked right past the barracks and, when I noticed, I had walked an extra couple of blocks. I refused lunch back at the barracks. I went to my friend from work. He asked why I had come home so early. I told him everything that the Lord had done for my soul, thinking he would rejoice with me, that he too would repent. I looked at him but he was yawning – he didn't understand me, just as in the past I didn't understand others. Finally, he asked,

"Is that true? How did it happen?"

I again told him the whole story in detail. "If you'd like," I said, "I can take you to a meeting. I'll pray for you, asking the Lord to forgive you."

I STAND AT MY POST A NEW MAN

There was not one of my acquaintances whom I didn't tell about my happiness, and to every single one of them, the news was similarly incomprehensible. In the evening, I headed to my post. The night watchman, who sat at the same post as I, arrived. He handed me a cigarette.

"No," I said, "I don't smoke now, because my sins have been forgiven."

He looked at me in amazement, even stepped back a little. I began to explain everything to him in detail, saying that his sins, too, would be forgiven if he asked the Lord to do so with faith. At the Aleksandrovskii Park where we were working, the public uses the park until two in the morning. When everyone had gone home, I called the watchman to me and again started to tell him about how Christ loved him. Walking through the park, I stopped at one spot to pray and invited him to join me; we took off our caps, knelt down, and I prayed to the Savior, praising him for forgiving my sins and asking that He turn the watchman too to His light. I finished the prayer but the watchman for some reason was not praying.

"Pray," I said, "God will forgive you too."

"No, I can't, I don't know how to pray," answered the watchman.

"Lord, teach him to believe and pray to You," I prayed, after which we got up and we went back to our posts.

There arose in my soul a strong desire to tell everyone I could about the Savior of sinners. Within a few days of my conversion, at my post, everyone knew that my sins had been forgiven. But this news was not taken in correctly, in a spiritual manner: everything that I told them was perverted and passed on from person to person in a very disfigured form. People started to openly abuse me, making fun of me in various ways, shouting "He's crazy!" The guard with whom I had prayed told the other guards:

"At our post, a policeman has gone crazy, telling everyone that his sins have been forgiven."

But the Lord gave me the strength to not be troubled and to not be ashamed to suffer vilification for His sake. A little while later, God gave me a brother, a caretaker (*dvornik*), who, like me, had found salvation in Christ, but whose wife did not yet believe. Now, together, we talked to people day and night about what the Lord had done to our souls, trying to convince everyone to repent. The Lord heard our prayers and granted our wish: the wife of cabby N. converted and she became, like us, a zealous witness for the Lord. Once several of us had gathered, we began to organize a small meeting in the apartment of the caretaker, Brother Dripan (he's now in America). Brother-preachers came to his place; outsiders also started to attend our meeting and, as best we could, we sang and prayed, and preachers spoke the Word of God there. The caretaker's wife converted, then the Shuiskii family, husband and wife. The conversion of these souls to the Lord was the best reward from the Lord for all misfortunes and sorrows. And then there began days of even greater testing. Someone reported to Panasiuk, the district superintendent of police (*pristav*), that at such and such a post there was a policeman who "has become a shtundist and has lured others in too." The superintendent ordered that I be removed from my post and my brother, the janitor, removed from his position too. Here's how it happened: one evening, I was standing at my post and saw the supervisor, Puzanov, coming toward me and saying:

"You need to leave your post, this is what the superintendent ordered, because you preach some sort of shtunda here. I don't have anything against you personally, you are a good man, but now you'll suffer for your convictions."

AT THE INTERROGATION WITH THE SUPERINTENDENT

I left my post and appeared at the superintendent's office. When he was told that I had arrived, he sent me an order through the policeman on duty: go to the barracks and don't go anywhere until we call you. So I went home. During that time, he was given various pieces of information about me. The policeman came and said, "Go, the superintendent wants to see you." As I entered his office, I saw that his two assistants, Pogrebniak and Parashchenko, were there with him.

"Do you [*ty*, the informal form of address] know the Orthodox faith?" the superintendent asked me.

"I know what I was taught," I replied.

"Well, then, why did you leave the faith of your parents and don't reverence icons?" I answered that one should bow only to God in spirit and truth (*v dukhe i istine*).

"Tell me, please, Parashchenko, what is Skaldin's mental capacity?" the superintendent asked his assistant.

"Good," he answered, "he's a reasonable person."

"And what rank were you during your military service?" he asked me.

"A cavalry sergeant major," I said.

"Well, go along, the Orthodox missionaries will also talk to you."

Back at the barracks, the policemen peppered me with questions: Why had I been removed from my post? Why had the superintendent summoned me? What had he said? In anticipation of my upcoming discussion with the missionaries, they began to scare me by saying that they would send me into exile, or to the fortress, if I didn't renounce my convictions during the meeting. Walking around the city, I would stop on the bridges and, looking down, would interrogate myself: Do I have enough strength to stand firm and to not renounce my convictions if, for those convictions, they were to throw me over this bridge? The missionary never showed up. The superintendent assigned me to a post at the Bul'varnii district gates – the toughest post where only fined and disgraced officers were sent. And now I was among them. I spent a few days at that post, patiently awaiting a pardon, but none came. Then I asked the supervisor, "What am I being punished for?" "You just chatter around here and you'll find out!" was the answer.[11] I began to wonder what was coming next. Once, the superintendent and police chief walked past me when I was standing at my post and they stopped and the superintendent pointed to me and asked the police chief, "What should we do with that policeman who's made himself into a shtundist?" I don't know what the police chief's answer was or what they said after that, but my heart was not calm and I kept waiting for something else to happen. The policemen with whom I worked and lived developed a real hatred for me, and some forbade me to come near their beds. They taunted me in myriad ways: I would come in from my shift and lie down to rest on my bed, and they would turn me out of my bed; I'd get up, lie down, and again they would upend my bed. Then I would sit on the bed and from all corners they would throw dirty rags and foot-cloths at me. I knew they did so in order to get a rise out of me, and so internally I prayed continually to the Lord to spare me from the devil and the Lord preserved me and I was completely calm. I felt sorry for them as people in the hold of an evil spirit – the spirit of enmity against a person who had done them no ill. I convinced many through patience; a few began to defend me, asked me to once again read the Gospel to them, bought themselves Gospels too, and in our spare time we would sit for hours discussing one verse or another. Denunciations again followed: "Skaldin converts policemen into shtundists or dukhobors." On 1 October there was a church service at the barracks. After the liturgy, everyone started to go up to the priest (*batiushka*) to kiss the cross, after which he sprinkled them with water. In accordance with my convictions I didn't participate, and so several ordinary policemen, concerned about my soul, tried by force to bring me to the cross; but after lengthy resistance on my part they gave up, and one of them loudly declared that it was not a sin to throw such an atheist through the window onto the road, a plan that he promised to make a reality.

I remained in disgrace and continued to serve at the same tough post. The challenge of the post lay in the fact that you couldn't take ten steps, you had to stand at attention, and as a result my legs started to swell. Since I still hadn't been relieved of this post, I decided to appeal for release from police service – and did so. A few days after I sent in my resignation, an order came: "Put Skaldin in the punishment cell for five days for rudeness to the public." When I asked when and to whom I had been rude, they didn't answer me. Our path is always thorny. And my path to the punishment cell was strewn with such difficulties, too: just as I was getting ready to leave the barracks, the policemen started whistling, shouting, swearing, and cursing me, began to drum on the samovar or on buckets – this is how I was met at the barracks. "I'm leading out the shtundist, sirs, I'm leading out the shtundist," shouted the policeman on duty as he led me to the punishment cell.

IN THE PUNISHMENT CELL

"Greetings, gentlemen," I greeted the policemen who were being punished for dereliction of duty as I entered the cell. "Hey, great, the shtundist has joined us!" – and right away various witticisms, mockery and even kicks rained down. "With smoke, with smoke, we'll fill up the shtunda with smoke," they said, and right away they encircled me and each of them tried to fill my mouth with tobacco smoke. "Let's fight," they said and straight away they piled on to me, knocked me off my feet, and after every fight like this, my sides hurt for a long time. I used to say, "Gentlemen, why do you beat me," and they answered, "and what are you going to do, complain about us? No, brother, shtundists don't do that – endure." Finally, they either became ashamed of taunting me or they lost interest, and things quieted down and became friendlier; I made use of this lull and began to preach the Gospel to them.

On the very day that I left the punishment cell, I was informed that I was released from service.

DEPARTURE FROM ODESSA

Upon receiving my documents, I thought of immediately heading to my wife in the city of Vasil'kov in order to tell the good news of Christ there, but, realizing that I had yet to be baptized and that I still didn't know the Gospel well, I decided to remain a little while longer in Odessa. During that time, I attended every meeting, visited brothers who were more versed in the Scriptures, asked anything and everything, and studied holy Scripture. I had heard at some point from villagers that the shtundists made you sign up with the blood of your ring finger, and now I remembered this. I wondered why the brothers didn't talk about this with me – perhaps it was only slander; so I decided I would go and ask the preacher; if he proved to me that it was necessary, well, then, I'd even sign in blood. I knew Brother Bubes best, so I went to him. I arrived and we greeted one another.

"So brother, you have some matter for me? Go ahead and ask whatever you like," said Bubes.

"Yes, I have a question," I said.

We sat for a long time reading the Gospel, but I just couldn't get my nerve up to ask about the blood question.

"Maybe you have something else to ask," said the brother.

"Yes, you know, when do I sign in blood, then?" I finally said.

He looked at me in amazement.

"What blood? We don't have any practice of signing up with blood – that's all human slander. If anyone signed up with blood, it was Christ the Savior, He signed up for us with His holy blood, poured out on the cross at Golgotha. And it was not blood from his finger but the blood of His entire immaculate Body."

"All the same, I need to stay a little longer in order to study the Bible and be baptized," I said, to which brother Bubes replied that it takes no more and no less than an entire lifetime to study the Bible, and as far as baptism went, it could be done in the summer, since it was inconvenient to do it in the winter, whether in a river or the sea. Having bid my brothers farewell, I travelled to Vasilkov.

IN VASILKOV

Upon arriving in the town of Vasilkov, I bought a bottle of vodka for my father-in-law, since I knew him to be fond of it.

When I arrived and we greeted one another, everyone was very happy to see me again in their house.

When they were preparing the table, I gave my present to my father-in-law – a present with a little red cap. He smiled when he saw it, lit a cigarette and suggested that I follow suit. I said to him, "I don't smoke anymore." When he heard this, that I had quit smoking, he looked at me for a long time in amazement; it seemed to me at the time that out of sheer amazement even his pupils had dilated – and, indeed, how could he not be amazed, when his son-in-law had smoked continually and now refused to smoke before supper. I was put in the place of honor at the table and everyone began to cross themselves; I remained faithful to my convictions and did not follow their example.

The goblet began to go around the table, words of greeting were spoken and wishes for all the best. I refused the goblet, saying that I didn't drink vodka now. When my father-in-law again heard this unpleasant news, "I don't drink," he stroked his beard, smoothed his moustache, cleared his throat, and loudly and clearly declared:

"I told you that he had fallen in with the shtunda – and yes, it's true that he's already a shtundist; look, he already doesn't smoke, doesn't drink, doesn't cross himself – and do you reverence icons?

"No," I answered, "we are to bow to God alone, and I bow to Him."

"There you go – see what he's become!"

The second day, their eighteen-year-old son Aleksandr Antonovich – who is now a preacher of the Gospel – and I began to discuss the Gospel and he began to agree with me. His mother heard this and forbade him to discuss with me and study the Gospel in such detail.

"Read it like you used to read it and don't listen to him – after all he's turned away from Christ and it's no sin to kill such people," she said.

My wife began to cry out of pity for me, that I had destroyed my soul. The women turned to a means they thought would turn me around and expel Satan from me.

They drew crosses with chalk on the doors and windows, and since they couldn't begin to make the sign of the cross on me that way, they signed me with the sign of the cross even when I wasn't noticing; for example, when I left one hut and went into another, my wife followed behind me on tiptoe and made the sign of the cross with the words, "Get out, Satan."

After a little while, I remained true to my convictions and my wife confronted me:

"Either return to your previous faith or we'll divorce, because I can't live with you like this."

At the same time, her mother came up to her, hugged her, and with tears in her eyes and a shaking voice, she said:

"He's ruined you, my child!"

I answered her with the words of the apostle Paul:

"If you want – live, and if you don't want to, then consider yourself free of me."

A few days later, my father-in-law said to me,

"Clear out of my house; I don't want you to live with us; it's enough that because of you I'm embarrassed to show my face outdoors. You have shamed me."

I asked to wait a bit while I found a new job. I went to Kiev to the field gendarme squadron in order to return to military service, but there were no openings and I couldn't wait for one. When I returned from Kiev, I went to the estate (*ekonomiia*) office to the manager whom I knew there, in order to get a job from him, but since it was winter, he too refused. Then I decided to go to Odessa.

PREPARATIONS FOR HEADING TO ODESSA

Since she didn't share my views, my wife began to debate with her mother what she should do: to go with me would be to give up praying before icons. I found out about this from her herself and promised that for my part I would give her full freedom of conscience.

"Do as you wish, pray to whomever you want and bow to whatever you want."

On the day of our departure, my wife decided not to bring icons with her and only asked that her parents bless her with them for the trip; in the end she decided that her parents should bless her only with bread and salt, and they did as she wished.

In bidding her farewell, her parents advised her not to join my faith.

Upon arriving in Odessa with my dear brothers in Christ, I stayed with brother Dripan on Novaia street and he joyfully took me in, fed me, and gave me a cozy corner – may the Lord reward him a hundredfold. The brothers worked hard to find me a job; I didn't find work often, at best one day a week, at the port among hopelessly debauched people. When they saw that I was new and unaccustomed to the work, they mocked me horribly. But the Lord sent solace and gave me a position: I began to work at the Shpolianskii rolling mill where K. F. Denisov worked (he has already died). At the plant they began to persecute me especially strongly, as a former policeman.

"Hey, you, bloodsucker, now you've enlightened yourself, shtundist!"

After these words, I got wet rags thrown at my eyes, full of sand that got in my eyes, and they laughed:

"Yeah, right, why didn't your God save you. After all, you're a shtundist and you're not allowed to get angry."

Then a big guy came up to me, turned and hit me in the face and looked at me to see what I would do.

The blood was rushing in my head from the powerful blow and I was seeing stars. When I came to, he said to me:

"So Christ teaches: to the person who hits you on one cheek, offer the second one too."

I readily agreed, but he didn't repeat the blow.

The next day this person came to me and asked for forgiveness.... I worked at that factory for about two years and had to put up with a lot of insults. A difficult time began as the war with Japan started and I was called up again for military service.

MILITARY SERVICE

I was drafted to the 4th field gendarme squadron in the city of Odessa. After receiving our uniforms and harnesses, we prepared to be shipped out. Before our departure the aide-de-camp (*ad"iutant*) asked me whether I would like to stay in Odessa. I answered that I would unwaveringly obey the will of the authorities and refused to make the choice myself. The next day, the order came to leave me in Odessa. I thanked the Lord for His care for me. My service in the above-mentioned Odessa squadron began. Since I held the senior rank among my comrades and was experienced in service, my comrades respected me. But when they found out that I was a "shtundist," they began to distrust me and to hold discussions with me about the word of God, during which they could not hold their ground. They reported my convictions to the superiors. The squadron commander was a German, Colonel Erdel', and he had nothing against my convictions.

At one point an announcement ran in the newspapers about an upcoming discussion with shtundists at the seminary.

My comrades impatiently looked forward to that day, and when I arrived from my meeting they forced me to go with them to the seminary. There were a lot of people there. The discussion was led by the rector of the seminary with someone we didn't know well, a petty trader known as "the scallop guy" (*grebiniuchnik*). He didn't belong to the Baptists. They discussed the baptism of infants. To the rector's question about where it is said in the Bible that it is forbidden to baptize children, the scallop guy couldn't say anything and they ridiculed him, and all shtundists with him. Then my comrades quickly pushed me forward and so I found myself right in front of the rector, who looked at me with amazement and asked,

"What would you like?"

I was silent and wanted to hang back.

"He's a shtundist too," my comrades answered for me.

"Aha, then tell me, where does it say in the Gospel that children should not be baptized?"

Then I turned to the audience and said:

"You heard, gentlemen, that this person did not point to where it says not to baptize children. I in turn ask you, Mr. Rector, where it says literally to baptize children?"

And since he could not point out the spot, the discussion was immediately drawn to a close with the singing of "It Is Right" (*Dostoino est'*). My comrades began to attend our meetings and to get to know the Word of God...

The days of freedom came. The Imperial Manifesto on freedom of conscience was proclaimed. I began freely and more actively to attend the meetings with my comrades. Brothers came to see me in the barracks. Soon my platoon leader and his wife turned to the Lord, which further heightened my joy. In the barracks, everyone loved me and called one another brothers. In my presence, people were ashamed to use foul language. But the enemy does not sleep. Someone reported to the command that because of me, all through the camps there was verbal conflict. I was ordered to keep quiet and not to speak of my convictions to anyone. If I did not obey, I would be sent to the front line of battle or imprisoned in the guard house.

"Send me wherever you like, I won't be quiet," I answered.

There were no results from this denunciation. I continued zealously to serve the Lord and honorably to do my duty. The command liked me.

After the peace treaty, although they gave me the option of extended military service, I refused and headed home to my family.

WORK FOR THE LORD

Because I had the desire to speak about the Lord, I along with others began to preach at meetings. At first it was hard, but later everything settled down. When V. G. Pavlov[12] arrived in Odessa, I was appointed an evangelist and began to work for the Lord. Then I had to move to Lozovaia station where I currently live with my family. There is a lot of work, and I pray to the Lord that He will give me more strength and zealousness for work in His field.

My house and I serve the Lord!

NOTES

1. Vasilii Skaldin, "Ot neviezhestva k istinie," *Slovo istiny* no. 31 (March 1914): 365–66; no. 32 (April 1914): 361–62; no. 33–34 (April 1914): 397–98; no. 36 (May 1914): 420–21; no. 37 (May 1914): 432–33.

2. Barge-haulers were considered to be the lowest of the low on the social scale and to lead dissolute lives.

3. Tiflis is present-day Tbilisi, the capital of Georgia.

4. Matt. 23:13.

5. Skaldin most likely refers here to a popular 450-page collection of religious "discussions, teachings, and pastoral instructions" aimed at village parishioners, which went to fourteen editions by 1906: *Vrazumitel': Izbrannye besedy, poucheniia I pastyrskie nastavleniia sel'skim prikhozhanam* (Moscow: V. A. Mavritskii, 1893).

6. Acts 8:30–31: So Philip ran to him, and heard him reading Isaiah the prophet, and asked, "Do you understand what you are reading?" And he said, "How can I, unless someone guides me?" And he invited Philip to come up and sit with him.

7. A working-class district of Odessa.

8. Skaldin refers here to St. Paul's praise of Gaius for his hospitality in Rom. 16:23.

9. A white, braided bread used for ritual occasions.

10. Translation of a classic eighteenth-century hymn "O happy day that fixed my choice," still used by Russian and Ukrainian evangelicals; see: http://songs.fleita.com/file.php?id=545 (accessed 5 November 2013).

11. The superintendent uses the Ukrainian expression *liaskaty zubamy*, which means "to chatter."

12. An important Baptist leader and editor of the journal where this conversion narrative was published.

SUGGESTED READINGS

Coleman, Heather J. *Russian Baptists and Spiritual Revolution, 1905–1929.* Bloomington: Indiana University Press, 2005.

Herrlinger, Page. *Working Souls: Russian Orthodoxy and Factory Labor in St. Petersburg, 1881–1917*. Bloomington, IN: Slavica, 2007.

Hernandez, Richard L. "The Confessions of Semen Kanatchikov: A Bolshevik Memoir as Spiritual Autobiography." *Russian Review* 60 no. 1 (January 2001): 13–35.

Rambo, Lewis R. *Understanding Religious Conversion*. New Haven, CT: Yale University Press, 1993.

Zhuk, Sergei I. *Russia's Lost Reformation: Peasants, Millennialism, and Radical Sects in Southern Russia and Ukraine, 1830–1917*. Baltimore: Johns Hopkins University Press, 2004.

Glossary and Abbreviations

verst (Russian *versta*) measure of distance equivalent to 3,500 feet or approximately one kilometer
volost (Russian volost') township
PSZ *Polnoe sobranie zakonov Rossiiskoi Imperii* (Complete Collection of Laws of the Russian Empire)
GAVO Gosudarstvennyi arkhiv Vladimirskoi Oblasti (State Archive of Vladimir Oblast), Vladimir
GMIR Gosudarstvennyi muzei istorii religii (State Museum of the History of Religion), St. Petersburg
OR RGB Otdel rukopisei Rossiiskoi gosudarstvennoi biblioteki (Manuscript Division, Russian State Library), Moscow
RGADA Rossiiskii gosudarstvennyi arkhiv drevnykh aktov (Russian State Archive of Ancient Acts), Moscow
RGIA Rossiiskii gosudarstvennyi istoricheskii arkhiv (Russian State Historical Archive), St. Petersburg
TsGIA SPb Tsentral'nyi Gosudarstvennyi istoricheskii arkhiv Sankt-Peterburga (Central State Historical Archive of St. Petersburg), St. Petersburg

Archival notation follows the accepted Russian form of abbreviation:

f. *fond* (collection)
op. *opis'* (inventory)
g. *god* (year)
otd. *otdelenie* (division)
koll. *kollektsiia* (collection)
k. *korobka* (box)
t. *tom* (volume)
vyp. *vypusk* (installment)
ch. *chast'* (part)
d. *delo* (file)
l., ll. *list, listy* (page, pages)
ob. *oborot* (verso)

Further Reading

On the Eastern Orthodox Tradition

Angold, Michael, ed. *Cambridge History of Christianity*. Vol. 5, *Eastern Christianity*. Cambridge: Cambridge University Press, 2006.

McGuckin, John Anthony. *The Orthodox Church: An Introduction to Its History, Doctrine, and Spiritual Culture*. Malden, MA: Blackwell, 2007.

———, ed. *The Encyclopedia of Eastern Orthodox Christianity*. Malden, MA: Wiley-Blackwell, 2011.

Ware, Timothy. *The Orthodox Church*. New ed. London: Penguin, 1997.

Other Primary Sources on Religion in Imperial Russia in English Translation

Belliustin, I. S. *Description of the Clergy in Rural Russia: The Memoir of a Nineteenth-Century Parish Priest*. Translated and introduced by Gregory L. Freeze. Ithaca, NY: Cornell University Press, 1985.

Bisha, Robin, Jehanne M. Gheith, Christine Holden, and William G. Wagner, eds. *Russian Women, 1698–1917: Experience and Expression. An Anthology of Sources*. Bloomington: Indiana University Press, 2002. Part 5.

Book of Needs of the Holy Orthodox Church with an Appendix Containing Offices for the Laying On of Hands. Translated by G. V. Shann. London: David Nutt, 1894.

Bulgakov, Sergei Nikolaevich. *A Bulgakov Anthology*. Edited by James Pain and Nicholas Zernov. London: SPCK, 1976.

Fedotov, G. P. *The Way of a Pilgrim and Other Classics of Russian Spirituality*. Mineola, NY: Dover Publications, 2003.

Gapon, George. *The Story of My Life*. New York: E. P. Dutton, 1906.

Muller, Alexander V., trans. and ed. *The Spiritual Regulation of Peter the Great*. Seattle: University of Washington Press, 1972.

Rosenthal, Bernice Glatzer, and Martha Bohachevsky-Chomiak, eds. *A Revolution of the Spirit: Crisis of Value in Russia, 1890–1924*. Newtonville, MA: Oriental Research Partners, 1990.

Rostislavov, Dmitrii Ivanovich. *Provincial Russia in the Age of Enlightenment: The Memoir of a Priest's Son*. Translated and edited by Alexander M. Martin. DeKalb: Northern Illinois University Press, 2002.

Sergieff, John Illytch [Father John of Kronstadt]. *My Life in Christ, or, Moments of spiritual serenity and contemplation, of reverent feeling, of earnest self-amendment, and of peace in God.* Translated by E. E. Goulaeff. London: Cassell, 1897.

Orthodoxy in Imperial Russia

Note: the emphasis here is on general works in English. Please see chapter bibliographies for further readings by topic.

Batalden, Stephen K., ed. *Seeking God: The Recovery of Religious Identity in Orthodox Russia, Ukraine, and Georgia.* DeKalb: Northern Illinois University Press, 1993.

——. *Russian Bible Wars: Modern Scriptural Translation and Cultural Authority.* Cambridge: Cambridge University Press, 2013.

Coleman, Heather J. "The 1908 Missionary Congress and the Problem of Cultural Power in Late Imperial Russia." *Jahrbücher für Geschichte Osteuropas* 52, no. 1 (2004): 70–91.

Cunningham, James W. *A Vanquished Hope: The Movement for Church Renewal in Russia, 1905–1906.* Crestwood, NY: St. Vladimir's Seminary Press, 1981.

Curtiss, John Shelton. *Church and State in Russia: The Last Years of the Empire 1900–1917.* New York: Columbia University Press, 1940.

Engelstein, Laura. *Slavophile Empire: Imperial Russia's Illiberal Path.* Ithaca, NY: Cornell University Press, 2009.

Evtuhov, Catherine. *The Cross and the Sickle: Sergei Bulgakov and the Fate of Russian Religious Philosophy, 1890–1920.* Ithaca, NY: Cornell University Press, 1997.

Freeze, Gregory L. *The Parish Clergy in Nineteenth-Century Russia: Crisis, Reform, Counter-Reform.* Princeton: Princeton University Press, 1983.

——. "Handmaiden of the State? The Church in Imperial Russia Reconsidered." *Journal of Ecclesiastical History* 36, no. 1 (January 1985): 78–103.

——. "Subversive Piety: Religion and the Political Crisis in Late Imperial Russia." *Journal of Modern History* 68 (June 1996): 308–50.

——. "Russian Orthodoxy: Church, People, and Politics in Imperial Russia." In *The Cambridge History of Russia.* Vol. 2, *Imperial Russia, 1689–1917.* Edited by Dominic Lieven. Cambridge: Cambridge University Press, 2006.

Florovsky, Georges. *Ways of Russian Theology.* Part 2, vol. 6 of *The Collected Works of Georges Florovsky.* Edited by Richard S. Haugh. Translated by Robert L. Nichols. Vaduz: Büchervertriebsanstalt, 1987.

Gatrall, Jefferson J. A., and Douglas Greenfield. *Alter Icons: The Russian Icon and Modernity.* University Park: Pennsylvania State University Press, 2010.

Geraci, Robert P., and Michael Khodarkovsky. *Of Religion and Empire: Missions, Conversion, and Tolerance in Tsarist Russia.* Ithaca, NY: Cornell University Press, 2001.

Heretz, Leonid. *Russia on the Eve of Modernity: Popular Religion and Traditional Culture Under the Last Tsars.* Cambridge: Cambridge University Press, 2008.

Himka, John-Paul, and Andriy Zayarnyuk, eds. *Letters from Heaven: Popular Religion in Russia and Ukraine.* Toronto: University of Toronto Press, 2006.

Hugues, Robert P., and Irina Paperno, eds. *California Slavic Studies XVII. Christianity and the Eastern Slavs.* Vol. 2,

Further Reading

Russian Culture in Modern Times. Berkeley: University of California Press, 1994.

Kivelson, Valerie A., and Robert H. Greene. *Orthodox Russia: Belief and Practice under the Tsars*. University Park: Pennsylvania State University, 2003.

Kornblatt, Judith Deutsch, and Richard F. Gustafson, *Russian Religious Thought*. Madison: University of Wisconsin Press, 1995.

Kornblatt, Judith Deutsch, and Patrick Lally Michelson, eds. *Thinking Orthodox in Modern Russia: Culture, History, Context*. Madison: University of Wisconsin Press, 2014.

Nicholas, Robert L., and Theofanis George Stavrou. *Russian Orthodoxy under the Old Regime*. Minneapolis: University of Minnesota Press, 1978.

Rock, Stella. *Popular Religion in Russia: "Double Belief" and the Making of an Academic Myth* Abingdon, UK: Routledge, 2007.

Steinberg, Mark D., and Heather J. Coleman, eds. *Sacred Stories: Religion and Spirituality in Modern Russia*. Bloomington: Indiana University Press, 2007.

Strickland, John. *The Making of Holy Russia: The Orthodox Church and Russian Nationalism Before the Revolution*. Jordanville, NY: Holy Trinity Publications, 2013.

Tarasov, Oleg. *Icon and Devotion: Sacred Spaces in Imperial Russia*. London: Reaktion Books, 2004.

Timberlake, Charles E., ed. *Religious and Secular Forces in Late Tsarist Russia: Essays in Honor of Donald W. Treadgold*. Seattle: University of Washington Press, 1992.

Valliere, Paul. *Modern Russian Theology: Bukharev, Soloviev, Bulgakov: Orthodox Theology in a New Key*. Grand Rapids, MI: Eerdmans, 2000.

Wagner, William. "The Transformation of Female Orthodox Monasticism in Nizhnii Novgorod Diocese, 1764–1929, in Comparative Perspective." *Journal of Modern History* 78 (December 2006): 793–845.

Contributors

NICHOLAS BREYFOGLE is Associate Professor of History at the Ohio State University; he is the author of *Heretics and Colonizers: Forging Russia's Empire in the South Caucasus* and co-editor of *Peopling the Russian Periphery: Borderland Colonization in Eurasian History*.

HEATHER J. COLEMAN is Associate Professor and Canada Research Chair in Imperial Russian History in the Department of History and Classics at the University of Alberta. She is the author of *Russian Baptists and Spiritual Revolution, 1905–1929* (IUP, 2005) and co-editor (with Mark D. Steinberg) of *Sacred Stories: Religion and Spirituality in Modern Russia* (IUP, 2007). She is the editor of *Canadian Slavonic Papers/Revue canadienne des slavistes*. She is currently completing a book on Orthodox parish priests in nineteenth-century Kiev province.

A. J. DEMOSKOFF is Assistant Professor of History at Briercrest College and Seminary in Caronport, Saskatchewan, and is completing a dissertation titled "Penance and Punishment: Monastic Incarceration in Imperial Russia."

GREGORY L. FREEZE is the Beinfield Professor of History at Brandeis University and the author of the forthcoming study *Bolsheviks and Believers, 1917–1941*.

AILEEN FRIESEN is a Social Sciences and Humanities Research Council of Canada Postdoctoral Fellow at the University of Illinois at Urbana-Champaign.

ROBERT H. GREENE is Associate Professor and Chair of History at the University of Montana and the author of *Bodies like Bright Stars: Saints and Relics in Orthodox Russia*.

PAGE HERRLINGER is Associate Professor of History at Bowdoin College and the author of *Working Souls: Russian Orthodoxy and Factory Labor in St. Petersburg, 1880–1917*.

SCOTT M. KENWORTHY is Associate Professor of Comparative Religion at Miami University (Ohio); he is the author of *The Heart of Russia: Trinity-Sergius, Monasticism and Society after 1825*.

NADIESZDA KIZENKO is Associate Professor of History at the University at Albany; she is the author of *A Prodigal Saint: Father John of Kronstadt and the Russian People* and other studies of Orthodox Christianity from 1666 to the present.

MARA KOZELSKY is Associate Professor of History at the University of South Alabama and the author of *Christianizing Crimea: Shaping Sacred Space in the Russian Empire and Beyond*.

LAURIE MANCHESTER is Associate Professor of History at Arizona State University and the author of *Holy Fathers, Secular Sons: Clergy, Intelligentsia and the Modern Self in Revolutionary Russia*.

IRINA PAERT is a senior researcher at the University of Tartu, Estonia, and the author of *Spiritual Elders: Charisma and Tradition in Russian Orthodoxy*.

ROY R. ROBSON is Professor of History at the University of the Sciences in Philadelphia and the author of *Solovki: The Story of Russia Told Through Its Most Remarkable Islands*, *Old Believers in Modern Russia*, and *Think World Religions*.

VERA SHEVZOV, Professor of Religion at Smith College, is the author of *Russian Orthodoxy on the Eve of Revolution* and numerous articles on various aspects of Russian Orthodoxy in modern Russia.

CHRISTINE D. WOROBEC is Board of Trustees and Distinguished Research Professor Emerita at Northern Illinois University and the author of *Possessed: Women, Witches, and Demons in Imperial Russia*.

Index

Italicized page numbers refer to figures.

academies, theological, 3, 8, 20n31, 132
adultery, 43, 156–57, 163
Adventists, 250
akathist, 131–33, 166, 274; in honor of icons, 12, 15, 131–34; in honor of the Mother of God, 92, 132, 240–41, 246–47; in the honor of saints, 89, 132. *See also* hymns
Akhtyrka, 277, 279
alcohol, 160, 212, 264
alcoholism, 222, 262
Alexander I, 1, 32
Alexander II, 2, 233, 237
Alexander III, 2, 141
Ammerman, Nancy T., 15
Amvrosii, elder, 231, 241
anointing of the sick, the rite of, 32–33, 35
Antichrist, 52–53; seal of, 191
apostasy, 43, 208, 212
archives, 31, 271
Arkhangelsk diocese, 44
Armenian Gregorian Church, 3
ascetics, women, 64
atheist, 304
Athos, Mount, 125
Austrian Empire, 107
authority, 8, 10, 48, 53–56, 73, 117, 127, 136, 158, 283, 309; of the bishop, 9; church, 16, 17, 44, 200, 229–30, 264; civil, 214; diocesan, 209, 235–37; ecclesiastical, 44–45, 172; of Kiev Metropolitan, 5; of the laity, 232; of Muscovite principality, 140; of the Orthodox church, 154, 264; police, 236; of the priest, 86, 88; religious, 10, 13, 231; reporting to, 25; sacramental, 85; secular, 43, 44, 45; spiritual, 241; of the Synod, 49, 221; Uniate, 126
autobiographies, 1, 15; of priests, 87; spiritual, 290; of worker, 289
autocracy, 2, 17
autocratic government, 85

Baikal, Lake, 95, 97
baptism, 87, 93, 126, 288, 306; and icons, 11; of infants, 310; and marriages, 9; and naming, 92; of Russia, 78–79; sacrament of, 121
Baptists, 219, 246, 250, 288, 289, 310
Barbara, Great Martyr, 132, 281
Battle of Sinope, 72
Belev convent, 60
Belgorod, 277–78
beliefs, 16, 32, 45, 59, 222; decline in, 199; exhibiting, 214; and love, 266; in miracles, 22, 192; pagan, 13; and practices, 22; religious, 97, 215, 250; sectarian, 43; and traditions, 298
benefactor, 59, 174, 218, 242

321

Bibikov, General Dmitrii, 121, 129n17, 129n19
Bible: reading of, 293–94; translation, 11, 32
Bogoslovskii Vestnik, 178
Bolkhovskii convent, 231
Book of Needs, 88, 109, 125–26
Boris, Saint, 132
Borispol, 277, 280
Borovskii Pafnut'evskii monastery, 44, 46
bribe-taker, 292
Bright Week, 67
Brothers' Monastery, Kiev, 281
Bulgaria, 116
Bulgarians, 72
bureaucracy: church, 10; state, 6
bursa (church school), 8–9, 111, 117
Byzantium, 132

canon law, 43, 153
canonization, 22, 193, 197
cantor, 90, 113–15, 117, 120–21, 180, 234, 258; and deacon, 116; payment to, 259; and priest, 274; and sons of priests, 118; St. Stephan as, 142; teaching by, 115. *See also* sacristan
Cassian, Saint, 64–65
Catherine II, 6, 115, 289
Catholicism, 3, 73, 123
Caves (Pecherskaia), Lavra, 24, 81, 280–81
censor, 24, 134, 243, 293
census (1897), 4
chastity, 91; preservation of, 139
Cheesefare Week, 28, 29n3, 66
Chernigov, 234, 258–59
Chernigov diocese, 231, 233
Chernigov province, 233, 236–37
Chersonesos, 73, 78
Christian duty, 46, 212–14, 218, 281
Christian tradition, 1; Eastern, 231, 248n9
Christianity, 51, 53, 76, 95, 272; conversion to, 4; early, 173; light of, 149; and native people, 192; Orthodox, 73, 140, 186; overthrown by, 101; Russian, 73; Slavic, 73; spread of, 198; traditional, 188; western, 12
Christmas, 258, 259
Chronicle of Nestor, 73
Chudov Monastery, 271, 284
church law, 43, 153
church-state relations, 6, 10, 17, 18n9, 44
Churikov, Brother Ioann, 14, 17, 262–64, 263
civilization, 249
clergy, 8–9, 52, 114, 208–10, 273; black and white, 7, 158; children of, 211; and churches, 147; culture of, 10; diocesan, 219, 222, 223; education of, 7–9, 117; estate structure, 7–8, 172–73; and factory youth, 215; and laity, 4, 12, 140, 213, 221, 224; local, 211, 236; material condition of, 210, 213, 260; members of, 43; and miraculous-working icons, 241–42, 246; and nobility, 121; Orthodox, 7, 107, 220, 272; and Orthodox mission, 255; parish, 7–8, 172–73, 214, 219, 260; and the peasantry, 118, 174; persecution of, 86; presence of, 131; professionalization of, 8; reports of, 218, 256; south Russian, 117; and state, 6, 209; treatment of, 212–14, 218, 260
colonists: German, 289; in Siberia, 249. *See also* Sibiriaki
colonization, 249, 250
Committee of Ministers, 289
communion, 11, 35, 124, 132, 214, 217t; and confession, 34, 43, 140, 208–209, 212–14, 216, 216t, 217t, 218, 240, 281; giving, 64, 93; partaking of, 161, 170n37; receiving, 214, 279
community, 1, 10, 16, 69n1, 250, 271; celibate, 58; conception of, 290; ecclesial, 10; evangelical, 290; German-language, 288, 289; interests of, 22; network of, 186; Old Belief, 251; Orthodox, 10, 192, 194–95; parish,

230; secular and scientific, 96; village, 117–20; women's, 59
community life, 12, 250
confession, 32, 93, 124, 125, 152, 157, 160, 166, 299; annual, 34, 152–53; confidence of, 6; failure to attend, 43, 44, 46; first, 152; formal, 64–65; as personal story of faith, 1, 14; preparation to, 27, 155, 161; silent, 27; spoken, 155; written, 14, 16, 152–55, 162. *See also* communion
confinement, 53, 56
conservative nationalist, 109–10, 173
Constantinople, 4–5
convent, 43, 64, 65; entering, 60; leaving, 59; and monasteries, 60. *See also* monastery; *names of individual convents*
conversion, 250, 255, 290, 301–302; to Christianity, 4; converts, 185, 290; personal, 288, 290; narrative, 17, 288–89; and revolutionary idea, 289; Uniate, 108, 121, 129n17
Counter-Reformation, 22
court: ecclesiastical, 43; secular, 44
crime, 6, 43–44
Crimean War, 2, 17, 72–74, 83n17
culture, 3, 110, 218; church, 4; clerical, 9–10; of iconic piety, 230–31; individualistic, 15; lament, 70n6; mass, 207; material, 12; peasant, 169n22; political, 15; popular, 14; Russian Orthodox, 185; storytelling, 131; Western, 1
cures, miraculous, 12, 14, 23–24, 192, 194

Danube River, 75, 76
Danubian Principalities, 72, 75
death, 62, 77, 108, 118, 181, 264, 284, 285; of Alexander II, 233; of Anna Fedorovna Golitsyna, 31, 33; anniversary of saint's, 140, 192–93; and baptism, 93; and confession, 93; conquering, 89; offending to, 296; preparation for, 34; shade of, 80, 148; and sickness, 32, 80, 162; and sin, 283; of St. Stefan, 140, 149
dechristianization, 208

declaration of Crimean War, 72, 74–75
Deist approach, 96
Descartes, 101
diaries, 1, 16; of priests, 10, 14, 16, 85–86, 174, 181; of Toviia, Archimandrite, 10, 16, 269, 271–72, 278–79, 282–83
diocesan congress, 209, 221, 223; Vladimir, 224
dissident, 133
dissent, religious, 250
divine revelation, 101
Dnieper River, 5, 109, 280–81
Dobrotoliubie, 58, 60, 67
doctrine, 11, 49, 272; Christian, 51; moral, 51, 54
domesticity, 61
Domnitskii monastery, 233, 236–37
Dostoevskii, Fedor, 110, 152
Dukhobors, 3, 304
dvoeverie (dual faith), 13

earthquake, 16, 95–101, 103–104
Easter, 27, 67, 162, 257–59
Eastern Church, 4, 32
Eastern Question, 72
Ecclesiastical Regulation, 1721, 6, 22
education, 2, 101, 110, 117, 166, 211, 250; and business, 108; of children, 181; Christian, 222; clerical, 86, 117; formal, 271–72; higher, 8; popular, 100, 210; primary, 3, 290; receiving, 172, 272; religious, 160; religious-moral, 221; seminary, 86; theological, 7, 8, 117, 118; and upbringing, 173. *See also bursa* (church school); literacy; seminary; academies, theological
Ekaterinburg diocese, 196
Elagin, Nikolai Vasilievich, 134
elders: church, 211, 236; Orthodox, 16; spiritual, 7, 58–65, 67, 144, 231, 285
Emancipation of the Serfs, 269
England, 72
Enlightener in the Spirit of Orthodoxy, 293
Enlightenment, 22, 96

environment: natural, 96–97; urban, 17, 263
Epicurus, 101
Epiphany, 258–59
estate, 23, 73, 172; clerical, 8, 86, 117, 172–73; social, 8, 117, 173
Eucharist, 32–33, 44, 46, 49, 153–54
Evangelicalism, 32, 288, 290
everyday life, 1, 74, 264
excommunication, 264
exile, 249, 303

factory, 25, 211, 289, 309; area, 215; population, 218, 222
faith, 4, 53, 64, 77–78, 157, 161–62, 190, 254, 267, 279, 300–301, 307, 308; abandonment of, 208; ancestral, 288; basis of, 149; brothers of, 76; changing, 253; Christian, 11, 52, 73, 75, 76, 91, 135, 136, 142–44, 200, 250; commitment to, 262; conscious, 13; decline of, 218–20, 222, 243, 244; dual, 13; and earthquake, 99, 103; and fear, 189; and good deeds, 80; and hope, 195, 201; indifference towards, 252; Jewish, 51; light of, 148; lives of, 17; and love, 82, 113; matters of, 34; and memory and identity, 18; and migrants, 215; and nationality, 114; Old Belief, 52, 55, 188; Orthodox, 12, 34, 75, 76, 199, 212, 230, 237, 243, 245, 246, 250, 253, 289, 303; outpost of, 193; and piety, 212, 219, 221; reanimation of, 110; and reason, 174; relationship between scripture, observation and, 96; religious, 16–17, 31; Russian, 75; and science, 265; and sectarian propaganda, 251; and social and civil ideals, 113; spirit of, 91; stories of, 1, 14, 15; strengthening in, 220; true, 91; truth of, 11; understanding of, 14, 174; virtues of, 139. *See also* Baptists
famine, 240, 241
Filaret, Metropolitan of Kiev, 123, 281, 287n13

Filippov, Nikolai Nikolaevich, 140, *141*, 142
Flavian, (Gorodetskii), Metropolitan of Kiev, 211
Florishchevaia Pustyn, 55
fornication, 43, 160, 164, 165
France, 72, 252
freedom: of conscience, 78, 308, 310; religious, 185

gender, 209; identity, 16
Gleb, Saint, 132
Golitsyna, Anna Fedorovna, 31–34
Golos, 113, 129n10
govenie, 152. *See also* confession
Great Reforms, 2–3, 8, 227n24; era of, 85
Greece, 6, 116, 125; Orthodox, 78
Greek Battalion, 77

hagiography, 172
healing, 23, 26–27, 32, 79, 237; confirmation of, 16; hope for, 230; miraculous, 22, 24–25; power, 263
heresy, 43, 60; Hungarian, 135–36
hesychasm, 58, 60, 61. *See also* quietude
Holy Mountain Monastery, 269
Holy Mysteries, 279, 281; partake of, 27, 34, 35, 66, 154, 160, 162; receiving, 46. *See also* communion
Holy Synod, 6, 24, 59, 204–206, 220; bureaucrat of, 108; and confessional records, 153; correspondence with, 9, 12; decision of, 201; decree of, 125; order of, 200; petitions to, 192–93, 196, 198, 201–202, 204, 229, 233, 237, 239; Over-Procurator of the, 195, 196, 198, 202, 204–206, 237–38, 243; Publication Commission of, 223; replacement of patriarch by, 22; reports to, 9, 44–45, 203, 233; representatives of, 153; session of, 202; telegram to, 193; and veneration of icons, 23, 233, 237–38, 239, 241–47
Holy Transfiguration Almshouse, 187

Index

Holy Week, 33, 35, 67, 179
homiletics, 74
homilies, 82n1, 90, 92, 188, 212; giving, 89, 93, 123, 124. *See also* sermons
hooliganism, 214
hromada (village community), 117, 119
humility, 33, 64, 65, 92, 286
hymns, 1, 89, 131–32, 258–59; in honor of icons, 11–12, 133–34, 135; in honor of saints, 132. *See also* akathist

Iakovlev monastery, 165
iconoclasm, 241
iconography, 231
icons, 11–12, 34, 37–38, 51, 79, 133, 187, 212, 257–59, 297; akathist in honor of, 12, 15; blessing with, 74, 81, 233, 290; iconostasis with, 294; miracle-working, 18, 24, 31, 97, 131, 134–35, 161, 229–31, 233–38, 278–279; painting of, 230, 242; praying before, 308; procession with, 222, 257, 259; prominence of, 229; relationship to, 154; reverencing, 303, 307; sermon about, 11; veneration of, 11, 23, 136, 163, 230–31, 235, 239, 244–47; visitation of, 230
identity, 16; national, , 18, 229; religious, 1; Russian, 75
ideology, 5, 14, 61, 185; revolutionary, 13; state, 17
Ignatius, Saint, 64
illness, 33, 38, 60, 94, 284; and death, 162; mental, 44; and miracle, 23; physical, 49, 263, 264; suffering from, 262; world of, 22
Incarnation, 11, 190, 229
individualism, 15
industrialization, 208–209
infidelity, 66
Innokentii (Borisov), Archbishop, 10, 17, 73–74, 76
innovation, 188, 231
insanity, 167; social, 215
Irkutsk, 95

Irkutsk diocese, 49
Isaiah, Saint, 165
Islam, 73, 76

Jerusalem, 76
Jewish faith, 51
Jews, 119, 120, 129n4, 154–55; and Poles, 109, 110, 120; Yiddish-speaking, 107
John (Ioann) of Kronstadt, 16, 152, 153, 262
John Chrysostom, Saint, 14, 74, 86, 88, 184, *186*, 188–89
John of the Ladder, Saint, 63–64, 67
John the Baptist, Saint, 132
journals, 3, 73, 108, 223, 271; and books, 180; Orthodox, 139; for priests, 3; religious, 23; scholarly, 3; secular, 109; theological, 86, 178. *See also* literacy; magazines; newspapers
Judgment Day, 25, 40

Kallistos, Saint, 64
Kaluga diocese, 45, 54
Kaluga province, 59, 69n3, 248n10
Kama River, 197, 198, 205
Karelia, 24
Kazan, 134, 167
Kazan icon of the Mother of God, 12, 15, 97, 131, *133*, 134–37, 239
Kharkov, 291
Kharkov province, 269, 279
Kiev, 5, 24, 27, 107, 115, 132, 276–82, 308
Kiev diocese, 10, 107, 109
Kiev province, 107–109, 292
Kiev Theological Academy, 108
Kievskaia starina, 108, 109
Kireevskii, Ivan, 60
Kirillo-Belozerskii monastery, 49
Kolochskii monastery, 175
Kormchii, 12, 139, 223
Kostroma, 163
Kronstadt, 161, 166
Kryzhanovskii, Evfimii Mikhailovich, 108–10, 115

laity, 13, 23, 98, 131, 213, 232; and clerics, 10; elders, 65; empowering, 210; and literacy, 3, 11; and monks, 60; petitions to, 10; practices and beliefs among, 22. *See also* clergy

landowner, 43, 60, 128, 175, 180, 294; and authorities, 127; noble, 193

laws, 255, 260; church, 43, 153; imperial, 48; of nature, 36, 96, 102–104; state, 6

Lent, 26, 66, 68, 132, 152, 156, 217, 240, 299

Leonid (St. Lev) of Optina, 59–61, 65, 67, 69n2

liberation movement, 218

library, 175, 178, 180; church, 139; parish, 174, 178; Pushkin Public, 180; school, 159

life, religious, 109, 143, 209, 221, 250; basis of, 252; condition of, 251, 253; Orthodox, 6; popular, 210; Russian, 208

Life of St. Basil the Younger, 32, 40n2

Life of St. Stefan of Perm, 15

Lisbon, 96

literacy, 3, 177, 208, 272, 274–75; rates, 2–3, 85. *See also* education; journals; magazines; newspapers

literature: anti-alcohol, 223; illegal, 218–19; theological, 214

Lithuania, diocese of, 193, 200

liturgy, 48–49, 52–53, 56, 90, 115–16, 120, 280, 286, 304; and akathist, 89, 92; attending, 55; church, 250; Divine, 49, 87, 89, 153, 273; function of, 131; knowledge of, 272; performing of, 8, 146, 222, 275; and prayer, 131; quotation from, 14; ringing for, 165; and rituals, 123; serving, 55, 88, 114, 119; the words of, 11

lived religion, 12–13

lives of saints, 1, 3, 139, 154, 173, 272, 275

Lubny, 277, 279

magazines, 3, 12, 289. *See also* journals; literacy; newspapers

Makarii, Saint, 59–60, 63, 65, 67, 69n3, 280

manuals, for priests, 86, 153

marriage, 9, 32, 60, 67, 91, 226n16, 255; performing, 256

Mary, Mother of God, 37, 135–37, 146, 157–58, 160–62, 247; appearance of, 136, 241–42; praying to, 161–62, 282, 285; service in honor of, 89; thanks to, 24, 134. *See also* akathist; Kazan icon of the Mother of God; Mother of God, icons of

McDannell, Colleen, 12

memoirs, 1, 74, 108, 271; of Toviia, Archimandrite, 10, 14, 269, 271–73, 282

Meyendorff, John, 32

migrant labor, 208, 213, 218, 219

migration, 254

Ministry of Education, 32, 221, 227n24

Ministry of Spiritual Affairs and Education, 32

miracle, 22–24, 31–32, 135–36, 192, 236–37, 240; attitude toward, 16; belief in, 23; existence of, 139; false, 22; of Resurrection, 36; posthumous, 22; Providential, 282; recognition of, 23; recording, 136, 247; records of, 194; reported, 230; stories, 1, 23–, 31–32, 192, 194. *See also* icons: miracle-working

mission, Orthodox anti-sectarian, 255

missionaries, 250, 251; missionary work, 140, 193, 197; Orthodox, 255, 303; of the Russian Baptist Union, 289

missionary council, 223, 251; Omsk Diocesan, 251

Missionerskoe obozrenie, 223

Mitrofan of Voronezh, Saint, 81

modern science, 16

modern state, 109

modernity, 15–16

modernization, 1–2, 16, 85

Mogila, Petr, Metropolitan of Kiev, 109, 125

Mohammed, 82, 104

Moldavia, 72, 125

Molokans, 3, 50, 250

Index

monastery, 7, 23, 43–44, 58, 123, 143, 210, 241; and cathedrals, 230, 231; and convent, 60; entering, 60, 275, 277, 282, 283; incarceration in, 43; network of, 208; Orthodox, 6, 43; retiring to, 276; travelling to, 18; visiting, 273. *See also* convent; *names of individual monasteries*

monasticism, 58, 271, 275, 283; resurgence of, 272; women's, 58–59, 61

Monday ladies, 90

morality, 85, 210, 222; ascetic, 226n16; degradation of, 213; and faith, 218–19, 220, 222; religious, 117

Moscow, 23, 27, 52, 141, 143, 148, 149, 194, 199, 205, 271, 284; devastation of, 197; holy sites in, 24; transferring relics from, 12, 198, 201, 202, 205; travel to, 147; veneration of relics in, 196

Moscow Church Council of 1549, 205

Moscow patriarchate, 5

Moscow province, 52, 59

Mother of God, icons of, 24, 37, 81, 133, 161, 230, 279; "Multiplier of Grains," 231, 232, 239–47. *See also* Kazan icon of the Mother of God

movements, religious, 104

multiconfessionality, 3

Muscovy, 5

Muslims, 76, 226n18

narrative: conversion, 17, 288–89; public, 1, 15; religious, 1, 14, 15, 17, 45, 109. *See also* hymns; lives of saints; sermons

National Day of Unity, 134

national identity, 18, 229

nationalism, 3

nationalization, 17

natural disaster, 95–96

neophyte, 58, 64

Nero, 53

New Testament, 11, 294. *See also* Old Testament

newspapers, 3, 73, 212, 309; church, 139; diocesan, 3, 98, 139, 172–73, 243. *See also* journals; literacy; magazines

Nicholas I, 2, 24, 53, 74–75, 79, 120, 126, 181; government of, 32; rule of, 17

Nicholas II, 2, 185, 193, 271

Nicholas, Saint, 132, 165, 248n8, 278; icon of, 79, 234, 239, 278

nihilism, peasant, 253

Nikon (Rozhdestvenskii), Archbishop, 271

Nikon (Sofiiskii), Bishop, 211, 226n14

Nikon, Patriarch, 52, 125, 185

Nizhnii Novgorod province, 24

nobility, 8, 118, 132, 180; Polish, 107, 121, 129n19; Russian, 31, 61

Novgorod, 81, 140

Novgorod diocese, 49

obedience, 64, 149, 158, 283–85; and devotion, 212; living in, 62

obituary, 10, 172–73, 175

objects: holy, 235, 240, 242–43, 245; sacred, 158, 197, 199, 201, 241, 247

October Manifesto, 185–86, 211, 310

Odessa, 73, 77, 243, 289, 292, 305, 308–309, 311

Official Nationality, 17

Old Belief (*raskol*), 3, 6, 23, 209, 216, 225n8

Old Believers, 185–88, 199, 208, 216, 246, 251

Old Testament, 11, 51, 154. *See also* New Testament

old time residents. *See Sibiriaki*

Omsk diocese, 252, 256

Omskie eparchial'nye vedomosti, 251

Optina Pustyn, 24, 59–60, 63, 65, 67–69, 231, 241, 243

Orel diocese, 231

Orel province, 60, 69n1, 289–90

organizations, religious, 15

Orlovskii, Ioann Mikhailovich, 172, 174–75

Orlovskii, Ivan, 172
Orsi, Robert, 13
Orthodox Church, 4, 6, 17, 81, 140, 155, 193, 230–31, 243–46, 247, 288; authority of, 154; bosom of, 210; contribution from, 73; devotion to, 264; institution of, 214; leaving, 290; members of, 216; and Orthodox religiosity, 18; pastors of, 220; reform in, 98; rights of, 75; rituals of, 154; role of, 18; sacraments of, 88, 214; self-identity within, 231; and Uniate Church, 107, 125; unity with, 212; unreliable for, 253. *See also* Orthodoxy; Russian Orthodox Church
Orthodox publishing houses, 139
Orthodoxy, 3–4, 6, 11–12, 14, 221; ancient, 109; and Autocracy and Nationality, 17; baptizing into, 4; bastion of, 208; and Christianity, 76; converting to, 108, 121, 168; defection from, 216; defending, 210; Eastern, 1; efforts to spread, 140; experience of, 11; and faith, 78; hostile to, 254; and Islam, 73; modern, 18, 132; nature, 14; purity of, 116; relicts of, 122; and religious history, 4; Russian, 13, 131, 188, 192, 254; spreader of, 199; as state religion, 212; status of, 209; storytelling culture of, 131; straying from, 185; studies of, 13; understanding of, 13; and Uniate faith, 122. *See also* Orthodox Church; Russian Orthodox Church
Ottoman Empire, 72, 75
Over-Procurator of the Holy Synod, 195, 196, 198, 202, 204–206, 237–38, 243

paganism, 14
Paisii Velichkovskii, Saint, 58
panikhida (requiem), 278
Panteleimon monastery, 297
Paraclete Hermitage, 271, 284
paradise, 32, 105, 297
parish, 8, 114, 120, 128, 181, 218, 220, 242; administering, 8; boundary of, 241; and clergy, 208, 224; circles, 221–22; condition in, 210; customs of, 126; and family networks, 8; head of, 121; inheritor of, 118, 119; leader of, 179; local, 44; location of, 122; majority of, 252; meeting the need of, 212; Orthodox, 126, 221, 255; and priest, 117; property-owner of, 118; and reforms, 7, 117; reinvigorating, 209; relocating to, 214; removing from, 127; reorganization of, 221; school, 210, 221, 227n24, 234; in Siberia, 17, 251, 252, 259–60; and Uniate authorities, 126
parishioners, 6, 9, 16, 85, 97–98, 126, 172, 176, 178–82, 211, 213, 217, 222, 250; clergy relationship to, 210; comforting, 72; demands from, 209; discussion with, 139, 174; and education, 72; heterogeneity of, 252; literacy of, 139; Orthodox, 85, 215; and pastors, 218, 220; participation in parish life, 221; piety of, 216; poor, 174; and priest, 10, 96, 119, 121–22, 127–28, 258; request of, 212; spiritual progress of, 87
passport, 24
pastoral care, 173–74, 177, 201; movement, 9
patriotism, 17, 75
Paul, Saint (the apostle), 98, 149, 307
peasantry, 13, 107, 113, 118, 129n11, 269
penance, 44, 90, 123, 125, 127, 181; church, 44–46; public, 43, 45
Pereiaslavl, 277, 279–80
Perm, 12, 143–44, 147–48, 192–93, 195–96, 198–202, 204–206
Perm diocese, 147, 196
Perm province, 55, 197–99, 204
persecution, 242–44, 246–47; of clergy, 86
Peter the Great, 6, 43, 52, 174, 181, 185; reign of, 72, 231
petitions, 22, 40, 55, 221, 223, 229; to Brother Ioann Churikov, 262, 264–65, 267. *See also* Holy Synod

Index

Philip, Saint, 90–91
philosophy, 98, 100–104; pagan, 101
Pietism, 31–32, 34
piety, 9, 10, 163, 209; acts of, 272; ancient, 185, 188; and beliefs, 32; Christian, 91–92; example of, 61; and faith, 212, 218–19, 221; feminization of, 86; iconic, 229–30; model, 172; and modernization, 16–17; personal, 87; popular, 209; rise in, 216
pilgrimages, 24, 43, 76, 272–73, 276
pilgrims, 7, 15, 18, 26, 241, 269, 272, 275; Russian Orthodox, 24
plant, 213, 308; and factory, 223
Pobedonostsev, Konstantin P., 108
Poland, 107, 113, 120, 197; invasion of, 196; and Jews, 109, 110, 120; Kingdom of, 108; partition of, 5, 107; slaughter of, 127; victory over, 134
Polish-Lithuanian Commonwealth, 5, 107–109
politics, 292; church, 174
Poltava, 259, 280
Poltava province, 255
Pontius Pilate, 295
pope, 4, 108, 122
populism, 174
Porte, 72, 75
practice, religious, 13–14, 250–52
prayer house, 255
Prayer Rule Before Holy Communion, 88
prayerbook, 37, 152. See also *Book of Needs*
preacher, 17, 74, 149, 176, 198, 222, 262, 302, 305, 307. See also clergy; priests; sermons
press, 3, 12, 227n26, 289; clerical, 85–86, 175; diocesan, 9; expansion of, 2. See also journals; literacy; newspapers
priests, 8, 35, 87, 88, 119, 178, 222, 258–59, 272–73; and bishops, 74, 132; Byzantine, 73; and cantor, 274; and church publicists, 12; confession to, 64, 65, 153, 155, 157, 164, 165; and Crimea War, 72; daughter of, 8, 118; and elders, 58; experience as, 251; former, 48; generation of, 114, 120, 121; ideals of, 10; and journals, 3, 113, 139; Kiev province, 108; and land, 9; and landlords, 118; local, 109, 147, 233; and miracle-working icon, 233–37, 242, 244; missionary, 251; officiating, 32; Orthodox, 85, 87, 96, 174; parish, 9, 10, 27, 31, 39, 153, 233, 250; and parishioners, 10, 96, 128; and peasants, 127–28; presence of, 218; reports of, 14, 211, 249; rural, 85, 107, 172, 174–75, 255; scholarly, 120; and seminary, 117; senior, 92; and sermons, 98, 152; sons of, 7, 8, 10, 107, 109, 110, 111, 114, 118; as spiritual mentors, 59; theologian, 123, 127, 128; Uniate, 121, 122, 126; values as, 109; widowed, 7. See also clergy; diaries: of priests; obituary
prior (*namestnik*), 10, 26, 27, 29, 269, 271, 281, 284–85
private life, 13
progress: of science, 104; spiritual, 59, 85, 87
propaganda: radical, 174, 208; of rationalist sects, 219; sectarian, 224, 251, 253–55
Protestant Reformation, 22
Protestantism, 3, 23, 31, 73
Providential view of nature, 96–97
Psalter, 51, 115, 123, 274–75
psalterist, 120–21, 123
public life, 13
publishing, 3, 139. See also literacy
punishment, 43–44, 53, 125, 190, 238, 265, 275, 304; God's, 96
purity, 52, 54, 91; of Orthodoxy, 116; ritual, 154
Pushkin, Alexander, 181

quietude, 280, 283–85

radicalism, 117; political, 17, 263
rationalism, scientific, 23, 31

reader, 3, 113, 139, 274; modern, 283; young, 142
reading huts, 3
refugees, 72
relics, 12, 28, 278, 280; cross with, 40; icon with, 37; kissing, 26, 28–29, 192; miraculous healing before, 25; praying before, 26; repatriation of, 18; of Stefan of Perm, Saint, 12, 192–202, 204–205; veneration of, 12, 197, 200–201, 205, 234, 279–81; visitation of, 24
religion, 6, 12–13, 14, 16, 53, 72, 174, 216, 250; attitude toward, 213; Christian, 48; elite, 13; ideas about, 16, 51; instructor in, 221; medieval, 60; members of other, 154; religious narrative, 1, 14, 15, 17, 45, 109; of peasantry, 13; popular, 13, 289; Russian, 13; Russian religious thought, 14; Siberian, 254; state, 4, 212
religiosity, 12, 182; Orthodox, 18; peasant, 14, 272
repentance, 45, 155, 283, 286, 299; focus on, 32; signs of, 43; and sinfulness, 152
resettlement, 196; movement, 254
resurrection, 12, 36, 132, 235
revolution: printing and reading, 2; revolutionary identities, 17; revolutionary movement, 85; Russian, 4, 271
Revolution of 1905, 2, 17, 215, 229, 231, 289; anxiety during, 209; upheavals of, 193
Revolution of 1917, 1, 4, 13, 17, 208
Riazan province, 257
rites, 8, 33, 50, 221–22, 253; administration of, 87, 252, 260; celebration of, 88, 92; of consecrated oil, 35; of the Divine Liturgy, 49, 273; fees for, 119; Orthodox, 32; payment for, 214; performance of, 9, 45, 88, 121, 211; and sacraments, 216
rituals, 11, 125, 126, 185, 187, 208; celebration of, 123; church, 6, 108–109; familial, 230; private, 125; Old Russia's, 188; Orthodox, 154, 250, 188; pre-Nikonian, 186; purification, 33
Roman Catholic Church, 16, 32, 155
Romania, 72
Rome, 107; bishop of, 4
Rostov, 142–43, 165
royal family, 269
Rukovodstvo dlia selskikh pastyrei, 3
rumors, 99–100, 120, 236, 271; spreading of, 67, 104
Russian Baptist Union, 289
Russian Bible Society, 32
Russian Orthodox Church, 3–4, 11, 14, 23, 32, 73, 85, 139; challenges for, 249; children of, 197; leaders of, 185; organ of, 44; persecuted by, 185; potential of, 7; representatives of, 251; returning to, 109; and Siberian settlers, 249; view of, 14. *See also* Orthodox Church; Orthodoxy
Russian Sisters of Mercy, 72, 79, 83n20
russification, 142

sacraments, 8, 32, 53, 55, 88, 213–17, 299; of baptism, 121; celebration of, 93; of confession and communion, 208, 216, 281; of Eucharist, 49; participating in, 60; performing, 52; and salvation, 264
sacristan, 8, 90, 114, 117, 153. *See also* cantor
sailors, 72, 74
sainthood, 22, 194
saints, 11, 33, 37, 89, 124, 139–40, 149, 158, 159–62, 205; assistance of, 194; canonization of, 193; celebrations dedicated to the memory of, 256; contact with, 192; dreams of, 24; false, 22; female, 132; and icon, 31; male, 132; medieval, 142; names of, 92; pledge to, 24; praying to, 26, 27, 264, 276–77, 282, 285, 297; recognized as, 12; relationship with, 12; reliquaries of, 22, 24; "spiritual hearing" of, 192; veneration of, 23, 272, 279, 281. *See also names of individual saints*

salvation, 16, 50, 53, 88, 137, 189, 219, 300; concept of, 59; and dignity, 62; eternal, 103, 221; finding, 302; and holy sacraments, 264; hope of, 286; human, 11; and mercy, 161; path to, 153, 199, 283; receiving, 52, 55; responsible for, 59; search for, 289; teaching on, 288
Samara province, 262
Sanctification, 22, 193, 197
Sarov monastery, 24
Schelling, F. W. J., 101
schism, 4, 6, 210, 212, 225n8
science, 100–103, 174, 180–81; and faith, 265; modern, 16; natural, 96, 101, 103; and natural disaster, 95; progress of, 104; and Protestantism, 31
Scientific Revolution, 96
sect, 50, 209, 244, 252, 288; Adventists, 250; converting, 255; Molokan, 50; Old Believer, 54; rationalist, 214, 219; re-baptizing, 52; recognizing, 254; shtundist, 289. *See also* Baptists; Molokans; Old Belief (*raskol*); shtundism
sectarianism, 17, 23, 216, 222, 255
sectarians, 199, 208, 216, 250, 253–55; group of, 251
Selenginskii monastery, 49
self, notions of, 15–17, 289
self-improvement, 85, 87
semi-constitutional system, 2, 289
seminarians, 16, 113, 121, 211, 226n12
seminary, 117, 121–22, 176, 211, 309; and clergy, 209; enrolled in, 175; graduated from, 176; memories of, 176; rector of, 7, 309; and schools, 8; theological, 120
Serafim of Sarov, relics of, 194
Serbia, 116, 125
Sergiev Posad, 23–24, 33
Sergius of Radonezh, 132, 138n5
sermons, 10, 12, 89–90, 105, 124, 139, 180, 210, 298–300; attributed to St. John of Chrysostom, 14, 188; Crimea War, 17, 72–74, 76, 79; delivering, 74, 152, 222;

about earthquakes, 16; emphasis on, 9; as a genre of communication, 98; giving, 123, 174; greeting with, 141; about icons, 11; Orthodox, 95; preparation of, 31; as public narrative, 1; reading, 73; reference to, 86; Sunday, 68. *See also* homilies
Sevastopol, 73–74, 77, 81
Sevsk convent, 66
Shakhovskaia, Anna A., 60–61, 65, 67, 69
shrines, 12, 18, 24, 192, 196, 201
shtundism, 114, 129n11
Siberia, 5, 10, 167, 168, 249–54, 256; migrants to, 17; neighboring territories, 196, 201; Russian, 95
Sibiriaki, 249, 256, 260
singing, 8, 35, 179, 297; church, 116; love of, 176; popular, 222
sins, 68, 80, 97, 124–25, 146, 154, 160–61, 166, 304, 307; absolution of, 64; categories of, 152; compunction for, 163; confessing, 65, 93–94, 124, 152, 153, 155; and crime, 43, 44; and death, 283; forgiveness of, 32, 40, 157, 187, 189, 297, 298, 300–302; hiding, 65; historical, 127; kinds of, 153; minimizing, 155; mortal, 157, 217; praying for, 265, 266, 297; punishment for, 96, 263, 265; remembering, 286; remission of, 285; revealing, 298; sexual, 43; and vice, 263; written list of, 153
Skaldin, Vasilii, 17, 289, 290, 303, 304
Slovo istiny, 289
Smolensk province, 69n1, 173
sobriety, 9, 263, 267
social injustice, 289
social order, 250
Solbinskaia Pustyn, 56
soldiers, 76, 82, 83n17, 122, 165, 296, 299; honored, 90; Orthodox, 77; Russian, 73; and sailors, 72, 74; wounded, 79; young, 291
Solovetskii monastery, 24, 44, 54
Sophia, Alekseyevna, 43

Spaso-Evfimiev monastery, 9, 14, 44, 47, 48–50, 55–56
spiritual guidance, 7, 58, 60, 210
spirituality, 60; clerical, 10; Orthodox, 11, 12
St. Alexander Nevskii Brotherhood, 225
St. Michael's Monastery, 281
St. Petersburg, 9–10, 107, 108, 229, 263, 266; outskirts of, 262
State Duma, 205, 209
Stefan of Perm, Saint, 12, 139–49, *141*, 192–202, 204–206
Stolypin, Petr, 197, 204
suicide, 168, 292
superstition, 23, 89, 104, 145, 147, 174, 181
Supral'skii monastery, 200
Suzdal, 9, 47, 48, 217t
Symeon, Saint, 64
Syria, 116

Tambov province, 50
Tauride peninsula, 76–77
Theodora, Saint, 32
Theodosian Concord, 187
theology, 86, 127, 180, 188, 192, 272; Hesychast, 61; mystical, 58; Orthodox, 11, 14; practical, 74
Third Rome, 5
Time of Troubles, 134, 138n5
Tobolsk province, 251
tolerance, religious, 289
Tolstoi, Lev, 152, 214, 226n16
Toviia, (Tsymbal), Archimandrite, 269, 270, 271–73, 282–83, 286n1. *See also* diaries: of Toviia, Archimandrite; memoirs: of Toviia, Archimandrite
tradition: Christian, 1; Eastern Christian, 231, 248n9; religious, 1, 173, 252
Transfiguration monastery, 279
Trans-Siberian Railway, 10, 249–50
trezvenniki, 9, 263, 267
Trinity Akhtyrskii monastery, 279, 282
Trinity Word, 271

Trinity-Sergius Lavra, 10, 23–25, 28, 33, 269, 271
Troitse-Odigitrievskaia Pustyn, 59
Tsagan steppe, 95
Tsarskoe Selo, 75
tserkovnost' (churchness), 10
Tula diocese, 60
Tula province, 24–25, 27
Turkey, 4, 72, 75, 76

Ufa, 239
Ufa diocese, 240
Ufa province, 240
Ukraine, 6, 109–10, 113, 155, 249, 289; Right-Bank, 5, 107–109, 115
Unction of Consecrated Oil, 32–33, 35
Uniate (Greek Catholic) Church, 107–108
uprising: peasant, 127; Polish (1831–1832), 113, 120

Valaam monastery, 24
Vasilii of Paria, Saint, 37, 41n10
vespers, 26, 112, 115, 119, 281
Viatka, 241
Viatka diocese, 196, 239, 244
Viatka province, 197, 239, 246
vice, 222–23, 263, 267
Viestnik Evropy, 113
village life, 249
violence, 9, 72
visions, 24, 34
Vladimir, 217t, 226n12
Vladimir, diocese, 16, 44, 208, 211, 218, 224
Vladimir, Grand Prince of Kiev, 4, 73, 76
Vladimir monastery, 246
Vladimir province, 208
Vologda diocese, 196
Vologda province, 142, 195, 197, 204
Voltaire, 96
Voronezh, 275
Voronezh province, 269

Voskresnoe chtenie, 90, 94n6
vows, 27, 80, 90, 104, 113; making, 166, 278; monastic, 7, 269

Wallachia, 72
White Sea, 24
women, 7, 12, 89, 90, 209, 212, 214, 249; bad, 291; and children, 145; educated, 154; married, 159; and men, 16, 60, 73, 131, 139, 154, 195, 222, 229–30, 296; Orthodox, 142; peasant, 113, 155; practice by, 61; religious, 58; rural and urban, 3; shrines of, 24; spiritual guidance by, 60; unmarried, 59; and workers, 14

workers, 14; accounts of, 289; factory, 215; houses for, 213; peasant, 17. *See also* factory
working class, 17, 262, 264
World War I, 2, 72
worship, 14, 55, 76, 222, 288; places of, 33, 145

zemstvo, 198, 204, 221, 227n24
Zhirovitskii Monastery, 161
Znamenskii Monastery, 271
Zosima, Saint, 58–59, 62–63, 69n1
Zyrians, 140–41, 143–46, 148–49, 197–98, 204–206

www.ingramcontent.com/pod-product-compliance
Lightning Source LLC
Chambersburg PA
CBHW070259240426
43661CB00057B/2592